W9-DHF-803

Globalization of Services

In an era of accelerating change in the world economy, services are assuming greater importance for the economies of both developed and developing countries. As technological developments allow increasing tradability of services, huge global firms are offering services across national boundaries. This important book explores the global impact of this economic phenomenon from both empirical and theoretical perspectives.

A range of international authors, including both academics and representatives of major international organizations offer contributions in two key areas:

- theories and paradigms of international business behaviour; the book questions whether traditional models of international business, which were developed with manufacturing industries in mind are applicable to the service sector, and suggests new directions for the direction of international business and management theory
- case studies covering a wide range of service industries, from consumer services such as hotels and airlines, to professional business-to-business services.

Globalization of Services therefore offers international business scholars both a wealth of new source material and a fresh perspective on the modern global service economy.

Yair Aharoni is Rector of the College of Management, Tel Aviv, and editor of *Coalitions and Competition: the Globalization of Professional Business Services* (Routledge 1993).
Lilach Nachum is Senior Research Fellow at ESRC Centre for Business Research, University of Cambridge. She is author of *The Origins of the International Competitiveness of Firms: the Impact of Location and Ownership in Professional Services* (Edward Elgar 1999).

Routledge Studies in International Business and the World Economy

Globalization of Services

Some implications for theory and practice

**Edited by Yair Aharoni
and Lilach Nachum**

London and New York

First published 2000
by Routledge
11 New Fetter Lane, London, EC4P 4EE

Simultaneously published in the USA and Canada
by Routledge
29 West 35th Street, New York, NY 10001

Routledge is an imprint of the Taylor & Francis Group

Typeset in Baskerville by
Curran Publishing Services Ltd, Norwich
Printed and bound in Great Britain by
St Edmundsbury Press, Bury St Edmunds, Suffolk

British Library Cataloguing in Publication Data
A catalogue record for this book is available
from the British Library

Library of Congress Cataloging in Publication Data
   Globalization of Services: some implications for theory and
   practice / by Y. Aharoni and L. Nachum (eds).
   352 pp. 15.6 x 23.4 cm
   Includes bibliographical references and index
   1. Service industries. 2. Competition, international.
   I. Aharoni, Yair. II. Nachum, Lilach
   HD9980.5.G58 2000
   338.4–dc21   99-088059

ISBN 0-415-22654-6

Contents

Figures

Tables

Contributors

Yair Aharoni, Rector of the College of Management, Academic Studies, Tel Aviv.

Charles Baden-Fuller, Professor of Strategy, City University Business School (CUBS), London.

Farok J. Contractor, Professor of International Business, Rutgers University.

David J. Cooper, Associate Professor, Center for Professional Service Firm Management, Faculty of Business, University of Alberta.

Peter Enderwick, Professor, Department of Marketing and International Management, University of Waikato.

Karin Fladmoe-Lindquist, Associate Professor, David Eccles School of Business, University of Utah.

Royston Greenwood, Professor, Center for Professional Service Firm Management, Faculty of Business, University of Alberta.

Robert Grosse, Director of the Research Center, Thunderbird, American Graduate School of International Management.

Bob Hinings, Professor, Center for Professional Service Firm Management, Faculty of Business, University of Alberta.

Dale B. Honeck, Secretary to the Working Party on Professional Services (July 1997 to April 1999), and to the Working Party on Domestic Regulation, World Trade Organization (WTO).

George Michael Klimis, Research Associate, City University Business School (CUBS), London.

Michel Kostecki, Director of the Enterprise Institute and Professor of Business Economics and Marketing, Université de Neuchâtel.

Martin Kretschmer, Fellow, Centre for Strategy Research, City University Business School (CUBS), London, and Leverhulme Senior Lecturer in Intellectual Property Policy and Management, Bournemouth University.

Sumit K. Kundu, Assistant Professor of International Business, Saint Louis University.

Bente R. Løwendahl, Associate Professor, Norwegian School of Management.

Padma Mallampally, Consultant to the Division on Investment, Technology and Enterprise, United Nations Conference on Trade and Development (UNCTAD), Geneva.

Lilach Nachum, Senior Research Fellow, ESRC Centre for Business Research, Cambridge University.

Teresa Rose, Associate Professor, Center for Professional Service Firm Management, Faculty of Business, University of Alberta.

Susan Segal-Horn, Professor of International Strategy, Canterbury Business School, University of Kent.

Tan Kim Seng, SIA Engineering Company, Singapore.

Hannu Seristö, Professor of International Business, Helsinki School of Economics and Business Administration.

Roger Wallis, Director of the Multimedia Research Group, City University Business School (CUBS), London.

Zbigniew Zimny, Staff Member, Division on Investment, Technology and Enterprise, United Nations Conference on Trade and Development (UNCTAD), Geneva.

1 Introduction

Setting the scene

Yair Aharoni

This book is published at the dawn of the twenty-first century. We have moved to a new millennium after gigantic and breathtaking technological advances made in the last century. It is often proposed that the pace, magnitude and direction of change will continue to accelerate in the global economy. Managers will have to cope with the rapid pace of changes by mobilizing human capital and increasing their adaptive capabilities. They will have to exploit and protect knowledge, facilitate its creation and mainly nurture systems to transfer this knowledge expeditiously within the organization. A major source of competitive advantage might be the reputation of the firm rather than any physical resources available to it. Moreover, the firm, rather than the country, would become the focus of attention of researchers attempting to understand the world economy.

In the world of the dawn of the twenty-first century, factors of production (with the possible exception of labour) are mobile across national borders. This mobility is facilitated by the interconnectedness of the world through a network of computers, high-speed telecommunications, fax, and other means. In an increasingly dynamic competitive global environment it has become almost impossible for any one firm to develop all the skills needed for effective competitive battle. Firms have become increasingly involved in strategic alliances and co-operative joint ventures. The nature of relationship among firms becomes at least as important as the organization of each one of them.

One manifestation of the changing nature of the global economy is the vast increase in the role of services as a per cent of GNP in both developed and developing economies. Between 1980 and 1997 the share of the services in gross domestic product has declined in only twenty-one out of more than 120 countries (World Bank 1999a). In all low income countries this share grew from 38 to 42 per cent; in middle income countries from 40 to 50. As to the developed countries, in the USA, this share grew from 58.3 per cent in 1960 to 64 per cent in 1980 and 71 per cent in 1997. In the Netherlands, the growth was from 60 per cent in 1980 to 70 per cent in 1997. Corresponding figures for the UK were 64 per cent to 71 per cent (World Bank 1999b).

Another development is the flourishing of huge global firms offering services across many countries in services previously considered non-tradable. Indeed, technological developments have allowed increasing tradability of services. These firms seem to enjoy advantages derived from the ownership of intangible assets such as organizational skills, technological knowledge, organizational capabilities, or the unique ability to transfer knowledge horizontally. These advantages are transferred from one country to another within the firm, not between firms. In fact, the international division of labour has shifted from country-based comparative advantage in one product or another to intra-firm division of labour. The multinational service firm can allocate skill-intensive operations to one country and low skill, labour-intensive operations to another (Gereffi and Korzeniewicz 1994). The creation, accumulation, transfer and protection of knowledge has become a major source of competitive advantage.

Services had to be performed in proximity to the consumer, and were therefore considered non-tradable for a long time. They also necessitate a close interaction between the supplier and the consumer, and the costs to the consumer include not only the price paid but also learning and other costs. Some of these costs are incurred in the inter-action phase while others are incurred in isolation (Hirsch 1989). Services are also intangible and non-storable and therefore cannot be transferred across national borders. Instead, they have to be produced at the time and place in which they are consumed. Therefore, in most services delivery to foreign markets must be achieved by establishing a presence in that market, often by foreign direct investment.

In the early 1990s, the service sector – long believed to be an unproductive and undesirable source of employment, and an arcane area of economic activities – became a focal point of world-wide attention among both researchers and policy makers. The Uruguay Round trade negotiations were the first to bring international trade in services under multilateral rules, summarized in the General Agreement of Trade in Services (GATS). Signatory governments made binding commitments with respect to market access and national treatment with regard to many services. The World Trade Organization (WTO) was created, and was given the responsibility to negotiate and police the rules of the game on trade and investment in services.

Parallel to the increase in the importance of services interest has shifted from an analysis of the service sector in a national setting to an examination of international trade and investment in services. There has been a surge of interest in looking for a better understanding of the reasons firms expand into the international arena: what is the motivation for such expansion, when do firms internationalize and how? Since the 1980s, there has been also a growing attention paid to questions such as the best and most effective ways of organizing, managing and transferring knowledge, as well as bench-marking best practices, within a multinational firm. Several notions held as axioms in the past have turned out to be obsolete. The degree to which generalizations based on the experience of mining or manufacturing firms is applicable to service organizations has been questioned. All in all, there has been a gradual shift from an economy of goods to an economy of services and to new products and services increasingly based on knowledge. These shifts have fundamental theoretical implications, as well as policy ramifications.

A brief review of the contributions

The editors approached most major scholars in the area of services and asked them to contribute to this volume. These contributions are grouped in three parts. The two chapters included in Part I summarize trends related to foreign investments in services and the institutional environment in which these transactions are taking place. Chapter 2, authored by Padma Mallampally and Zbigniew Zimney, two of the senior economists in UNCTAD, summarizes trends and patterns of foreign direct investments in services. It also examines the underlying reasons for the globalization of services. The authors note the rapid growth in the share of foreign direct investments in services, that grew from less than 25 per cent of total stock at the beginning of the 1970 to almost a half of that stock in 1995. The shift toward services is remarkable mainly in developing countries, in which the share of services doubled from 20 to 41 per cent of the FDI stock. The figures available on services by industry for three developed countries – the United States, Germany and the United Kingdom – show a significant difference among them. One reason for this difference is the composition of service industries. Note that FDI statistics do not include franchising or management contracts and thus underestimate significantly the globalization of service firms and service industries.

Although FDI in services are rapidly growing the globalization of service firms, the authors argue, still lags behind that of the manufacturing sector. One reason, they suggest, may be that the service sector became open to FDI only recently, much later than in mining or manufacturing. Moreover, as indicated, much of the FDI in services is undertaken by industrial firms. Finance and trade-related services dominate the FDI stock in services. In these two sectors, a significant portion of the activities are financial and marketing subsidiaries of non service firms. Increasingly manufacturing firms perceive their comparative advantage in product development and marketing activities. A possible different explanation may be that services are dominated by non FDI organizational forms. Note the growth of franchising reported in Karin Fladmoe-Lindquist's chapter (Chapter 9) and that of both management contracts and franchising in hotels, analysed by Contractor and Kundu.

Outward FDI in services came from many developed countries and went mainly to other developed countries. As to inward investments, about a fifth went to the United States, later increasing to about 30 per cent. The next important region has been Western Europe while in Japan the stock has been very small. In the 1990s there has been a major growth in inward investments in developing countries.

The authors note that the first wave of the international expansion of service MNEs came in response to international expansion of other MNEs when service firms followed their clients. They also note that the service sector has grown and some of its components such as telecommunications have become very sophisticated. In addition, the marketing of goods have become based on increased service inputs. A second reason, they argue, has been an increased competitive advantage of some service firms. A third is the change in policies of governments and the growing liberalization of markets for services. Finally, services have become more tradable as a result of technological advances such as electronic commerce.

Chapter 3, authored by Dale Honeck, provides a critical overview of the work of the Working Party on Professional Services (WPPS). The WPPS created the Guidelines for Mutual Recognition Agreements and the Disciplines on Domestic Regulation in the Accountancy Sector. Honeck, who has been a member of the WTO Secretariat, is very well equipped to provide a panoramic view of the motivations, problems and achievements of the negotiations. He tells the story of the role of the WTO in the development of regulatory disciplines in professional services. More exactly, the development of guidelines for mutual recognition arrangements and disciplines on domestic regulation, both in the accounting sector.

Since business firms as well as consumers are heavily affected by government's regulation of services, a thorough understanding of the process by which specific WTO disciplines are developed is of great importance. In this introduction, I shall not attempt to summarize the rich details of both the positive and negative aspects of the process. Rather, some of the major points will be highlighted.

Professional business services are subject to regulation, required for the protection of the public interest to ensure adequate standards of competence and integrity. Article IV of the GATS calls for preventing regulations from unduly restricting trade. Regulations must also be based on transparent and objective criteria. This article refers to three types of regulation: licensing requirements, qualification requirements and procedures, and technical standards. Other relevant articles of GATS are those related to market access and national treatment. The author notes that most developing countries were reluctant to discuss market access issues. Further, the negotiations were difficult and time consuming. To date, technical standards is the area where the least progress was made in respect to the creation of discipline. It might be hoped that the learning process of achieving the agreement on disciplines might reduce the time needed to achieve such disciplines on additional professional services. This process may be accelerated if international professional associations would provide technical expertise, even though only governments can participate in WTO activities directly. One conclusion from the experience to date is that the limited resources of the delegations as well as the WTO secretariat are potential barriers to the creation of regulatory disciplines.

Part II of the book includes theoretical contributions on services. My co-editor, Lilach Nachum, has contributed a chapter on foreign direct investments and the link between the location advantage of home countries and competitiveness of firms (Chapter 4). Nachum asserts that firms of particular nationalities tend to excel in certain activities in a manner that reflects the resources abundant in the country of origin. Firms then use their location-based ownership advantages to gain competitive advantage in foreign markets. The foreign activities of firms weaken the traditional link between the resources of home countries and the ownership advantages of firms, as a result of the generation of knowledge by all parts of the MNEs and the diminishing dominant position of the headquarters, which were typical in the past. The ability of MNEs to generate knowledge in all its units is allowing the competitiveness of firms to flourish, in part, independently from that of the home country. Nachum suggests that even under these circumstances, home countries continue to affect the competitiveness of firms, but this impact is considerably weaker compared with the situations in which firms either served markets via exports, or operated overseas with very centralized organizational structure, in which knowledge was flowing in one direction: from the headquarters to the affiliates. If location advantage of the home country declines, national firms may maintain their strength by foreign investment. Alternatively, the national firms may remain focused domestically and lose their lead in the industry. If the location advantages are sustained, national firms may create barriers to the entry of foreign firms. Alternatively foreign firms may get access to similar advantage by investing in the advantageous country. These possibilities are tested by examining five professional services industries: advertising, management consulting, engineering consulting, accounting, and law.

The analyses conducted in her chapter show the different circumstances under which FDI affects the link between the advantages of professional service firms and their home countries and the competitiveness of firms. The foreign activities of firms enable them to develop advantages which are not related, or at least not directly so, to the location advantages of their home countries. Outward FDI may thus strengthen the ownership advantages of firms independent of the location advantages of their home countries. Inward FDI enable firms to get access to resources not available in their home country and to develop strength based on the location advantages of foreign countries. FDI thus weakens the link between the location advantages of home countries and the ownership advantages of firms, which tends to be strong when firms operate only or mainly within their home countries.

In Chapter 5, David Cooper *et al.* focus on the globalization process and international structural arrangements of the Big Five accounting firms. They point out that if contingency theory as proposed by Lawrence and Lorsch (1967) or Thompson (1967) is applied, then firms facing similar environment would display similar organizational mechanisms to achieve the required integration and differentiation. In fact, they argue, firms did not. There is more than one successful response, or way of organizing, to the same set of environmental conditions. The way chosen, they argue, depends on the early history of the firm. More specifically, decisions made in the early life of the organization in terms of governance, domain, design and recruitment help to explain differences in present-day structures. These assertions are supported by a rich and detailed account of the history of two of the 'Big Five' firms (KPMG and Arthur Andersen), contrasting the differences between the two. At the same time, it is also pointed out that the historical partnership structure has restricted the centralized control of expansion. The analysis of these authors raise the ancient question: is the leader the creator of history or is history determined by events? The authors themselves build on the idea of sedimentation. That is, they see history 'as a process involving disruption amidst continuity'.

My own contribution to this volume (Chapter 6) deals with the role of reputation. The major argument of the chapter is that professional business services are of the nature of credence. Therefore, clients find it extremely hard to assess quality, competence, reliability and other factors they deem important in choosing a service supplier. At the same time, the cost of switching suppliers is quite substantial and the consequences of choosing the 'wrong' supplier may be devastating. Therefore, clients look for means to assess quality of service. When one employs an individual, or a small firm, trustworthiness may be easier to assess, based on interpersonal relations. In a global environment, firms attempt to gain a reputation for the firm as such, not for the individual professionals. The chapter analyses the ways in which reputation is built in such context, from the point of view of professional service firms as well as this of their clients.

Professional business firms attempt to sell their competence and build reputation. They may emphasize service to clients and attempt to differentiate themselves from competitors as offering a better service. However, more often than not, the clients use surrogates such as size or age of the firm or the list of its major clients to assess quality. Thus, large firms gain a major competitive advantage as a result of their size. In contrast to Bente Løwendahl's stress on ethical standards, my contribution argues that the client cannot judge quality of service, but shows that under these conditions, as predicted by elaboration likelihood model (ELM) theory, other variables will be used. This is not to say that ethical standards are not important, but to stress that they do not differentiate among firms and thus cannot be used to assess quality of a professional service.

Bente R. Løwendahl, in Chapter 7, compares and contrasts the globalization of professional business service firms with that of the more traditional manufacturing multinationals. Her chapter starts with an overview of the major differences between professional business firms and other knowledge-intensive service firms. She emphasizes the commitment to the delivery of customized tailored service based on a careful and ethically sound professional judgement to the client. For her, this commitment is the major difference between a professional service firm and other knowledge-intensive firms such as banks. High ethical standards are necessary because the client generally does not have sufficient knowledge to judge the quality of the service delivered. In addition, the delivery involves a high degree of discretion and personal judgement by experts involved.

The chapter by Løwendahl is based on the theoretical contributions of Porter (1986). Porter discusses globalization in terms of market characteristics on the one hand and the characteristics of the value-creating activities of the firm on the other. Løwendahl argues that the value chain developed by Porter is not appropriate for the analysis of value creation activities in professional service firms. Instead, she posits that the value creation activities are based on three core processes:

- selling a 'credible promise';
- delivering what was promised;
- learning from the process to improve both efficiency and effectiveness in future projects.

Professional service firms, according to her, do not compete on price and costs nor do they create value by the transformation of tangible inputs into output. Professional service firms globalize because they perceive size and globalization as proxies for high quality and hence reputation. They may need to cater to demands of global clients who demand consistent services at multiple sites, or to serve local clients with global problems. They may choose global strategies also to achieve credibility or to learn from a large number of diverse projects. In some cases, the reason for globalization is even more mundane and idiosyncratic such as personal preferences of partners. The organization of the professional service firm depends fundamentally on the organization of the client firm activities it is expected to support. Value creation takes place in interaction with the client and the costs of logistics and transportation emphasized by Porter are very different. The key question in deciding to create a local office is the duration and frequency of client's demand rather than the cost of operating a local office.

In Chapter 8, Martin Kretschmer *et al.* describe and analyse the forces hypothesized to determine the current appropriation of intellectual property in music. Music is interesting because the issue of intellectual property rights is particularly problematic in this industry. These rights are recognized not only with regard to the publishing but also for any performance of the music and even the integration of the music into new contexts. Global enforcement of such property rights is difficult, more than in other industries. Recent technological changes, mainly digitization and the increasing use of the internet for selling music, coupled with deregulation of the industry, have further complicated the protection of intellectual property rights.

The authors claim the 'allocation of intellectual property rights is essentially a result of bargaining power in the process of "bringing music to the market"'. They identify four major trends at the heart of the industry:

- commodification (turning the music into a product);
- globalization (exploitation of the music rights globally);
- delivery (of the product to the consumer);
- royalty management (necessitating the resources to monitor secondary usage).

The existing allocation of rights, they argue, is a result of historical accident. New technologies and changes in regulation would lead to different allocation of the rights. A budding process of these changes led, they argue, to a different allocation in Japan where intellectual property rights are stretched between the production company and the media channel. The authors discuss briefly the possible scenarios for change, including the advance of internet retailing.

An important mechanism for international expansion of service firms has been through franchising agreements. Chapter 9, by Karin Fladmoe-Lindquist, is a thorough analysis of international franchising. She demonstrates that franchising is a very efficient means to achieve international business expansion. She also proposes that a major contribution of franchising is the creation of linkages and network relationships. She views foreign direct investments as a system of relationships needed to attain resources not otherwise available. This approach emphasizes the interdependence of all franchisees: poor performance by one may reflect on all others. This mutual dependence means a need to develop formal as well as informal connections among the parties.

Fladmoe-Lindquist discusses in detail four particular elements deemed of great importance in understanding international foreign direct investment. These four are:

- shared identity among the various franchisee units, enhancing reputation and making further opportunities more desirable;
- collective learning: a system wide collective learning and knowledge transfer across franchisees;
- franchisee partner status partners with a high status that can provide a significant access to political or business systems: thus the connections of the local partner are emphasized;

- franchise network culture or a set of common and shared beliefs, norms and language that helps to control the possibility of free riding.

All in all, the analysis of this chapter expands the transnational approach to franchising. It is stressed that FDI can be seen as a source of resources and that the development of a set of relationships and routines.

Robert Grosse speculates, in Chapter 10, on the role of knowledge creation and transfer. He posits that the globalization and even the viability of service firms depends on their ability to produce, transfer and guard from competitors knowledge they use in providing the services to clients. Knowledge cannot always be protected by legal means such as patents or copyrights. Grosse and his students interviewed 110 managers in three industries whose target clients are other businesses rather than final consumers. These were management consulting, advertising agencies and commercial banks. These managers operated in Latin America (seventy-two managers), and thirty-eight affiliates in industrial countries (France, Japan, Spain and the United Kingdom). The researchers found that more than half of the business of these service firms in any country outside the home country was generated from multinational firms rather than from local ones. The knowledge emphasized as a key to their competitiveness was knowledge of the clients and relationships with them. They also emphasized capabilities such as global scope of the service firm's affiliate network; methodologies for producing services; knowledge of the market for the services; management skills and technical/specialized information and relationship with clients. These types of knowledge were embodied in the people of the firm, highlighting the importance of maintaining the loyalty of key personnel as a means to protect the knowledge base of the firm. Grosse stresses that the use of teams is one way to protect knowledge as well as to transfer knowledge horizontally within the firm. Other methods of knowledge transfer are more technical e.g. electronic mail, telephone, or fax, as well as training.

Part III comprises some case studies of internationalization of services in different industries, Seng and Enderwick analyse global competition in aircraft maintenance, repair and overhaul services (MRO). The MRO industry, they show, has established product and service quality as a major ingredient of competition, it moved to become global, and became mature with a considerable over-capacity world-wide. With increased competition in the airlines business – fuelled by the deregulation and privatization – firms were required also to cut costs and propose lower prices. One result has been the outsourcing of MRO activities.

The industry is shown to be composed of three major groups: airline-owned, independent operators (many of which went through a series of mergers). They were also acquired by the third group who seems to dominate the field: the original equipment manufacturers (OEM). The airline recession meant stiff competition of engine OEMs for new engine orders and a move to engine maintenance on a global scale, acquiring outsourced airlines maintenance activities as well as independents. As they increase their aftermarket focus, OEMs are hypothesized to become the dominant group in the industry. Tan Kim Seng and Peter Enderwick trace the activities of one airline-owned firm, one independent firm and three OEMs in Chapter 11. Interestingly, both the airline subsidiary and the independent firm were acquired by engine manufacturers, all of which have been moving from their traditional role of providing warranty repair to an aggressive expansion into the MRO business.

In Chapter 12 Hannu Seristö analyses the international strategic alliances among airlines. His chapter thus complements that of Seng and Enderwick. He seeks to answer two related questions: what are the drivers of international airline alliances and what are the objectives of international alliances? Seristö starts with a description of the changes in the airline industry. These changes have made it essential for most airlines to secure presence in a larger market and to seek growth. Airlines also seek to reduce operational costs. At the same time, government regulation in the industry make alliances the only feasible way to seek presence in foreign markets: mergers have been tightly controlled, foreign ownership has been restricted and has been problematic also as a result of government to government bilateral agreements. Seristö analyses case histories of several airlines and, based on his study, proposes a model for airline alliances objectives.

Drivers of international alliances appear to be the need for presence in large markets, the regulation and the pressure for a better utilization of resources. Objectives of alliance include market presence, regulation evasion, resource utilization learning and competitor taming. In the last section of his chapter, Seristö discusses lessons for other industries suggesting four major variables:

- the nature of the competition;
- differentiation possibilities;
- cost structure;
- key factors of success.

In Chapter 13 Michel Kostecki describes the ways DHL Worldwide Express, the largest express carrier, attempts to solve the difficulties of facing ill-managed customs offices mainly in Central and Eastern Europe. According to this case, the primary external reason for late delivery is inefficient customs control and procedures. While enjoying many improvements in the operations of banks, distribution chains or other trade-related services in the private sector, Kostecki argues, the countries of Central Europe suffer from inefficiencies in the public sector and in particular in the customs service that hinders their economic development. In a world of a rapidly changing trading environment in which electronic trading and just-in-time supply are gaining ground, Kostecki calls for a major reform and complete rethinking of the role of customs to provide remedy to the procrastination of the customs as well as to the increased problem of fraud and malpractice.

Hotel chains have a long history of operating beyond national borders. Some of them started international operations more than a hundred years ago. Certain hotel chains are extremely global. Others are not. The globalization of hotels is the subject of two chapters.

Farok Contractor and Sumit Kundu's contribution (Chapter 14) is a part of a major study analysing the globalization of hotels. In their chapter, they concentrate on three research questions: first, why is there a wide variation in the proportion of rooms outside the home country (that ranged in their sample of hotels between 3 and 96 per cent)? The second research question searches for an explanation for the determinants of strategy in relying on inter-firm co-operation as opposed to equity investments. It asks: what determines the optimum choice of organization mode for a particular hotel property? The third research question asks what facilitates franchising, and explains its coverage. Two sets of explanatory variables were used to answer the three research questions: firm-specific attributes (including both firms' characteristics and strategic factors) and country-specific variables.

The explanation to the variability in the degree of international operations was tested by a step-wise regression function. The most relevant variables were size, international experience, and geographic proximity to foreign markets. Unexpectedly, size had a negative sign. Unlike previous studies, factors such as global reservation system did not show strong statistical association in explaining the degree of internationalization of hotel chains.

Non-equity modes account world-wide for more than 65 per cent of foreign operations. Franchising is more frequent in North America. In contrast, equity ownership is more common in Asia. Non-equity modes were found to be preferred in high income nations and in higher risk environment. The propensity to franchise was explained by firm characteristics and by market conditions. Thus, international experience is negatively correlated with the propensity to franchise. The only country variable found to be significant was GDP per capita. Franchising propensity rises with level of economic development. Further, the more experienced hotel chains preferred equity modes. So did executives who place a higher importance of control over daily management. Global reservation systems enable a firm to build and control a network of contractual alliances.

Contractor and Kundu observed a considerable amount of overlap amongst the firm-specific, country-specific, and strategic factors in explaining the variation in the degree of internationalization, organizational forms, and location patterns for the global hotel business. They conclude by drawing the implications of their findings, notably those related to the preference of hotel multinationals for contractual relationships, to firms competing in other global industries.

In Chapter 15 Susan Segal-Horn presents a case study of a major French hotel chain: Novotel. The case study demonstrates how core competence is developed and nurtured in a well known global hotel chain. Her chapter describes the process of identifying, building and then rebuilding competencies within Novotel. The analysis provides an illustration of the internal mechanisms by which core competencies are identified, developed and then internally transferred within an multinational service business. It demonstrates how core competencies are path dependent, in that the firm's history has contributed to the competencies they now possess. These pathways build on complex processes of organizational learning, which are themselves contingent upon earlier stages of learning, investment and development.

Implications and generalizations

The chapters assembled in this volume provide a rich summary of both theory and practical experience regarding the globalization of the services. These have important implications for the theory of multinational enterprises, for the practical operations of these enterprises as well as for policies of governments and international institutions.

Implications for theory

Received theory of multinational firms see the foreign investment as based on the availability of firm-specific advantages. Since the seminal work of Hymer (1960, 1976), it has been assumed that a firm must possess some unique advantages and that these advantages explain the ability of the firm to overcome the additional costs of operating across national borders and still be competitive. Another stream of studies emphasized the foreign investment process as a stream of learning by doing. One example is my earlier contribution (Aharoni 1966). Another is Johanson and Vahlne (1977). Both works emphasized the process of decisions. This process consists of gradual knowledge acquisition leading to the commitment of resources. Initial investments are in – physically or psychologically – close countries. With the accumulation of experience comes more knowledge and self confidence leading to more investments. Several papers in this volume propose a third important variable: that of early history. In other words, the process of experiential learning is heavily affected by the history of the firm and its first steps in the international arena. Thus, Cooper *et al.* demonstrate the importance of history by contrasting the development of KPMG and Arthur Andersen. Fladmoe-Lindquist stresses the importance of a network, with shared identity, collective learning, impact on political systems of some partners and network culture. Segal-Horn emphasizes history in the process of creating core competence.

In earlier studies, based on extractive or manufacturing firms, competitive advantages were often achieved by economies of scale, or by the creation of expensive international distribution networks. In the world at the start of the twenty-first century, we shift from an economy of goods to an economy of ideas and of knowledge. In such an economy, the firm is portrayed as a solution to fundamental problem of information processing (e.g. Alchian and Demsetz 1972; Casson 1997). Moreover a firm may acquire and gain a competitive advantage by the acquisition of knowledge and mainly by its transfer within the organization. Kogut and Zander (1992, 1993) proposed that multinational enterprises are able to transfer knowledge that cannot be fully codified economically through 'a set of higher order organizing principles'. Gupta and Govindarajan (1991, 1993) posit that the degree of interdependence of subsidiaries depends on how much of the knowledge they require is held within the subsidiary, how much is received from other subsidiaries or other parts of the firm, and how much they supply to other parts. It is thus important to understand where the knowledge is generated and how it is transferred. The intangible nature of services and the heavy reliance of some services on knowledge make the value of knowledge particularly important for these firms. This was clearly reflected in the data reported by Grosse, where all the major competitive advantages identified by the service firms in his sample were related to knowledge of different kinds.

Moreover, a multinational may create new knowledge in host countries' subsidiaries, not in the home country. This is obvious in cases in which a multinational creates an R&D centre in the Silicon valley, or any other knowledge centre. It is possible also when an accounting firm concentrates some of its experts in a certain location, or when all the consultants share and transfer knowledge by e-mail. In these cases the knowledge is not generated, nor is it necessarily accumulated, at headquarters. The ability of an MNE to transfer knowledge across many countries and cultures within the organization has become the major component of the firm-specific advantage of these firms.

These firms have become a powerful repository of knowledge but mainly an effective agent of the creation of new knowledge and the transfer of exiting one. One consequence of this new role of the affiliates is that the advantages of multinational enterprises are no longer related to the home country as they used to be in the past. Hu (1992) may have been right in pointing out that the global companies are in reality national companies with international operations. The home country environment allowed the creation of the firm-specific advantages, be it through standardization, or through any combination of resources, capabilities and innovation. Nachum's chapter suggests that the competitiveness of firms is becoming less dependent upon the comparative advantages of their home countries, thus eroding the explanatory power of the latter for the patterns of international competition. These developments are particularly notable in services, since the need to respond to local demand, so critical in some service industries, limits the value of knowledge generated in the headquarters and yields great autonomy for the affiliates. In this sense, organizations learn, and are not bound, at least not fully, by their history. They are also affected by changing environment, as shown by Kretschmer *et al.*, Seng and Enderwick, and Seristö.

The globalization of service industries, notably some professional service industries, brings about new forms of organization of international business activity, which do not exist in manufacturing. In the production of goods, MNEs are a cluster of firms incorporated under the laws of different countries, all of which are wholly or partially owned subsidiaries of a parent firm. In contrast, the expansion of professional service MNEs to new markets is often achieved by a network of several autonomous partnerships. Each partnership gives up some of its autonomy to achieve minimum common standards, and to gain more reputation and thus work. These organization forms are unique characteristics of these firms, and they have important implications for the ways advantages are generated in international competition and diffused within the multinational enterprise. Cooper *et al.* illustrate some of these processes in the context of accounting multinationals.

There are many other examples of networks. Holders of credit cards travel internationally. Therefore, the value of the card is enhanced if it can be used all over the globe. Credit card firms established and maintain a multinational network of establishments honouring the card. Banks maintain a world-wide network of ATM machines. Network arrangements are common in hotel, retail or foods outlets in which franchising is paramount. The MNE sells a package of management know-how and marketing technology: maintaining common standards of service, cleanliness or food preparation. These values are infused to each franchisee, who benefits from the reputation of the firm and from access to its international systems. Reduced or poor quality in one country can damage the reputation of the firm in all parts of the world. In other words, there is an important externality problem in reputation. All in all, there is an increased trend for loosely structured networks of different service firms that join together to achieve a certain purpose, while competing in other areas. In this volume, Fladmoe-Lindquist analyses the advantage of network in franchising and Contractor and Kundu discuss network in hotels. My chapter analyses the role of reputation. A similar network is portrayed in strategic alliances examples in airlines analysed by Seristö. In all these cases, the advantages of multinational operations are not based on ownership.

Services may also be delivered through goods or may be embodied in goods. Therefore, the official statistics simply underestimate the role of services. The more complex the operation of the good, the higher the service component in it and the greater the probability that consumers would buy the product based both on preproduction services such as R&D or market research but mainly based on specific post-sales services (e.g. a maintenance contract) that are deemed indispensable. Giarini (1994) noted that the pure cost of production of most products is very seldom higher than 20 or 30 per cent of the final price. More than 70 or 80 per cent of the price represents the costs of pre-production services such as research and development, planning and maintenance or post-production services such as distribution, as well as services related to the utilization of the products, such as maintenance contracts. In Giarini's terms, values are no longer a result of products which exist materially, but instead are attributed to the performance of a product or a service integrated into a system.

All in all, the MNE of the future, in particular in services, may gain its competitive advantage from different sources than those assumed to be essential in earlier studies. This raises an interesting question: to what extent are earlier theoretical contributions still relevant? Ricardo was not aware of computers or internet and thus could not conceive of a firm as an accumulation or depository of knowledge. More generally, firms operated within a certain technological and institutional environment. Changes in the environment shift the factors creating competitive advantage as shown by Kostecki and by Kretschmer *et al.* in their respective chapters.

A related theoretical question is the degree of determinism assumed. Readers may note the contrast between those who stress unique characteristics and idiosyncratic characterization of the industry or even the firm they analyse, and those looking for generalizability of knowledge. Many theories posit that there is a linear relation among events. Thus, in many economic theories the competitive success of the firm depends on its ability to carry out certain tasks. A firm will be global because the industry is global. Porter (1986) focuses on key activities and tells the reader where each should be located, emphasizing the costs of transportation and co-ordination. Other theories emphasize firm-specific advantages, the ability to develop and sustain certain resources, the ability of a firm to continuously tap into the knowledge developed in relevant centres of the world, the role of leaders, the importance of learning, or the unique contribution of administrative heritage. Segal-Horn stresses core competence. Nachum attempts to combine the two, but still assumes country's resources help create ownership advantage. Of course, the explanation could be related to demand factors rather than to resources. Thus, it may be that the demand for management consulting caused the concentration of leading firms in the United States while that for engineering services was more diffused across countries. Note that Lawrence and Lorsch's (1967) contingency theory ideas came as a revolt against the sweeping generalizations of the classical theory. Cooper *et al.*, however, find these contingencies not accurate enough to depict the accounting industry. This raises a fundamental question: can a new multinational firm be started from any country, or are we bound to some location advantages from certain developed countries?

A more fundamental question is the generalizability of theories developed on the basis of the experience of multinationals in the extractive and manufacturing industries to multinational service enterprises, as well as the degree to which services themselves are similar. It is often argued that many of the frameworks and the models formulated on the basis of the experience of the manufacturing multinational firm need to be assessed for their applicability in the new environment and for their generalizability. Thus, Bartlett and Ghoshal (1989) posit that firms must become transnationals and many authors question the validity of generalizations driven from the experience of manufacturing multinationals to service global firms. As one example, most research on the operation of multinational firms has seen the primary task of the firm as tangible, repeated, measurable, and defined by the producer. All of these attributes are not applicable to a professional business service firm. These firms offer an intangible service that is generally customized and is based on a close interaction between client and the supplier of the service. Producing MNEs sometimes gain competitive advantage over uni-national firms by reaching global economies of scale or scope. The reason some professional business service MNEs are able to operate globally is very different. The supply of services – such as legal counseling, executive search, or management consulting – is highly dependent on the skills of individuals, with little or no economies of scale or of scope, and few possibilities of standardization. Yet some firms in each of these fields have turned out to be very successful global operators (while thousands of others continue to confine their services to one nation or region). These firms certainly possess some more subtle firm-specific advantages, that come from the possession of specific knowledge and competence that compete to clients' benefits and is difficult to imitate by rivals and more difficult to unravel.

The importance of differences between manufacturing and services presented here is not shared by all the authors. In fact, there is a whole array of implicit and explicit differences in point of view on this topic in the different chapters of the book. Grosse uses a standard value-added chain with application to advertising. He explores similarities of motivations of manufacturing and service firms in going abroad (resource seeking and market seeking). Nachum argues that professional services can be analysed as a special case within existing theories and do not require different theories. She also suggests considerable similarity between professional services and some manufacturing industries (notably knowledge-intensive industries), greater than the similarity between professional services and some other service industries. In contrast, Løwendahl rejects the applicability of theories developed based on manufacturing experience to the domain of professional business service firms and see them as very unique, even in comparison to knowledge based services. Cooper *et al.* also emphasize the inadequacy of manufacturing-based paradigm. Other authors, too, tend to emphasize the differences. As a generalization, economists tend to search for similarities while researchers in strategy tend to emphasize unique characteristics. We still need to find an optimum between the level of generalizations and the need to learn more from specific and unique cases.

Different authors analyse a wide range of service industries that differ, among other things, in terms of the nature of their customers (final consumers versus other businesses), and in terms of the nature of their output (a combination of tangibles and intangibles in services such as hotels and airlines, while only intangibles in professional services). These differences have important implications for the conceptualisations of the authors of the nature of foreign activity in the respective industries.

While we do not yet have a general theory of direct foreign investments, four points are clear. First, ownership advantages, or firm-specific advantages, are all services-based for both service and producing multinationals. These advantages are expected to stem from such services as R&D, marketing or access to and ability to use effectively information systems. In a large pharmaceutical multinational, the direct manufacturing costs of the drugs is trivial relative to sale prices. Value is added through service activities: R&D, clinical clearance through regulatory bodies, or a distribution system. The only ownership advantage that may not be based on services is economies of scale and scope.

Second, the literature stresses the importance of internalizing as the major – if not the only – reason for multinational advantage (Rugman 1980). The idea of internalizing, and the derivative issue of reducing transaction costs, seem to have lost much of the favour of those authors dealing with strategy. More and more experts call for an increased outsourcing of all but the core activities. As Quinn *et al.* point out 'other outside service groups can often provide greater economies of scale, flexibility and levels of expertise for specialized overhead services than virtually any company can achieve internally' (1990: 81). To be sure, outsourcing means opportunities for global service MNEs that would follow the producing MNEs world-wide. These observations point to the limit of internalizing, yet not necessarily to the efficacy of markets, but rather to the advantages of networks.

Third, much has been written about alternative modes of entry into the international market. Service firms did not follow the classical process proposed by Johanson and Vahlne (1977). Rather, many of them started by creating a network of independent operators and/or strategic alliances. Contractor and Kundu in this volume attempt to analyse the reasons for this behaviour.

Fourth, specific forms of knowledge and, mainly, the ability to transfer this specific knowledge across countries, thus leveraging the original competitive advantage, have become the major source of competitive advantage. Indeed, the importance of knowledge and its accumulation and transfer is becoming a major cornerstone of FDI theory. As pointed out by Bartlett and Ghoshal (1989) one reason firms are successful in foreign operations is that they continuously learn from all parts of their network. Løwendahl even takes the extreme position that a firm may become global in order to be able to learn from a large number of diverse projects, not because of the demands of global clients. All in all, knowledge and learning are becoming a cornerstone of international business theory.

Obviously, certain factors are more important in one type of service firm than in others. Thus, in some, financial resources are a key factor: banks find it necessary to merge to maintain international competitiveness. In others, consistency must be assured. Thus, auditing firm services are used by third parties, and must use consistent rules. Lawyers or medical doctors service clients, and clients alone. In these cases, consistency is less important. One result is a quest for a common set of policies, procedures and performance measures. Another is the different ability to differentiate the services offered. Auditing, for example, is perceived more as akin to commodity than information services consulting.

Finally the environment in which the firms are operating is an important variable. Airlines use strategic alliances because of the limitations they face in exploiting ownership as a result of government regulations.

Implications for multinational enterprises and for governments

One major development in all professional business service firms is that the increasing competition caused all of them to cross boundaries and invade each other's territories. Accounting firms attempt to increase their market share in strategy advice, engineering consulting firms tend to move to management consulting; lawyers advise on management, and management consultants advise on mergers and acquisitions or engage in executive search. Large companies attempt to become even bigger by recruiting different experts and by acquiring small firms specializing in these different fields. However, efforts to create diversified 'mega firms' have not been very successful and many oppose these trends on ethical grounds. Thus, the *Financial Times* reported, a proposal that lawyers be allowed to work along side non-lawyers in fee-sharing multi-disciplinary partnerships (MDPs) is stirring controversy within the profession. Some believe professional service firms must offer 'one stop shops' in which the client would be able to get advice on accounting, tax, real estate, management, information, or legal issues. Others vehemently oppose this, believing such partnerships compromise the independence of the legal advice offered. The American Bar Association postponed voting on the issue until at least the year 2000. However, such practices are common already in Europe. In fact, accounting firms are today among the largest providers of legal services. Arthur Andersen is one of the three biggest legal service suppliers, employing 2,400 lawyers in thirty-four countries. Accountants already provide many different services, and the clashes between auditors and management consultants have been increasing (Eaglesham 1999).

In the information age, professional service firms – almost by definition – will find many new business opportunities. To some extent, these opportunities may mean a strong need to restructure and adapt the organization if not its basic values. Another important issue is whether or not the partnership form will be abolished in favour of incorporation. The lure of big money through public offering of shares is very tempting! Even if the partnership form persists, it is important to speculate whether partners will continue to hold the same ethical standards. I have elaborated on these questions in another paper (Aharoni 1999).

In addition, firms find that their future growth depends on serving markets in developing countries. China and India, the two most populous countries in the world, cannot be ignored. The rate of growth in the developed, mature markets of the world is very low and the major growth (and opportunities) may be found in countries that until recently were considered to enjoy too little income per capita. The marketing of services in these countries presents many obstacles. Firms will have to learn to operate across greater cultural distances, within alien legal systems and across seemingly insurmountable cultural differences. The experience of some firms, particularly in the United States, in operating in multicultural societies may give these firms some competitive edge.

Finally, multinational professional business firms must listen to their customers and understand not only their declared needs but also their way of thinking. My chapter on reputation seems to demonstrate that attempting to convince customers they will receive great service may be less important than acquiring other firms and achieving large size. Still, the quality of service and the competence of professionals is important. A more general implication is that the focus of economic activities is rapidly changing to trade in knowledge, ideas and information intensive services. The ramifications to the way firms are organized and managed are manifold.

One implication of increasing globalization is that governments will have to augment their co-operation to streamline the flows of goods across borders but mainly to regulate cross border funds flow effectively, to agree on rules for mutual recognition, and to create new rules. The chapter by Kostecki shows the degree to which rules written decades ago hinder development of free flows of goods and services today. The chapter by Honeck tells the saga of achieving even very rudimentary rules for regulating services and controlling licenses. Both show how very far are we from the global village envisioned by Marshall McLuhan and how important are institutions, rules, regulations and laws in invigorating a true seamless global flows of factors of production. Kretschmer *et al.* see the distribution of intellectual property rights as dependent on the mutual bargaining power of the parties involved. They believe the bargaining power of the artists will increase and the collecting societies are in a precarious situation since monitoring of use involves much less transaction costs. Of course, the music industry is not alone in facing rapid changes in technology, deregulation and other changes in institutions. Many of the conclusions offered by Kretchmer *et al.* are very relevant to other industries as well. Some of the implications for airlines are discussed by Seristö.

The role of government in regulating services has undergone a major revolution recently. Policy changes, in particular deregulation, induced global operations by creating new opportunities for market access. Protective policies have in many cases fragmented the markets and the opening of these markets to foreign competition has allowed great advantages to those firms that were first to be deregulated. Further, the immediate aftermath of deregulation has been a major restructure of the deregulated industries (Mahini and Turcq 1994). In many cases, deregulation has resulted in the dominance of a few giant global players.

Mallampally and Zimny rightly emphasize government policies as a major reason for the expansion of direct foreign investments in services. Only a few decades ago, governments in both developed and developing countries guarded zealously many of their service industries against the onslaught of foreign competition. Industries such as telecommunications were maintained as a local monopoly, and banking or advertising, and certainly education and health were considered strategically, politically, or culturally sensitive. The liberalization of the markets, in particular after the fiscal problems in Latin America and as a result of the transition of the socialist economies, have changed all that, allowing more global competition and strengthening some of the service MNEs.

Conclusions

This introduction has only touched upon the many fascinating new ideas presented by the various authors in this volume. If there is one theme that dominates all the contribution it seems to be the fast paces of changes in technology, in governmental policies and in the core competence of firms leading to competitive advantage.

References

Aharoni, Y. (1966) *The Foreign Investment Decision Process*, Boston: Harvard Business School Press.

—— (1999) 'Internationalization of Professional Services: Implications for Accounting Firms', in D. Brock, C. R. Hinings and M. Powell (eds) *Restructuring the Professional Organization: Accounting, Health and Law*, London:Routledge.

Alchian, A. and Demsetz, H. (1972) 'Production, Information Costs and Economic Organization', *American Economic Review* 62: 777–95.

Bartlett, C. and Ghosal, S.(1989) *Managing Across Borders: The Transnational Solution*, Boston: Harvard Business School Press.

Casson, M. (1997) *Information and Organization: A New Perspective on the Theory of the Firm*, Oxford: Clarendon.

Eaglesham, J. (1999) 'Massed Ranks of Accountants Throw Lawyers Defences into Disarray', *Financial Times*, 11 August.

Gereffi, G. and Korzeniewicz, M. (eds) (1994) *Commodity Chains and Global Capitalism*, London: Greenwood.

Giarini, O. (1994) 'The Service Economy: Challenges and Opportunities in Business Firms', in M. M. Kostecki (ed.) *Marketing Strategies for Services*, 23–40, London: Pergamon.

Gupta, A. K., and Govindarajan, V. (1991) 'Knowledge Flows and the Structure of Control Within Multinational Corporations', *Academy of Management Review* 16: 768–92.

—— (1993) 'Coalignment Between Knowledge Flows Patterns and Strategic Systems and Processes Within MNCs', in P. Lorange, B. Chakravarthy, J. Roos, and A. Van de Ven (eds) *Implementing Strategic Processes: Change, Learning and Co-operation*, Oxford: Blackwell, 329–46.

Hirsch, S. (1989) 'Services and Service Intensity in International Trade', *Weltwirtschaftliches Archiv* 125: 45–60.

Hu, Y. S. (1992) 'Global Stateless Corporations Are National Firms with International Operations', *California Management Review* 34 (2) (winter): 107–26.

Hymer, S. H. (1960, 1976) *The International Operation of National Firms: a Study of Direct Investment*, PhD thesis, MIT, published by the MIT Press.

Johanson J. and Vahlne, J. (1977) 'The Internationalization Process of the Firm – a Model of Knowledge Development and Increasing Foreign Market Commitments', *Journal of International Business Studies* 8: 23–32.

Kogut, B. and Zander, U. (1992) 'Knowledge of the Firm, Combinative Capabilities and the Replication of Technology', *Organization Science* 3: 383–87.

—— (1993) 'Knowledge of the Firm and the Evolutionary Theory of the Multinational Corporation', *Journal of International Business* 24: 625–45.

Lawrence, J. and Lorsch, L. (1967) *Organization and Environment*, George, Ontario: Irwin-Dorsey.

Mahini, A. and Turcq, D. (1994) 'The Three Faces of European Deregulation', *The McKinsey Quarterly* 3: 143–58.

Porter, M. E. (ed.) (1986) *Competition in Global Industries*, 15–60, Cambridge, Mass: Harvard Business School Press.

Quinn, J. B., Doorley, T. and Paquette, P. (1990) 'Beyond Products: Services-Based Strategy', *Harvard Business Review*, March/April, 58–67.

Quinn, J. B. and Paquette, P. (1990) 'Technology in Services: Creating Organizational Revolutions', *Sloan Management Review* 31 (2)(winter.): 81–95.

Rugman, A. M. (1980) 'Internationalization as a General Theory of Foreign Direct Investment: a Re-Appraisal of the Literature', *Weltwirtschaftliches Archiv*, Band 115, Heft 2.

Thompson, J. D. (1967) *Organisations in Action*, New York: McGraw Hill.

World Bank (1999a) *World Development Report*, Oxford: Oxford University Press.

World Bank (1999b) *World Development Indicators*, Oxford: Oxford University Press.

Part I

The globalization of service industries

2 Foreign direct investment in services

Trends and patterns

Padma Mallampally and Zbigniew Zimny

Introduction

The purpose of this paper is to examine trends and patterns of foreign direct investment (FDI) in services, and their underlying reasons so as to shed some light on the globalization of services, as far as FDI is concerned. Globalization involves, among other things, the international expansion of firms' activities through trade, FDI and other modes (such as licensing, subcontracting or franchising) of accessing markets, resources and assets and reducing costs. FDI has increased particularly rapidly in recent decades and, as a result, sales of foreign affiliates have become larger than exports for delivering products to international markets (UNCTAD 1998: 2). FDI has also become one of the key channels for international technology transfer.

The importance of FDI as an instrument of globalization is much greater in service industries than in manufacturing, because many services are not tradable and establishing foreign affiliates is often the only mode of accessing foreign markets. In addition, other reasons for serving foreign markets through foreign affiliates, such as the need for proximity to clients for effective delivery or because of regulations requiring local presence, common to both service and goods industries, are stronger in the former than in the latter. Because of the limited tradability of many services, the pursuit of cost-reducing and asset- and resource-seeking objectives by TNCs is limited, in services industries, to FDI in information-intensive services that can be traded along computer-communication networks.

Growth and types of services FDI

The rapid growth of FDI, more rapid than the growth of production and trade, has been one of the key driving forces of globalization. This growth has, in fact, been driven by FDI in services. As a result, the sectoral composition of global FDI has shifted towards services. During the 1950s, FDI was concentrated in the primary sector and resource-based manufacturing (UNCTC 1989: 8). Today, it is mainly in services and manufacturing. The shift towards services was quite steady during the 1970s and 1980s and continued into the 1990s: services represented less than a quarter of the stock of FDI of major home and host countries at the beginning of the 1970, 40 per cent in 1985 and around half in 1995 (Figure 2.1).

This dynamic growth and increasing share of services in FDI are indicative of various types of services globalization through FDI. These include:

- globalization of service TNCs – and the service industries they represent – which takes place when service parent firms in an industry undertake FDI in the same industry;
- globalization of corporate services by firms in manufacturing and primary sectors: when in-house services are performed by separate units located abroad;
- globalization of corporate services by service TNCs investing abroad in service affiliates in service industries different from the industry of the

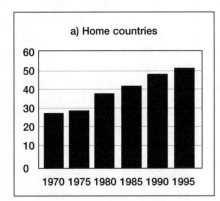

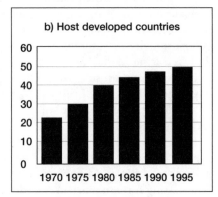

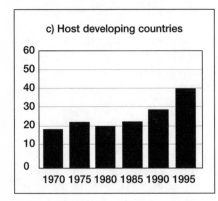

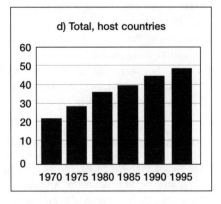

Figure 2.1 The share of FDI stock in services in total FDI stock in principal home and host countries, 1970–95 (%)

Source: Annex table

parent firm, to produce services in-house (e.g. data services) or to diversify activities (Hood and Peters 1997);

- establishment of affiliates abroad by parent firms from all sectors, not to produce services but to perform certain functions for parent companies or corporate networks. Financial affiliates in tax havens and transportation affiliates offering flags of convenience are of this type. Services FDI data typically include holding companies which may or may not engage in services production abroad. From the viewpoint of corporations, holdings may perform management services (therefore some countries classify them under 'property management');[1]

- affiliates in services industries which do not fall under any of the above types of services FDI such as FDI in real estate.

The relative importance of these various types of services FDI cannot be ascertained in a systematic or comprehensive manner due to limitations on the availability of data. Only a few countries publish data that shed light on services FDI by industry, and especially data throwing light on the extent to which FDI in services results from the globalization of the services sector (that is, FDI undertaken by service parent firms within the services sector: in the same industry or other service industries) and globalization of corporate services by parent firms in goods industries. Data are available for the United States, Germany, and, to a limited extent, the United Kingdom (Figure 2.2, page 28). For the United States they show that, by the mid-1990s, not more than half of the FDI stock in services was controlled by service TNCs, and at least half by companies from other sectors; this ratio had not changed since 1977. Exclusion of holding companies from the United States data does not alter this ratio much. For both Germany and the United Kingdom, around a maximum of 80 per cent of services FDI was under control of service TNCs. Exclusion of holding companies, possible for Germany, brings the ratio closer to that of the United States ratio: services TNCs control only 60 per cent of FDI stock in services.

More instructive are figures disaggregated by service industries.[2] It is in trading and financial services other than banking and insurance that the role of service TNCs in the globalization of the respective services is the smallest and the role of TNCs from other sectors the greatest. Typically, the stock of FDI in these services is several times greater than the FDI stock controlled by parent firms in these industries: six times greater in Germany and over three times greater in the United States in the case of outward stock in the mid-1990s. If the latter data are disaggregated into wholesale and retail trading, the ratios are, respectively, six and one, indicating that inter-sectoral origin of FDI is typical for wholesale rather than retail trading.[3] Data available for Germany for 1985 and 1996 show little change in the ratio. For Germany, this ratio is much higher for other financial services: in 1996, FDI stock in other financial services was twenty-three times higher than the total FDI stock controlled by TNCs in financial services other than banking and finance, a

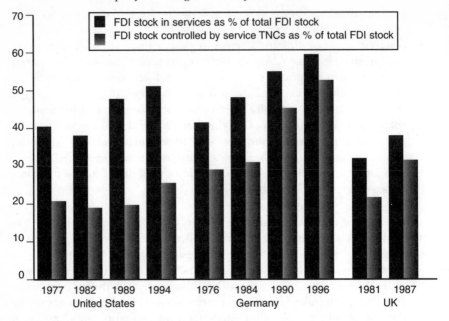

Figure 2.2 Outward FDI in services and by services parent firms from the United
States, Germany and the United Kingdom, various years (%)

Source: UNCTAT 1993 and author's calculations based on national sources

doubling from the level of twelve times in 1985. In the United States the ratio
was greater than three in 1994 (Table 2.1).

In other service industries (leaving holdings aside) these ratios are first,
generally smaller than in trading and other financial services. In the United
States, in a group of industries including business services such as advertising and computer and data processing services, rentals, health services
and hotels, the ratio was 1:8. In Germany, in the insurance industry, it was
1:6. Secondly, for a number of service industries such as banking, communication, construction and public utilities, they were smaller than one,
indicating that parent firms in these industries had FDI in industries
different from their own. For example, parent firms in banking had
affiliates in other financial services and parent firms in telecommunication,
in data services and manufacturing. In the United States these investments
were at least twice as large as those in the same industry. Data on holdings
for the two countries show different ratios: in the United States, FDI stock
in holdings is fifteen times larger than the stock controlled by parent
holding companies, while in Germany the ratio is only one fifth. Given that
holdings are typically included in the aggregate data on the services sector,
they can distort averages for the entire sector, as noted.

Foreign-direct-investment data underestimate the globalization of
services firms and service industries in two respects. First, as they are

collected on the basis of a definition according to minimum equity capital stakes (typically above 10 per cent), they cannot capture globalization through non-equity arrangements, which in a number of service industries play a very important role in the global expansion of firms, more important than equity-based forms. International restaurant networks, especially fast-food networks, car rentals and retail trading networks are frequently based on franchising arrangements. Management contracts are used in the hotel industry (together with equity forms) and partnerships rather than equity links in business services such as business consultancy, engineering or legal services. Second, data on the stock of FDI in services do not capture global-ization of services TNCs that undertake FDI in non-service industries: in manufacturing or in mining. Although the incidence of this is much smaller than the expansion of manufacturing TNCs into services such as trading and financial services, it can take place, as the examples given above indicate.

In spite of the rapid expansion of FDI in services, the degree of globalization of the services sector as measured by the globalization of service firms *per se* (Table 2.2) or the services sectors of host countries through FDI (Table 2.3) still lags behind that in the manufacturing sector. The explanation can be two-fold. First, as discussed later in this chapter, the growth of the services sector in national economies and the building up of

Table 2.1 Outward FDI by industry of parent firm and by industry of foreign affiliate: Germany and the United States (billions of currencies and ratio)

Industry	Germany 1996			United States 1994		
	FDI stock, DM billion			FDI stock, $ billion		
	By industry of parent	By industry of affiliate	Ratio	By industry of parent	By industry of affiliate	Ratio
	1	2	3=2:1	1	2	3=2:1
Trading	12.2	69.8	5.7	20.2	69.2	3.4
Financial						
Services	68.4	128.00	1.9	87.5	114.1	1.3
Banking	50.4	45.5	0.9	34.6	25.9	0.7
Insurance	15.4	24.7	1.6	34.1	27.1	0.8
Other finance	2.5	56.9	22.8	18.8	61.1	3.3
Holdings	145.6	26.6	0.2	6.7	101.7	15.2
Transport	3.8	3.3	0.9	2.9	4.5	1.6
Communication	3.2	1.9	0.6	17.9	6.8	0.4
Construction	2.2	1.8	0.8	2.9	1	0.3
Public utilities	4.4	2.4	0.5	5.6	2.5	0.4
Memorandum:						
Manufacturing	186.7	127.1	0.7	347.7	201.8	0.6
Primary sector	3.7	6.1	1.6	95.3	75.8	0.8

Source: Authors' calculations based on national sources

Note
In the case of the United States, the primary sector includes petroleum industry services

Table 2.2 Degree of transnationalization of United States transnational corporations (%)

Industry of parent company	Share of foreign affiliates in total assets of TNCs				Share of foreign affiliate in total sales of TNCs			
	1982	1989	1994	1996	1982	1989	1994	1996
ALL INDUSTRIES	26	24	28	–	29	29	31	–
All excluding banking	22	22	26	28	28	29	31	33
Manufacturing	27	27	33	35	30	34	37	39
SERVICES								
Banking	36	28	34	–	43	30	31	–
Finance, insurance and real estate	10	13	20	20	15	19	21	22
Finance	–	12	31	34	18	14	21	22
Insurance	–	11	10	9	12	17	12	12
Trade	16	16	15	24	19	19	14	–
Wholesale	25	19	20	31	25	21	17	26
Retail	11	14	12	15	13	18	11	–
Transportation, communication and public utilities	5	10	13	16	6	7	13	14
Transportation	–	4	10	9	–	4	9	10
Communication	–	14	16	19	–	9	17	17
Public utilities	–	–	9	15	–	–	6	10
Construction	24	29	39	49	27	20	27	32
Business and other services	15	20	19	23	16	19	20	26
Services total	24	21	24	–	20	19	18	–
Services excluding banking	10	14	18	20	15	17	17	23

Source: United States Department of Commerce, *United States Direct Investment Abroad*, Benchmark Surveys, various issues

Note
Dash indicates that data are not available

Table 2.3 Transnationalization of the service sectors of selected host countries (%)

Host economy	Year	Foreign affiliates as % of total	
		Services[a]	Manufacturing
a) Value-added			
Finland	1996	3.6	13.3
Japan	1995	0.4	2.5
Sweden	1994	3.4	18.0
United States	1996	3.1	8.7
China	1996	0.5	19.1
India	1991	0.5	12.2
Mexico	1993	1.6	64.0
Taiwan Province of China	1995	21.5	37.3
b) Employment			
Austria	1996	6.3	19.8
Finland	1997	5.1	12.5
Germany	1996	2.5	13.0
Japan	1995	0.2	1.2
Sweden	1996	4.4	18.0
United States	1996	2.6	10.8
Brazil	1995	1.2	13.4
Hong Kong, China	1994	14.3	16.0
Indonesia	1996	0.4	4.7
Mexico	1993	0.7	17.9
Sri Lanka	1996	5.7	54.4
Taiwan Province of China	1995	7.6	21.1
Viet Nam	1995	1.5	14.9

Source: UNCTAD FDI/TNC data base

Note

a Data shown for services refer to non-manufacturing, that is, to the primary and tertiary sectors. Since FDI in the primary sector in most of the countries in the table is negligible, the figures reflect the transnationalization of the service sector

competitive advantages by services firms are relatively recent phenomena. Thus, service firms historically have been small and domestically focused. As indicated above, a good part of FDI in services is undertaken by manufacturing firms, and does not reflect the globalization of services firms in their own right, linking service parents to service affiliates (although, of course, the establishment of affiliates by manufacturing firms represents globalization of services as such, as part of the value added chain of manufacturing firms). This is why much of the services FDI expansion has taken place in the financial and trading services. And second, countries have liberalized their policies with respect to FDI in services relatively recently, compared to FDI in the extractive and manufacturing sectors. So the expansion of FDI in services in modern times has a relatively short history: though the relative importance of FDI is growing, more time is needed for services FDI relative to the activities of service firms or service industries in host countries (and home countries) to catch up with the manufacturing-sector ratios.[4]

Table 2.4 The composition of FDI stock in services, major home and host countries[a], 1990–95 (US$ billion and %)

Industry/sector	1990	1991	1992	1993	1994	1995
a) Outward stock			Value			
Tertiary, total	686	775	817	913	1013	1160
Finance	332	357	399	468	510	575
Trading	125	140	147	157	169	184
Other	230	279	272	288	334	401
			Composition			
Tertiary, total	100	100	100	100	100	100
Finance	48	46	49	51	50	50
Trading	18	18	18	17	17	16
Other	34	36	33	32	33	35
b) Inward stock			Value			
Tertiary, total	478	521	512	572	636	723
Finance	162	178	180	236	249	334
Trading	154	170	169	182	203	201
Other	162	174	163	154	183	188
			Composition			
Tertiary, total	100	100	100	100	100	100
Finance	34	34	35	41	39	46
Trading	32	33	33	32	32	28
Other	34	33	32	27	29	26

Source: Authors' calculations based on national sources

Note
a Australia, France, Germany, Italy, the Netherlands, United Kingdom, United States for both outward and inward stock; Canada and Japan for outward stock
Figures have been rounded up and totals may reflect this

Industry and country patterns

Industries

Within the services sector, finance- and trade-related activities dominate the FDI stock in services of most home and host countries: during the 1990s they consistently accounted for two thirds of the FDI stock of major home countries, while their share in the inward stock of major host developed countries increased from two thirds in 1990 to three quarters by 1995 on account of the growing share of financial services (Table 2.4). It seems that these shares were even higher in the mid-1980s, not only in developed but also in host developing countries, exceeding in many individual countries 80 per cent (UNCTC 1989: 167–9). This domination is not surprising, given that financial TNCs (banks and insurance companies) and trading companies (for example, Japanese *sogo shosha* and *chaebols* from the Republic of Korea) are among the most prominent transnational service corporations and, as mentioned before, that petroleum and manufacturing companies have invested heavily in wholesale and marketing affiliates and TNCs from all sectors tend to establish their own finance-related foreign affiliates.[5] In addition, while most service industries, including financial services like banking, insurance, and trading services performed by independent companies, such as retailers or trading intermediaries were, until not long ago, heavily regulated and often closed to foreign competition, internalized financial and trading functions were not regulated in a similar manner. This was because they did not pose an immediate competitive threat to domestic service industries in host countries, and foreign affiliates performing these functions in support of trade or FDI were considered necessary for doing business. Moreover, not competing directly with other service companies, but rather servicing units of their own corporate networks, these affiliates did not need to exhibit strong ownership-specific advantages over service companies of host countries.

The principal task of finance-related affiliates established by non-financial corporations in the trading, manufacturing and petroleum industries as well as by banks or insurance companies is to improve the efficiency of the financial management of their corporate systems by such means as facilitating the flow of funds among the various entities of a corporate system; providing consumer credit to boost sales (e.g. cars); investing surplus funds as profitably as possible; raising funds locally; and utilizing the facilities offered by tax havens. Insurance companies also establish finance affiliates in major financial centres to invest their parent corporations funds in foreign securities. The growth of finance-related services has also been fuelled by the growth of holding companies. Holding companies are a popular conduit of FDI for all types of TNCs and are often motivated by tax reasons. They are typically responsible for certain aspects of the financial management and administration of a corporate system as a whole, supplying it with buying, accounting or management services. Since their assets include those of both service and non-service TNCs, their inclusion in the category of finance-related services FDI inflates the size of that category to a certain extent (UNCTC 1989: 20–1).

As regards FDI in trading services, as shown earlier, it is also dominated by marketing affiliates established by parent firms in manufacturing rather than by transnational trading companies. Investment in trading affiliates by manufacturing firms is in line with the theory which explains the international expansion of firms as a sequential, step by step process, in which establishing a trading affiliate abroad is one of the steps, following arm's length exports and preceding FDI (Johanson and Vahnle 1993; UNCTAD 1996). The trading affiliate does not have to be dismantled once an affiliate in goods-production is itself established: it may even grow or new trading affiliates may be established to distribute goods produced by the foreign affiliate in place of those imported from the parent. So trading affiliates are needed to support both international trade and FDI in manufacturing and, as these two expand, they lead to FDI in trading, apart from that resulting from the expansion of transnational trading corporations. During the 1980s and 1990s, the balance between the role of marketing affiliates and independent trading corporations appears to have shifted in favour of the former, because of the declining importance of commodity traders and because, among others, 'a growing number of leading manufacturers appears to perceive their comparative advantage increasingly in distribution, product development, marketing and similar activities' (UNCTC 1989: 25–6). Downstream integration into distribution and marketing activities has become a widely embraced strategy for large manufacturers producing differentiated and marketing-intensive products, in order to internalize transaction costs and the advantages arising from the producer-specific knowledge of their products. Trade-mark and brand-name considerations, as well as the growing importance of global marketing strategies, have become a major investment determinant for the establishment of marketing affiliates. This trend has been fostered by the fact that trade marks and brand names are normally granted for an indefinite period, in contrast to patents and copyrights. In industries such as petroleum, office equipment and computers, pharmaceuticals, and food and beverages, the major TNCs have established global networks of marketing affiliates.

Although, as indicated, FDI in other service industries can also be undertaken by both service TNCs and industrial TNCs (e.g. in transportation or data services) in none of them is the part accounted for by non-service TNCs as large as that in trading and other financial services and, by and large, FDI in these other industries reflects the global expansion of services TNCs. Initially, however, the expansion of services TNCs began on a large scale, because the globalization of industrial activities in the primary and manufacturing sectors through trade and FDI required not only an increasing reliance on services which could be undertaken in-house (such as trading or finance) – leading to FDI in services by non-service firms – but also on other services supplied at home by independent companies, such as accounting and business consultancy services, advertising and legal and banking services. Therefore the first wave of the international expansion of service TNCs took place when they followed their clients – TNCs in primary and manufacturing industries – abroad. Their ownership-specific advantages consisted of the intimate knowledge of their clients' needs and the ability to provide their clients with services of known quality anywhere in the world (Nachum 1999: 77–9). In the process, service TNCs gained experience and discovered the advantages of operating internationally, which they built upon to find new customers and penetrate new markets. As a result, many service firms which followed their industrial counterparts abroad expanded to provide services to others, becoming transnational in their own right by the beginning of the 1980s.

By the late 1980s and the 1990s, the number of service industries open to FDI was considerably expanded (see later in this chapter). This should have led to a greater diversification of the industry composition of FDI in services towards services other than trading and financial services. Surprisingly, however, the FDI data for the largest home and host countries do not indicate that this has happened (Table 2.4). The share of services other than financial and trading services in the outward stock of these countries has been stable at one third of the total stock in services while in the inward stock it even declined between 1990 and 1995 from one third to one quarter. Thus any changes that have occurred have apparently taken place at the level of individual services industries rather than groups of industries.

Data for the United States, by far the largest home and host country for the services FDI stock, give an idea about trends in this regard for the United States, and for other home countries to the extent that the latter invest in services in the United States. Ranking industries by FDI-stock increases between 1990 and 1997, FDI in public utilities is observed to have grown the fastest, with an increase in outward FDI of over ten times; that is followed by outward FDI stock in communication (five times), car rentals and business services (both over four times). Even though both telecommunications and public utilities are capital-intensive industries with companies of large size, their FDI expansion has not yet changed significantly the composition of services FDI, because this expansion began from a low absolute level. (The share of both these industries in the outward FDI stock of services increased three times from 1 per cent to 3 per cent.) It is interesting that among financial services neither insurance nor banking expanded particularly rapidly: the former grew slightly above and the latter below the average growth for all industries. As regards United States inward FDI, which throws light on FDI by other countries, mainly Western Europe and Japan, the fastest growth was in health services (ten times), followed by telecommunications services (five times), other financial services (more than four times), business services including accounting, R&D and management and public relations services (four times), and public utilities (three times). Apart from other financial services, accounting for 10 per cent of the United States inward stock in services in 1997, the shares of the other fast-growing categories did not exceed 2 per cent in that year. FDI in banking grew at a rate slightly above the average rate for the total FDI stock while FDI in insurance increased considerably more and, as a result its share in the total United States services FDI stock increased from 14 to 19 per cent between 1990 and 1997 (Table 2.5).

Although such detailed breakdown of FDI data is not available for other countries, the United States data probably highlight pretty well the dynamic industries for services FDI in and by other countries as well. They include telecommunication services, public utilities, various business services and financial services other than banking and insurance. For a number of countries, both home and host, they may also include banking and insurance services (in some countries such as Germany and France these have grown at above average rates). Given that deregulation of air transportation services is beginning to take hold in Western Europe and other countries, this industry is another candidate for the future dynamic expansion of FDI.

Table 2.5 United States service industries with fastest-growing FDI, 1990–97 (%)

Industry	FDI stock index index, 1997 (1990=100)	Share of total FDI stock in services	
		1990	1997
a) Outward stock			
Public utilities	1064	1	3
Communication	520	1	3
Car rental services	451	0	1
Business services[a]	411	3	4
Finance except banking	356	11	17
Other[b]	305	1	1
Transportation	242	1	1
Management	240	1	1
Petroleum related services	234	5	5
Holding companies	234	31	31
Insurance	229	9	8
Hotels	207	1	1
Construction	195	0	0
Retail trade	178	3	2
Banking	166	10	7
Wholesale trade	158	21	14
Engineering and architectural services	157	0	0
Film, TV, etc.	127	1	1
Real estate	64	1	0
Health services	36	0	0
Memorandum			
Total FDI stock in services	236	100	100
FDI stock in all industries	200		
b) Inward stock			
Health services	1003	0	1
Communication	526	1	2
Finance except banking	421	4	10
Accounting, research and management services	402	0	1
Holding companies	318	1	2
Public utilities	299	1	2
Other[c]	283	1	2
Insurance	255	14	19
Business services[a]	288	3	4
Transportation	255	1	1
Banking	201	9	10
Petroleum related services	178	4	4
Retail trade	174	5	4
Wholesale trade	172	26	24
Real estate	98	18	9
Hotels	97	5	3
Film, TV, etc.	70	5	2
Construction	60	2	1
Engineering etc.	56	1	0
Memorandum			
Total FDI stock in services	183	100	100
FDI stock in all industries	173		

Table 2.5 (Continued)

Source: United States, Department of Commerce, Bureau of Economic Analysis, Survey of
　　　Current Business, various issues

Notes
a Advertising; equipment rental, excluding automotive and computers; computer and data
　processing services; other business services such as services to buildings
b Automotive parking; amusement and recreation services; legal, educational and
　accounting services; research and development services; repair and other services provided
　on a commercial basis
c Car rental and parking services; repair services; amusement and recreation services; legal
　and educational services; other services provided on a commercial basis

Countries

The long-term reorientation of FDI towards the services sector has occurred
in almost all home developed countries. In 1995, the share of services in total
FDI stock of nine major home countries was higher than in 1985 and earlier
years, ranging from 40 per cent in the United Kingdom to 65 per cent in Italy
and Japan (see annex table). In four of the countries, the high shares already
reached in 1990 stopped growing further in the 1990s. Apart from that, the
greatest change in the home country pattern of FDI in services has been the
loss of the dominance by the United States and the catching up of West
European countries and Japan as large home countries for services FDI.
Having reached the status of a mature services economy well ahead of other
developed countries, in 1970, the United States dominated the outward stock
of services FDI of the nine principal home countries, accounting for almost
two-thirds of it. By 1990, this share fell to 29 per cent (in spite of the rapid
growth of services FDI from the United States) to increase to 32 per cent in
1995. In 1970, the FDI stock in services of the five countries (Japan, Germany,
United Kingdom, France and the Netherlands) following the United States
as large home countries (in 1995) was only over 40 per cent of the United
States stock; it increased to 111 per cent by 1985 and 213 per cent in 1990,
declining to 174 per cent in 1995.

Services FDI was the most dynamic component in the rapid build-up of the
outward FDI stock of Japan, especially during the 1980s. Apart from the
expansion of Japanese *sogo shosha* – general trading companies – the 1980s
witnessed a remarkable expansion of Japanese banks and securities
companies into foreign markets and the beginnings of a more cautious
expansion of insurance companies. This expansion was fuelled by a strong
capital base generated by a large and profitable domestic market, high
savings rate, a strong currency and a substantial balance of payments surplus.
Other areas of rapid expansion for Japanese firms included real estate
(especially in the United States where Japan's FDI stock increased fifteen
times between 1985 and 1990: from $1 billion to $15 billion), advertising,
data services and fast-food. As in the case of many United States service TNCs
fifteen to twenty years earlier, Japanese service TNCs were pulled abroad by
the rapid expansion of industrial TNCs – their major home clients. In the

1990s, as a result of the recession in many of the host countries for Japanese FDI (which resulted, among others, in losses from real estate investment in the United States), slowing down of the Japanese economy and a financial crisis in Japan, the growth of services FDI by Japanese TNCs slowed down, although Japan remained the second largest home country for services FDI after the United States.

Western European firms were quite well established among TNCs in many of the important service industries such as banking, insurance and reinsurance, publishing, airlines and other transportation already in the 1980s. They also rivalled Japanese TNCs in wholesale trading. Their foreign expansion was greatly facilitated by the Single Market programme of the then European Community (now European Union) announced by the mid-1980s and implemented in the second half of the 1980s and early 1990s. The restructuring of many service industries followed, leading, among others to accelerated intra-EU FDI flows in services between the mid-1980s and early 1990s (UNCTC 1991: 19–20). Another area of expansion of West European FDI in services has been the United States market: partly to support rapidly growing FDI in manufacturing and partly reflecting the expansion of European service TNCs in their own right, among others, in response to the expansion of United States transnational service corporations on their own markets and to benefit from huge, though competitive United States market. This expansion was also encouraged by the strength of European currencies *vis-à-vis* the dollar.

The expansion of services FDI, undertaken by TNCs from developed countries, has taken place mainly in other developed countries and, mirroring the growth of outward stocks, the inward stocks of FDI in services have also grown considerably in all principal developed host countries (Figure 2.1). But the pattern of inward FDI has been different. First, it has never been dominated by the United States, although, since 1975, that country has been the largest host country to services FDI.[6] In the 1970s, the United States accounted for one-fifth of the stock held by principal developed and developing host countries and in the 1990s this share increased to over 30 per cent. Secondly, Japan is missing from the picture, with its small stock of total FDI and rapidly growing but still very small services FDI stock. So the expansion of inward FDI has taken place mainly in the United States and Western Europe and, beginning in the second half of the 1980s, in the markets of developing countries. Until then, developing countries, to the extent to which they permitted FDI to play a role in their economies, concentrated their policy efforts on manufacturing FDI and the share of services remained at a relatively low level: one-fifth of their inward stock of FDI. Most of it was, most likely, in goods-FDI- and trade- supporting trading and financial services. When developing countries began to liberalize FDI, especially in producer services, in an effort to increase their competitiveness, the share of services in their inward stock of FDI began to grow quickly: it rose to 30 per cent in 1990 and to over 40 per cent in 1995. Between 1990 and

1995, when the inward stock of FDI in services in principal developed countries, affected by the recession of the early 1990s, increased only by 40 per cent, the stock in developing countries increased by three times, thus fuelling the expansion of services FDI into the 1990s. Countries in transition, also seeking to attract FDI as part of the transition process are a new group of host countries where services FDI has been growing rapidly, although, compared to world-wide stock, it still remains at a low absolute level (UNCTAD 1998: 274).

Explanatory factors

The upward trend in services FDI and the pattern of globalization of service industries through FDI reflect the interaction of several factors influencing firms' decisions with respect to internationalization of their service activities. Viewed in the framework of the eclectic paradigm (Dunning 1989), the main factors influencing the trends relate to the location-specific advantages of countries and ownership-specific advantages of TNCs in services. Shifts in economic structure resulting from changes in demand and supply conditions due to economic growth and development have greatly increased the importance of services in national economies and expanded the size of markets for services. Since most services are both intangible and non-storable and, hence, not transportable over distances, they are not tradable at arm's length across borders; thus, except for services that can be delivered through cross-border movement of customers (such as tourism or education), or through the cross-border movement, for limited periods of time, of individual service-providers (for example, expert consultants, musicians, or household helpers) or of groups of providers and equipment (as in the special case of trans-portation services), product delivery of these services to foreign markets is impossible without the establishment of service facilities in those markets. The expansion of national services markets world-wide therefore represents a major improvement in location-specific advantages stimulating FDI in services.

At the same time, in order for firms to exploit foreign markets through FDI, minimum competitive strengths over local firms delivering the same services are necessary. Thus, a second factor explaining the trends and patterns in services FDI is the extent to which firms in different service industries of countries have been able to build up and strengthen their competitive advantages for investing abroad and the strategies they adopt with regard to their internationalization. Moreover, since FDI cannot take place unless foreign firms are allowed to enter and operate without serious impediments, policy changes with respect to the services sector and the rules and regulations governing foreign service providers are a third important factor underlying the trends and patterns in services. Finally, the rapid development of telecommunication and data technologies and their application to the cross-border delivery of information-intensive services not only improves the ease and reduces the costs for firms to undertake

FDI in order to deliver services to foreign markets, but also enables some services to be traded at arm's length. This can reduce the need for firms to rely on FDI to deliver services and exploit location-specific resources, while, at the same time, enabling TNCs to distribute their service activities internationally along efficiency-oriented lines to take advantage of low-cost locations for sourcing information-intensive service inputs. The effects of this increased tradability of service products on services FDI and its pattern are only just beginning to be felt.

Structural change and the growth of services markets

The services sector, already quite important, has grown further in importance in most countries of the world in recent decades. Growth in real income per capita has increased the demand for consumer services, especially in the developed economies but also in many developing countries. At the same time, technological advances have increased the importance of many services as inputs into the production of goods and other services. Services output has grown faster than goods output in industrialized countries, although only slightly faster than manufacturing output.[7] The share of services in GDP has increased in both developed and developing countries: for example, according to one comparison that included thirteen developed economies and forty-one developing countries, in 1985, the share of services averaged 65 per cent for developed countries, as compared with 55 per cent in 1965; for developing countries, the average shares of services in GDP in those two years were 47 per cent and 42 per cent, respectively (Dunning 1989: 5). Developed countries, in particular, have become largely service economies, with services accounting for more than 60 per cent of GDP by the 1990s.[8]

The expansion in the demand for and supply of services to the extent mentioned above would not have been possible without the profound qualitative changes that have taken place in many services during the past two to three decades. The technological-, information- and knowledge-intensity of many services has increased greatly. Revolutionary changes have taken place in financial services, transportation, telecommunications, tourism, and professional business services. For example, telecommunications, based until not long ago on simple electro-mechanical means and relatively unimportant as an industry, have become a sophisticated set of activities that are in wide demand by both households and firms. Accounting, once perceived mainly as book-keeping, has evolved into a complex activity of importance for firms in all countries as a basis for informed management. The increasing role of intermediate or producer services – in particular, information-based services – in the production and diversification of services is part of this process of qualitative change.

The growing economic importance of services also derives from the fact that goods have become technically more complicated and are sold in both domestic and world markets under much more competitive conditions than a decade or two ago. As a result, the final value of goods consists increasingly of various service inputs necessary for competing in such markets. For example, marketing, distribution and after-sale maintenance and servicing activities are important elements in the value of physical products such as copying machines, aircraft, or power-plant equipment.

All this has increased the size of national markets for services, providing an inducement for increasing FDI, as well as domestic investment, in service industries. As FDI is the most convenient mode of delivering many non-tradable services to foreign markets, and the prospects for export-oriented production based on resource availability, cost or efficiency conditions are low in many services, market size is the major location-specific advantage for FDI in services; the growth of FDI can thus be expected to occur as a natural consequence of the growth of markets in many service industries, as long as there are firms that have the competitive strengths necessary to compete with local service providers in foreign countries that permit them to do so. In addition, growing international trade and FDI in the goods-producing sectors that have, as discussed earlier, traditionally been followed by FDI in services, continue to provide an impetus to increased FDI by services TNCs.

Changes in the competitive advantages and internationalization strategies of TNCs

Until two or three decades ago, in many service industries, the competitive advantages of foreign firms seeking to establish local presence or operations in a country were not sufficient to compensate for the additional costs of serving a foreign market (Dunning 1989: 37). This meant that services FDI was largely confined to investment in trade-supporting, client-following, specialized or niche services. As shown in the first part of this chapter, investments in trading and finance affiliates to serve home-country and other firms involved in trade, and TNC affiliates in the primary and manufacturing sectors, have been (and continue to be) the major areas of TNC activity in services.

In recent years, however, qualitative changes have taken place in service industries, increasing the information and knowledge content of service products that, along with the revolution in communication and information technologies, have redefined the parameters related to firm-level decisions regarding FDI in several services. They have created a pattern of ownership-specific advantages in favour of the firms that have been at the forefront of those changes, enabling them to invest abroad successfully. Furthermore, by gaining experience in foreign markets and exploiting economies arising specifically from the greater flexibility offered by multinationality (Dunning 1993: 81), these TNCs have added to their initial competitive advantages. The reduction in costs of co-ordinating cross-border decision-making and management due to advances in telecommunications and information services have further strengthened the competitive advantages of TNCs in services. Moreover, as TNCs globalize their activities in services in an attempt to meet the needs of their transnational and other clients, many of them develop a distinctive quality image, often captured in reputation, increasing the tendency for their competitive advantages to become more firm specific.

Many of the firm-specific competitive advantages underlying services FDI and its growth are based on knowledge: technological, managerial, financial, marketing, or organizational (Dunning 1989: chapter IV). Information- and human capital-intensive services such as banking, finance, telematics, business and professional services embody a common pool of tacit or codifiable knowledge - 'soft technology' – that is specific to the firm, or the collective human resources or personnel of a firm. The knowledge-intensity and advisory content of large service firms in these information-intensive producer services gives them a competitive advantage which is often captured in their name, which connotes quality standards or technical capabilities and provides a basis for the growth of their FDI. Firm-specific advantages in the form of knowledge related to organizing activities and providing services to meet consumers' needs, captured in brand names and trademarks, also explain the growth of TNC activities in consumer services such as hotels, fast-food chains, car rentals and retail stores. In some industries (such as stockbroking, foreign exchange and securities dealing, business consultancy, commodity-broking, data-processing, -provision and -transmission) tech-nology, and information-gathering and processing capabilities embodied in machines have become a principal source of competitive advantage. In addition, economies of scale and scope in operations (as distinct from knowledge generation), form the basis of the competitive advantages accumulated by TNCs in some industries, such as insurance, international trade and banking, professional business services, and retailing, although there may be limits to the extent to which such economies apply.[9] The quest for economies of scale related to knowledge generation, information gathering, processing and transmittal, and to more conventional sources such as specialization and differential procurement and financing costs probably drives many of the mergers and acquisitions that have become a popular mode of entry of TNCs into host countries, especially developed countries. In 1996 and 1997, the value of cross-border mergers and acquisitions in the services sector was $155 billion and $113 billion, as compared with $96 billion and $117 billion in manufacturing (UNCTAD 1998: 423).

As already noted, the range of internationalization options open to corporations as regards expanding the markets for the services they provide is often limited to FDI or other forms of international production because many services are not tradable at arm's length across borders. Under conditions of growing demand for services and growing scope for firms in service industries to build up competitive advantages, one would therefore expect that FDI would expand rapidly – more rapidly than international trade in services – as, indeed, has been the case.[12] Nevertheless, as the data in the earlier parts of this chapter show, the impact of the new sources of competitiveness for TNCs in services is not yet clearly evident in the patterns of FDI by ownership and industry. As discussed, the reasons for this include, among others, the role played by non-equity forms of investment in the global expansion of services firms. Industries in which non-equity arrangements tend to dominate include services in which the performance requirements can be successfully codified into agreements and the knowledge satisfactorily separated from the finance or capital components, for control by the parent firm. The form of the preferred non-equity arrangements varies, from management service contracts in the case of hotels (Contractor and Kundu 1998) to networks of firms that co-operate as regards minimum quality, customers referral, and sharing a common name, but stop short of common ownership, as in the case of several professional business services (Aharoni 1993). Taking services as a whole, over the past couple of decades, there have been factors both encouraging internalized modes of internationalization and those working in the opposite direction.

Furthermore, the growing importance of created-asset seeking investments for TNCs generally is providing an additional basis for FDI in services beyond those of market-seeking and client-following to deliver services through local presence. The availability of natural and/or human resources in potential host countries has always been important in determining FDI decisions in some service industries, such as tourist hotels and financial institutions (which require adequate local facilities and trained labour, as well as proximity to customers and suppliers); more recently, thanks to the increased tradability along computer-communication lines of information-intensive services, the availability of created assets – primarily skilled and talented human resources at reasonable cost – to produce services not just for the domestic market but for export is increasing in importance for FDI in some information- and knowledge-intensive services. Like TNCs in manufacturing industries such as electronics and automobiles, TNCs in services such as computer systems, banking, insurance, and air transport are beginning to follow integrated international production strategies; activities at various points of the value chain – such as computer programmes, financial advice, claims processing, or accounting – are undertaken in foreign affiliates and vertically integrated with other activities conducted in other affiliates or in the parent firm.

In several service industries, competitive pressures forcing larger TNCs to adopt strategies of following other companies to establish a presence abroad have also contributed to increased FDI by TNCs in important markets aimed at strengthening their respective international market positions *vis-à-vis* major competitors (Dunning 1989: 38–9). The industries mainly affected by this kind of strategies include banking and other financial services and, in some locations, other services such as management consultancy, advertising, air transportation and hotels. The increasing importance of these strategies, as well as the other competitiveness-related factors discussed above have contributed to the diversification, discussed earlier in this chapter, of the home-country distribution of services FDI that was dominated not long ago by the United States.

Changes in policies

One of the most striking developments affecting the globalization of services during the past two decades or so has been the revision of government policies towards the services sector (UNCTAD and The World Bank 1994). Two or three decades ago, governments of both developed and developing economies strictly controlled the extent and form of foreign (and often, domestic private) involvement in major services such as telecommunications, transport, banking and advertising, considered to be strategically, politically, or culturally sensitive industries, as well as in community services such as education, health and public utilities. The qualitative changes in service industries mentioned earlier, coupled, in some cases, with financial constraints affecting state-owned service enterprises have forced governments to review their protectionist policies and set in motion a process of liberalization of policies with respect to domestic as well as international production and provision of services. Domestic as well as foreign competition are increasingly viewed as tools for increasing the efficiency and productivity of service industries, which in turn are recognized as being critical for economic performance generally. Openness to FDI is, in turn, viewed as an important means for injecting and maintaining competition, especially in oligopolistic services markets.

There is no doubt that the opening up of the markets of developed countries has been a major factor encouraging TNCs to exploit their competitive advantages through FDI. In particular, the creation of the Single Market in Europe provided a powerful inducement for both European-Community and the non-European-Community TNCs to invest in the service industries of the European Community countries. This is not surprising, since the single market is, in fact, mostly about services: while the European Community started to dismantle barriers to trade and FDI in goods some thirty years ago, obstacles to trade and FDI in services remained untouched until the 1992 Single Market programme came into force. The essence of the programme was to remove not only the remaining barriers to intra-Community movement of goods but also to remove barriers to the movement of people (including professionals in heavily regulated professions), services and firms. By including services and tackling not only border obstacles to international movements of goods and services but also internal national regulations impeding them, and initiating the deregulation of a number of service industries in the Communities, the programme has led to the opening up of services markets on a large scale for the first time since the establishment of the European Economic Community. Service firms acquired a large geographical space for expansion in Europe while being, at the same time, exposed to competition from firms of other countries. The mere announcement of the Single Market and the beginning of the removal of obstacles in the late 1980s led to a massive reorganization of the Community's service industries and created substantial interest on the part of TNCs from all major home countries in positioning themselves in the large and dynamic European market.

Substantial liberalization of policies with respect to FDI has also taken place in developing countries, particularly those in Latin America, partly as a result of privatization programmes. This has enabled impressive increases in FDI in services, reflected in the rising shares of services in countries such as Argentina, Brazil and Mexico. Although the extent and pace of liberalization varies widely among developing countries and among industries, there has been an overall movement towards liberalizing FDI policies, both horizontally and sectorally in services (UNCTAD and World Bank 1994: 20–30), some of it driven by economic crises and financial pressures. The completion of the Uruguay Round and the adoption of the General Agreement on Trade in Services have undoubtedly provided a potent channel for further liberalization of developing countries' policies related to FDI in services. The adoption of the GATS protocols on basic telecommunications (in February 1998) and on financial services (in March 1999) are likely to affect FDI policies of developing countries in these two major service industries substantially.

Implications of the increasing tradability of services

Technological advances in telecommunication and computer technologies and computer communications in the past two decades have greatly enhanced the abilities for processing and transporting information between geographic locations. These advances in computer communications contribute to the cross-border tradability of information-intensive services by making it possible for information-intensive services or parts thereof to be transported across borders and delivered to foreign customers without the local presence of the provider.

The increased tradability of services has implications for the extent and pattern of FDI in services. These are not, however, straightforward and cannot be generalized for all services. At the aggregate or general level, to the extent that FDI and trade are complementary (as trends in the two flows suggest), the increased tradability of services can be expected to increase FDI. On the other hand, if specific services that could not previously be delivered to foreign markets without the presence of a service provider can now, because of the ease and low-cost of conveying information across borders, be traded without or with limited local presence, FDI in those services could decline.

The degree of tradability and actual trade – or electronic commerce – fostered by the advent and progress of computer-communication systems is likely to vary considerably among service products within industries. In the banking industry, for example, although the use of computerized methods and telematization have made most banking service products technically transportable, a much smaller number of retail banking service products are actually traded internationally, as compared with corporate banking products (UNCTAD 1994: 122). In the insurance industry, there is some evidence to suggest that the potential of information technology has not been used extensively for trade but rather, for increasing the efficiency of the existing structure of international insurance business, which relies heavily on FDI (UN–TCMD 1993). Nevertheless, to the extent that some service products become tradable, the pattern and nature of FDI in services can be expected to be affected. A major implication of this is the prospect for splitting up the value added chain, undertaking export-oriented FDI and engaging in integrated international production in, or involving, services, comparable to that observed in the manufacturing sector. In particular, labour- or human-resource-intensive service inputs can be produced by TNCs, both services firms and manufacturers in their affiliates or under non-equity arrangements with local firms in human-resource-abundant locations and integrated with capital- or technology-intensive services and other products produced elsewhere. This is already taking place in a noticeable manner in the case of services such as computer software, accounting and data processing.[11] This has both benefits and costs for host countries. It creates new opportunities for attracting FDI. At the same time, the likelihood of FDI involving replication of home-country facilities, with comparable productivity, diminishes as TNCs seek to take advantage of low-cost factors of production available in host countries.

Conclusion

Foreign direct investment in services has played a key role in the rapid growth of FDI and international production that constitutes a driving force of the process of globalization. The sectoral composition of world FDI has shifted steadily towards services during the past three decades. The dynamic growth of FDI in services and the increasing share of services in world FDI reflect a variety of ways in which FDI in the services sector is made, by services as well as other firms, and a diversification of home and host countries for FDI in services. Available data indicate that a substantial part of FDI in services taken as a whole is still controlled by firms from other sectors. Data disaggregated by service industry indicate that the intersectoral origin of FDI in services applies mostly to trading services and financial services other than banking and insurance. Considering services as a whole, however, despite the rapid growth of FDI in services, the degree of globalization of the services sector – as measured by the globalization of services firms themselves, or as measured by the globalization of the services sectors of host countries – lags behind that of the manufacturing sector, among others, because of the relatively shorter history of the expansion of FDI in services as compared with that in manufacturing.

The upward trend in services FDI and the patterns observed in the globalization of service industries through FDI involve the interaction of several factors influencing firms' decisions with respect to the internationalization of service activities. Changes in the location-specific advantages of potential host countries as well as ownership-specific advantages of firms for competing abroad have been conducive to increased FDI in services. Most importantly, markets for services have grown significantly as a result of economic growth and structural change, and countries have liberalized their policies with respect to the entry and operations of foreign firms in services while, at the same time, qualitative changes in service industries have strengthened the abilities of firms to build up firm-specific advantages necessary for competing with local firms in host countries. In addition, the growing tradability of information-intensive services is generating scope for efficiency-seeking and created-asset seeking FDI in services, extending the inducements for FDI in services beyond those related to the quest for markets. Overall, these factors are likely to sustain the continued importance of services FDI in the globalization of economic activity, with important potential consequences for patterns of production, growth and development of the countries involved.

Notes

The responsibility for the contents of this paper and the views expressed in it is entirely the authors' own and cannot be attributed to the organization with which they are associated.

1 Holding companies can also be 'letter box' companies that do not perform any specific function along the value-added chain of production but are registered in tax havens (host countries offering tax advantages) or companies established in financial markets to provide access to these markets for corporate networks (Eurostat 1998). Needless to say, TNCs in manufacturing establish foreign affiliates in the form of holding companies. For example, in 1996, in France, shares of outward FDI by manufacturing TNCs accounted for by holding companies ranged from 1 per cent in the chemical industry to one quarter in mechanical industries (Dreyfus 1998: 146).

2 Aggregate figures may be distorted to the extent to which service parent firms control goods-producing affiliates (which is however much less frequent than industrial firms controlling service affiliates) and, as mentioned above, by the importance of holding companies in the services data.

3 It may, however, be that the ratio in retailing results not from homogeneity but from balanced intersectoral investment, that is, retail TNCs chains controlling the stock in manufacturing affiliates (to provide supplies) of the same size as the stock in retail affiliates controlled by manufacturing firms.

4 Historically, FDI in some service industries was important: trading houses, banks, insurance companies were among the first companies to establish foreign affiliates. In the 1870s, the first wave of the expansion of industrial firms abroad was accompanied by FDI in railroads and public utilities, particularly in colonial territories. In the interwar period, much of the United States FDI in Latin America was in transportation, communication and public utilities (Whichard 1981: 39-56; Lipsey 1999: 8).

5 Another reason may be the comparatively large size of these industries and firms in these industries, resulting in larger FDI per foreign affiliate, which was found to be several times greater in trading and financial services than in service TNCs in industries such as advertising or business consultancy. In other capital-intensive

48   *Padma Mallampally and Zbigniew Zimny*

service industries with large firms such as telecommunication or public utilities, until not long ago, FDI was restricted to a greater extent than in trading or finance in many countries (UNCTC 1989: 27).

6 In 1970, Canada had larger stock of both total FDI and services FDI than the United States.

7 See, for example, Jacques Nusbaumer (1987: 10–11). See World Bank (1998: 212–3) for country-wise data on the share of the services and other sectors in GDP in 1980 and 1997.

8 Excluding construction and utilities (electricity, gas and water), services accounted for 62 per cent of total value added in developed economies and 49 per cent of value added in developing economies in 1988–90. If construction and utilities are included, the shares rose to 72 per cent and 58 per cent, respectively (UNCTAD and The World Bank 1994: 7).

9 In the case of insurance, which has been considered one of the industries in which TNCs are particularly likely to benefit from economies of scale, a recent study found that TNCs achieve economies of scale only up to a point, and that the most internationally diversified insurers suffer diseconomies. (See Katrishen and Scordis 1998: 305–23).

10 For instance, the value of services sold abroad by majority-owned affiliates of United States companies rose at a higher rate than the value of United States cross-border sales of private services in every year since 1987 (United States, Department of Commerce, Bureau of Economic Analysis, October 1998).

11 For some examples, see UNCTAD (1993: Part Two).

References

Aharoni, Y. (1993) 'Ownerships, Networks and Coalitions', in Yair Aharoni (ed.) *Coalitions and Competitions: The Globalization of Professional Business Services*, 121–42, London: Routlege.

Contractor, F. J. and Kundu, S. K. (1998) 'Modal Choices in a World of Alliances: Analyzing Organizational Forms in the International Hotel Sector', *Journal of International Business Studies*, vol.29, no.2, second quarter: 325–57.

Deutsche Bundesbank (1998) *International Capital Links*. Special Statistical Publication 10, Frankfurt am Main: Deutsche Bundesbank.

Dreyfus, A. (1998) 'Stock des investissements direct francais a l'etranger au 31 decembre 1996', *Bulletin de la Banque de France*, no. 52, April 1998, Paris: Banque de France.

Dunning, J. H. (1989) *Transnational Corporations and the Growth of Services: Some Theoretical and Empirical Issues*, UNCTC Current Studies, series A, no. 9,New York: United Nations.

—— (1993) *Multinational Enterprises and the Global Economy*, Wokingham, England: Addison-Wesley.

Dunning, J. H. and J.A. Cantwell (1987) *The IRM Directory of Statistics of International Investment and Production*, London: Macmillan.

Eurostat (1998) *European Union Direct Investment Data*, Luxembourg: European Commission.

O'Farrell, P. N. (1995) 'Manufacturing demand for business services', *Cambridge Journal of Economics* 19: 523–34.

Hood, N. and Peters, E. (1997) 'Globalization, corporate strategies and service industry development', mimeo.

Johanson, J. and Vahnle, J. E. (1993) 'The internationalization of the firm: four Swedish cases', in P. J. Buckley and P. Ghauri (eds) *The Internationalization of the*

Firm, London: Academic Press.

Katrishen, F. K. and Scordis, N. A. (1998) 'Economies of Scale in Services: a Study of Multinational Insurers', *Journal of International Business Studies*, vol. 29, no. 2, second quarter: 305–23.

Lipsey, R. E. (1999) 'The role of foreign direct investment in international capital flows', National Bureau of Economic Research, working paper 7094, Cambridge, MA: NBER.

Nachum, L. (1999) *The Origins of the International Competitiveness of Firms: the Impact of Location and Ownership in Professional Service Industries*, Cheltenham: Edward Elgar.

Nusbaumer, J. (1987) *Services in the Global Economy*, Boston: Kluwer International.

OECD (1998) *International Direct Investment Statistics Yearbook*, Paris: OECD.

UN-TCMD (United Nations, Transnational Corporations and Management Division), Department of Economic and Social Development (1993) *International Tradability in Insurance Services: Implications for Foreign Direct Investment in Services*, New York: United Nations.

UNCTAD (United Nations Conference on Trade and Development) (1993) *World Investment Report 1993: Transnational Corporations and Integrated International Production*, New York: United Nations.

—— (1994a) *The Tradability of Banking Services: Impact and Implications*, Geneva: United Nations.

—— (1994b) *World Investment Directory. Vol. IV: Latin America and the Caribbean*, New York: United Nations.

—— (1996) *World Investment Report 1996: Investment, Trade and International Policy Arrangements*, New York and Geneva: United Nations.

—— (1998) *World Investment Report 1998: Trends and Determinants*, New York and Geneva: United Nations.

UNCTAD and The World Bank (1994) *Liberalizing International Transactions in Services: a Handbook*, New York and Geneva: United Nations.

United Nations (1978) *Transnational Corporations in World Development: a Re-examination*, New York: United Nations.

—— (1993) *World Investment Directory 1992. Vol. III: Developed Countries*, New York: United Nations.

UNCTC (United Nations Centre on Transnational Corporations) (1989) *Foreign Direct Investment and Transnational Corporations in Services*, New York: United Nations.

—— (1991) *World Investment Report 1991: the Triad in Foreign Direct Investment*, New York: United Nations.

—— (1992) *World Investment Directory 1992. Vol. I: Asia and the Pacific*, New York: United Nations.

United States, Department of Commerce (1998) *US Direct Investment Abroad. 1994 Benchmark Survey, Final Results*, Washington, D.C.: United States Department of Commerce.

United States, Department of Commerce, Bureau of Economic Analysis (1998) 'U.S. International Sales and Purchases of Private Services: U.S. Cross-Border Transactions in 1997 and Sales by Affiliates in 1996', *Survey of Current Business*, October.

Whichard, O. G. (1981) 'Trends in the United States direct investment position abroad, 1950–1979', *Survey of Current Business*, vol. 61 (February 1981): 39–56.

World Bank (1998) *World Development Report 1998/1999: Knowledge for Development*, New York: Oxford University Press.

Annex Table Foreign direct investment stock in services in principal home and host countries, 1970–95 ($ billion and %)

	1970			1975			1980			1985			1990			1995		
	Total FDI	Servs	Share of servs %	Total FDI	Servs	Share of servs %	Total FDI	Servs	Share of servs %	Total FDI	Servs	Share of servs %	Total FDI	Servs	Share of servs %	Total FDI	Servs	Share of servs %
A. Home countries																		
United States	75.5	24.6	33	124.2	35.6	29	220.2	85.7	39	251	103.1	41	423.2	200.1	47	711.6	374.8	53
Japan[a]	3.6	1.4	39	10.6	4.1	39	19.6	8.5	43	43.9	24.3	55	201.4	136.5	68	306.8	199.1	65
Germany	7.3	1.1	15	20.8 b	8.6 b	41	43.1	20.7	48	60.0	31.4	52	155.1	90.9	59	262.2	144.6	55
UK	21.8	5.1	23	31.6	8.5	27	85.9	31.1	36	87.6	30.5	35	229.3	96.1	42	302.8	120.7	40
France	—	—	—	3.4	1.3	38	12.2	5.3	43	28.3	12.3	43	110.1	55.9	51	184.4	99.4	54
Netherlands	15.6	2.1	13	19.9	2.9	15	42.1	8.0	19	49.6	16.8	34	107.7	46.9	44	178.5	88.3	49
Italy	3.3	1.6	48	3.3	1.3	39	6.9	2.1	30	14.1	7.5	53	56.1	31.7	57	97.0	62.9	65
Canada	6.5	2.1	32	10.4	2.9	28	22.6	5.8	26	38.7	13.6	35	84.8	15.3	18	118.3	51.2	43
Australia	0.6	0.2	33	1.1	0.4	36	2.3	1.0	43	6.7	3.3	49	29.8	16.1	54	36.7	18.4	50
Total	134.2	38.2	28	225.3	65.6	29	454.9	168.2	37	579.9	242.8	42	1397.5	689.5	49	2198.3	1159.4	53
B. Host countries																		
Developed countries																		
United States	13.3	4.1	31	27.7	10.1	36	83.0	37.1	45	184.6	94.8	51	403.7	200.7	50	560.0	300.6	54
UK[c,d]	9.7	1.6	16	24.5	4.6	19	30.0	13.9	46	44.5	11.3	25	203.9	83.7	41	200.0	93.2	47
Germany	9.2	1.7	18	26.9 b	9.0 b	33	36.6	14.7	40	36.9	18.4	50	93.4	59.4	64	162.0	92.1	57
France	—	—	—	4.9	2.9	59	15.4	9.5	62	19.2	12.1	63	77.4	44.7	58	143.7	86.0	60
Netherlands	7.3	2.0	27	9.8	2.7	28	19.2	7.6	40	25.1	11.6	46	72.4	33.1	46	92.1	51.8	56
Australia	—	—	—	8.8	3.8	43	12.9	5.9	46	25.0	13.1	52	70.4	37.4	53	91.9	42.1	46
Spain	—	—	—	2.4	0.5	21	5.1	1.3	25	8.9	2.8	31	41.9	19.3	46	84.4 e	39.2 e	46
Italy	6.2	1.9	31	9.1	2.6	29	8.9	2.8	31	19.0	7.1	37	58.0	33.8	58	63.4	37.1	59
Canada	26.1	5.8	22	36.8	9.0	24	51.6	12.9	25	62.4	18.1	29	108.0	35.4	33	122.8	33.3	27
Japan[a]	1.0	0.1	10	1.5	0.3	20	3.3	0.7	21	4.7	1.3	28	9.9	3.6	36	33.5	15.0	45
Total	72.8	17.2	24	152.4	45.5	30	266.0	106.4	40	430.3	190.6	44	1139.0	551.1	48	1553.8	790.4	51

Annex Table continued

	1970 Total FDI	1970 Servs	1970 Share of servs %	1975 Total FDI	1975 Servs	1975 Share of servs %	1980 Total FDI	1980 Servs	1980 Share of servs %	1985 Total FDI	1985 Servs	1985 Share of servs %	1990 Total FDI	1990 Servs	1990 Share of servs %	1995 Total FDI	1995 Servs	1995 Share of servs %
Developing economies																		
China	—	—	—	—	—	—	4.7	0.6	13	10.8	4.6	43	20.9f	8.4f	40	131.2a	47.4a	36
Singapore	0.6	0.30	50	2.2	1.2	55	6.2	2.8	45	13.0	6.7	52	26.8g	15.4g	57	59.6	37.9	64
Mexico	2.8	0.50h	18	4.6	0.8	17	8.5	1.5	18	14.6	2.9	20	30.3	7.6	25	41.1	20.9	51
Brazil	2.9h	0.50	17	7.3	1.6	22	17.5	3.8	22	25.7	5.5	21	37.1	10.3	28	42.5	18.4	43
Argentina	—	—	—	3.5b	0.9b	26	5.3	1.2	23	6.6	1.6	24	6.9g	3.4g	49	24.6	13.1	53
Thailand	—	—	—	0.5	0.3	60	1.0	0.5	55	2.0	1.0	49	5.5g	2.7g	49	17.4	10.0	57
Indonesia	0.4	0.02	5	4.4	0.3	7	10.3	0.4	4	24.9	0.7	3	38.9	1.1	3	37.3	6.4	17
Taiwan, Pr. China	—	—	—	0.8	0.1	13	2.4	0.2	6	2.9	0.3	10	11.5	3.0	26	15.7a	4.9a	31
Chile	—	—	—	0.04	0.01	25	0.9	0.2	22	2.3	0.7	30	6.2	1.9	31	14.7	3.8	26
Korea, Rep.	0.1h	0.03h	21	0.7b	0.1b	14	1.1	0.4	36	1.8	0.6	33	4.0f	1.5f	38	9.6ii	3.2ii	33
Venezuela	—	—	—	1.3	0.4	31	1.6	0.5	31	1.5	0.3	20	3.9	0.6	15	6.8	2.7	40
Colombia	0.5	0.13	26	0.63	0.18	29	1.1	0.3	23	2.2	0.4	18	3.5	0.4	11	12.1	2.3	19
Philippines	—	—	—	0.36	0.16	45	1.2	0.4	33	1.3	0.3	23	1.6g	0.3g	19	6.1	1.7	28
Total	7.3	1.48	20	26.33	6.05	23	61.8	12.7	21	109.6	25.6	23	197.1	56.6	29	418.7	172.7	41
Grand Total	80.1	18.68	23	178.73	51.55	29	327.8	119.1	36	539.9	216.2	40	1336.1	607.7	45	1972.5	963.1	49

Sources: Compiled by the authors on the basis of OECD, *International Direct Investment Statistics Yearbook*, various issues; United Nations, *World Investment Directory*, various issues; UNCTAD FDI/TNC data base; United Nations, 1978; and national sources.

Note: The home countries in the table represented, in 1995, 79% of the world stock of FDI. The host countries shown accounted for 76% of the world inward stock. Host developed countries accounted for 81% of the total stock of developed countries and host developing countries for 67% of the stock of developing countries. Countries are ranked by the size of FDI stock in services in 1995.

a Stock in services was estimated by applying the industry composition of FDI based on approvals to actual total stock figures. b 1976. c Data are for 1971, 1974, 1981 and 1984 instead of the years indicated in columns. d Source: Dunning (1987). e Calculated by adding flow figures to 1990 stock. f 1988. g 1989. h 1971. ii 1994. Dash indicates data not available.

3 Developing regulatory disciplines in professional services

The role of the World Trade Organization

Dale B. Honeck

Introduction

The Uruguay Round trade negotiations that led to the creation of the World Trade Organization (WTO) brought services trade under multilateral rules for the first time.[1] In the context of the General Agreement on Trade in Services (GATS), one of the major Uruguay Round achievements, governments made legally binding commitments with respect to market access and national treatment in a wide range of services sectors, including professional services. Recognizing the potentially restrictive effects of domestic regulatory measures, WTO Members also agreed on the need to develop specific disciplines to ensure that government regulations are not unduly trade restrictive. The result was Article VI: 4 of the GATS, which refers to three types of regulation (licensing requirements, qualification requirements and procedures, and technical standards) and mandates the development of 'any necessary disciplines'.

Recognizing as well that government regulation is especially pervasive in professional services, the first step in implementing the mandate of GATS Article VI: 4 was the *Ministerial Decision on Professional Services*, and the establishment of the Working Party on Professional Services (WPPS). After several years of difficult discussions, especially in regard to the coverage of Article VI with respect to the market access and national treatment provisions of Articles XVI and XVII of the GATS, WTO Members succeeded in creating the *Guidelines for Mutual Recognition Agreements or Arrangements in the Accountancy Sector*, released in May 1997, followed by the *Disciplines on Domestic Regulation in the Accountancy Sector* in December 1998. Both the guidelines and the disciplines are general in scope, and potentially could be applied across the entire range of professional services.

In addition to the introduction, this chapter has four main parts: the first part describes the initial activities of the WPPS; the second details the development of the disciplines on domestic regulation; the third speculates on future regulatory initiatives in the GATS context; and the fourth presents general conclusions. Each of these four parts is divided into descriptive and analytical sections, respectively. The immediate focus of this chapter is on accountancy, as this was the services sector where work on regulatory disciplines has mainly occurred, but the analysis is generally applicable to all professional services, and perhaps even to services trade in general.[2]

Together with providing a critical overview of the WPPS work on domestic regulation, this chapter helps explain why multilateral regulatory disciplines are needed, why the WTO provides an appropriate forum to create such disciplines, and what are the likely effects on trade. In this regard, it is important to note that both international corporations and locally-based producers, together with consumers, are heavily affected by government regulation of services, not only in respect to business activities in specific services sectors, but also in regard to the wide range of services inputs required by virtually all firms. Consequently, the implications of the WTO work on domestic regulation are of widespread importance. By examining in some detail both the positive and negative aspects of the process for creating the disciplines in accountancy, it should be possible to better assess the requirements for, and potential obstacles to, the development of further regulatory disciplines, both for professional services and other services sectors.

WPPS initial activities

Descriptive summary

Article VI: 4 of the GATS states,

> With a view to ensuring that measures relating to qualification requirements and procedures, technical standards and licensing requirements do not constitute unnecessary barriers to trade in services, the Council for Trade in Services shall, through appropriate bodies it may establish, develop any necessary disciplines. Such disciplines shall aim to ensure that such requirements are, *inter alia*:
>
> (a) based on objective and transparent criteria, such as competence and the ability to supply the service;
> (b) not more burdensome than necessary to ensure the quality of the service;
> (c) in the case of licensing procedures, not in themselves a restriction on the supply of the service.

The ministerial-level *Decision on Professional Services*, which was presented to, and approved by, trade negotiators in the final hours of the Uruguay Round negotiations, has three main aspects: first, it required the immediate implementation of the work programme mandated in Article VI: 4; second, it established the Working Party on Professional Services (WPPS) in order to implement the work programme; and third, it gave priority to the development of multilateral disciplines in the accountancy sector. Accountancy was chosen primarily as a result of lobbying efforts (via government delegations) by the International Federation of Accountants (IFAC), the private-sector international industry association for the profession.[3]

In respect to the priority given to accountancy, the mandate of the WPPS under the Decision on Professional Services had three parts:

1   the development of disciplines on domestic regulation (in accordance with the requirements of GATS Article VI: 4);
2   concentration on the use of international standards;
3   the establishment of guidelines for the recognition of qualifications.

Following the selection of a Chairperson, the first priority of the WPPS was to determine a work programme. As noted in the minutes of the early WPPS meetings (i.e. WTO documents S/WPPS/M1 through M/10), the WTO Secretariat prepared two background documents as preparation for discussion of the work programme. Members subsequently made a substantial number of written submissions, both on a formal and informal basis.[4]

IFAC, the International Accounting Standards Committee (IASC), OECD, UNCTAD, and others, beginning in October 1995, gave presentations and provided detailed written information concerning their work on professional and accountancy services.[5] A list of eight 'Issues Proposed for Consideration' was assembled by the Secretariat in January 1996 from submissions and statements by delegations, together with WPPS discussions; delegates were invited by the Chairperson to indicate how they wished the WPPS to address the issues listed. Some delegations also suggested that, as a complement to the Article VI: 4 negotiations on domestic regulation, Members improve their market access and national treatment commitments. The Secretariat was requested to prepare a background paper on the relevance of existing GATT provisions, particularly the Agreements on Technical Barriers to Trade (TBT) and Import Licensing Procedures.

Some Members, noting that little regulatory information was available from developing countries, requested that a questionnaire be developed; a draft was circulated on 16 February 1996, and quickly finalized. The WPPS decided that the questionnaire should be responded to voluntarily. Countries not respondents to previous accountancy questionnaires from the OECD, IFAC, and other bodies were invited to complete the entire WTO questionnaire, with other Members asked to respond only to new questions not contained in other surveys. A total of forty-four Members (counting the fifteen EC Members separately) responded to the questionnaire, including many of the larger developing countries. UNCTAD also presented information concerning thirty-seven developing countries in July 1996 (S/WPPS/W/8).

The WTO Secretariat was subsequently asked to create a synthesis of questionnaire responses, structured according to the January 1996 list of issues for consideration. Members also requested that the synthesis draw a distinction between GATS Article VI measures (domestic regulation), and those of Articles XVI (market access) and XVII (national treatment). The synthesis was released as document S/WPPS/W/11, in May 1997. In discussing this document, Members stated that a practical working distinction was needed between measures pertaining to Article VI: 4 and those pertaining to Articles XVI and XVII. At the same time, the minutes of the discussion state that delegations were of the view that 'This did not mean, however, that the Working Party should refrain from addressing Article XVI and XVII issues, but simply that it would work on them differently' (S/WPPS/M/9, p.2.).

In regard to work on the second part of the WPPS mandate (i.e. the use of international standards), presentations were made by IFAC, IASC and the International Organization of Securities Commissions (IOSCO) in July 1996.[6] Among the views expressed in informal papers, one Member made the statement that the GATS could not become a forum that would result in mandatory use of what originally were non-binding, voluntary standards. Some delegations also questioned whether IFAC and IASC were 'representative organizations' (i.e. open to at least all the Members of the WTO), as required under GATS Article VI: 5. Despite such differences of opinion, the Singapore Ministerial Declaration of 13 December 1996 did include the statement: 'We encourage the successful completion of international standards in the accountancy sector by IFAC, IASC and IOSCO'.

In respect to the third part of the WPPS mandate (i.e. the establishment of guidelines for the recognition of qualifications), Members provided substantial amounts of information. Their focus was primarily on bilateral mutual recognition agreements (MRAs), rather than on multilateral procedures. One delegation, however, did submit an informal paper on 'competency based assessment' in regard to Article VI: 6. The WPPS meeting minutes (S/WPPS/M/5) state that, 'participants had different views as to whether the approach that should be taken was more related to paragraph 6 of Article VI (Domestic Regulation) or to Article VII on Recognition'. The WPPS Chairperson suggested considering Article VI issues first, then Article VII issues, but delegations preferred to focus on Article VII issues. Members then proceeded to specify the substantive elements needed for recognition guidelines. A number of WTO Members consistently stated they preferred the guidelines to be non-binding (i.e. to be used voluntarily to assist in the negotiations of MRAs).

The final version of the MRA guidelines was released in May 1997, and is entitled *Guidelines for Mutual Recognition Agreements or Arrangements in the Accountancy Sector* (WTO document S/L/38, dated 28 May 1997). As required by Members, the Guidelines are voluntary. According to the introduction to the MRA Guidelines, 'The most common way to achieve recognition has been through bilateral agreements'. The Guidelines further state, 'There are differences in education and examination standards, experience requirements, regulatory influence and various other matters, all of which make implementing recognition on a multilateral basis extremely difficult'. The core elements of the Guidelines, in addition to a reminder of the notification requirements under Article VII of the GATS, are recommendations on the form and content of MRAs. The Guidelines state that MRAs should clearly identify the:

- participants
- purpose of the agreement; scope of the agreement
- details of the mutual recognition provisions, including eligibility requirements for recognition as well as specification of the conditions under which any additional supplementary requirements may be applied
- mechanisms for implementation
- further licensing or related requirements, and
- terms for revision of the agreement.

Analysis

The main motivating factor for the creation of GATS Article VI: 4, and the *Decision on Professional Services*, was the fact that trade in professional services is severely handicapped by a maze of regulations at the national and sub-national levels. As observed in the Secretariat background paper S/WPPS/W/2 (p. 1), however, 'It is clear that most if not all service industries, and particularly the professions, will always be subject to regulation; protection of the public interest requires the maintenance of adequate standards of competence and integrity'. It should also be noted that the preamble of the GATS explicitly recognizes the rights of governments to regulate; nonetheless, the GATS does set specific rules, in Article VI and elsewhere, to prevent regulations from unduly restricting trade.

A careful reading of the initial paragraphs of the *Decision on Professional Services* implies that the multilateral disciplines to be established under GATS Article VI: 4 are distinct from specific commitments: after recognizing the impact of regulatory measures on trade, the *Decision* states that trade ministers desired 'to establish multilateral disciplines with a view to ensuring that, when specific commitments are undertaken, such regulatory measures do not constitute unnecessary barriers to the supply of professional services'. In regard to the development of disciplines in accountancy, however, the same *Decision* is less clear, stating that the Working Party shall concentrate on 'developing multilateral disciplines *relating to* market access' (emphasis added). Nonetheless, it is unlikely that the latter text intended to contradict the initial references.[7]

In the January 1996 list of 'Issues Proposed for Consideration', no attempt was made to distinguish between GATS Article VI measures (domestic regulation) and those of Articles XVI (market access) and XVII (national treatment). Some informal papers by delegations also made no distinction between these issues. Other informal papers, although noting that market access and national treatment issues are covered by Article XVI and XVII, nonetheless advocated that they be addressed by the WPPS. The minutes of the third WPPS meeting (S/WPPS/M/3, p. 2), which immediately preceded the listing of issues, observed that 'A number of delegations questioned the need for, and the feasibility of, the idea that the working party could provide a forum for continuing the liberalization of trade in accountancy services that was begun in the Uruguay Round'.

The efforts made by some WTO Members to initiate market access/national treatment negotiations in the WPPS were reflected in spoken interventions in meetings, written submissions, and in the initial selection of issues for consideration. The fact that the financial services, telecommunications and other post-Uruguay Round negotiations all included market access and national treatment issues undoubtedly added to the level of confusion. Apparently equally important was the fact that GATS Article VI: 4 does not explicitly make a distinction between Article VI and Articles XVI/XVII-related regulatory measures. Procedurally, Members could have conducted market access/national treatment negotiations in parallel with the WPPS work, had they so wished.

A question that arises is why Members did not have substantial formal discussions in WPPS meetings of such crucial issues as arguments for and against alternative approaches to regulation. For example, among the most significant topics raised in the informal papers by Members, but not substantially discussed or included in the January list of issues, was the question of 'de-linking' regulatory measures, i.e. no longer requiring citizenship, residency or local qualifications as prior conditions for permission to invest in and manage local firms. Anecdotal evidence suggests that Members were reluctant to discuss specific regulatory approaches in the WPPS, for fear that their own national regulations might be identified as trade-restrictive.

The predominant viewpoint of Members regarding international standards, as stated in one informal paper, was that the WPPS should stay informed of developments in the area of international accounting standards. As a whole, the WPPS preferred to receive updates of the progress made by the International Federation of Accountants (IFAC) and the International Accounting Standards Committee (IASC), rather than encourage the use and acceptance of international accountancy standards as part of trade in accountancy services. At least one Member, however, was of the opinion that the WPPS could make a major contribution towards promoting the emergence of the newly revised accounting standards, and ensuring that they could be used by firms with a preference for such standards. In the final analysis, it should be noted that the mandate of the Decision specifically refers to the *use of* international standards (emphasis added). The Singapore Ministerial statement supporting the creation of international standards, while helpful, might therefore be considered as an interim step in fulfilment of the WPPS mandate.

In respect to the MRA Guidelines, it is interesting to note that the *Decision on Professional Services* actually refers to the establishment of guidelines for the recognition of qualifications in respect to Article VI: 6, and not specifically to the development of guidelines for MRAs.[8] It may, therefore, be argued that the Guidelines only partially facilitate the mandate stated in the *Decision*. A question remains why Members did not try to further define the 'adequate procedures' to verify the competence of foreign professionals required in Article VI: 6. Although the Guidelines appear to have had little effect to date in accelerating the low level of accountancy MRAs currently in place (see endnote 12), ultimately their main contribution will be to focus greater attention, at both the government and industry levels, on the issue of creating MRAs as a means of facilitating trade in professional services. In the event that a substantial number of MRAs are created according to the Guidelines, the use of a common format would help promote the eventual consolidation of such agreements.

The rate of progress by the WPPS, at least in private-sector terms, was somewhat slow in the initial stages. The number of meetings and pace of work later picked up significantly following the submission of draft disciplines by Members (see the next section). To be fair, it should be noted that both delegations and the WTO Secretariat were burdened by other pressing work, especially the WTO negotiations on telecommunications and financial services. Another factor was undoubtedly the difficulties of familiarizing trade negotiators with the technical complexities of the accountancy sector; at the same time, the accountancy profession evidently had some difficulties in understanding the complexities of developing multilateral trade disciplines according to GATS requirements.

As noted earlier, accountancy services were selected as the initial area of work by the WPPS, primarily as a result of the previous lobbying efforts by IFAC. Once the work was under way, IFAC was evidently one of the major motivating forces pushing the work forward, by presenting seminars and providing detailed written information to the WPPS. Internally, IFAC organized a 'GATS Task Force' for the purpose of consolidating the views of its member bodies. The accountancy industry's main concern, however, was primarily market access issues, with actual Article VI: 4 issues of a more secondary interest.

Development of multilateral disciplines on domestic regulation

Descriptive summary

Five separate proposals for disciplines on domestic regulation in the accountancy sector were formally submitted by WTO Members, the first being a US paper entitled, *Elements to be Addressed in Developing Disciplines for Professional Services: Accountancy Sector* (S/WPPS/W/15, dated 20 June 1997). The paper gave priority to the accountancy sector, and noted that 'a great many of the elements could have broader applicability'. The disciplines suggested by the United States were categorized according to the three main principles of Article VI: 4, i.e. objective and transparent criteria, not more burdensome than necessary, and not more restrictive than necessary (for licensing procedures). As part of the examples of possible disciplines, no mention was made in the proposal of international standards.

The second proposal was submitted by a group of four Latin American countries: Brazil, Chile, Colombia and Mexico (S/WPPS/W/16, dated 24 June 1997). The disciplines proposed in the paper were categorized according to types of measures mentioned in Article VI: 4, specifically licensing requirements, qualification and licensing procedures, and technical standards. Measures relating to qualification requirements were not included, as these were considered to reflect differences in educational, legal and cultural systems, about which it was 'not possible to make value judgements'. The paper pointed out that the development of disciplines should take due account, in particular, of legitimate general policy objectives. In this respect, the paper stated, it may be appropriate to also consider the additional costs which may be incurred in implementing such alternatives when considering the issue of less-trade-restrictive alternatives to current regulatory measures.

The European Communities submitted the third proposal for multilateral disciplines (S/WPPS/W/17, dated 25 June 1997). Like the previous proposals, the suggested EC disciplines were not based on the January 1996 WPPS listing of major issues, using instead the categories of qualification requirements, and licensing requirements and procedures. As with the US proposal, no mention was made of possible disciplines on technical standards. In regard to qualification procedures, the EC paper stated,

> given the complexity and detailed nature of the issues, the possibilities of drawing up multilateral disciplines in this field are rather limited. The existence or non-existence of an MRA between two countries will always be the major influence on the ability of foreign professionals to practise.

The paper also observed that 'The issues of nationality, citizenship and of entry and stay should be set aside at this stage as being issues clearly related to Article XVI, XVII and the Annex on the Movement of Natural Persons'.

The Australian proposal was the most detailed of the proposals by delegations (S/WPPS/W/18, dated 16 July 1997), including sections on scope, definitions and general transparency provisions, in addition to the categories of qualification requirements and procedures, other licensing requirements, licensing procedures, and licensing appeals. Again, however, no mention was made of possible disciplines on technical standards. India submitted the fifth and last of the proposals (S/WPPS/W/19, dated 5 September 1997). It was not intended to be comprehensive, but rather to highlight preliminary areas of concern. In addition to sections on scope and transparency, suggested disciplines were classified according to the categories of qualification requirements and procedures, licensing requirements, licensing procedures, and a final category of citizenship, nationality and residency requirements.

The Indian proposal included the statement, 'The GATS recognizes that the Member shall have certain domestic policy choices with regard to measures of general application affecting trade in services. Therefore, there is the need to strike an appropriate balance between the areas which should fall under the ambit of the Member's domestic policy domain and the areas to be regulated by the multilateral disciplines'. The next paragraph continued by stating, 'Considering that such multilateral disciplines would require considerable administrative burden by way of bringing domestic regulation in line with agreed multilateral disciplines, and putting appropriate administrative machinery in place, developing country Members should be allowed sufficient time to comply with such multilateral disciplines even after they undertake specific commitments in the accountancy sector.'

Informal written comments on the first four papers (from a developed country) were circulated in July 1997. In addition to comments on specific proposals in the drafts, they included a statement to the effect that the WPPS should find the most appropriate balance between those aspects which should be left to domestic policy choices and those to be regulated by multilateral disciplines. The comments also noted that the WPPS should be fully mindful of the administrative burden which the disciplines may require of Members.

Prior to the submissions by Members, the International Federation of Accountants (IFAC) had sent a letter to the Chairman of the WPPS, who then circulated it in May 1997 as an unofficial paper, containing draft accountancy disciplines on licensing requirements and licensing procedures. A second letter, with additional suggested disciplines on qualification requirements, qualification procedures and technical standards, was similarly circulated in September 1997. In both IFAC submissions, the main categories were further sub-divided on the basis of the main Article VI: 4 principles, in other words, that measures should be transparent; based on objective criteria; not more burdensome than necessary; and, in the case of licensing procedures, not in themselves a restriction on the supply of the service. Of the proposals by Members, only Australia followed the IFAC sub-division of categories, while the US proposal, as noted above, was based entirely on the sub-categories alone. In terms of content, the IFAC sugges-tions were the most detailed and extensive of the proposals.

In July 1997, at the request of WTO Members, the four proposals (at the time) were consolidated by the Secretariat into a single side-by-side informal text, classified by main categories (including scope, definitions, and a category entitled citizenship, nationality, residency and movement of natural persons), with separate columns detailing each of the proposals. The Secretariat was then asked to refine the text to eliminate duplication, to add the additional elements from the Indian proposal and to incor-porate the informal comments. This informal text, dated 15 August 1997, was accepted by Members as the starting-point for negotiations.

Subsequent revisions to the consolidated text, including both additions and deletions, were made only on the basis of consensus, i.e. as long as none of the Members raised an objection. As reflected in the minutes of the WPPS meetings at the time (S/WPPS/M/10–24), the major topics of discussion in the context of creating the accountancy disciplines were: the addition of general provisions to the draft text; concerns relating to stating the intended objectives of regulatory measures; concerns relating to permitting trading partners to comment on proposed domestic regulations; and objections to the inclusion of measures relating to market access and national treatment.

Between October 1997 and July 1998, a total of ten revisions of the draft disciplines were prepared by the WTO Secretariat at the request of the WPPS (discussions were typically conducted on an informal basis). The most signif-icant change to the draft text was the movement to a separate annex (subsequently not included in the final text) of provisions which appeared to involve existing GATS measures related to transparency, the scheduling of specific commitments, etc. Other changes included the consolidation of 'General Provisions' as a separate category, the elimination of sub-categories and the definitions section (a number of definitions were incorporated into the text), and the grouping of all transparency provisions together in a single category. IFAC also suggested revisions to the draft text, some of which were included in the revisions suggested by WTO Members.

In regard to legal applicability, most Members quickly decided, and continued to assert subsequently, that they wished the disciplines in accountancy to be legally binding. Somewhat later, they also decided that the disciplines would be applicable only to those with specific commit-ments in accountancy. The general feeling was that Members would be more willing to create stronger disciplines if they were applicable only to those with specific commitments.

Deciding the legal form of the accountancy disciplines was another major task required of the WPPS. Unlike previous GATS negotiations, for example those in financial services or telecommunications, where the main issues were market access and national treatment, and the outcome was always expected to be put by Members into their schedules of commitments, the legal form of the accountancy disciplines is a precedent under the GATS (detailed information on the scheduling of GATS commitments is presented on the WTO web-site). Article VI: 4 makes no mention of legal form in regard to the regulatory disciplines which are to be developed.

To address the legal form issue, Members requested an options paper by Secretariat. The alternatives initially presented were a GATS Annex or a 'reference paper' (as used in the telecommunications negotiations) to be inscribed in the additional commitments column of Members' schedules. A third option, consisting of adopting the accountancy disciplines by means of a Decision by the Council for Trade in Services was also suggested in an informal proposal. In discussing the legal form issue, Members initially stated a preference for a GATS Annex. However, discussions of the difficulties related to procedures for ratification by national legislatures led Members to shift their preferences. For several months, Members subsequently were undecided between the reference paper and Council Decision options (the compromise they achieved is detailed below).

The *Disciplines on Domestic Regulation in the Accountancy Sector*, after agreement had been reached within the WPPS, were adopted by the Council for Trade in Services on 14 December, and subsequently issued as WTO document S/L/64, dated 17 December 1998. The disciplines are rather concise, comprising only twenty-six paragraphs in four pages (six pages with the appendix). They are divided into eight sections: Objectives, General Provisions, Transparency (five measures), Licensing Requirements (six measures), Licensing Procedures (five measures), Qualification Requirements (three measures), Qualification Procedures (three measures) and Technical Standards (two measures).

The main achievements of the accountancy disciplines, relative to the current Article VI: 4 provisions, are found in paragraphs one, two, five, and six. Paragraph one, for example, confirms that that Article VI disciplines are separate and distinct from measures under Articles XVI and XVII. Paragraph two is the most important element of the disciplines, as it mandates a 'necessity test' for all applicable regulatory measures, i.e. the requirement that regulatory measures shall not be more trade-restrictive than necessary to fulfil a specified legitimate objective. Examples of such legitimate objectives mentioned in the disciplines are the protection of consumers (including all users of accounting services and the public generally), the quality of the service, professional competence and the integrity of the profession. In paragraph five, Members are required to explain upon request the specific objectives intended by their accountancy regulations. Finally, in paragraph six, Members are asked to provide an opportunity for trading partners to comment upon proposed accountancy regulations, and to give consideration to such comments.

The Decision of the Council for Trade in Services adopting the accountancy disciplines was issued as WTO document S/L/63, dated 15 December 1998. As a response to the situation mentioned above, the Decision is composed of three elements. The first element is a statement that the disciplines have been adopted by the Council, and the specification that they are applicable to Members who have scheduled specific commitments on accountancy. The second element of the Council Decision is the statement that Members will continue their work on domestic regulation, aiming to develop general disciplines for professional services while retaining the possibility to develop additional sectoral disciplines. Before the end of the new round of services negotiations, which commenced in January 2000, all the disciplines developed by the WPPS are to be integrated into the GATS and will then become legally binding. Consequently, the accountancy disciplines did not have immediate legal effect. The final element is a 'standstill provision', effective immediately, under which all WTO Members, including those without GATS commitments in the accountancy sector, have agreed, consistent with their existing legislation, not to take new measures which would be in violation of the accountancy disciplines.

Analysis

When analysing the accountancy negotiations, it is interesting to observe that several of the most active developing country participants in the negotiations had not yet scheduled commitments for accountancy, and therefore would not be directly affected by the disciplines created in the WPPS. It should be presumed that they were interested in adding accountancy commitments to their GATS schedules, but were probably unwilling to give up future negotiating capital. If this was the case, an important opportunity for expanding and accelerating the accountancy negotiations may have been lost.

Another important characteristic of the process was that both developing and developed countries were highly concerned about the potential costs and administrative burden of implementing disciplines. Comments made by Members during the negotiations also implied a general unwillingness to change existing domestic laws simply for the sake of creating the accountancy disciplines. Unfortunately, there was insufficient discussion of the potential gains from the creation of disciplines. In this respect, more active participation of the major users of international accountancy services, e.g. multinational corporations via their industry associations, could have helped bring the issue of the expected gains from liberalization more to the attention of WTO Members.

As with the earlier stages of the WPPS work, there was an initial attempt by some Members to include obvious market access and national treatment issues in the proposed accountancy disciplines (in addition to some actual confusion over what types of measures were to be covered by the disciplines). This evidently caused delays in the process of creating the disciplines, as other Members firmly resisted the inclusion. Most developing countries, as reflected in the Latin American proposal for accountancy disciplines, were clearly reluctant to discuss market access issues. Some countries were even reluctant to discuss the creation of Article VI: 4 disciplines for any aspects other than transparency; this may simply have reflected the lack of previous opportunity and resources for certain developing countries to develop their internal policy positions. On the other hand, it may also have reflected an attempt by some Members to protect national development policies. Some developing countries also feared that the regulatory disciplines might override items in their GATS Schedules.

Again as with the earlier stages of the WPPS work, there was little formal discussion of some of the most important issues regarding trade in professional services, even when raised in formal proposals. For example, the US proposal had stated, 'Citizenship and most aspects of residency requirements are generally not regarded as objective. The rationale for these requirements and possible alternatives for achieving the same objectives need to be discussed in the WPPS'. It should be noted that developed countries have already extensively debated most of these issues within the OECD context, but developing countries to date have evidently not held a similar range of discussions, either within UNCTAD or other major organizations.

The results of the negotiations on regulatory disciplines were said to be disappointing to the accountancy industry, and several WTO Members as well.[9] This is presumably due primarily to the lack of market access and national treatment provisions. As noted above, Members were generally unwilling to discuss these issues in parallel with the work on domestic regulation. A second aspect was the very limited opportunity for political trade-offs due to the narrow framework: negotiations were limited to one aspect (Article VI: 4-related issues) of a single professional services sector. Interestingly, the five proposals by Members for accountancy disciplines (see page 59), upon which the accountancy disciplines were based, had a very distinct advantage: the suggested disciplines from these proposals were automatically included in the initial draft text, as part of the consolidation of proposals by the Secretariat. Subsequently, revisions to the consolidated text could only be made if no other Members raised an objection. For this reason, the lack of disciplines on international standards in the initial proposals was a major shortcoming, as it later proved nearly impossible to make major additions in sensitive areas.

In comparing these initial five proposals, the structure of the disciplines proposed by the United States, which apparently led to a complicated discussion in the WPPS on definitions of 'objectivity and transparency', seems somewhat confusing. Many of the proposed US measures were in the form of guidelines rather than actual disciplines; several of the suggested disciplines also included provisions duplicating existing GATS requirements, e.g. transparency provisions, while others contained Articles XVI and XVII-related measures involving market access and national treatment.

A question that arises is why the Australian proposal, and perhaps the US proposal as well, did not contain disciplines regarding technical standards. The simple answer is that it was evidently too controversial at the time. In the view of the author, however, Members should at least have been willing to acknowledge the status quo in regard to international standards in accountancy, i.e. that they are widely incorporated (on a voluntary basis) into technical standards at the national level.[10]

When examining the role of the accountancy industry in the creation of the accountancy disciplines (i.e. as represented by IFAC), the initial observation is the high level of patience displayed during what was a rather long process. As described above, the industry encouraged the WTO to adopt the disciplines it believed were required. IFAC was (naturally) narrowly focused on the needs of the accountancy industry; WTO Members had a wider perspective, including awareness of the precedent-setting effect for other services sectors of creating disciplines in accountancy.[11] Consequently, IFAC's proposed measures ultimately needed to be adapted and modified to conform to the legal requirements of the GATS. From the industry's perspective, this adaptation was needlessly complex, i.e. the distinctions made between measures covered under GATS Article VI and those covered under Articles XVI and XVII were considered to be artificial. As noted earlier, however, a careful reading of the Ministerial *Decision on Professional Services* clearly implies that regulatory disciplines created under Article VI: 4 are distinct from specific commitments. In addition, a legal separation is essential, as GATS Article VI: 4 and Articles XVI and XVII impose different kinds of requirements on Members.

At first glance, it may appear that the current disciplines have largely failed to address many of the main trade barriers in accountancy (and professional services in general), e.g. local accreditation requirements for the ownership and management of firms. Under the disciplines for licensing requirements, for example, no mention is made of this issue. Upon closer examination, however, it will be seen that such requirements must first satisfy the strict criteria of paragraph two, i.e. that measures must not be more trade-restrictive than necessary to fulfil a legitimate objective. Under paragraph five, Members must respond to requests to explain the specific objectives intended by their regulations. Although more precise disciplines might be preferable, and are likely to be considered in the future, these two existing disciplines do provide a starting-point for requiring Members to re-evaluate measures that are viewed by trading partners as overly restrictive.

While the accountancy disciplines in their current form are quite simple, they do address the most fundamental means by which trade in accountancy (or other professional services) could be obstructed. In this regard, they serve as an indicator to other services sectors that the WTO is at some point likely to address their regulatory barriers as well. The disciplines are also well-suited to serve as the foundation for the subsequent development of horizontally applicable disciplines for professional services as a whole (or even for trade in services in general), as well for the development of more specific sectoral measures.

Regarding the legal form of the accountancy disciplines, the use of a Council Decision, while disappointing in that it lacked immediate legal enforceability, was nonetheless probably the best approach, considering that most Members stated that their ultimate preference is the creation of a GATS annex. Use of the 'reference paper' approach might actually have set a negative precedent for the creation of additional disciplines in the future, i.e. by permitting selective participation by Members and by potentially allowing the possibility of 'picking and choosing' which disciplines to apply. Also, the presence of a reference paper in individual schedules of commitments might have obstructed subsequent efforts to create an annex. Postponing the creation of an annex until the upcoming round of services negotiations greatly increases the likelihood that countries such as India, Indonesia, and the Philippines, which actively participated in developing the disciplines, but had not yet made specific commitments, will be legally bound by the accountancy disciplines upon their entry into force, having by this point added commitments to their GATS schedules.

Future WTO negotiations

Descriptive summary

The December 1998 Council Decision on accountancy stated that 'the Working Party shall aim to develop general disciplines for professional services, while retaining the possibility to develop or revise sectoral disciplines'. At the time, Members discussed sending the accountancy disciplines and MRA guidelines to other professions for discussion and consideration. Options such as developing additional questionnaires were also mentioned in WPPS meetings at the end of 1998.

WTO Members subsequently embarked upon a major expansion of their efforts to develop regulatory disciplines under Article VI: 4. An formal paper by New Zealand (S/C/W/66, dated 17 November 1998) earlier noted that the Council had not yet held broad discussions of Article VI: 4 issues, and urged that these take place as a matter of priority. As a preliminary measure, the paper suggested that the Secretariat prepare a background paper examining the relevant issues. The suggestion was later accepted, with some Members stating that work on general VI: 4 issues should not prejudice the work of the WPPS. Two Secretariat papers were prepared: 'Article VI: 4 of the GATS: Disciplines on Domestic Regulation applicable to all Services' (S/C/W/96) and 'International Regulatory Initiatives In Services' (S/C/W/97), both dated 1 March 1999.

The *Decision on Domestic Regulation* was adopted by the Council for Trade in Services on 26 April 1999 (WTO document S/L/70). The *Decision* replaced the WPPS with a new Working Party on Domestic Regulation. The new Working Party is mandated to develop generally applicable disciplines, and may develop disciplines as appropriate for individual sectors or groups of sectors, including professional services. Following the preparation of background papers by the Secretariat, one of the first steps of the new Working Party has been the examination of the accountancy disciplines (more specifically the principles embodied in the accountancy disciplines) in respect to their potential application across all GATS sectors. This was expected to be followed by an overview by Members of existing GATS and other WTO measures on domestic regulation, as well as an examination of work to date in other fora.

New negotiations in services (including a review of all exemptions) are mandated to begin in the year 2000. For professional services, it might be assumed that there is a possibility of rather quickly creating horizontal disciplines under Article VI: 4, considering that the accountancy measures are very general and potentially easily applicable to most other professional services sectors. Compared with the previous Uruguay Round negotiations on professional services, which focused primarily on commercial presence, greater attention is likely to be paid to the movement of natural persons (i.e. individual services suppliers) and regulatory issues in the upcoming negotiations.

Market access and national treatment negotiations in professional services are more likely to be conducted on a sectoral basis, rather than a 'formula approach' for professional services as a whole. In the view of the author, discussions of further sectoral-level regulatory disciplines are unlikely to occur until the final stages of the next round (i.e. in connection with the conclusions of individual sectoral market access/national treatment negotiations).

Analysis

A number of developing countries, including India, are likely to support the expected push by the United States and other developed countries to improve upon the accountancy results, primarily because of their own export interests, especially under Mode 4 (movement of natural persons). Together with the expectation of inevitable legislative changes resulting from the upcoming round of services negotiations, the (larger-scale) horizontal approach to additional negotiations on domestic regulation should overcome the general unwillingness shown in the accountancy negotiations to change existing domestic laws for the sake of creating regulatory disciplines. Another potential advantage is the much greater opportunity for trade-offs in future negotiations, in respect to both discussions on horizontal disciplines under Article VI: 4 as well as market-access/national-treatment negotiations in the context of the next round. These trade-offs could occur both within and across sectors.

As noted above, the negotiations on accountancy were difficult and time-consuming. Perhaps a cautious approach was inevitable for any such new area; future negotiations, however, may well proceed more rapidly, now that some experience has been acquired. Members, for example, will already have had the experience and background information from the WPPS discussions on Articles XVI and XVII-related issues. Also, unlike accountancy, no specific 'areas of concentration' for further professional services negotiations were specified under the *Decision on Professional Services.*

Concerning horizontal discussions of regulatory disciplines, the crucial question is the following: to what degree are the accountancy disciplines actually applicable to professional services as a whole and, ultimately, across all services sectors? The very general nature of the accountancy disciplines, as described in the analysis part of the previous section, strongly implies that they could rather easily be applied on a much broader scale. The main issues addressed by the principles embodied in the accountancy disciplines (e.g. the necessity test and transparency), are common to apparently all services sectors.

Concurrently with the examination of the horizontal applicability of the accountancy disciplines, Members would benefit from thoroughly discussing the major regulatory issues identified by the WPPS, such as possible alternatives to local qualification requirements for firm ownership and management. The expected costs and potential benefits of each alternative should be carefully considered, with an effort to reach common understandings among Members wherever possible. The relevant market access and national treatment issues, such as nationality and permanent residency requirements, should be carefully discussed as well.

Additional work is also needed in the area of recognition procedures. If, as stated in the introduction to MRA Guidelines, 'The most common way to achieve recognition has been through bilateral agreements', the question remains of why are there so few existing arrangements for accountancy and professional services as a whole.[12] WTO Members should discuss this issue thoroughly, seeking comments from the profession and academics as well. One of the priorities in regard to the development of horizontal disciplines should be to discuss the 'adequate procedures' requirement of Article VI:6, and attempt to define what these should include. Members should also consider alternatives to bilateral MRAs, attempting perhaps in the next round of negotiations to consider plurilateral MRAs in specific professional services sectors.[13]

Regarding the legal form of the regulatory disciplines developed under GATS Article VI:4, an annex to the GATS is the stated goal of most Members. As discussed above, an annex is also probably the best way to ensure the widest level of participation by Members, as well as the adoption of disciplines without selective changes or deletions. During the Uruguay Round negotiations, the possibility of adding an annex on professional services to the GATS was examined and rejected by Members (see S/WPPS/W/1, p.1); attitudes, however, may have changed since that time. In this regard, it should be noted that the only specific reference to professional services in the GATS is in Article VI: 6 (see endnote 8). Assuming that substantial progress is made in the wider discussions of potential VI:4 disciplines covering all services, there is nothing to prevent creation of a GATS annex on domestic regulation as a whole, perhaps with specific disciplines on professional services as a separate section.

General conclusions

The value of creating regulatory disciplines in professional services is similar to that of scheduling market-access and national-treatment commitments: they help ensure greater transparency, predictability and irreversibility of policies for both trading partners and domestic producers. By providing greater opportunity for domestic users to obtain world-class services at internationally competitive prices, regulatory disciplines have the potential for enhancing domestic productivity and efficiency, as well as increasing the scope and quality of the services locally available. Both domestic and foreign service producers should be able to take advantage of expanded economies of scale, to the benefit of their clients and the domestic economy as a whole.

Advantages of creating horizontal rather than sectoral disciplines include the greater simplicity and transparency of application for all parties concerned, i.e. regulators, service providers and consumers. The total time required for developing disciplines should be considerably reduced, and 'economies of scale' could be achieved in regard to the activities of business federations, consumer groups and others concerned with professional services or services in general. At the sectoral level, it is undoubtedly easier for protectionist-minded trade associations, regulators, etc. to block efforts to create disciplines by focusing narrowly on the possible difficulties for some, rather than on the expected benefits for the majority. The advantage of sectoral-level negotiations is the ability to address any specific characteristics of particular sectors that may be inappropriate for horizontal-level negotiations; consequently, such negotiations should be held after horizontal negotiations.

For the small and medium-sized firms of both developing and developed countries, regulatory disciplines would help to ease (and expand) their cross-border trade. Firms will increasingly be able to work in neighbouring countries, as well as to form regional networks. Consequently, these smaller-scale firms should be able to expand the scope and efficiency of their activities, thereby increasing their ability to compete (at least locally) with the networks of larger international firms. Developing countries should also be able to expand the service exports of independent professionals. Another likelihood that arises is that the creation of disciplines on domestic regulation will accelerate international regulatory harmonization.

In addition to the protectionist concerns noted above, barriers to the development of additional disciplines on service regulations potentially include 'infant industry' and 'strategic industry' policies at the national level.[14] There may also be national or cultural sensitivities to allowing foreigners to perform certain services. In some cases, it is not always clear whether governments and the professions have fully accepted the arguments and evidence regarding the benefits of trade liberalization. Concerns have been expressed by some governments, as well, over making internationally binding the technical standards which are currently being created by private-sector associations; one option in this regard is to increase the role of governments in the international standards-making process.

Less obvious, but equally significant, potential barriers to the creation of regulatory disciplines at the WTO include the limited resources of both delegations and the WTO Secretariat. Developing- and even developed-country delegations have repeatedly complained about the difficulties of keeping pace with the ever-increasing workload. WTO Secretariat resources are also quite limited (the WTO Trade in Services Division has less than a dozen professionals). In response, Members will evidently need to make some decisions in regard to increasing WTO-related resources, and/or delegating responsibilities elsewhere. For example, they could consider having international professional associations and other organizations do some of the preliminary work, e.g. the development of initial proposals, and even some test implementations, on a voluntary basis. Greater technical assistance would also need to be provided to developing countries.

The value of the WTO's role in respect to the development of regulatory disciplines includes the fact that it can give legal enforceability to measures which would undoubtedly remain voluntary if implemented at the level of the international trade or professional associations. In this respect, it should be noted that, as difficult and perhaps incomplete as the WTO process has been to date, apparently no other government-level international organizations have yet been able to develop binding disciplines regarding international trade in professional services. WTO negotiations also help overcome the usual reluctance of individual governments to make changes unilaterally; they can even assist in achieving domestic consensus in situations where majority, but not universal, agreement exists.

Complementing the role of the WTO, international professional associations can provide the technical expertise and practical experience that are otherwise unlikely to be available, either in the WTO Secretariat or in delegations. Perhaps even more important, the private sector can typically provide the initial impetus to launch the process, as well as the continued motivation to see the development of disciplines through to their conclusion. As mentioned above, international associations might also be able to serve as the 'testing ground' for the development and implementation of new disciplines and other measures to promote services trade. In fact, some argument could be made that new disciplines should not be brought to the WTO until they have first been thoroughly discussed at the level of the international associations.

Finally, it should be observed that only governments can participate in WTO activities directly. Therefore, the private sector can exert influence only to the extent that it is able to convince governments to act on its behalf, bearing in mind that governments will act on the basis of the perceived benefits for society as a whole, and not simply for an individual services sector.[15] Depending on the situation, it may often be necessary to persuade a number of governments to act collectively. While the existence of trade and professional associations at the international level is extremely helpful for representing the world-wide interests of a particular services sector, it is unlikely to be sufficient in itself in regard to the creation of regulatory disciplines. Active efforts at the national level are undoubtedly essential for convincing governments to act.

Notes

The views expressed in this article are strictly those of the author acting in his personal capacity, and not those of the WTO or its Members. The author would like to specifically thank the following people for their comments: Rolf Adlung, Maria Alejandra Aristeguieta de Alvarez, Julian Arkell, Bernard Ascher, David Hartridge, Juan Marchetti, Rhonda Piggott, Ann-Mary Redmond, Vincent Sacchetti, Michael Stone, Claude Trolliet, Peter Walton, and John Williams.

1 Extensive information about the WTO and the Uruguay Round trade agreements – including most of the documents referred to in this chapter – is available on the WTO Internet site (http://www.wto.org).
2 Work on regulatory disciplines has also occurred in the context of the telecommunications negotiations.
3 In addition, as stated in the WTO Secretariat background paper *Functions of the Working Party on Professional Services in relation to Accountancy* (document S/WPPS/W/1, dated 27 June 1995), 'This profession is already more integrated on the international level than most, not withstanding the existence of important domestic regulatory structures, and international trade in accountancy services shows considerable potential for growth' (p. 1).
4 WTO Members typically have the option to submit documents formally or informally. Informal documents (called 'non-papers') do not receive WTO document numbers and may remain permanently restricted; formal papers are given WTO document numbers, and are subsequently derestricted for public access. Only derestricted formal documents are quoted and referenced in this article.
5 Information from the OECD and UNCTAD was circulated as formal documents, i.e. S/WPPS/W/4 and W/5, respectively, as these organizations have Observer status in the WTO. As non-governmental organizations, IFAC and IASC presentations were made informally, with accompanying documentation circulated as informal documents. No written records are kept for informal WTO meetings or presentations.

6 Detailed information concerning IFAC activities and organizational structure is available at the IFAC Internet site (http://www.ifac.org). Information on IASC and IOSCO is available at (http://www.iasc.org.uk) and (http://www.iosco.org), respectively.

7 The 1995 Secretariat background paper (S/WPPS/W/1) noted, 'The objective of Article VI:4 of the GATS is to ensure that regulations applied to services in the form of qualification requirements, technical standards, and licensing requirements do not constitute unnecessary barriers to trade. In general these measures are to be distinguished from limitations on market access and national treatment which would be scheduled under Articles XVI and XVII respectively' (pp. 1–2). Unfortunately, this point did not seem to provoke substantial discussion at the time.

8 The mandate under the WPPS was to concentrate on 'facilitating the effective application of paragraph 6 of Article VI of the Agreement by establishing guidelines for the recognition of qualifications'. Article VI:6 states 'In sectors where specific commitments regarding professional services are undertaken, each Member shall provide for adequate procedures to verify the competence of professionals of any other Member'.

9 See, for example, *Financial Times* (letters to the editor), 'Accountancy disciplines in danger of being world trade battleground', 11 March 1998. Comparison of the original IFAC proposals and the actual resulting disciplines reveals that the majority of IFAC requests were actually achieved. Most of these successful requests, however, concerned transparency issues as opposed to more controversial topics.

10 The second IFAC letter contained a proposal that reliance on international standards shall be encouraged, as well as another measure saying national standard-setting authorities should explain, if requested, the reasons for differences between their national standards and international standards.

11 As only governments are able to submit proposals to the WTO for formal consideration, the first hurdle the profession faced was to succeed in persuading Members to incorporate IFAC proposals into WPPS submissions. Delegates, despite the fact they did not always have the technical expertise required, sometimes reacted unfavourably to the strong role played by the profession.

12 The recent background paper prepared by the WTO Secretariat on accountancy services (S/C/W/73, dated 3 December 1998) stated that the number of recognition arrangements notified to the WTO, which specifically mentioned accountancy (4), appeared to be remarkably small (p. 10).

13 It should be remembered that GATS Article VII is about recognition procedures as a whole, and does not simply concern bilateral MRAs.

14 In this regard, however, market access and national treatment issues are likely to play a greater role.

15 In this regard, it must be remembered that, in some cases, governments need to resist the protectionist efforts of industry associations and other lobbyist groups.

Part II
Theory

4 FDI, the location advantages of countries and the competitiveness of TNCs

US FDI in professional service industries

Lilach Nachum

Introduction

The different patterns of national participation in international economic activity suggest that firms of particular nationalities tend to excel in certain activities, in a manner that reflects the resources abundant in their countries of origin. This implies that home country characteristics are important determinants of firms' abilities to create ownership advantages and of their subsequent competitive positions in international markets. Empirical studies indeed show that home countries affect the competitiveness of firms more than any other location in which the firms operate (Porter 1990; Dunning 1996; Pauly and Reich 1997; Nachum and Rolle 1999a, 1999b; Nachum 1999).

This link between the characteristics of home countries and the competitiveness of firms is particularly strong when firms are active only or mainly in their home countries and serve foreign markets by exports. Under such circumstances, locationally advantageous countries are likely to be the home for internationally competitive firms in particular industries, and when countries lose their location advantages, firms will respond by a corresponding loss of their ownership advantages.

However, when firms implement large parts of their value added activities outside their home countries, the link between the characteristics of the home countries and the ownership advantages of firms is likely to be weakened (Cantwell 1989, 1990). Such an outcome is particularly likely when the foreign activities are organized, as is increasingly common among TNCs, in a manner in which the affiliates enjoy a considerable amount of managerial autonomy and share the responsibility for knowledge generation for the benefit of the TNCs as a whole (Bartlett and Ghoshal 1989; Doz and Prahald 1991; Nohira and Ghoshal 1997). Under such circumstances, the conditions in the home country are likely to have less impact on the competitiveness of the TNCs as a whole. Consequently, changes in the location advantages of countries may not necessarily be reflected in corresponding changes in the competitiveness of national firms. A loss of a country's location advantages in a particular industry thus may not always imply a corresponding deterioration of the ownership advantages of a country's firms and their position in an industry. Rather, when countries lose their location advantage their firms may maintain their strength via activities in foreign countries. Likewise, a country's firms may not be the only beneficiaries from the location advantages of their home country. Foreign firms may gain access to these advantages via foreign investment and may develop similar ownership advantages.

In this chapter I seek to examine the implications of the foreign activities of firms for the link between the location advantages of home countries and the competitiveness of firms. I address questions such as: to what extent and under what conditions can firms compensate for deteriorating location advantages in their home country and maintain their lead in an industry through investment in foreign countries? Under what conditions does the dominance in the industry shift to firms based in another country whose location advantages are increasing? To what extent and under what conditions can firms reap the benefits of another locationally advantageous country, and when are these exclusive to national firms?

These questions are examined with reference to professional service industries, where the most internationally competitive firms are originated from very few countries. These industries have also been characterized by intense FDI activity, notably in more recent decades, making them a most interesting case for the examination of the questions addressed here.

FDI and the link between the advantages of firms and countries

FDI theory suggests that firms develop their ownership advantages based on the resources abundant in their home countries. Thus, firms based in a locationally advantageous country would develop strong ownership advantages, and those would enable them to compete successfully in international markets.[1] In his discussion of the type of advantages required for international operation, Hymer (1960/1976) implicitly implied a national origin for these advantages. He conceived the advantages that enable firms to compete successfully in international markets to arise from favourable access to certain resources abundant in their home countries, which are denied, or not available under similar conditions, to firms located in other countries. Later attempts (Vernon 1966) regarded the capabilities of firms in using physical and human assets to create ownership advantages, and particularly their capacity to innovate new products and processes, as country-specific in origin. Dunning maintained that the ownership advantages of one country's firms reflect the resource endowments and institutional framework of their home countries. Hence, differences among countries in the configuration of these resources explain the different structure of the foreign activities of firms of different nationalities (Dunning 1979, 1988, 1993). More recently, there has been a renaissance of interest in the link between the advantages of firms and the characteristics of their home countries and a realization that the globalization and integration of the world economy has not undermined the value of advantages gained in the home countries. This renewed interest was led by Porter (1990) and the stream of studies that have sought to test and extend his Diamond of national attributes (Rugman and D'Cruz 1993; Hadgetts 1993; Cartwright 1993; Jense *et al.* 1994). Empirical studies have illustrated the similarity between firms originating from the same country and the differences across countries, and have attempted to attribute these differences to specific conditions facing firms in their home country (Kogut 1993; Schroath *et al.* 1993; Shane 1994; Dunning 1996; Yip *et al.* 1997; Zaheer and Zaheer 1997; Nachum 1999).

FDI theory also suggests that the competitive position of firms in the international market is determined by their ownership advantages. Ownership advantages are distinctive capabilities that distinguish the firm possessing them from its actual and potential rivals. Such advantages enable firms to perform in unique ways, not available to their competitors, and to acquire dominant position in their market. They enable the firm to capture market share and to grow faster than other firms in their industry and to expand more rapidly than the general rate of growth of markets. Following the seminal work of Hymer (1960/1976), the possession of ownership advantages has been considered as the factor determining the ability of firms to operate abroad and their competitive position in international markets (see, among others, Dunning 1993; Lall 1980; Cantwell 1990).

Based on the links established above between the location advantages of countries and the ownership advantages of firms, and between the latter and the competitive position of firms, Figure 4.1 presents several possible combinations resulting from dynamic changes in the location advantages of home countries and the ownership advantages of national firms and draws their implications for the competitive position of firms.[2]

In an economic world in which firms operate within their home countries and serve foreign markets via exports, their ownership advantages would tend to reflect the location advantages of their home countries. Thus, a locationally advantageous country would have firms with strong ownership advantages and sustained competitive position, as described in the upper right box of Figure 4.1. If the home countries lose their location advantages, their firms would respond by a corresponding loss of their ownership advantages, as described in the low left box of Figure 4.1. Only when the ownership advantages of firms are influenced by the conditions in foreign countries, as a result of their activities in these countries, can a discrepancy between the location advantages of the home countries and the ownership advantages of firms arise. Such situations are described in the upper left box and the lower right box of Figure 4.1.

When countries which were locationally advantageous in certain industries, and became the home for the leading firms in these industries, lose their advantages, their firms may maintain their competitive position through FDI (the situation described in the upper left box). Firms originated from a country that was historically strong may thus retain their lead, even at a time when the conditions that gave rise to this dominance are deteriorating (Cantwell 1990). An example of such a development is suggested by the activities of Japanese manufacturers who have moved parts of their production abroad in response to increased labour costs at home, and have maintained the strength of their ownership advantages via FDI. However, advantages gained by investment in a foreign country may not be as strong as those gained at home (Hu 1992), because they are not as exclusive as the latter. Firms of other nationalities can similarly gain access to the location advantages of a foreign country and develop similar ownership advantages. Most notably, indigenous firms of the host country are likely to have favourable access to these resources, as they enjoy the advantage of operating within a system more familiar to them and are often also favoured by various government policies. Therefore such advantages are unlikely

Location advantages of home countries

DECLINE	SUSTAINED	
National firms maintain their strength via investment abroad. The firms are likely to share their dominance in the global industry with firms of other nationalities, because their sources of advantages are no longer exclusive.	National firms are strong enough to create barriers to entry and prevent foreign firms from getting access to the conditions that gave rise to their initial strength. The dominance of firms in the industry is maintained.	S U S T A I N E D
National firms remain focused domestically and lose their relative strength and their lead in an industry.	Foreign firms get access to similar advantages via investment in the locationally advantageous country, and weaken the relative strength of national firms.	D E C L I N E

Ownership advantages of national firms

Figure 4.1 FDI, the advantages of firms and countries, and the international competitiveness of firms

to provide as strong a position in an industry, and the lead of firms is likely to be shared with firms of other nationalities.

The second possible response of firms to a decline in the location advantages of their home countries is a corresponding loss of ownership advantages (the lower left box in Figure 4.1). Under this scenario, a country's firms will lose some or all of their past dominance in an industry. Such developments are likely when firms maintain most of their activities in the home country, which no longer provides the advantages it did in the past, and serve foreign markets mainly or only via exports. They can also result from the inability of firms to use the resources abundant in foreign countries as the basis for their ownership advantages. Examples for such a loss of a country's dominant position in an industry and the movement of the lead to firms based in other countries are abundant (the UK car industry for one).

When the location advantages of home countries are strong and sustained over time, they tend to attract foreign firms. The outcome of this investment depends on the relative strength of the ownership advantages of national firms *vis-à-vis* those of the foreign firms. Two scenarios might be possible. One, which is described in the lower right box, is that foreign firms are strong enough to compete successfully against national firms. In this case, they are likely to develop ownership advantages similar to those of the national firms and to gain a strong competitive position in the industry. Some Japanese investment in the US illustrates this scenario. This investment enabled Japanese TNCs in certain industries to develop ownership advantages that are in many ways similar to those of US firms and to threaten their lead in the relevant industries. The investment of UK advertising agencies in the US, notably during the 1980s, is also of this kind. As a result of this investment, UK agencies have increased their size and acquired managerial and organizational skills of running a large international network. Part of the recent strength of UK agencies can be attributed to the capabilities they have developed in their US operations. Under such circumstances, a country may maintain its location advantages, or even become more locationally advantageous, but the relative strength of the ownership advantages of its own firms would diminish and the country patterns would tend to dissipate over time (Cantwell 1990). However, such a development depends on the extent to which foreign firms are able to benefit from the location advantages of a foreign country in a manner similar to the benefits accruing to national firms. It has been argued (Porter 1990; Hu 1992) that national firms enjoy favourable access to the resources available in their home countries and foreign firms cannot benefit from these resources to the same degree.

It is also possible, as described in the upper right box, that the strength of national firms creates high barriers to entry and prevents foreign investment. Foreign firms are unable to compete successfully in the locationally advantageous country and the ownership advantages of national firms remain strong and sustained over time. The US computer and management consulting industries, in which the US receives small amounts of FDI, despite its apparent location advantages, suggest examples of such a situation.

In what follows, I use the framework presented in Figure 4.1 to examine the impact of FDI on the changing competitive position of firms in five professional service industries: advertising, management consulting, engineering consulting, accounting and law.

The choice of professional services and the country patterns in these industries

Professional service industries are particularly interesting for the examination of the issues addressed here. The advantages of professional service firms are based exclusively on intangible, often mobile assets, whose ties to any particular location, including the home country, are not evident. Consequently, there seems to be no reason for a link between the advantages of firms and the characteristics of their home countries. Nonetheless, the leading firms in many of these industries originate from very few countries and their dominant position in their industries is often sustained in spite of the rapid expansion of international activity during the last few decades in these industries. Traditional explanations, based on relative abundance of tangible factors of production, cannot provide a satisfactory explanation for these patterns. These industries thus provide an opportunity to examine different aspects of the ways in which home countries affect the advantages of firms. Such aspects are of special interest when the advantages of firms in a growing number of manufacturing and service industries increasingly derive from intangible, partly mobile, assets.

Figure 4.2 presents the national distribution of the leading TNCs (ranked according to total world-wide revenues) in several professional service industries, based on the lists of the top firms, published annually in industry publications.[3] The sources of the data were followed in determining the nationality of firms. They tend to use the location of the headquarters as a proxy for the nationality of a firm, because it is usually the centre of a firm's activities. However, such an approach is somewhat obscure in industries where partnership is the dominant ownership form (as in accounting, law and to a lesser extent in management consulting). Firms owned by their partners are networks which group separate, locally-owned partnerships, with no common equity base, and each has its own managerial structure and work routines (Post 1996). The nationality of these networks cannot be identified in a manner similar to that of corporations. The common practice used in this regard by the industry publications which list the top firms, and which is adopted here, is to link firms to the country in which the dominant partnership is located.

The diversification activities of firms, notably those of the originally accountancy 'Big Eight' (later 'Big Six') into management consulting and law, have often blurred the boundaries between these industries. This

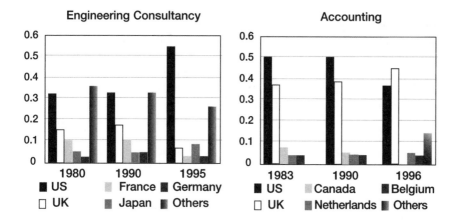

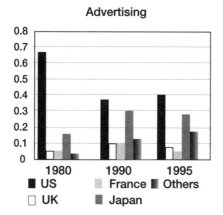

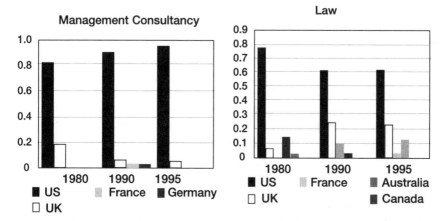

Figure 4.2 The national distribution of the leading TNCs in selected professional
   service industries, 1980–96: share of a country's TNCs in the top TNCs
   globally in an industry

Source: Various issues of *Advertising Age, Consultants News, Engineering News Record* (ENR),
   International Financial Law Review, International Accounting Bulletin

trend is not new, having its origins at the end of the nineteenth century (Kippings and Sauviat 1996), but in recent decades it has reached such a significant magnitude that the position of the established management consultancies and law firms has been challenged. For example, in 1996, Arthur Andersen, one of the 'Big Six' accounting firms, was the fastest growing law firm in the UK (*The Economist* 1996). As a result of these developments, several of the top firms that comprise the lists summarized in Figure 4.2 appear in more than one industry.

The presentation in Figure 4.2 suggests a considerable variation across the industries in terms of the national distribution of the leading TNCs. Some industries are dominated by TNCs from a single or very few countries, while in others the lead in the industry is taken by TNCs originating from a large number of countries. The management consulting industry, strongly dominated by US firms, illustrates the former, while the engineering consulting industry provides an example of the latter, at least historically. Furthermore, the dominance of firms of a particular nationality is more sustained over time in some industries than in others. For example, US management consulting firms have maintained their lead in the industry and have slightly increased it during the last decades. By contrast, the share of US advertising agencies among the top agencies had diminished by 1995 to only two-thirds of its size in 1980, and the lead in the industry is shared by firms originating from several countries. In the rest of the paper, I seek to examine how the foreign activities of firms in these industries have influenced these patterns and their dynamic changes over time.

Some statistical testing

The US is the only country that publishes FDI data for individual professional service industries, and it is thus the only country for which the issues addressed here can be examined statistically. Table 4.1 (pages 84–5) presents several measures for the location advantages of the US, the ownership advantages of US firms, and inward and outward US FDI data in selected professional service industries over the last two decades. Elsewhere (Nachum 1999: Chapter 3) I have developed the theoretical arguments for the choice of the first two constructs and their operations as the most powerful measures for the location advantages of countries in professional service industries. I have also shown empirically their explanatory power for the competitive position of firms in several professional service industries. The argument underlying the choice of the import/export ratio is that increase (decrease) in the ratio indicates that a country's location advantages are becoming more (less) attractive than those of competing countries (see Dunning 1988 for a similar use of this ratio).[4] Various measures of performance are commonly used as indicators of ownership advantages (see Dunning 1988; Cantwell 1989, 1990). In Nachum (1999: Chapter 4) I have discussed the theoretical foundations for the use of these indicators and I have shown their link with the possession of ownership advantages of advertising agencies. The data in Table 4.1 is used to examine the various possible influences of FDI on the links between the location advantages of countries, the ownership advantages of firms and their subsequent competitive position, as summarized in Figure 4.1.

The data in Table 4.1 illustrate considerable variation across the industries and over time in terms of the location advantages of the US, the ownership advantages of US firms and the investment position of the US. The three indicators of location advantages suggest that the US possesses strong location advantages in the management consulting industry. The ownership advantages of US management consulting firms have been strong relative to those of their main competitors, strong enough to prevent inward FDI to the US and to enable US firms to become successful outward investors (Table 4.1). This scenario corresponds to the situation described in the upper right box of Figure 4.1, in which the strong ownership advantages of national firms prevent foreign firms from investing in a country and, at the same time, enable them to compete successfully in foreign countries. The dominant position of US firms in the management consulting industry is thus sustained over time, and they are able to strengthen their ownership advantages via outward FDI.

A similar situation seems also to describe the accounting and law industries. The US is locationally advantageous in these industries, and its advantages have intensified during the last two decades. The ownership advantages of US firms, although somewhat weakened, have remained strong. Registered FDI activity in these industries is moderate (compared with the other professional service industries).[5] The partial picture provided by the available data, along with anecdotal observations regarding the patterns of international activity in these industries (see Spar 1997 for law; Post 1996 for accounting), suggests strong FDI outflows from the US with only moderate FDI inward flows. The strong ownership advantages of US firms in these industries have enabled them to develop a strong competitive position in international markets and to create barriers to entry to foreign firms seeking to invest in the US.[6] As in the management consulting industries, the situation in these industries also corresponds to the scenario described in the upper right box of Figure 4.1, in which national firms prevent foreign firms from gaining access to the favourable resources in their home country and maintain their lead in an industry.

The data presented in Table 4.1 suggest that both the location advantages of the US and the ownership advantages of US firms are moderate in the engineering consulting industry, with the former somewhat improving and the latter deteriorating in more recent years. Weaker ownership advantages of US firms, along with improving location advantages, have attracted foreign firms to invest in the US (Table 4.1). This situation corresponds most closely to the right lower box in Figure 4.1, in which the location advantages of the home country are sustained but national firms

Table 4.1 The location advantages of the US, the ownership advantages of US firms, and inward and outward US FDI: selected professional service industries, 1980–95

	Advertising			Management consulting			Engineering consulting			Accounting			Law		
	1980	1990	1995	1980	1990	1995	1980	1990	1995	1980	1990	1995	1980	1990	1995
Location advantages (Relative Location Advantages (RLAs) and ratios)															
Abundance of qualified employees (RLAqe)[1]	n.a.	1.427	n.a.	n.a.	1.297	n.a.	n.a.	0.680	n.a.	n.a.	n.a.	n.a.	n.a.	1.051	n.a.
Size of domestic market (RLAms)[2]	n.a.	n.a.	n.a.	n.a.	1.811	1.724	0.791	0.925	0.953	n.a.	n.a.	n.a.	n.a.	1.594	1.452
Imports/exports ratio[3]	0.819	1.869	1.286	0.196	0.381	0.368	0.396	0.196	0.119	1.380	0.478	0.836	0.412	0.246	0.270
Ownership advantages (averages of the US sample relative to the average of the group of the leading TNCs in an industry)[4]															
Performance[5]	1.13	1.16	1.18	n.a.	1.05	1.03	n.a.	n.a.	1.11	(1.58)[8]	1.40	1.16	(1.03)[9]	1.12	1.05
Growth[6]	–	0.57	1.07	–	n.a.	0.97	–	n.a.	n.a.	–	0.82	-0.28	–	1.40	0.00
Multinationality[7]	n.a.	n.a.	n.a.	n.a.	n.a.	n.a.	0.87	0.74	0.67	1.17	1.11	0.96	n.a.	1.03	0.82
FDI (sales of non-bank affiliates in million US$, and ratios)[10]															
Inward FDI	83	2,871	3,316	n.a.	526	1,262	594	3,897	6,253	0	0	2	n.a.	0	26
Outward FDI	1,738	5,006	6,470	1,847	n.a.	5,307	3,322	6,105	7,467	277	378	499	58	330	222
Inward/outward	0.04	0.57	0.51	n.a.	n.a.	0.19	0.18	0.64	0.84	–	–	0.00	n.a.	–	0.11

Sources :
Location advantages: various issues of UNESCO Statistical Yearbook (UNESCO, Paris); European Commission, Panorama of EU Industry (Brussels, The European Commission); FIDIC (the international association of engineering consulting), unpublished data; FEE (Federation of European Accountants), unpublished data; U.S. Dept. of Commerce, Statistical Abstracts of the US 1996 (US Bureau of the Census, Washington D.C., 1996); U.S. Bureau of Labour Statistics, Monthly Labour Review (US Bureau of Labour Statistics, Washington D.C.); UK Central Statistical Office, Employment Gazette (Harrington Kilbride, London); OECD, Labour Force Statistics 1974–1994 (OECD, Paris, 1996). US Bureau of Commerce, Survey of Current Business (Washington D.C.)
Ownership advantages: as for Figure 2
FDI: various issues of US Department of Commerce, Inward FDI in the US and US Direct Investment Abroad (Washington D.C.: Government Printing Office)

Notes to table 4.1

1 Calculated as follows:

$$RLAqe = \frac{\text{Number of graduates in field i in country j / total number of graduates in country j}}{\text{Number of graduates in field i in all countries / total number of graduates in all countries}}$$

Where: RLA: Relative Location Advantages. RLA can get any value between 0 and infinity. When 0<RLA<1 the country is comparatively disadvantaged in terms of qualified employees. When RLA>1 the country is comparatively advantaged. qe: abundance of qualified employees. i: fields of study: Advertising: graduates in mass communication and fine and applied arts. Management consulting: graduates in commercial and business administration. Engineering consulting: graduates in engineering. Law: graduates in law. j: countries (the countries which are the centres of economic activity in professional service industries).

2 Calculated as follows:

$$RLAms = \frac{\text{No. of employees in industry i in country j / total service employment in country j}}{\text{No. of employees in industry i in all countries / total service employment in all countries}}$$

Where: RLA: Relative Location Advantages (specification as in 1 above). ms: market size. i: industries (the professional service industries included in the study). j: countries (the countries which are the centres of economic activity in professional service industries and for which data are available)

3 The smaller the ratio (i.e. exports exceeds imports), the more locationally advantageous is the US. 1980 data from 1985.
4 US firms possess strong ownership advantages in a particular industry when their average is larger than the average for the whole sample, i.e. the ratio is larger than 1.
5 Performance is measured by revenues, except for law for which such data are not available and number of partners is used.
6 Growth rates are calculated as the average annual increase of revenues (number of partners in law). 1990 cells present growth data for 1980–1990. 1995 cells present growth data for 1990–1995.
7 Multinationality is measured by the share of revenues outside the US in total revenues in advertising, management consulting and engineering consulting. Due to lack of such data, in accounting multinationality is measured by number of countries in which a firm has member firms and in law by number of foreign offices.
8 As of 1983, the earliest date for which such data are available.
9 As of 1988, the earliest date for which such data are available.
10 Flows were judged more adequate than stocks in the case of professional services to measure the FDI activity, as they provide a better measure of the magnitude of business activity.

are losing the relative strength of their ownership advantages, as foreign firms gain access to the conditions which initially gave the rise to these advantages. Inward FDI thus prevents the exclusive access of national firms to the resources abundant in their home country.

The imports/exports ratio in advertising suggests that the location advantages of the US deteriorated between 1980 and 1990, with some recovery during the 1990s (Table 4.1). This situation has facilitated the outward investment of US agencies, who were able to strengthen their ownership advantages at a time when the location advantages of the US were diminishing. These developments correspond most closely to the situation described in the upper left box in Figure 4.1, where the home country is losing its location advantages but national firms maintain the strength of their ownership advantages via FDI. However, as advantages gained in a foreign country are not as exclusive as those gained in the home country, the lead in the industry is taken by firms from a larger number of countries, as happened in the advertising industry during the 1990s.

In order to examine more systematically the impact of FDI on the international competitiveness of TNCs, we construct a model that links the international competitiveness of US TNCs as the dependent variable with several potentially significant explanatory variables. The latter include the location advantages of the US, the ownership advantages of US firms, and inward and outward FDI, measured at the level of individual professional service industries, and over time.

The model is of the form:

$$C_{jt} = f(L_{jt};\ O_{jt};\ IF_{jt};\ OF_{jt}) + E_{jt}$$

where:

- C = Competitiveness, measured by the US shares of the leading TNCs world-wide.
- L = Location advantages of the US, measured by import/export ratios.
- O = Ownership advantages of US firms, measured by the growth of revenues of US TNCs relative to the average growth of the leading TNCs in an industry.[7]
- IF = Inward FDI, measured by sales of non-bank foreign affiliates in the US.
- OF = Outward FDI, measured by sales of US affiliates abroad.
- E = Random error.
- j = Industries. J=1 . . . 5: advertising, management consulting, engineering consulting, accounting and law.
- t = Time (T = 1 . . . 12: 1985–1996.)[8]

The results of the estimation of the model by means of multiple regression analyses are presented in Table 4.2.

Table 4.2 FDI, the advantages of firms and countries, and the competitiveness of firms[a]

		coefficient	std error	t stat	p-value
A model without FDI[b]					
Location advantages (import/export)		0.1230	0.1199	1.03	0.324
Ownership advantages (growth)		0.6289	0.1241	5.07	0.000
Adj. R-Square	0.5092				
p-value	0.000				
A model with FDI					
Location advantages (import/export)		Not significant[c]			
Ownership advantages (growth)		0.5505	0.1336	4.12	0.001
Inward FDI		-0.0001	0.0000	-1.49	0.161
Outward FDI		0.0001	0.0000	1.78	0.100
Adj. R-Square	0.5058				
p-value	0.000				
N (in both models)	57				

Notes
a Missing values were estimated from available observations by estimating a model based on the complete variables, and using it to estimate missing data
b Both models yielded better fit without an intercept
c The exclusion of this variable improved the overall fit of the model

The models explain a considerable portion of the variation in competitiveness among US professional service industries and are highly significant (p-values = 0.000 in both models). However, the model loses some of its explanatory power when FDI variables are included, and these variables are insignificant. The location advantages and the ownership advantages lose some of their explanatory power in the model with FDI, though they remain of similar magnitude and similar direction of causality. These findings suggest that FDI weakens somewhat the link between the location advantages of countries and the competitiveness of US professional service TNCs. FDI does not have a significant impact on the competitiveness of US TNCs on its own. Rather, it affects the competitiveness of US TNCs indirectly, via its impact on the location advantages of the US and on the ownership advantages of US firms.

Location advantages are not significant in both models, a finding that may reflect, at least partially, the limitations of a trade-based measure in professional service industries. It might also be attributed to the fact that US TNCs have well-developed international activities, and, as previous research has shown, at this stage the location advantages of the home countries are less critical for the competitiveness of firms (Cantwell 1990; Dunning 1996; Nachum 1999). By contrast, ownership advantages possess strong explanatory power for the variation in competitiveness, and explain most of this variation in both models. The emphasis thus moves from the location advantages of the US to the ownership advantages of US firms and to their ability to tap into foreign resources as the critical determinants of their competitive position.

The direction of causality between the FDI variables and competitiveness, the dependent variable, is most interesting. Inward FDI has negative sign (i.e. acts to diminish the competitiveness of US firms), while outward FDI strengthens it. This is in line with the arguments summarized in Figure 4.1, according to which inward FDI may threaten the competitive position of firms as it gives foreign firms access to the resources that provided their initial strength. Outward FDI acts to strengthen the competitiveness of firms when it enables them to benefit from resources available in foreign countries. However, this interpretation should be taken with great caution, as FDI variables are not significant.

Conclusion and possible generalizations

The analyses conducted in this paper have shown the different circumstances under which FDI affects the link between the advantages of firms and their home countries and the competitiveness of firms. The foreign activities of firms enable them to develop advantages which are not related, or at least not directly so, to the location advantages of their home countries. Outward FDI may thus strengthen the ownership advantages of firms independent of the location advantages of their home countries. Inward FDI may allow firms to get access to resources not available in their home country and to develop strength based on the location advantages of foreign countries. FDI thus weakens the link between the location advantages of home countries and the ownership advantages of firms, which tends to be strong when firms operate only or mainly within their home countries.

Thus, US advertising agencies were able to maintain the strength of their ownership advantages at a time when the US has been losing some of its location advantages. In a similar manner, an increase in the location advantages of the US in the engineering consulting industry has facilitated a substantial increase in inward flows to the US rather than strengthened the ownership advantages of US engineering consulting TNCs. In these industries, FDI has created some discrepancy between the location advantages of the US and the ownership advantages of US TNCs. In the three other industries analysed (management consulting, accounting, and law), there seems to be a close link between the location advantages of the US and the ownership advantages of US TNCs, with changes in the former reflected pretty well in the latter.

However, the results of the regression analyses suggest that, on a whole, FDI weakens only slightly the link between the location advantages of the US and the competitiveness of US professional service TNCs. Both inward and outward FDI do not possess significant explanatory power for the competitiveness of US TNCs, after taking account of the advantages of firms and countries. The inclusion of FDI has diminished the overall explanatory power of the model, as well as of the individual explanatory variables, but this change is moderate. This implies that FDI by itself does not influence the competitiveness of US professional service firms. Rather, this impact is exercised via the influence of FDI on the location advantages of the US and on the ownership advantages of US firms. These findings suggest that the foreign activities of firms have only a moderate effect on their competitiveness, and the ownership advantages which firms develop in their home countries have the dominant influence on their competitiveness.

The interpretation of these findings should be made in light of the nature of foreign activity in professional services, which is likely to weaken the links between the headquarters and the affiliates and consequently the impact of home countries on the competitiveness of the TNCs as a whole. First, the overwhelming shares of foreign activities in professional services are of the market-seeking type and have a horizontal nature, in which the affiliates implement the complete value creation process in their market, with limited linkages with the headquarters. Second, the need for deep knowledge of the local market and the clients served in these markets often rules out the possibility for tight control of the remote headquarters over the affiliates. Third, The partnership structure common in some professional service industries (notably accounting, legal services and to a lesser extent management consulting) further diminishes the links between the various parts of these networks, which have no ownership ties. These characteristics are likely to lead to considerable independence of the affiliates from the headquarters and to weaken the impact of advantages generated in the home countries on the affiliates and on the TNCs as a whole.

Future research may examine the extent to which the findings reported here, based on several US professional service industries, can be generalized to other industries and countries. To the extent that there are differences across industries in terms of the impact of FDI on the competitiveness of firms, they may not be related to a distinction between services and manufacturing, which is often made in such context. Professional service firms often have more in common with manufacturing firms than with other service firms. For instance, like professional services, manufacturing firms are increasingly relying on intangible assets as critical for their competitive position (such as knowledge in technologically advanced manufacturing industries).[9] By contrast, professional service firms differ from other service firms in some critical aspects, such as the role of cheap labour in consumer services and of human capital in professional services. The increasing reliance of firms in a growing number of industries on intangible assets as the most critical factors shaping their behaviour and affecting their competitiveness (Stewart 1997; Skandia 1998) suggests that the findings of this research are intuitively appealing to a large number of other industries.

It is also likely that certain characteristics of the US limit the validity of the findings to other countries. Notable among them is the large size of the US, as well as the age and international maturity of US TNCs, which are likely to create a unique combination of advantages of firms and countries, and to lead to a different effect of FDI on them.

Notes

1 This conceptualization is based on the assumption that causality goes from the resources of home countries to the ownership advantages of national firms, and a possible impact of the latter on the former is usually ignored. In many cases, however, circular and accumulated causation between country characteristics and the advantages of firms, in which the two are not independent of each other (Cantwell 1989), better describes the process of the development of ownership advantages by firms. It seems likely that at least under certain circumstances, firms shape the mobile and immobile resources of their home countries, which in turn affect their ownership advantages. The assumption that causality goes from countries to firms may apply more often than not, but may not always be a valid assumption (see Nachum 1999 for a discussion of the specific conditions under which this assumption may hold).

2 Figure 4.1 is based on the combination of extremes of the two dimensions. Obviously, they are both continuous. In reality, the strength of the location advantages of countries and the ownership advantages of firms are expected to vary across the entire spectrum between these two extremes.

3 Law firms are ranked according to number of partners because revenue data are not available. Subject to data availability, the ranking of advertising agencies, engineering consulting and law is based on the lists of the largest fifty TNCs in these industries. In management consulting the top forty firms are used, and in accounting the top thirty firms in 1983 and 1990 and the top forty-two firms in 1995.

4 The low tradability of professional services might question the use of this ratio. However, the large increase in US trade in professional services suggests that considerable cross-border activity in these industries is taking place via trade. In 1996, business, professional and technical services were among the fastest growing categories of US service trade, with exports and imports reaching $19.2 and $5.2 billions respectively. Both have increased more than four times during the last decade (Survey of Current Business 1997).

5 A main reason for this situation is the ownership structure common in the law and accounting industries. As partnerships, the 'affiliates' are often owned by the partners in the foreign country and do not have ownership links with the parent firm. Thus, the activities of these 'affiliates' are not registered as FDI.

6 A main reason for this situation is the ownership structure common in the law and accounting industries. As partnerships, the 'affiliates' are often owned by the partners in the foreign country and do not have ownership links with the parent firm. Thus, the activities of these 'affiliates' are not registered as FDI.

7 The more common indicator of ownership advantages (i.e., some measure of international activity), was judged to be inadequate for US TNCs, where the home market usually accounts for higher shares of activity compared with TNCs of other nationalities.

8 In law from 1988, the earliest date for which data is available to calculate the dependent variable.

9 This approach is somewhat in contrast to the more common view which tends to emphasis the differences between professional service industries and most other industries (see for example Løwendhal's chapter in this book. See also Maister 1993). Professional service firms certainly have some unique attributes, which distinguish them from firms in other industries, both manufacturing and services. But in as much as their most salient characteristic is their sole reliance on intangible assets, notably knowledge, as both their input and output, and their subsequent dependence on their employees who hold these assets, professional service firms share common attributes with firms in other industries, with similar characteristics, notably high tech manufacturing firms.

References

Bartlett, C. A. and Ghoshal, S. (1989) *Managing Across Borders: the Transnational Solution*, Boston: Harvard Business School Press.

Cantwell, J. (1989) *Technological Innovation and Multinational Corporations*, Oxford: Basil Blackwell.

—— (1990) 'The Growing Internationalization of Industry: a Comparison of the Changing Structure of Company Activity in the Major Industrialised Countries', in A. Webster and J.H. Dunning (eds) (1990) *Structural Change in the World Economy*, London and New York: Routledge.

Cartwright, W. R. (1993) 'Multiple Linked "Diamonds" and the International Competitiveness of Export-dependent Industries: the New Zealand Experience', *Management International Review* 33 (2): 55–71.

Doz, Y. L. and Prahalad, C. K. (1991) 'Managing DMNCs: A Search for a New Paradigm', *Strategic Management Journal* 12, special issue, 145–64.

Dunning, J. H. (1979) 'Explaining Changing Patterns of International Production: in Defence of the Eclectic Theory', *Oxford Bulletin of Economics and Statistics*, November: 34–48.

—— (1988) *Multinationals, Technology and Competitiveness*, London: Allen and Unwin.

—— (1993) *Multinational Enterprises and the Global Economy*, Wokingham: Addison-Wesley.

—— (1996) 'The Geographical Sources of the Competitiveness of Firms: Some Results of a New Survey', *Transnational Corporations*, December, 5 (3): 1–30.

Economist (1996) 'The Globalisation of Corporate Law: Red Tape Around the World', 23 November: 81–2.

Hadgetts, R. M. (1993) 'Porter's Diamond Framework in a Mexican Context', *Management International Review* 33 (2): 41–55.

Hu, Y. S. (1992) 'Global or Stateless Corporations are National Firms with International Operations', *California Management Review*, winter: 107–26.

Hymer, S. H. (1960/1976) *The International Operation of National Firms: A Study of Direct Investment*. Ph.D. Thesis, MIT (published under the same title by the MIT Press in 1976).

Jense, N., Brouthers, K. and Nakos, G. (1994) 'Porter Diamond or Multiple Diamond: Competitive Advantage in Small European Countries', in Yamin, M., Burton, F., and Cross, A. R. (eds) *The Changing European Environment*, proceedings of the 21st annual conference of the UK Academy of International Business, Manchester.

Kipping, M. and Sauviat, C. (1996) 'Global Management Consultancies: Their Evolution and Structure', Reading University, discussion papers.

Kogut, B. (1993) *Country Competitiveness: Technology and the Organisation of Work*, Oxford: Oxford University Press.

Lall, S. (1980) 'Monopolistic Advantages and Foreign Involvement by US Manufacturing Industry', *Oxford Economic Papers*, March: 102–22.

Maister, D. (1993) *Managing the Professional Service Firm*, New York: Free Press.

Nachum, L. (1999) *The Origins of the International Competitiveness of Firms: the Impact of Location and Ownership in Professional Service Industries*, Aldershot and Brookfield: Edward Elgar.

Nachum, L. and Rolle, J. D. (1999a) 'Home Country and Firm-specific Ownership Advantages: a Study of US, UK and French Advertising Agencies', *International Business Review* 8 (5) Forthcoming.

—— (1999b) 'The National Origin of the Ownership Advantages of Firms: a Case Study of the Advertising Industry', *The Service Industries Journal* 19 (4).

Nohira, N. and Ghoshal, S. (1997) *The Differentiated Network: Organising Multinational Corporations for Value Creation*, San Francisco: Jossey-Bass.

Pauly, L. W. and Reich, S. (1997) 'National Structures and Multinational Corporate Behaviour: Enduring Differences in the Age of Globalisation', *International Organisation* 51 (1): 1–30.

Porter, M. (1990) *The Competitive Advantage of Nations*, New York: The Free Press.

Post, H. A. (1996) 'Internationalisation and Professionalization in Accounting Services', *International Studies of Management and Organisation* 26 (2): 80–103.

Rugman, A. M. and D'Cruz, J. R. (1993) 'The 'Double Diamond' Model of International Competitiveness: The Canadian Experience', *Management International Review* 33 (2): 17–41.

Skandia (1998) 'Human Capital in Transformation', Supplement to Skandia's 1998 Annual Report, Stockholm: Skandia.

Schroath, F. W., Hu, M. Y. and Chen, H. (1993) 'Country-of-origin Effects of Foreign Investments in the People's Republic of China', *Journal of International Business Studies* 24 (2): 277–90.

Shane, S. (1994) 'The Effect of National Culture on the Choice between Licensing and Direct Foreign Investment', *Strategic Management Journal* 15: 627–42.

Spar, D. (1997) 'Lawyers Abroad: the Internationalisation of Legal Practice', *California Management Review* 39 (3): 8–28.

Stewart, T. A. (1997) *Intellectual Capital: The New Wealth of Organisations*, London: Nicholas Brealey.

Survey of Current Business (1997) 'US International Sales and Purchases of Private Services', October: 95–111.

Vernon, R. (1966) 'International Investment and International Trade in the Product Cycle', *Quarterly Journal of Economics*, May: 190–207.

Yip, S. G., Johansson, K. J. and Roos, J. (1997) 'Effects of nationality on global strategy', *Management International Review* 37 (4): 365–85.

Zaheer, S. and Zaheer, A. (1997) 'Country Effects on Information Seeking in Global Electronic Networks', *Journal of International Business Studies* 28 (1): 77–100.

5 History and contingency in international accounting firms

David J. Cooper, Teresa Rose, Royston Greenwood and Bob Hinings

There has been tremendous interest in understanding why and how organizations expand into the global arena. Recent interest has been in gaining an understanding of how multinational companies (MNCs) are best organized and managed to be effective in the global arena (e.g. Bartlett and Ghoshal 1989; Evans 1993; Hedlund 1986, 1994; Nohria and Ghoshal 1994, 1997; Pralahad and Doz 1987). This chapter emphasizes the importance of history in understanding the current organization of MNCs, and how these organizations are changing. In addition, we cast doubt on deterministic versions of contingency theory as providing explanations of the role of history (Chandler 1977; Chandler and Daems 1979).

Despite increased interest in MNCs in recent years, there is still little work done on the organization and management processes of MNCs other than in manufacturing, and most research has adopted an economic orientation. There has been limited attention given to services generally, and, until very recently, little attention paid to the internationalization process and international structural and managerial arrangements of professional service firms (Aharoni 1993, 1995; Greenwood *et al.* 1999; Løwendahl 1997; McKee and Garner 1996).

The lack of attention to professional service firms (e.g. accounting, law, architectural, engineering, and management consulting firms) is unfortunate for three reasons. First, these firms are increasingly important to society and the world economy. The service sector is continuously increasing its share of GDP, employment, and international trade, and thus contributing extensively to economic activity. About two thirds of GDP in developed countries and close to one half of GDP in developing countries is accounted for by services (Aharoni 1993). The world market for business services was predicted to be over $800 billion in 1996. The fee income of the Big Six at that time was $43.7 billion. Profitability for the partners in the Big Six (now Five) firms has been twice that of mid-sized accounting and consulting firms (Aharoni 1999).

McKee and Garner describe the importance of the Big Six Accounting firms, as follows:

They act as facilitators of economic activity within nations at various levels of development . . . carry their facilitative impacts beyond national boundaries into the world economy. As important as the facilitative functions of services may be, it must be remembered that those same services 'are actually being traded in that economy and in many instances have become internationalized in their own right'. The firms in question [the Big Six] are unique in their ability to supply such a wide range of services to so many jurisdictions. This uniqueness has made them major players in the global economy, capable of major impacts within and between individual jurisdictions.

(McKee and Garner 1996: 90)

Furthermore, the activities of the Big Five bring increasing opportunities for these firms to significantly impact government policy, for example in privatization, government restructuring and policy advice. Strange (1996) indicates other important roles, such as brokers in large mergers, tax consultants supporting big business, and corporate financiers, that increase the importance of these firms in the world economy.

Second, the lack of attention on professional services is unfortunate because many of the firms are finding it difficult to keep up with the intensely changing environment. These firms, at present, have little in terms of strategic management models or even reflective accounts of their activities over recent years to guide present decision making (Løwendahl 1997). The firms stand to gain from a critical analysis of their international organization and management responses to global pressures to date.

The third reason the lack of attention on professional service firms is unfortunate is that they have different historical origins and structural characteristics than firms upon which theories of MNCs are based. Thus existing theories of the MNC need to be assessed for their generalizability. Expanded theoretical models may be required (Løwendahl 1997).

Purpose

The general purpose of this chapter is to increase our understanding of professional service firms' international structures and management processes; to indicate the limitations of contingency theory to explain these structures; and show how history affects present organizational arrangements and future opportunities. Specifically we focus on the globalization processes and the international structural arrangements and management processes of the Big Five accounting firms (more recently referred to as the Big Five advisory firms).

Contingency theory argues that there is a best way to organize, dependent on environmental conditions (Lawrence and Lorsch 1967), scale (Pugh and Hickson 1976) and the task (Thompson 1967). Contingency theory is still argued to be the most promising approach to organization theory (Donaldson 1985, 1995) and forms the basis of current work in international management – for example Bartlett and Ghoshal (1989) and Nohria and Ghoshal, (1997). Lawrence and Lorsch (1967) argue that increased environmental uncertainty and complexity requires an organization to differentiate such that each part of the organization attends to an aspect of a heterogeneous environment. Greater interdependence of the units is then required to avoid conflict and pressured decision-making. Increased interdependence requires more co-ordinating devices and an appropriate level of overall integration. Specifically, Lawrence and Lorsch state: 'It is the appropriateness of the three-way relationships between uncertainty and diversity of the environment, the degree of organizational differentiation, and the state of integration and conflict resolution achieved which will lead to effective functioning' (Lawrence and Lorsch 1967: 209).

They emphasize an objective set of structural arrangements and co-ordination devices to match certain environment characteristics. Thompson (1967) stresses that the appropriate co-ordination devices are dependent on the nature of the technological core. Organizations must buffer their technological core (primary tasks). There is an appropriate structure derived through the relationship between core technology and buffering activities in response to the environment. The goal of management and administration has to be the effective alignment of structure, technology, and environment. For professional service firms, the implication of contingency theory is that the Big Five accounting firms, facing similar environments, would display similar organizational mechanisms to achieve the differentiation and integration required for success.

Previous analysis of the Big Five accounting firms (Greenwood *et al.* 1999) suggests that there has not been just one successful organizational response to the same environmental conditions. This suggests limitations in the contingency argument. A starting premise for this paper is that organizational history may help in understanding the international organizational features of the Big Five accounting firms (Turley 1994). Allen and McDermott (1993) have made a convincing argument that the present situation for any one of the Big Five firms is dependent on its historical context. Supporting this idea, Bartlett and Ghoshal (1989) have argued that an organization's 'administrative heritage' is an important factor shaping the international arrangements of MNCs. They suggest:

> The influence of a nation's history, infrastructure and culture permeates all aspects of life within the country including the norms, values, and behaviors of managers in its national companies. Nationally influenced behavioral characteristics become an ingrained part of each company's 'way of doing things' and shape its international organization structure

and processes. . . . Early choices about products, markets, and modes of operation are locked in through decisions about asset configuration and organization structure, constraining future options.

(Bartlett and Ghoshal 1989: 42, 45)

Kimberly (1987) argues those decisions made relatively early in an organization's history account for its structure and processes and also shape its responses to present opportunities and challenges. However, he argues that not all decisions in the early life of an organization are of equal significance. Drawing on Kimberly (1987), we discuss how the early decisions on their governance form (partnership), domain in which they operate (the industries and clients they focus on), initial expertise and organization design have shaped and are continuing to shape the Big Five accounting firms' international organizational arrangements and behaviours. Following Bartlett and Ghoshal (1989), we also examine the role that national history, infrastructure and culture has played in shaping international structure and processes.

There are many ways in which we could explore the history of these firms. Many of the official histories adopt a teleological approach, implying that the history of these firms has been a general progression to the current state. History is also depicted therein as a story of 'great men', and this approach would seem to resonate with Kimberley's call (1987) for a biographical approach to organizational analysis. However, these approaches to history are not consistent with modern approaches to history, particularly those that seek to unsettle common conceptions and unproblematic visions of historical progress. Thus writers such as Merino (1998) and Napier (1998) stress the value of more theoretically informed histories in providing explanations and rationales for the events and activities that traditional histories emphasize. Because we rely extensively on official firm histories, it is difficult to adopt a modern approach to history, but we can, at least, acknowledge the need for theoretical explanations for the developments that took place. Broadly, we start from the position that the choices made at the inception of the large accounting firms was a product of their national circumstances and the ideas current at the time about appropriate modes of organizing: 'Men make their own history, but they do not make it just as they please; they do not make it under circumstances chosen by themselves, but under circumstances directly encountered, given and transmitted by the past' (Marx 1852).

Thus, we analyse history in two ways. First, we look at the impact of partnership form, the professional skill requirements of the task, and the high client interdependence involved in the professional service task and assess how these have generally impacted the international structures and processes of the Big Five accounting firms. Later, we look at the present international arrangements of two firms and explain their organizational realities in the specifics of their early circumstances and decisions.

This chapter proceeds as follows. In the next section we describe the methodology used for this study. Subsequently, in the third section we compare the organization history of the Big Five advisory firms to other MNCs in terms of early decisions about governance form, domain, design, and expertise. Then, in the fourth section, we discuss the transnational environment that has been facing the Big Five advisory firms since the 1980's. The fifth section describes in detail two distinct organizational arrangements in response to the environment pressures by two of the largest business advisory firms. In the sixth section, we describe each firm's unique history and discuss how their organizational responses in that broad context. In the discussion section we describe how each firm's history both limits and facilitates their current responses to their present global challenges, summarize the understanding we gained of the organizational arrangements of the Big Five, and provide suggestions for future research.

Importantly, our analysis shows how decisions in the early life of these organizations in terms of governance, domain, design and recruitment helps to explain the different present day structures and responses of international professional service firms. However, following Marx's quotation above, we do not argue that a firm's history is an iron cage for the international organizational arrangements related to present and future challenges.

Methodology

This chapter draws on a long standing and ongoing program of research which examines the practices of professional service firms (notably, law, engineering, consulting and accounting firms) with the predominant focus on the Big Five accounting firms. Our primary source of data for this paper was interviews. We draw on over 130 interviews conducted in numerous countries (Australia, Belgium, Canada, Hong Kong, Malaysia, Netherlands, Singapore, UK and USA) to understand the firms' international organizational arrangements. Interviewees held key managerial roles in the international firms or served key global clients between 1989 and 1996. Interviews ranged from one to three hours in length. Often second and third interviews captured changes that occurred over time. Most interviews were audio taped and fully transcribed. In addition to the interview data, reports and documents such as strategic plans, annual reports and directories, office procedure manuals, process reports, client service manuals, and client proposals were collected and analysed. Qualitative data analysis software (Richards and Richards 1992) facilitated the analysis of both types of data.

We produced descriptions of the Big Five advisory firms' orientations, organizational structures and decision processes which reflected their governance, domain, design and expertise focus. We were particularly interested in these firms' strategic orientation; the relative autonomy and self-sufficiency of member firms; and the nature of control in the firms. A semi-structured interview schedule was used. Interviewees described the international organization and their international role. The goal was to obtain as much information as possible on the structural configuration and how it functioned. We paid particular attention to what they said were critical processes (such as strategic decisions, including investment decisions, budgeting and resource allocation decisions, human resource practices, and other managerial practices supporting service to international clients).

We also obtained information on the historic configuration of assets, the distribution of responsibility over time, and the historic norms, values and preferences of partners over time. Capturing the details of important decisions taken by the organization in the early years of its history was of particular importance, asking how and why current managerial arrangements had, and were, evolving. This material was augmented with biographical and historical accounts of accounting firms (e.g. Allen and McDermott 1993; Cypert 1991; Richards 1981; Wise 1981; Watt 1982), despite the teleological and managerialist assumptions such histories implicitly adopt.

We first discuss generally the historical nature of the Big Five advisory firms and then provide detailed information on two of the firms (Andersen Worldwide and KPMG) to show different, but both successful, international organizational responses to a common environment. The descriptions of the firms depict their international organizational arrangements and processes and important elements of their histories up to June 1996. Because they are continually adapting their arrangements in anticipation and response to evolving market circumstances, aspects of their international arrangements may already be superseded. However, our purpose was to gain an understanding of the breadth of those arrangements and the responses of the firms to their history and environmental pressures. It was not to evaluate the firms *vis-à-vis* one another, or with others in the industry. These two firms, as well as the rest of the Big Five accounting firms, are highly successful, as far as can be assessed through the limited, un-audited information on growth and revenues they provide.

History of the Big Five accounting firms

To understand organizational behaviour, both the unique and the common characteristics of their history must be considered. Specifically, Kimberly (1987) argues that decisions undertaken relatively early in the life of an organization, relating to governance, domain, expertise and design, impact on future behaviour. We begin by assessing the common history of the Big Five accounting firms along these four dimensions.

Governance

Under governance we will discuss two elements: the partnership form and the role of social controls. The origin of the Big Five advisory firms is mostly the professional partnership, with unlimited liability. In these arrangements, the partners are simultaneously the operators, managers and owners of the firm (Greenwood *et al.* 1990). Authority is widely and horizontally held. Power is decentralized. Partners with equivalent skills are replicated in every market so the partners can stay close to the clients and be responsive to their needs. In many jurisdictions, despite partners' fears of legal liability and thus desire for legal protection, these firms have been and continue to be legally bound to this partnership form.

While there have been recent moves to make the Big Five firms more like corporations, democratic governance structures have predominated for partners in these firms. The CEO (managing partner) of the international firm is elected. He (it has never been a woman) then chooses an Executive Committee, which is subject to the oversight of a Partnership Board. The broad contours of this governance structure have existed since the inception of the international firm, and tend to mirror the typical governance structure of national firms.

The professional business advisory firms expanded into the global sphere by forming associations across borders between national partnerships (each a legal entity in itself, and often comprising a number of local firms). The international relationships have increased in formalization over time in all the firms, but more in some firms than others (Daniels *et al.* 1989). Partnership and expansion through association has resulted in an organizational configuration which is best described as a complex network structure. In this, a large number of loosely coupled connections among various firms support the firm's goals of providing service to clients' businesses, enhancing the network's reputation to ensure ongoing business and thereby maximizing the profits available for the partners. This network mode of expansion has meant that there has been limited commitment of resources to support international expansion initiated from the centre.

These firms have adapted to demands upon them, co-ordinated themselves and safeguarded exchanges among themselves and others involved in serving clients by using social mechanisms rather more than authority, bureaucratic or legal rules, or standards. Jones *et al.* (1997) refer to this as network governance. Social mechanisms have included institutional interventions that set industry-specific and professional knowledge standards (e.g. professional training and examinations and accounting standards setting agencies). Other social mechanisms have included processes within the firms and between the firms in areas where governments have left considerable discretion to the professionals to monitor and control themselves, such as self regulating requirements, firm socialization and inter-office exchanges. The firms' behaviour, notably their expansion through association, has also been guided by the importance of reputation. Size has been positively correlated with reputation in the eyes of clients. The characteristics, skills, and consistency of individuals as well as the firm have been key to repeat business. Thus, collective sanctions and processes restricting undesirable behaviour have been important elements of the way advisory firms have been governed. Member firms have been removed from the international network (no longer allowed to use the name of the firm; no longer eligible for assistance from the international firm, no longer accessed for referral work) in all the Big Five.

Domain

The Big Five firms' initial product/service domain was audit/accounting, tax, and bankruptcy services (Jones 1981). These services are highly knowledge intensive and require a high level of education; they involve a high degree of customization and require the individual providing the service to use extensive discretion and personal judgment in the delivery of the services (Gibbins and Mason 1988). They require a high degree of interaction between the professional delivering the service and the client being served and are delivered within the constraints of professional norms (e.g. codes of conduct). Furthermore, audit/accounting, tax, and bankruptcy have traditionally interfaced with law and economics, both as partners and bodies of knowledge. Traditional service offerings have been highly impacted by external forces (e.g. court interventions and professional standards) whereby rules, procedures, mandates, and monitoring have impinged on organizational choice.

The legal basis of knowledge and the core domain of legal compliance in audit, tax, and bankruptcy continue to affect the core values and domain of current businesses in Big Five firms. For example, partners in one firm stated that they have had the expertise to be a global travel business. They made a conscious decision not to enter that market because it is inconsistent with professional status and core domain. Core domain values (e.g. objectivity, neutrality, independence) continue to be important in positioning the type of consulting work they engage in (Hanson 1989). Further, it is only very recently that non-audit partners have been able to be elected to senior positions in firm management.

These firms' original market focus was the local client, but that could also involve international activity. Unlike other types of MNCs, where overseas expansion was to secure supplies of resources and raw materials, or to provide additional markets for production capabilities requiring stable and high demand (Bartlett and Ghoshal 1989), the professional advisory firms first went overseas to service existing clients (Cypert 1991; Daniels *et al.* 1989).[1]

Expertise

The original experts of the Big Five were all part of the common profession of audit and this service has unique characteristics. For example, audit work is characterized by a great deal of consistency. It is required by law, has specific statutory requirements, and is not threatened by economic downturn to the same extent as other business services. A client comes to the firm and a service team is assembled. The work is fairly reactive. Successful auditors tend to have a strong technical ability, rooted in the disciplines of audit, tax, finance, law and economics. But perhaps even more crucial for success has been the ability to get along with clients and to be trusted by partners. Note, however, the expertise has often been more about maintaining good client relations than about getting new audit business.

It is relatively easy for a single audit approach to be applied worldwide. The audit is a product that can be easily taken to the client and replicated in a number of markets. Thus each of the Big Five has developed a world-wide computer audit methodology. Barrett *et al.*(1997) indicate how the standardized, commodified approach is used to emphasize to clients the consistency, quality, and responsiveness of service. There is a great deal of internal control by the firm over the audit task, and its execution flows directly from professional audit expertise. Historically, the training of new accountants has been centred on the audit and accounting task; thus accountants all operated similarly and trusted that each office of the firm operated similarly. Furthermore, the auditor/client relationship is one in which the auditor gets the client through a legal process and often attempts to reduce the client's exposure to risk. The relationship with the client is often long-term. The client is seen frequently and the firm becomes quite familiar with the client's organizational processes. Although the client's experience of the audit process is important, it is not critical in bringing the next job to the firm.

Historically, the experts and the 'gatekeepers' of these firms, the accountants/auditors, have made decisions regarding international expansion and organizational arrangements. A federative type organization makes good sense to partners of traditional services who see themselves as mediating on a long term basis between their clients and the firm.

A third distinguishing characteristic of the expertise in the Big Five is that historically partners have placed a high value on their autonomy. Few partners have wanted managerial responsibility, and few have been good at managing. For example, integrated human resource management systems have been promoted as essential for knowledge creation and sharing in professional service firms (Evans and Doz 1992; Doz and Pralahad 1986; Taylor *et al.* 1996). Despite the importance of knowledge sharing and transfer, accounting professionals have been foremost technical experts and client-centred. Individuals have not trained for management functions and historically the greatest financial and status rewards have not been found there. Løwendahl (1997) talks about a paradox where professionals do not want to be managers. Auditors have highly valued their professional training and the freedom provided by the professional designation. The desire has been to apply their body of knowledge, skills, and experience to client problems. Because they have not trained to manage they often have not done it well (Ferner *et al.* 1995). Essentially professionals in these firms have been highly resistant to any attempts at formal organization (Starbuck 1992) and they have been resistant to managers who do not have an accounting designation (Løwendahl 1997).

Design

The designs of the Big Five firms from their earliest days are best described as networks based on interlocking partnerships. A number of large national firms, themselves an extensive network of local offices, comprise these international firms. This network has been, and continues to be, an alternative arrangement that is more congruent with partnership form (Greenwood *et al.* forthcoming) than with a hierarchical arrangement. The networks have been held together by a large number of lateral co-ordination mechanisms, involving a vast number of committees, task forces, project teams, and steering groups. These lateral supporting mechanisms may pertain to industry specialism such that there will be an international mining committee, or task groups may form to deal with ethical standards throughout the firm. Other groups form to focus on and advance a particular practice area, or attend to a technological decision that will affect the firm. These various groups evolve at the discretion of individual partners and are similarly dissolved when partners involved deem the group has served its purpose. Consequently, extensive overlapping of industry, service, client, and geographical groupings occurs within all the firms. Historically the network of lateral structures has emphasized the collegial mechanisms used to promote co-operation within advisory firms, and to promote the normative attachment of professionals to their organizations. In recent years, every Big Five network structure has strengthened the international firm, which is somewhat of a separate legal entity that attempts to influence horizontal relationships among all the separate national firms. More formal and central control mechanisms have been introduced over time due to the need for higher level integration to serve the large global clients (Ferner *et al.* 1995).

Most research on MNCs has assumed a hierarchical, centrally controlled firm that expands through wholly or partially owned subsidiaries. Typical mechanisms for integration and control (such as hierarchical decision-making, employee transfers) are assumed, with top management playing the primary role in ensuring all participants are motivated to share knowledge (for example through incentive systems). The historical partnership structure of the Big Five firms has restricted the centralized control of expansion. The relative autonomy of member firms has meant that a single, simple and clear governance structure has not been possible. Typical mechanisms for integration (e.g. co-ordinated and enforced planning) have not been sufficient or have not even existed. The regulatory and institutional influences have not allowed the international firms the same control over local units as in other MNCs. Professional knowledge and training means that accountants resist many efforts to control them or restrict their discretion about which clients to serve, and how to serve them.

Furthermore, most MNC research has assumed the primary task of a company is tangible, repeated, measurable, and defined by the producers. The traditional services of accounting firms have not been defined by these characteristics; instead these firms have to respond to multiple clients, each requiring a customized service and the partners must work interactively with the client in identifying their needs and devising solutions. Many multinational companies take a tangible and measurable product which is produced world-wide and use mechanisms for data management (such as information systems, business and managers performance measures, resource allocation procedures and budget processes), human resource management (e.g. employee transfers, reward and punishment systems), and centralized conflict resolution to internationalize the product (Doz and Pralahad 1992). However, because of the unique characteristics and histories of the Big Five, the same control mechanisms to simultaneously achieve global efficiency, local responsiveness and innovation, do not work. The subsequent two sections provide details of the uncertain and complex environment these firms have faced in recent years and their differential organizational responses in light of their historical origins.

The transnational environment

For a number of years, the Big Five firms have faced a transnational environment where the firms need to continuously adapt structurally and managerially to achieve high levels of co-ordination and to create and safeguard knowledge in order to remain competitive (Jones *et al.* 1997). The transnational environment is specifically characterized by the following conditions.

First, advances in technology and communication have underpinned various reorganizations in many companies, including the professional business advisory firms. The most recent bout of corporate reorganizing began in the early 1980s and continued throughout the 1990s. In the 1980s companies began to get more specialized, joining forces with other firms through multiple mergers and acquisitions and expanding into the international arena (Allen and McDermott 1993; Cypert 1991). The pressures on the professional service firms for restructuring have been two-sided. These firms have sought to take their clients through these major changes and in doing so, have been pressured to specialize, expand through large-scale mergers, and gain international capability themselves.

Second, the firms have sought substantive, industry-specific knowledge. Technological advances have enabled them to provide better quality traditional services and to offer additional and more specialized services. Advances in technology have put pressure on the firms to specialize in assisting clients with the implementation and integration of systems, thereby creating a very lucrative but demanding market. Technology has simultaneously created pressure for the firms themselves to update their technological systems and create integrated systems (such as Groupware) globally within the firms (Allen and McDermott 1993).

Third, competition for the Big Five has become intense over recent years. Audit, once the central activity of the firms, is a decreasing percentage of revenues. For the period 1988–95 profitability from audit and accounting services declined. The increase in competition for audits occurred for a number of reasons. Corporate mergers and takeovers have resulted in fewer clients needing audit services. The firms are concerned that the remaining large clients may have an increased propensity to switch auditors for a better deal (Greenwood *et al.* 1993); this has further heightened competition. The audit itself has become standardized and commodified which has resulted in increased competition and difficulty for suppliers to differentiate their audit and accounting services. There has been a relaxation of advertising constraints on professional service firms. Finally, the increase in litigation on the audits conducted by firms has made audit and accounting more risky and hence less desirable, or desirable only in the context of particular types of clients.

Simultaneously with the decline in audit and accounting opportunities there has been significant growth in the business services market. Clients have demanded services such as valuations, and insolvency and management consulting. There has been an increase in the demand for management consulting and information technology services which has put significant pressure on the firms to achieve a higher level of overall integration among their member firms (Greenwood and Hinings 1996). In addition to a demand for single services on a worldwide basis, there is a demand for arrays of single services to be integrated. Clients now have multiple needs, spanning multiple disciplines (e.g. audit, tax, and consulting). Partners have had to find ways to simultaneously deliver a spectrum of services in an integrated fashion, while providing efficient and effective points of contact.

Clients have become increasingly interested in value-adding services. This requires the firms to build specialized, industry-specific, knowledge. The firms have sought to identify and harness relevant expertise world-wide, and efficiently and effectively bring it together in ways they have not before. The Big Five firms have developed teams of people who have experience and skills in an industry and provide services to that industry no matter where the people are located. People from different disciplines and functions, but specializing in a particular industry, are pooled together to form specialized units with a wide expertise base in the industry.

The diversification of services along with the support of technology, however, has allowed all types of practitioners (e.g. lawyers, financial planners, tax advisors, and accountants) to offer consulting services as well as to cross over into each other's service areas. All these groups have access to highly developed software systems, specialist knowledge, and skills in client management. These groups have been increasingly competing with each other. Along with new services and strong competition across all the firms' service areas, there has been pressure on the Big Five firms to develop and launch highly successful marketing plans (an activity which was largely unpracticed and often seen as being in contradiction to professional values until recent years).

To increase specialist services and attend to increased competitiveness, especially locally, all the Big Five firms have felt, like the companies they serve, the pressure to strengthen themselves through consolidation. This is evident by the mergers in the late 1980s and the merger of Price Waterhouse and

Coopers and Lybrand in 1998. Mergers are a response to the continuous felt pressure to have a strong global position and the important role size plays in being global. Global positioning in the Big Five firms, as in many of their client organizations, is seen as strategically important. Attaining a high level integration of services across country boundaries has been a predominant pre-occupation in advisory firms over a number of years.

A fourth important aspect of the advisory firm's environment has been the pressure for increased harmonization of national accounting standards. For example, the International Accounting Standards Committee (IASC) sought to increase harmonization of standards and, by 1993, had professional bodies from seventy-eight countries as members (McKee and Garner 1996). Although standards still remain more nationally specific than internationally similar, the Big Five have to ensure that their technical solutions are consistent world-wide.

Organizational responses to the transnational environment

Deterministic versions of contingency theory argue that for an organization to be effective the right set of structural arrangements and co-ordination devices must align with specific environment circumstances.[2] Consequently, one would predict that the Big Five accounting firms, having many things common to their origin and facing similar environment circumstances, would be similar in terms of the way they differentiate and integrate. However, this is not what we find. In this section we look at the way the firms are similarly responding to their environment, but also at the ways in which their responses vary.

The common response of the Big Five firms to the changed market has been a movement away from audit and accounting services; an increased strategic focus on developing and implementing new services; and an increased focus on internal differentiation horizontally, functionally, geographically and demographically. Structurally there has been movement toward a more defined hierarchy (implementation of formal and centralized processes) yet with continued collegial structures. The firms have been driving for a more strategic capability grounded in a more authoritative style of decision-making. The time horizons for strategic planning have become longer and there appears to be more accountability for achieving targets. An important commonality among the firms in terms of their attempts to improve their global service is that all are developing extensive client management systems in order to serve their global clients better. There are few differences in their rationales for such systems and very few differences in their conceptualizations of the role of lead partner (the integral component of all the client management systems). Differences do exist, however, between the client management systems in terms of the extent to which authority is granted to lead partners (those given primary responsibility for ensuring that the client receives the very best service possible).

We now examine two dominant organizational responses to the changing transnational environment by the Big Five accounting firms. We look at the relationship between the centres of these firms' international operations (the international firms) and the periphery offices (the local and national offices). We analyse Andersen Worldwide's and KPMG's international arrangements in terms that Greenwood *et al.* (1990) refer to as strategic, marketing, financial, and operational orientation. Strategic orientation refers to the extent to which the international firm defines for its offices the range and scope of marketing initiatives, fixes offices' relative emphasis, or evaluates the competitive positions of the various offices. Market and financial orientation refers to the extent to which the international firm sets clear financial targets for offices and holds offices accountable for the targets set or the tolerance around accountability. Operational orientation refers to the extent to which the international firm is involved in basic functions of the national or local offices such as marketing and human resources. It is important to note that the term international headquarters, however, is somewhat different than a typical manufacturing MNC in that for the Big Five, the headquarters comprises the International Office (i.e. the full-time staff) and the various International Committees, which are used to oversee the international firm and to carry out many of its functions.

Andersen Worldwide

Andersen Worldwide perceives itself to be an integrated international organization, whose constitutive entities operate in multiple countries. It does not conceptualize itself as an aggregation of national firms. Partners emphasize that each of the firm's business units – Arthur Andersen and Andersen Consulting – operate in a highly co-ordinated way, and in no way operates like a franchise. Of course, the world firm comprises many local legal entities, connected by a complex of inter-firm agreements. As one senior partner in Arthur Andersen said, 'we are separate legal entities, but we are an integrated global multi-disciplinary firm'. Admission to full partnership is to the Andersen Worldwide international partnership.[3] The international firm is a cost sharing entity with income guarantees among partners. Under the pressure to provide services worldwide, each business unit emphasizes worldwide standardization of quality and integration of services, and does so through a strong international management structure. Each is tightly structured and places formal authority in a concentrated manner at the hierarchical apex of the firm. The distribution of power is clearly intended to favour the international management entity, not the national firms. Market share and financial targets are set both for the worldwide Arthur Andersen business unit and for each national member firm in a way not found in any of the other Big Five firms. For example each national member firm is wired into the business unit's central financial and operating system, which provides extensive, timely, operating data on a monthly basis.

The financial information system illustrates how a single and consistent set of mechanisms permeates the organization, providing centralized knowledge of local performance and offering the possibility of making strategic adjustments across countries in an effort to sustain global results. Arthur Andersen not only has a more tightly structured and hierarchically arranged international organization than any of the other Big Five advisory firms, in addition, its senior management team has the authority and is expected to act assertively and decisively. The authority of the hierarchy is indicated in the following comment by a senior executive: 'There's a tremendous amount of management authority which is given to what we call the leadership group of the firm. . . . I really have a true global responsibility. . . . I have executive authority to commit the firm.'

Operationally speaking, Arthur Andersen spends considerable sums on training their professionals and they have world-class facilities for doing so. One partner stated that the firm depended on the quality of their people and their ongoing professional development. Training and management development is seen as central to their goals of remaining a leading accounting and consulting firm. This training brings consistency and high level integration across countries.

The firm has reasons beyond technical standardization for the intensive training they employ; it wants to socialize its personnel into its values and norms, thus developing a deep-rooted commitment to the firm's organization and way of doing things. Training is treated as a vehicle for developing normative commitment to the firm. One reason why Arthur Andersen has found it possible to develop a firm-wide culture is because its professionals progress through standardized training programs, many of them delivered at the firm's world training centre. The training centre is seen as both a technology transfer point and as a crucial mechanism for the dissemination of the firm's values. One manager at the centre expressed it as follows: 'They're very tied to using the center as the cultural glue that holds the place together. They're very conscious of trying to do that in such a way that it holds the individual nationalities together.'

Arthur Andersen is one of two business units in Andersen Worldwide. The other, Andersen Consulting is a management and IT consulting firm, and has about half as many partners as the accounting unit. Growing tensions between the traditional gatekeepers of service, the accountants, and the management consultants who over time are bringing in the higher revenues, have made the two divisions the only feasible way to capitalize on, and meet the challenges of, clients' demands for diverse and quality services (Stevens 1991; Whitford 1997). Andersen Consulting targets Fortune 500 companies and competes with the likes of IBM, EDS, Bain and McKinsey. And, although originally entrenched in information technology consulting, the consulting division has expanded into a number of other areas, such as change management. 85 per cent of the consulting profits stay within the business unit and are shared worldwide, and 15 per cent is shared with the accounting business unit worldwide.

In summary, Arthur Andersen is an integrated international management entity whose member firms operate in multiple countries. The firm is fairly unicentric, built on full-service, self-sufficient national units. The relationship between these national units and the international organization is clear, with explicit accountability to the international entity. Arthur Andersen achieves integration through a combination of three mechanisms: a hierarchy of authority, reinforced by explicit information systems that provide and monitor the market and financial performance of each national unit; a mosaic of overlapping lateral structures (culminating in the business unit leadership team and ultimately in the Andersen Worldwide Board of Partners); and a strong organizational culture, deliberately managed through intensive training and development. The firm's strong culture is characteristic of US based cultures and reflects the founder's beliefs. The strong US based culture means that there is an acceptance that power is unequally distributed in organizations, and needs to be. Therefore the greater central control in this firm is accepted. The firm is relatively uneasy with ambiguous situations, so there is greater formalization and less tolerance of diverse viewpoints and ways of operating than in the other Big Five. The strong US based culture is seen in the emphasis on individualism versus collectivism, where individual initiative and achievement is important and there is considerable pressure for partners to attain high level training. There is a strong push for universal values throughout the firm. The US based culture is further seen in the emphasis on ambition, high performance standards, achievement, and in the idea that 'big' and 'fast' are important (Hofstede 1980).

KPMG

KPMG's international organization is quite different from Andersen Worldwide but is similar to the rest of the Big Five in the mid-1990s. Senior partners of KPMG perceive the firm to be a confederation of national practices.[4] They have a strong global presence in each of the major markets of the world and they have common goals, objectives, values, and interests. They suggest that they are the only truly global firm. They see the federation as a strength, not a disadvantage or a weakness.

In KPMG, admission to the partnership is at the national level. The partners share profits nationally and the international firm is a cost-sharing entity. The international office is comparatively small (in staffing and budget) and has a decision-making style that is primarily supportive and administrative, rather than directive and authoritative. The international office has approximately fifty staff, supported by under 0.5 per cent of worldwide revenues. Those inside the international office recognize their primary role as that of assisting the international firm to develop a common level of service capability and of delivery to clients, not to promote a one-firm structure. The head office provides support to the national firms.

An influential component of KPMG's international headquarters is the Executive Committee, to which the International Executive Partner (who heads the international office) reports. The Executive Committee decides on how the global network will be developed, including which new markets will be entered. It assesses merger opportunities. The committee is responsible for the development of client management systems; for the development, implementation and support of new ideas and processes; for managing litigation risk; and for ensuring the reputation of the firm is maintained.

Critically, however, the Executive Committee in KPMG has little formal authority to develop and enforce a global strategy. There are no systems providing the Executive Committee with detailed market and financial information on the performance of each national firm. Neither targets nor goals are set for the national firms. There is no international monitoring of national firm performance or appraisal of each national firm's managing partner. Policies adopted by the international firm are implemented at the discretion of each national firm.

The constrained authority of the international office and of the central committees in KPMG is reflected in two principles embodied in the governance structures of the firm, principles which emphasize the accountability of the international firm to the national firm. First, most of the work carried out by the international firm is conducted through committees that embody the principle of territorial representation. For example, the Board of Partners is comprised of the thirty-three heads of the largest national firms, which produce 97 per cent of worldwide revenues. The Board elects its own Chairman, Vice Chairman and the Executive Committee, which has eleven members. Typically, the Executive Committee will include the heads of the largest national firms (for example in the UK, US, Netherlands, Germany and France). In other words, the most senior governing structures of the International Firm are, *de facto*, directly accountable to the national practices by virtue of the representative structure of the Board and the Executive Committee. How far representatives act as representatives of national interests depends on the issue. Accountability of the International Firm to the national practices is solidified through international executive positions that are usually for fixed terms (though renewable) and are often combined with other national responsibilities. The chairmen of international committees are appointed for three years and continue to carry a client load. Members of the Executive Committee are national executive partners and are engaged at least as much, and probably more, in running their national firms than in running the International Firm. Until recently, the only full-time executive positions were within the International Office, which services the committee structure. The Chief Executive is the full-time head of the International Firm. Despite these developments, the role of the International Office in KPMG contrasts with that of Andersen Worldwide, which is much more clearly the strategic hub of the firm.

Second, KPMG's large expenditures on training are different from the format and training in Andersen. For KPMG training traditionally has served a twofold purpose: first to standardize methodologies so that clients will receive a similar standard of service worldwide and ensure that services provided to international clients are seamlessly delivered despite national boundaries; second, to maintain and improve the knowledge and skills of the workforce, thus improving the asset stock of the firm. Training and management development is primarily a cognitive activity intended to improve technical competence and develop standardized approaches. However, in Europe, KPMG is developing courses aimed at strengthening 'our unity as a firm' to strengthen values. Yet, although a process is underway to rationalize and co-ordinate training programmes traditionally designed and delivered by each national firm, mandatory training at the global level remains comparatively rare. Instead, facilities are available to national firms, and essentially are used voluntarily.

In response to clients' demands for industry specialization, all the Big Five have devised industry business units. These structures link regions and service areas. Individuals from different disciplines, but specializing in a particular industry, are pooled together to provide more coherent service to clients in specialized industries. However, KPMG makes industry specialization a priority and it is the dominant way in which it responds to its market.

KPMG's focus on industry specialization is likely to culminate in the development of new global structures. For example, one model takes partners out of their national practices, essentially purchasing them through a transfer pricing mechanism. Royalties go back to the professionals' originating firms. The idea is for these global partners to take on very large client engagements in a new industry or new market. The partners propose, organize, run, control, and bill a project. Profit sharing will be global within the structure. The idea is that global structure will form around new markets or new services. Essentially the global structure is an evolution of the firm's industry focus whereby the relationships among the firms are further codified and routinized for a select group of global clients.

In summary, KPMG is an association of full-service, self-sufficient national units. The firm is multi-centric. The relationship between the international and national firms is one in which the International Firm is an appendage to legally independent national firms. There is no parent firm. The degree of integration sought emphasizes two mechanisms: training focused upon the promotion of consistent service methods, and lateral structures (culminating in the Board of Partners) supported by a small international administration. Decision-making is based on discussion and negotiation, and adoption of international practices tends to be voluntary rather than mandatory. Formal, hierarchical authority is avoided as a means of achieving international integration. There is an increasingly extensive array of lateral mechanisms that allows Andersen Worldwide and KPMG (and all the advisory firms) to survive. In Andersen these lateral structures complement the most hierarchical arrangements of any of the firms. Lateral structures replace hierarchical arrangements in KPMG. The culture of the organization is characteristic of a European based MNC. There is a very high priority on consensus decision-making and much less tolerance of hierarchical arrangements and centralized control (Hofstede 1980).

How history has shaped the international organization

Why do two firms in the same industry, facing the same environmental challenges have quite distinct organizational realities? Part of the answer relates to the historical characteristics of these two firms. Here we discuss the unique origins of these two firms in terms of expertise, governance, design, domain and critical decisions, and/or cultural origins and explain some of the differences in their present organizational arrangements with those observations of each one's history.[5]

Andersen Worldwide

Expertise

The influence of Arthur Andersen himself, is still found in the international organization. Andersen came from a middle class background and is regarded as having a strong work ethic. He pushed boundaries, excelling academically and becoming the first academic to enter one of the major firms. He made recruitment a priority and from the inception of the firm intentionally recruited people similar to himself, creating a homogenous group of individuals who shared many values.

Early in the firm's history Andersen infused his passion for education into the firm by creating an extensive training program for all professional staff and extending it to all offices to assure uniform training of personnel and common procedures. In the 1930s training was expanded to offer industry specific courses, thus offering services much broader than traditional audit and accounting. In the 1950s the firm pushed forward with developing career opportunities, formal evaluation procedures, promotion by merit, and informal working relationships (referred to as an open-door policy).

Design

The firm expanded across the United States in the 1920s. That initial and extensive growth period was through internal expansion rather than acquisition. Although international expansion began in the 1920s the first major international thrust occurred in the following decade. The firm solidified 'working agreements' with a number of firms that themselves had extensive offices. Representation was gained in Europe, South America, Australia and

Canada. There were attempts to tie all working agreements together and put the US firm as the hub, in other words to form a worldwide organization. This firm, on numerous occasions throughout its history, has contemplated international expansion through merger activity. As early as 1935 the partners questioned the usefulness of absorbing personnel and partners involved in acquisitions. Meeting reports indicate that the partners intended to grow internally rather than through merger opportunities. There is a long history of this firm consistently valuing internal growth and common training thereby reinforcing the homogeneity of people in the firm.

The war interrupted the movement toward forming a single worldwide firm. In fact, some of the ties among firms prior to the war were damaged. Some offices were shut down; other operations were disrupted. Shortly after the war Andersen put in place a strategy for a worldwide firm. In 1946, shortly before his death, Andersen articulated his international vision in a memo:

> We must have as we have never had before, a united family, whether the offices are within or outside the borders of the United States, and we must be tied together as a continuing organization, making for better service to the outside world. Basically this is the philosophy that underlies the new and broader organization concept, which will have to be bolstered a little later in men, in vehicles for training and in continuity of relationships. It is not enough to have men in London, Mexico City and Paris: they must be tied to some general program that involves the entire organization so they, too, feel that kinship of understanding and responsibility that I am trying to introduce into the firm. We have operated much too long on an individual-office basis. We must now have a larger, overall-organization view.
>
> (Arthur Andersen 1988: 75)

The above statement highlights the firm's origins in the US. During the 1950s the firm sought continued homogeneity of its members by treating those in rapidly expanding networks of new offices around the world exactly as US counterparts. The founders and those that followed consistently focused on attaining a single organizational structure. They were not comfortable with the level of control that could be achieved in acquisition circumstances and they questioned the level of client service that could be achieved by a less centralized organization. The firm did try occasionally to make acquisitions, but most talks broke down and any acquisitions were less than satisfactory. The attitude within the firm remained favourable to internal growth, especially international. In a meeting in 1958, the partners re-committed to the firm's philosophy of creating a strong centralized management along with sufficient local autonomy deemed necessary to serve clients. They agreed, consistent with the past, to invest significant amounts into training, research, and development of specialized services and to invest in new offices in key cities throughout the world. In one meeting in 1958 they 'staunchly opposed the "loose federation" of offices and local focus that characterized the structure of other large firms' and they stood four-square behind the tough, driving management style of Arthur Andersen and his successor, Leonard Spacek (Arthur Andersen 1988: 102).

One interviewee emphasized the importance of the 'one-firm' firm to the founders, by relaying an event that occurred in the mid-1950s. The story goes that a large US global client complained about the service they were receiving in London. Spacek went there and, on finding the partners' corridor locked, he broke the contract then and there. Oxbridge graduates were then hired to work with Andersen partners from the US, as a way of avoiding the 'old boys' attitudes of the accounting profession in the UK. Thereafter, Spacek believed the firm needed to create a worldwide profit pool, not because of strategy, but because there was no other way to set up offices around the world. Otherwise, the young, ambitious US partners would not move and the firm felt that standards could only be reached by that kind of US partner mobility.

Also in the 1950s there was an explicit drive for unity through a conscious search for symbols and logos to support the building of common ties and creation of a unified worldwide firm. The symbol or logo was to represent confidentiality, privacy, security, orderliness, characteristics the leaders aspired for the firm. In the 1970s the firm established Arthur Andersen and Co. Société Cooperative (SC) in Switzerland to maintain a single-firm focus, despite nationalist and protectionist attitudes. This structure is an administrative entity that co-ordinates the activities of the various firms of the Andersen Worldwide organization, sets policy, establishes and monitors worldwide quality standards and co-ordinates training for all Arthur Andersen personnel (Arthur Andersen 1988: 139). Each partner is part of a national member firm but also a partner in SC. Throughout the 1970s the firm increased its client's base faster than internal growth would allow and once again contemplated acquisitions. Again, in most of the cases it decided against the acquisition, or was not successful in completing one, although it made two acquisitions that strengthened the firm in the UK and South Africa.

Domain: market and services

One very significant feature of Andersen's has been its broad range of services: it has always derived more revenue from non-accounting and audit services than other major accounting firms have. This feature began when the firm was founded. Andersen emphasized financial investigations. Their experience in this area positioned Andersen's to capitalize on the extensive amount of work available during the merger activity in the 1920s. At a regional meeting of the American Institute of Accountants as early as 1925, Andersen stated the need for accountants to have a broad role:

It is in bringing a balanced view to bear upon the problems of the undertaking and in assisting management in matters of business analysis that the accountant will have his greatest opportunities for service. It is my profound conviction that the accountant of the future will prosper and consolidate his position in the business world in proportion to his breadth of vision and willingness to accept these responsibilities of larger service to industry.

(Arthur Andersen 1988: 29)

Andersen pushed the firm to undertake work outside the usual range of accounting services, into areas such as labour relations, supply sourcing, production facilities, product and markets advise, and consulting about organizational and management effectiveness. By the 1950s the firm was developing practices that were foreign to the rest of the accounting industry. Many of these practices were related to personnel issues. Also beginning about 1953 the firm began to tap into technology and the systems market. Although they were into many new services, their eight consulting niches lacked focus (Stevens 1991).

By the 1960s, the management consulting services work, especially its information systems work, was central to the firm and its relations with many of its clients. The growth of the systems practice highlighted different philosophies between offices engaged in systems work and those concentrating on other work, and perhaps more significantly, between audit and tax personnel and management consultants. In the early 1960s a rule requiring two years audit experience for all new consultants was rescinded. The message was that it was no longer important for everyone to think and act like an accountant. While the decision was a cost saving measure it can also be seen as reflecting tensions between professional groups.

Throughout the 1960s there was a never-ending supply of information technology and systems integration work. A critical meeting in 1968 decided to bring more uniformity and cohesion to the consulting practice. Each consulting niche would have its own director and its own training program, thus forming a group of consultants with little diversity across locations. Conflicts between consultants and accountants grew over firm domain. Although accounting work contributed well over half of aggregate fees, the consulting practice was growing at twice the rate of accounting. Different requirements in terms of compensation, appropriate firm structure, and problems with access to capital, created such substantial friction that a critical decision was made in 1989 to have the consulting practice in many of the substantial markets in the world operate under a different name (Whitford 1997). Management responsibilities were split at the office level, so that not all the functions within the office reported to the managing partner (who, under professional regulations, had to be a qualified accountant).

KPMG

The history of KPMG is more difficult to present, as the current firm is an amalgamation of many predecessor firms. However, two firms have been particularly dominant and thus we focus on early decisions in terms of governance, expertise, domain and design of these two firms.

Peat Marwick International

A British and an American firm formed Peat Marwick International (PMI) in 1911. The two firms maintained separate names until they adopted the name of PMI in 1925. In its early years PMI pushed internationally, targeting English-speaking countries. They were structured as a single partnership, with single profit sharing. The firm was a 'tightly knit family of firms' (Cypert 1991: 64) and had an international partner exchange program to increase understanding of colleagues across borders. In the 1970s there was a push into new services but then there was a vote of the partners explicitly against continued expansion into diverse service areas, and a renewed focus on doing auditing better. This provided for tighter, quality controls, but cautious growth.

KMG history

The other part of KPMG's history lies in the history of a firm originating in Amsterdam in 1917. One of this firm's early leaders pushed industry specialization and they offered a wide range of services, especially to the banking and export industries. This leader was 'fiercely independent' (Cypert 1991) and instilled the same qualities to other partners and employees. The firm's early focus was on following major global clients to the financial centres of Europe and South America. In the firm's early years they unified Europe by forming a mini-trading bloc. The firm was bound together by numerous international agreements and shared profits nationally: it was a loose international federation. It had two levels of standards, one national (standards that were at least equal to those in any of the countries in which the firm operated) and one international (in accordance with the firm's international audit manual).

KMG also had different categories of representation, indicating the extent to which an office represented the international firm and drew upon the international firm. The member firms could choose the extent of their involvement in the umbrella organization. Member firms could quite easily withdraw from the organization. The firm stressed localism while pushing toward being global. The commitment to independent firms and localism appears to have been entrenched by one of the founders of the firm. A partner describes him this way:

He had a unique perspective for an American. He was raised in the

Midwest, worked on both coasts, served as senior partner for the firm's operations in West Germany, married a German, and traveled the world. His vision for the global organization he would one day head was a business without borders . . . a collection of strong national firms, each firmly grounded in its own country but linked by people and technology and each with a commitment to its own firm and the international organization.

By the mid-1980s this firm was a loosely knit collection of national entities, held together primarily through a Swiss *Verein*. It had a logo, which it licensed to national practices. The member firms' practices were fiercely independent. Most member firms did not have a formal international business plan. An intensive study by a leading consulting company advised the firm to move away from such a degree of local independence if it wanted to be a strong player in the global economy.

The merger between PMI and KMG

The two firms were following similar strategies, one with a strong European presence and the other with strong representation in Anglo-Saxon locations. The firms agreed to merge in 1987 through the creation of a new structure so that neither was taken over by the other. The agreed upon international structure was the professional partnership. PMI had profit sharing throughout Europe while KMG had many national practices organized as corporations. The commitment was to a federation rather than a more centralized form of governance. The international firm formed by the merger did not have an authoritative role. In terms of domain, the merger provided global reach and coverage and specific strength in Europe. There was complementarity in terms of their markets with PMI having strength in the financial sector and KMG was strong in the manufacturing sector. The combined firm focused on industry specialization, building on their financial and manufacturing expertise and moving into insurance, real estate, merchandising, health care, high technology, government and education. Its operational focus was to automate the audit and the firm was first among the Big Six to monitor client service. Expertise seemingly intensified around industry specialties.

Discussion

An historical explanation for differences between firms' international responses

The two firms have come to their present international arrangements very much in line with the early decisions they made in terms of governance, expertise, domain and design. In the case of Andersen Worldwide, these arrangements include: the high degree of international centralization and high level of integration (capacity for global efficiency of each business unit); broad service domain and information systems predominance; a highly developed and autonomous management consulting entity; and homogenous values. These arrangements are very much in line with early decisions. The firm's present organizational structure reflects the original aspirations of the founder of the firm, his conscious hiring of individuals like himself (to form a highly homogenous group), his commitment to education and training (further supporting homogeneity), and his belief in the broad role of accountants and therefore the early development of management consulting services. The firm does not derive its innovative capacity from multiplicity and diversity of people as much as it does through its efficiency and technical competence, especially in systems work.

Its history supports Arthur Andersen's ability to be globally efficient, to serve many global clients simultaneously, to integrate member firms quickly across borders through highly developed systems, and to compete in a market that is broader than the other Big Five accounting firms. Its history supports learning through standardization and rapid and extensive transmission of best practices largely defined technically, rather than through cultural sensitivity or local responsiveness. The strong focus on management consulting services and the conflicts between different types of professionals has limited the ability for one part of the Andersen Worldwide organization to gain clients through the other. In fact, Andersen Consulting may further separate from Andersen Worldwide (Whitford 1997) and the accounting side (Arthur Andersen) has developed significant consulting services within it.

In KPMG, the federative form, national profit sharing arrangement, regional consulting practices, and highly developed industry and regional focus reflects important decisions by the two original firms and was reinforced by the merger in 1989. KPMG is locally responsive and this ties closely to the values of both founding firms. KMG particularly sought local firm autonomy in order to facilitate local responsiveness. The higher commitment to audit and accounting reflects PMI's long-standing preoccupation with standards, quality, and monitoring of client service. This firm's strong regional focus and tendency to integrate only to the level necessary for the task at hand (e.g. high integration for the small group of highly global clients) reflects KMG's early success in forming an economic union among European firms. KPMG's relative difficulty in being globally efficient results from the original commitment to autonomy. Its innovative capacity lies in its early support for multiplicity and diversity rather than in its technological sophistication.

The International Firm of KPMG has increasingly been organizing itself to be more globally efficient and responsive to diversified, global clients. It is experienced at forming and later disbanding committees and other structures to respond to its environment. Its limitation lies in the numbers of global clients it can handle at one time and its capacity to organize itself for these types of clients. Their strong local roots support them in capitalizing on local opportunities and reaping the benefit of serving multiple cultures from each culture's perspective. The challenge lies in capitalizing and communicating on local knowledge. The degree of member firm autonomy in KPMG raises the possibility that a member firm simply may not comply or work in the best interest of the global firm. Non-compliance is not always identified, and, when identified, is difficult to monitor and control by the International Firm (Rose 1998).

We have portrayed two, highly successful, professional advisory firms that have faced the same environmental conditions but responded quite differently. This indicates the limitations of the contingency argument which argues there is one best way of organizing for a specific set of environment factors (Lawrence and Lorsch 1967; Thompson 1967). A firm's early decisions in terms of governance, expertise, design and domain helps explain how two highly successful firms can respond differently to the same environment. Our cases also show that current practices are the result not only of the early decisions in the history of the organization but also the result of the ongoing historical trajectories of these firms. For example, although early decisions in the histories of the two firms that merged to form KPMG are important, decisions concerning governance, domain, design and expertise at the time of the merger have also impacted its present international arrangements and future opportunities. For example, KPMG's renewed focus on regionalization and industry specialization will likely affect future opportunities. Unlike Andersen Worldwide, KPMG is unlikely to become a competitor in the large global consulting industry.

Sedimentation and change

The analyses of the two firms raises the general question whether there are turning points along the path of any organization whereby certain factors in the early history of the organization begin to matter less and significant events along the way better explain the present circumstances and future options available to the firm. This suggests that history cannot be seen as a linear process, or that history has its own logic, for example that it offers a story of progress, such as the pursuit of increased efficiency.

Instead, we feel it may be more appropriate to build on the idea of sedimentation, which has been applied to the study of organizational change in Cooper *et al.* (1996). That is, history is better understood as a process involving disruption amidst continuity. Using a geological analogy, organizations evolve through a series of layered features, practices and ideas. Some layers are quickly eroded and thus temporary, but even these tend to leave traces. Other layers are more permanent, and this chapter argues that the values, features and practices that are laid down early in the life of organizations tend to endure, especially those relating to form of governance, operational domain, understanding of appropriate expertise, and organizational design. In many ways, this sedimented view of change and history is similar to neo-institutional theories of change (Greenwood and Hinings 1996), where transformations are seen to occur in the context of inertia.

Features unaffected by history

A comparison of each firm's history and present international arrangements also raises the question whether there are aspects of the international structure which are unaffected by early decisions. We note that neither early decisions in terms of governance, design, domain or expertise, method of growth (internal versus. merger) nor the national origins of the International Office seems to matter much for the number or type of lateral mechanisms devised. The extensive array of lateral mechanisms is pervasive in all the Big Five firms. One partner's comments summarize well what we have been told repeatedly:

> What I am saying is the support mechanisms are getting better because they need to get better because there is a real element of speed to market in all of this. You can't take three days to figure out an answer to a simple question anymore because people won't tolerate it. The fundamentals of it don't change other than the fact that there is a lot more need for team work because issues are too complex now for one sort of guru type person to answer anything. So you need teams and that is a big change and a big issue. But you need the support infra- structure as well because the issues are complex enough and you need to respond quickly. That is the pressure we are under internationally. Where clients are well organized internationally, we are challenged to keep up with them.

Through our analysis of each firm's history and its international arrange- ments we question whether there are additional dimensions of history that are important. In professional advisory firms, unlike other MNCs, the role of the client in defining and facilitating the task, monitoring the task, and essen- tially defining the structural possibilities for service (usually mirroring the clients' structure) makes every client's history and the history of every client/firm relationship a potential factor impacting present organizational arrangements and potential directions of the firm. The lateral mechanisms developed and implemented by the firms are strongly influenced by the structure and nature of the demand of each client (Rose 1998).

This implies that firms may break away from aspects of their histories when under significant pressure. To what extent are the constraints of organiza- tional history reduced when firms are under specific conditions (e.g. when they enter into new services or new markets; when they have extraordinary political, economic, competitive or client pressure to organize in a certain way)? Each of the firms, because of clients' demands, is forming linkages with other professional service providers and even competitors. As this external network continues to evolve and become more complex, the historical relationships not only with clients, but also with competitors and other professional service providers will impact international organizational structures. To better understand the full impact of a firm's historical trajectory on international organizational arrangements and processes we will need to focus on the history of relations (both internal and external relations). For example, we need to ask:

- What aspects of an organization's history matter most and particularly what historical relationships have the most impact on organizational arrangements?
- What do they matter for?
- When do certain historical events impact international structure and for how long?
- What mitigates the impact of certain events or relationships?

We have shown firm history is an important factor shaping the present structural arrangements and future opportunities of these firms. To date theoretical glances at the implications of firm history for international firms generally and for professional service firms specifically have assumed too simple a conceptualization of history. They conceive of a single easily identifiable organization history that is associated with a parent company's cultural origin (Bartlett and Ghoshal 1989), or with the firm's growth pattern (Greenwood *et al.* 1999), or the firms earliest decisions in terms of governance, domain, expertise and design (Kimberly 1987).

We have begun to show that the international arrangements of these firms are impacted by the historical relationships between partners and non-partners; between colleagues of different disciplines; between geographic areas (some regions have had profit sharing and others have not; some areas have accommodated international strategy and some have not), and between parties external to the firms (i.e. clients, competitors, other professional service providers, regulators). The totality of these relationships in any one of the Big Five Firms is complex. There are multiple histories and to understand, for example, the international arrangements of these firms, requires a rich appreciation of the past.

A good understanding of the Big Five accounting firms and a guide to their practices entails a comprehensive examination of their history. Previts and Merino state:

> while accountancy has achieved a position of unquestioned importance in the US economic and social order, it continues to face growing responsibility to mutual fund business investors, management, traditional shareholders, clients, employees, an society as a whole, but in a worldwide capital market context. The challenges facing accountants today are both reflective of the issues of the past

and driven by society's present demands, formed by the legislative and institutional character of the capital market and the related market for information-based services. As each generation finds for itself a path through this network of conflicting obligations and expectations, history, as fact and as interpretation, provides by analogy the only catalogue of experience to guide us.

(Previts and Merino 1998: 423)

History is more than a guide to the future; it provides an explanation for the present. But we need to move beyond the type of linear and deterministic history that has underpinned contingency theory. Although the business history of Chandler (e.g. 1966, 1977) has been used to support both Williamson's transaction cost economics (1975) and the contingency theory of Lawrence and Lorsch (1967), it is too linear, teleological and functionalist (Du Boff and Herman 1980) to provide serious historical explanation. Instead, we might return to a more process view of history and of contingency, such as that offered by Burns and Stalker (1961). International arrangements need to be seen and studied more as processes than as immobile structures aligning to environment characteristics. Our understanding of these firms will increase as we organize our interpretations of the social experiences in these firms, over time, in dynamic ways instead of structural ways. Burns and Stalker (1961) state:

It is in this way, by perceiving behaviour as a medium of the *constant interplay and mutual redefinition of individual identities and social institutions*, that it is possible to begin to grasp the nature of the changes, developments, and historical processes through which we move and which we help create.

(Burns and Stalker 1961: xvi; emphasis added)

Notes

The authors acknowledge the financial support of the Social Sciences and Humanities Research Council and the co-operation of the accounting firms involved in our study

1 The importance of mirroring clients' investments overseas is illustrated by the recent forays in China, Eastern Europe, and elsewhere (see Cooper, *et al.* 1998).
2 This section draws extensively on our previous work (Greenwood *et al.* 1999). It provides a thorough description of the present international structure and processes in these firms and thus provides an important basis for us to explain the impact of the early decisions these firms made.
3 There are, increasingly, different categories of partners, notably national and international.
4 Turley (1994: 14) provides a sharp illustration of the independence of the national firms, by reminding us that they have the freedom to change their affiliation. Several national firms have changed affiliation as a result of mergers.
5 For the information in this section we have drawn extensively on the firms'

histories, all of which are publicly available. As we have indicated previously, these sources tend to offer a teleological focus on practices and events, and are rather weak in terms of explanation.

References

Aharoni, Y. (1999), 'Internationalization of Professional Services: Implications for Accounting Firms', in D. Brock, M. Powell and C. R. Hinings (eds) *Re-structuring the Professional Organization: Accounting, Health, and Law*, London: Routledge.

—— (1995) 'A Note on the Horizontal Movement of Knowledge Within Organizations', paper presented at the Conference on Change in Knowledge Based Organizations, University of Alberta, Edmonton, May.

—— (1993) *Coalitions and Competition: the Globalization of Professional Business Services*, New York: Routledge.

Allen, D. and McDermott, K. (1993) *Accounting for Success: a History of Price Waterhouse 1890–1990*, Boston: Harvard Business School Press.

Arthur Andersen and Co. (1988) *A Vision of Grandeur*, Chicago: Arthur Andersen.

Barrett, M., Cooper, D. J. and Jamal, K., (1997) 'That's Close Enough and the Friction of Space', paper presented at the Accounting, Time and Space Conference, Copenhagen.

Bartlett, C. and Ghoshal, S. (1989) *Managing Across Borders: the Transnational Solution*, Boston: Harvard Business School Press.

Bartlett, C., Doz, Y. and Hedlund, G. (1990) *Managing the Global Firm*, London: Routledge.

Burns, T. and Stalker, G. (1961) *The Management of Innovation*, London: Tavistock.

Chandler, A. D. (1966) *Strategy and Structure: Chapters in the History of the American Industrial Enterprise*, Garden City, N.Y.: Doubleday.

—— (1977) *The Visible Hand*, Cambridge, Mass.: Harvard University Press.

Chandler, A.D. and Daems, H. (1979) 'Administrative Coordination, Allocation and Monitoring: a Comparative Analysis of the Emergence of Accounting and Organization in the USA and Europe', *Accounting, Organizations and Society* 4: 3–20.

Cooper, D. J., Greenwood, R., Hinings, B. and Brown, J. (1998) 'Globalization and Nationalism in the Multinational Accounting Firm: the Case of Opening Markets in Eastern Europe', *Accounting, Organizations and Society* 23: 531–41.

Cooper, D. J., Hinings, B., Greenwood, R. and Brown, J. L. (1996) 'Sedimentation and Transformation in Organizational Change: the Case of Canadian Law Firms', *Organization Studies* 17 (4): 623–47.

Cypert, S. (1991) *Following the Money: the Inside Story of Accounting's First Mega-merger*, New York: Amacom.

Daniels, P., Thrift, N. and Leyshon, A. (1989) 'Internationalisation of Professional Services: Accountancy Conglomerates', in P. Enderwick (ed.), *Multinational Service Firms*, 79–105, London: Routledge.

Donaldson, L. (1985) *In Defence of Organization Theory: a Reply to the Critics*, Cambridge: Cambridge University Press.

—— (1995) *American Anti-management Theories of Organization: a Critique of Paradigm Proliferaton*, Cambridge: Cambridge University Press.

Doz, Y. and Pralahad, C. (1986) 'Controlled Variety: a Challenge for Human Resource Management in the MNC', *Human Resource Management* 25: 55–71.

—— (1992) 'Headquarters Influence and Strategic Control in MNCs', in C. Bartlett and S. Ghoshal (eds), *Transnational Management: Text, Cases and Readings in Cross-Border Management*: 552–66. Boston: Irwin.

Du Boff, R. B. and Herman, E. F. (1980) 'Alfred Chandler's New Business History', *Politics and Society*.

Evans, P. (1993) 'Dosing the glue: Applying Human Resource Technology to Build the Global Organization', *Research in Personnel and Human Resource Management* 3: 21–54.

Evans, P. and Doz, Y. (1992) Dualities: A Paradigm for Human Resource and Organizational Development in Complex Multinationals, in Pucik, N. Tichy, and M. Barnett (eds), *Globalization Management: Creating and Leading the Competitive Organization*, New York: Wiley.

Ferner, A., Edwards, P., and Sisson, K. (1995) 'Coming Unstuck? In search of the Corporate Glue in an International Professional Service Firm', *Human Resource Management Journal* 34: 343–61.

Gibbins, M. and Mason, A. (1988) *Professional Judgement in Financial Reporting*, Toronto: Canadian Institute of Chartered Accountants.

Greenwood, R., Cooper, D. J., Hinings, C. R. and Brown, B. (1993) 'Biggest is Best? Strategic Assumptions and Actions in the Canadian Audit Industry', *Canadian Journal of Administrative Sciences* 10: 308–21.

Greenwood, R. and Hinings, C. R. (1996) 'Understanding Radical Organizational Change: Bringing Together the Old and New Institutionalism', *The Academy of Management Review* 21: 1022–54.

Greenwood, R., Hinings, B. and Brown, J. (1990) 'P²-form Strategic Management: Corporate Practice in Professional Partnerships', *Academy of Management Journal* 33 (4): 725–55.

Greenwood, R., Hinings, B., and Cooper, D. J. (forthcoming) 'An Institutional Theory of Change: Contextual and Interpretive Dynamics in the Accounting Industry', in W. Powell and D. Jones (eds), *Bending the Bars of the Iron Cage: Institutional Dynamics and Processes*, Chicago: University of Chicago Press.

Greenwood, R., Rose, T., Hinings, B., Cooper, D. J. and Brown, J. (1999) 'The Global Management of Professional Services: The Example of Accounting', in S. Clegg, E. Ibarra, and L. Bueno (eds), *Theories of Management Process: Making Sense Through Difference*, Beverly Hills, Calif.: Sage.

Hanson, J. D. (1989) 'Internationalisation of the Accounting Firm', in A. G. Hopwood (ed.) *International Pressures for Accounting Change*, 43–56, London: Prentice Hall

Hedlund, G. (1994) 'A Model of Knowledge Management and the N-form Corporation', *Strategic Management Journal* 15: 73–90.

—— (1986) 'The Hypermodern MNC – Heterarchy?', *Human Resource Management* 24 (1): 9–35.

Hofstede, G. (1980) *Cultures Consequences: International Differences in Work-related Values*, Beverly Hills, Calif.: Sage.

Jones, C., Hesterly, W. and Borgatti, S. (1997) 'A General Theory of Network Governance: Exchange Conditions and Social Mechanisms', *Academy of Management Review* 22 (4): 911–45.

Jones, E. (1981) *Accountancy and the British Economy, 1870–1945: A History of Ernst and Whinney*, Oxford: Batsford.

Kimberly, J. (1987) 'The Study of Organization: Toward a Biographical Perspective', in J. W. Lorsch (ed.), *Handbook of Organizational Behavior*, Englewoods, N.J.: Prentice Hall.

Lawrence J., and Lorsch, L. (1967) *Organization and Environment*, Georgetown, Ontario: Irwin-Dorsey.

Løwendahl, B. (1997) *Strategic Management of Professional Service Firms*, Denmark: Munksgaard International.

Marx, K. (1852) 'The Eighteenth Brumaire of Louis Napoleon', reprinted in K. Marx and F. Engels, *Selected Works*, London: Lawrence and Wishart, 1968.

McKee, D., and Garner, D. (1996) *Accounting Services, Growth, and Change in the Pacific Basin*, Westport, Conn.: Quorum.

Merino, B. (1998) 'Critical Theory and Accounting History: Challenges and Opportunities', *Critical Perspectives on Accounting* 9 (6): 603–16.

Napier, C., (1998) 'Giving an Account of Accounting History: a Reply to Keenan', *Critical Perspectives on Accounting* 9 (6): 685–700.

Nohria, N. and Ghoshal, S. (1997) *Differentiated Networks*, San Francisco: Jossey-Bass.

—— (1994) 'Differentiated Fit and Shared Values: Alternatives for Managing Head-quarters–Subsidiary Relations', *Strategic Management Journal* 15: 491–502.

Post, H. (1995) 'Internationalisation of Professional Services: a Study of Large Dutch Accounting and Software Firms', paper presented at European International Business Association Conference, Urbino, Italy.

Prahalad, C. and Doz, Y. (1987) *The Multinational Mission*, New York: The Free Press.

Previts, G. and Merino, B. (1998) *A History of Accountancy in the United States: the Cultural Significance of Accounting*, Columbus: Ohio State University Press.

Pugh, D. S. and Hickson, D. J, (1976) *Organizational Structure in its Context: the Aston Program I*, Farnborough, UK: Saxon House.

Richards, A. B. (1981) *Touche Ross and Co., 1899–1981*, London: Touche Ross and Co.

Richards, L. and Richards, T. (1992) *Nud*ist: User guide: Version 3.0*, Aptos, Calif.: Aladdin Systems Inc.

Rose, T. (1998) *Co-ordination and Integration Processes in Global Business Advisory Firms: the Role of Global Clients*, unpublished doctoral dissertation, University of Alberta, Edmonton.

Starbuck, W. H. (1992) 'Learning by Knowledge-intensive Firms', *Journal of Management Studies* 29: 741–60.

Stevens, M. (1991) *The Big Six*, New York: Simon and Schuster.

Strange, S. (1996) *The Retreat of the State: The Diffusion of Power in the World Economy*, Cambridge: Cambridge University Press.

Taylor, S., Beechler, S. and Napier, N. (1996) 'Toward an Integrative Model of Strategic Human Resource Management', *Academy of Management Review* 21 (4): 959–85.

Thompson, J. (1967) *Organization in Action: Social Science Bases of Administrative Theory*, New York: McGraw-Hill.

Turley, S. (1994) 'The Theory of the International Development of Accounting Firms', paper presented at 4th Maastricht Audit Research Symposium, 25–25 October, Maastricht.

Watt, M. (1982) *The First Seventy-five Years*, Toronto: Price Waterhouse.

Whitford, D. (1997) 'Arthur, ArthurY', *Fortune*, 10 November: 169–78.

Williamson, O. E. (1975) *Markets and Hierachies: Analysis and Antitrust Implications*, New York: Free Press.

Wise, T. A. (1981) *Peat Marwick Mitchell and Co.: 85 years*, New York: Peat Marwick Mitchell.

6 The role of reputation in global professional business services

Yair Aharoni

Introduction

It is a generally accepted axiom of international business theory that a multinational firm must possess some ownership or firm-specific advantages over uni-national firms in order to be able to compete despite the higher costs of operating in more than one national market. These advantages are often assumed to come from global economies of scale or of scope. The competitive advantages that allow service firms to operate as multinationals are perhaps more subtle and thus more difficult to unravel. In the case of professional business service firms (PBS), the supply of services – such as legal counseling, valuation, executive search, or management consulting – is highly dependent on the skills of individuals, with little or no economies of scale or of scope, and few possibilities of standardization. Yet some firms in each of these fields have turned out to be very successful global operators (while thousands of others continue to confine their services to one nation or region).

Indeed, one characteristic of professional business services is that one finds in the same industry a few global firms and a multitude of small firms supplying services on a local basis. The received theory of international production including the eclectic approach (Dunning 1993) is not always sufficient to explain this coexistence of two types of firms in the same industry.

This chapter focuses on one possible explanation for this dichotomy. Its major hypothesis is that – at least in the supply of professional business services – all clients face a major problem of uncertainty as to the quality of the service supplied. Because of the uncertainty, clients resort to some surrogates to assess quality, such as relying on reputation. Excellent global reputation is, therefore, required to achieve global competitive advantage. Reputation itself is not measured nor perceived directly. It is assumed to exist because of a multitude of variables. An analysis of the role of reputation, given uncertainty, in professional business services may shed some light on the reasons for successful globalization strategy. To be sure, the perception of reputation is necessary but not sufficient: the success of firms would depend also on their ability to implement a strategy, and maintain inner systems to enhance reputation by maintaining quality and by achieving a 'one firm' culture.

Three theoretical questions are of interest and are discussed in this chapter. One is to find out how consumers decide on a provider of a professional business service given information asymmetry and how their loyalty is sustained. The answer to this question may be the key to understand global competitive advantage. A second is how the provider can influence such a decision. This is a derivative of the first question. The final question is, how can a system be designed to reduce firms' ability to get abnormally high returns by selling low-quality service at a high-quality price and reduce the temptation for other firms to enter only because of these high returns.

Other contributors to this volume discuss in detail the characteristics of professional business services and the specific attributes of their operations. Therefore, it is assumed that readers are familiar with these characteristics and attributes. This chapter concentrates on the analysis of the meaning of reputation and its significance for both individual professionals and for large professional business service firms. It starts by discussing the reasons for globalization of professional services and the reasons customers perceive the choice of a supplier of professional business service as risky and uncertain. It makes a distinction between individual and firm's reputation. It elaborates on the ways customers perceive quality of service and how customer's loyalty is attained and nurtured. It also discusses some surrogates used given uncertainty, such as firm size, age, or the recommendations of experts. Finally, reputation is shown to be a powerful constraint on cheating.

The internationalization of professional business service firms

As early as the end of the last century, 'Undoubtedly, increased British investments, which required close scrutiny given the wild, free-wheeling business environment in the United States in the 1880s, brought English professional accountants to the United States' (Previts and Merino 1979: 137). Since the end of the nineteenth century, auditors 'followed a parallel path to the evolution of the businesses which they served' (Jones 1981: 108). Later, in particular after 1950, firms 'have come under growing pressure to follow their transnational clients, wherever the latter have chosen to go and do business' (UNCTC 1990: 145).

By the 1980s, the trend towards globalization and the belief among service companies that they must follow their clients throughout the world had become pervasive. One result of this was cross-border investment, including the acquisition of companies in foreign countries. The largest firms grew, sometimes by acquisitions, and increased their market share.

In some cases (for example architects and design engineers, as well as construction contractors), the international expansion was a result of growing demand from newly independent nations that launched ambitious development projects but lacked the expertise in designing and managing them. Falling work loads at home pushed many to look for opportunities overseas, and these opportunities escalated as a result of the petro-dollar availability, mainly in the Middle East but also in Latin America. In design engineering firms, the major advantage for multinational operations might have been reliance on government financing or tie-ins to government aid (Strassmann and Wells 1988: 179). In civil engineering, technology is universal and very little technological advantage is possible. Still, one may have advantages in management methods or in specialized construction, such as large fuel-cell power plants or hazardous waste management technology (Strassmann and Wells 1988: 36) or in project management of a large project. Large architectural consulting firms may operate abroad by temporarily moving professional workers. In these cases, wholly-owned subsidiaries were set up abroad to manage the project. Later they might have continued and won more contracts from local clients. 'Forty percent of the firms in Seymour's international sample entered foreign markets to undertake work for home country clients' (Seymour 1986: 163–4, as quoted in Strassmann and Wells 1988: 227).

Another reason for an increased internationalization of professional business service firms is the rising trend toward what has come to be known as the 'virtual corporation' or 'a company in a box'. This future PBS firm is expected to farm out almost all functions and rely on computer-based networks to create an interrelated network of suppliers, providers or vendors, each of which is an expert in some specific function, operating only in the area of its 'core competence'. All functions except the core competencies must be outsourced. The firm thus rents most of the services it needs: from data processing to telemarketing, from billing and collection to publishing or employee training. An airline can operate not only with leased airplanes and contracted flying and ground crews, but also by using outside vendors for almost all other operations, be it baggage tracking or passenger reservations.

Reputation, asserts Nachum (1999: 28) 'is largely location-specific'. Thus, the reputation developed in one country will not translate automatically into similar advantage at another location. However, multinational professional business service firms do transfer reputation. They start their world wide expansion by offering their services to existing multinational clients in other than the home country. Existing clients know the firm and its reputation. With time additional customers are recruited. Still, the servicing of other multinationals is the major market of the global professional service firms. In the case of such global firms, the ability to give services globally is part and parcel of a perception of high reputation and an indicator of competence and commitment to service the customer. Global firms are able to transfer reputation from one geographical market to another. In fact, the major advantage of the giant global accounting, consulting or advertising firm is that clients believe these firms connote high quality.

Individual and firm's reputation

'Reputation' is defined by the *Concise English Dictionary of Current English* as:

> **reputation** – n. what is generally said or believed about a person's or thing's character (has not justified his reputation; has a reputation for integrity; place has a bad reputation); state of being well reported of, credit, distinction, respectability, good report (persons of reputation); the credit or discredit of doing or of being (has the reputation of swindling his customers, of being the best shot in England).

Note that the dictionary definition relates to 'said or believed'. It does not necessarily relate to an objective truth. Moreover, a reputation of an individual or of a firm is based on a set of different attributes, or an intersection of these attributes, and different assessors may use different attributes in looking at reputation. Davis (1992) suggests one possible list of such attributes. *Fortune*, in a survey of corporations (reported by Sprout 1991), looked at:

- quality of management; quality of products and services
- innovativeness
- long-term investment values
- financial soundness
- ability to attract, develop and retain talented people
- responsibility to the community and to the environment and
- wide use of corporate assets.

The weights assigned to each are not very clear.

Fombrun and Shanley (1990) examined and refined the results of a survey of reputation made by *Fortune*. They found reputation to be predictable from measures of profitability, size and visibility, which accounted for 27–35 per cent of the variation in reputation. Fombrun and Shanley (1990) rank ordered certain attributes in terms of their impact on reputation as follows:

1   profitability and risk
2   market value
3   media visibility
4   dividend yield
5   size
6   charitable foundations and contributions, and advertising.

Reputation is thus a multi-dimensional attribute, signaled by a whole array of variables. Often, it signals quality of service and a high level of integrity. Individuals and firms must have a reputation of being experts, of giving good service, of caring, being reliable and competent. The customers, as pointed out by Gronroos (1990), expect the supplier to give quality service. The quality is perceived to include both process (how) and technical (what) dimensions.

Why is reputation an important if not the sole component of competitive advantage in a global professional business service firm? The reason is twofold.

First, the selection of the provider of professional service is of critical importance, since they affect crucial outcomes. Faulty architectural planning, incompetent accounting advice, or bad legal guidance may be very costly and even jeopardize the survival of the client (Day and Barksdale 1994). Choosing the right supplier of heart surgery is of life or death importance. The higher the price of a wrong selection, the greater the perceived risk. Such a risk is even greater if the client believes there is a big difference in the quality of the service to be received from different professionals. Not all surgeons are perceived as equally competent. In contrast, it is said that auditors are less able to be perceived as very different from other auditors. The higher the perceived differentiation, the greater the salience of perceived quality and reputation. The more complex the service and the more it is based on unique knowledge, the more difficult it is for the consumer to assess quality. How can one judge the quality of one dentist compared to another? After all dentists are licensed and are able to give reasonable service of a certain minimum quality. Who is to say which dentist gives a superb service and how is this fact assessed by a layperson? An architectural design cannot be judged before it is delivered. If one needs to be operated on how does one judge who is the best surgeon?

Second, because of the intangible nature of the service it is difficult for a consumer to assess the quality of the service delivered. In most cases, there is a high level of uncertainty in the minds of service consumers about outcomes. In many cases, this is true not only before the service is purchased but even long after it is delivered. When a client calls on an architect to design a building, it is virtually impossible to anticipate exactly every detail in the execution of this order. The cost may escalate unpredictably, the structure may be faulty, or major repairs might be needed. The problem is exacerbated when a firm with many different professionals (and presumably heterogeneous level of competence) is employed. Clients will thus appreciate consistency of service quality, not only high quality levels, but may find it extremely difficult to assess service consistency and quality. When this is the case, the perception of quality and the belief that consistency is assured become extremely important. The combination of difficulty in judging quality and the crucial importance of outcomes makes reputation extremely valuable. In this sense, global reputation, if maintained and assured, gives firms an important firm-specific advantage. The problem of assessing quality of service is exacerbated when a firm has to be evaluated. In advertising, it is impossible to measure precisely the impact of an advertising campaign on sales. How can a customer say which advertising agency would deliver superior service? In management consulting, the quality of the advice given may be apparent only many years after the service was delivered (Aharoni 1997). Darby and Karni (1973) use a typology of search, experience and credence goods. While the quality of search goods can be established before the actual purchase, the quality of experience goods can be ascertained only on the basis of actual use (e.g. food in restaurants). In the case of credence goods, quality cannot be learnt even after acquisition and use. Professional services are of the nature of credence. Most clients cannot tell the quality of a tooth-filling for quite a long time. When consumers move to a new town in a different country, they face an even higher level of uncertainty in deciding which dentist to use. Lawyers are expected to use their skills to deliver quality service. Yet the quality of the service is difficult to assess.

In most professional business service situations, the service delivered is unique. A doctor's (or a lawyer's) advice to one person is unique under a set of circumstances, and the service is one of a kind. Many professional business service firms are extremely customized, based on creativity, innovation, or pioneering of new concepts and techniques or non-routine ways of solving a problem: that is, expertise. Others are much more routine, but are still based on judgment, knowledge and mainly experience. Many are based on availability of human resources (e.g. to carry out a market survey in a standard procedure but in an efficient way). Any specific firm may specialize in one of these 'three Es': expertise, experience and efficiency (Maister 1986). Expertise is crucial when the client has high risk, complex and unusual problems. The client wants professional skills and creativity in handling the problem. The fee is usually higher, and the work is of 'brain surgeon' type. In other types of problems, termed by Maister 'gray hair', the client looks for a firm that can bring past experience to bear in solving the problem. The third type are problems in which the professional business firm is expected to execute promptly and efficiently. This third type is characteristic of most of the audit functions, some basic architectural designs, market research and so on. In all of these cases, the service generates high perceived uncertainty.

A unique service must be delivered by experts with a high level of knowledge. As a result, there is a high variability in the way the service is provided among different service providers and even in different service situations supplied by the same individual provider. In addition, professional business service firms are highly dependent on the loyal and continuous service of very skilled individuals who may or may not agree to continue their working relationship with the firm. The ability to attract high quality professionals and then to maintain relationships with them is of utmost importance. The service provider possesses recognized expertise. In some cases, mainly in small firms, the reputation is that of an individual. Most large firms were able to make the reputation related to the firm rather than to specific individuals. As a result, firms sometimes 'sell' clients (e.g. in case of acquisition) assuming the clients will remain with the new firm. The turmoil in Saatchi and Saatchi points to the difficulties of firms maintaining the reputation when they lose some key personnel. The Saatchi brothers left the firm to start a new firm, and expected many valuable employees and clients to follow them. More generally, a PBS firm as an entity may have difficulty in capturing the economic rent of its senior staff. It is thus typically organized as a partnership or a corporation in which the senior staff has a significant equity share. When senior executives perceive their share as not commensurate with their contributions, they tend to leave hoping clients will follow them. Within the firm, quality monitoring is achieved by allowing power of inspection to other parts of the firm, for example, through peer review: quality does not have to be controlled by a central office. The review is made by persons from other countries, but not necessarily from 'headquarters'.

Because of these considerations, there are great gains to be achieved in a multinational professional business service firm from the training of individuals that inculcates a similar culture and method of operations, systems, procedures and problem-solving among employees in different countries. The skill intensity and the low barriers to leaving the firm make human resource management extremely important. This also makes global operations based on hierarchical relations, as in most producing MNEs, much less likely (Aharoni 1993). The importance of recruiting, developing, educating and maintaining the loyalty of the professionals who will be supplying the services cannot be overstated. Effective human resource management is essential to achieve better selection methods in recruiting, more efficient training, greater socialization, better career design and higher levels of loyalty. Technology is transferred through training efforts, and firms want to assure those trained will remain. They also attempt to inculcate a similar culture and methods of operations among their many employees in different countries.

To be able to operate a global giant firm, the set of individual expertise, must be converted into a firm reputation. The reputation of a professional business firm may be based on the availability of certain professionals. A major challenge is to create a strategic asset by transferring individual reputations to a firm's asset. In other words, to shift the relationships from the level of an individual to the reputation of the firm. If a firm is able to create the reputation that the firm itself is trustworthy, then it has a major competitive advantage. The clients would accept any employee of the firm as reliable, possessing high professional capability, customer oriented and committed to excellent service of high quality. The individual professionals become relatively anonymous; clients choose the firm, not the individual.

Professional business service firms prefer long-term relationships with the client. In fact, the loyalty of clients is a major strategic objective of these firms. Short-term assignments with no repeat business increase marketing costs and reduce capacity utilization. In large professional business firms, repeat business is said to constitute 80 per cent of the work, and referrals are important, underscoring the importance of past experience, as well as that of the reputation of the firm. The client must believe that the professional service is both necessary and that it is well conceived. In a small professional business service firm marketing is largely based on personal ties and recommendations of previous clients. Individual professionals and clients develop personal relations. Clients' satisfaction is strongly affected by the nature of interpersonal encounters (Bitner 1990). Failures in interpersonal interaction is a major reason for switching (Richman 1996).

In a large firm, marketing is done also by publishing articles in journals widely read by business executives, publishing house organ journals (such as the *McKinsey Quarterly*), mailing such journals or other papers to prospective clients, systematically seeking social contacts with prospective clients, utilizing other personal contacts (e.g. executives who used to work as consultants may turn to their old firm when they need consulting services: a major advantage of McKinsey is said to lie in that fact) but mainly by gaining an image of the firm's professional reputation, so that risk-averse clients would employ the firm. As long as the firm was small, and its partner knew the clients intimately, reputation could have been based on trust and on personal integrity of the individual professionals. Large global multinationals must be able to gain a reputation for the name of the firm that in turn reflects on the individuals. A client may have heard of the Mayo Clinic and therefore assumes that the doctors employed there are highly proficient. A client may employ McKinsey consultants because the name of the firm carries with it prestige. The reputation of the firm for a high quality service becomes the major reason for the employment of these firms by clients.

All in all there are pervasive differences between professional business firms and other service providers. Professional business service firms must develop unique solutions that are fine tuned and well adapted to the clients' needs (Micheline 1992). Customer retention and loyalty is a major strategic objective, given the high switching costs. Firms like to be differentiated from their competitors. However, differentiation is not easily achieved since the number of possible ways to provide a professional service is quite limited. At the same time, clients are very uncertain about outcomes, and these outcomes are of crucial importance. In small firms, customers stress interpersonal relations. In large, and in particular in the multinational firm, reputation is attributed to the firm rather than to the specific individual. Professional business service firms are naturally interested in gaining customers. They are also interested in maintaining the loyalty of existing customers over time and preferably getting more business from existing customers. The professional business service firms would also want their existing customers to recommend the service to prospective customers thus growing as a result of word of mouth. At least until recently, these firms could not advertise, and had to rely on creating customer's loyalty through reputation. How do clients evaluate performance or judge reputation?

Clients' perceptions of suppliers

How do clients choose one supplier of professional business services over another? How does the client decide which provider will deliver a superb service? Researchers of consumers' behaviour in services agree that clients are guided by expectations or by their beliefs and opinions. Most also agree that consumers judge services on the basis of several components. Thus Gronroos (1990) distinguishes between a technical component (what will be performed) and a process related component (how the service is performed). Parasuraman *et al.* (1988) divide between 'objective' and 'subjective/perceived' quality. They developed an instrument (*servqual*) to measure service quality along five dimensions: tangibles, responsiveness, assurance, empathy, and reliability. When these measures are used in practice to assess reputation for high quality service, it may be found that the measures used are less direct. Pallais and Good (1996) report that business firms rate their accountants mainly on the basis of responsiveness, trustworthiness and interpersonal responsiveness. They suggest that clients of CPAs would increase their consumption of accounting services if they perceive the CPA as knowledgeable and competent and because of relations formed with the accountant as well as personal characteristics of the accountant. Clients are willing to pay a premium for responsiveness to needs, effective interaction with the audit committee and trustworthiness. Other studies emphasize attributes such as quality, responsiveness, competence, and willingness to serve.

All professionals are considered reasonably competent, and a minimum acceptable level of competence is guaranteed in most cases by the need for very specific training and a governmental certification. Still the recipient of the service lacks both experience and knowledge and thus has difficulties in assessing the ability of a certain professional to supply above average or superb quality service. Whatever evaluation is done, it is subjective and based on perceptions of quality or on credence. Patterson *et al.* (1997) found that customer satisfaction by business firms is influenced by many variables, including level of expertise of the buyer, prior attitudes regarding the provider of the service, the importance of the purchase decision. Van-der-Walt *et al.* (1994) found that firms that form a closer relationship with their accountants stress effectiveness, personal service, image and a broad range of services. When the provider supplies services across national borders in many countries, these issues are becoming even more acute. From the provider's point of view, it is essential to create clients loyalty to the firm rather to any individual supplier. The client lacking other sources base expectations on prior experience, or on word of mouth communication about service quality.

Source credibility is known to have moderated the effects of claim extremity. If a source is considered credible, the probability that a message claim will be accepted is enhanced (Ajzen and Fishbein 1980). If a firm is considered trustworthy, it has a great advantage in terms of credibility. Goldberg and Hartwick (1990), in a classroom experiment using students as subjects, have shown that when subjects formed a negative image of a firm they found advertising less credible. Rowney and Zenisek (1980) show that authors with higher reputation enjoy a higher probability of their manuscripts being accepted to journals of the Canadian Psychological Association.

Klein and Leffler (1981) assume that consumers learn about low quality of goods immediately after purchase and that they disseminate this knowledge to other potential customers. Given that assumption, firms would be motivated to produce high quality goods and price them so that the stream of earnings would be higher than the one-shot wealth creation of cheating on quality. In other words, firms would invest in reputational capital. To protect the high prices from erosion by potential entrants, the firms would invest in advertising to create firm-specific assets.

Rogerson (1983) also shows that high quality may lead to higher prices, much above marginal cost. He also adds the hypothesis that high quality firms would have more clients. A larger client base implies, of course, larger size. These and other models are theoretical and conceptual. They do predict financial losses as a result of a reduction in quality and, therefore, strong incentives to maintain 'reputational capital'.

Theories on consumer behaviour often assume that persons make at least some decisions based on their overall attitudes toward the supplier of the service. Aaker and Myers noted that 'brand attitude is the pillar on which the sales and profit fortune of a giant corporation rest' (Aaker and Myers 1987: 160). Attitude change may come as a result of learning and comprehending information about the central merits of the object under consideration ('central route') or because of rewards, punishments and effective experience, without thinking about the information central to the merit of the attitude issue ('peripheral route'). Petty and Cacioppo (1980, 1981, 1986) posited that the central and peripheral routes are part of an elaboration likelihood continuum. The elaboration likelihood model (ELM) argues that people form what they perceive as correct attitudes in different ways. Thinking based on the message and detailed examination of arguments are grouped under what they term the central route.

Attitudes formed through the central route are expected to be persistent When ability to process information is mitigated, the peripheral route is assumed to be used, such as heuristic retrieved from memory ('experts are usually correct'), or attribution reasoning.

The ELM is a theory of attitude formation and change. According to this theory people can adopt attitudes not on the basis of persuasive arguments but on some mechanisms of persuasion mediating. If the likelihood of an elaboration of an argument is low, the peripheral route will be selected. Thus, an attitude about a product can be formed by the information contents of an advertisement (the central route). In other cases a character appearing in the advertisement may be the more important determinant of an opinion forming. The Heuristic Systematic Model (HSM) (Eagley and Chaiken 1993) posits that clients use heuristic cues: their judgement is mediated by decision rules. Thus size of the supplier firm may be interpreted as an indicator of competence and reliability.

Research on attitudes and on attitude changes has been vast, indicating that the process of attitude change is complex, pervasive and diverse. Clearly, as noted by Haas-Wilson (1990), consumers have no clear, rational way of deciding which service provider to choose. Clients use a multidimensional construct to decide on service suppliers. They use central as well as peripheral criteria or heuristic cues. There are several factors that affect the purchase of a certain service: price, availability, consumer characteristics, image and so on. It is unclear how consumers decide on the relative costs and benefits of acquiring more information and experience on different attributes. Again, in professional business services even past performance is not necessarily a guarantee of future success; the services are unique and are delivered by different persons at different times. The fact that a certain lawyer from a certain firm was successful in a certain litigation is no guarantee of the future success of the same lawyer in other cases and certainly not a guarantee of the success of another lawyer just because he/she is a partner or an employee in the same firm. Again, the non-professional would find it very hard to evaluate the service, even after using it.

Surrogates to reputation

Consumers may choose a service that has a competitive advantage if they are sure of the existence of such an advantage. Otherwise, the client's sense of risk is mitigated by behaving as other persons behave (and therefore purchasing service from firms with large client bases) or choosing firms reputed to be excellent on the basis of word-of-mouth. Services are associated with their providers more so than products with their manufacturers (Bromley 1993: Chapter 8). Customers' actions are governed by their subjective perceptions and beliefs. Based on the arguments of attitude change, it seems reasonable to assume that when one does not have any objective basis to ascertain quality, one relies on subjective evaluation of reputation. Since reputation is not easily assessed, clients may perceive it as correlated with other peripheral variables: more measurable by clients or judged based on heuristic cues. One is age (Nachum 1999), another is size. Doney and Cannon (1997) found purchasing managers tend to select a service supplier based largely on the size of the supplier. Since size is often seen as signaling quality assurance, larger firms (or networks) may have an important advantage over smaller firms. More generally, a positive opinion is shaped on the basis of some variables that may or may not be related to the quality of the service. Thus, a client may form a positive opinion of a lawyer because of the atmosphere in the waiting room, or because the lawyer is prompt in keeping appointments or because the lawyer was appointed a professor. A client may perceive an architect to be the best because of the opinion of another client, accepted as more knowledgeable or as an opinion leader. Further the client's perception of risk is reduced by signaling that other persons are behaving in the same way. Other surrogates may be the amount of work done *pro bono*, past performance, recommendations of past clients, attestations of opinion leaders, or existence of certain famous clients ('By Appointment to the King' or auditing of Fortune 500 firms). A large firm may have, *ceteris paribus*, a larger reputation than a small firm. A veteran firm may be perceived as having a greater reputation by virtue of its age.

More often than not, reputation is a result of size. Indeed, a growing literature claims that larger firms can offer better quality and greater growth. DeAngelo (1981) claims that a larger client base allows competitive advantage for an auditing firm. Indeed, it is generally accepted among accountants that being a member of the 'Big Five' (previously the 'Big Six' and the 'Big Eight') offers competitive advantage. Greenwood *et al.* (1993) claim that, even within this elite group, the ranking is of great importance. Auditing is a very mature industry, and is largely considered a commodity. 'In the eyes of the clients, an audit is an audit, and often little or no added value is perceived in choosing one firm over another' (Palmer 1989: 85). Still, very large client firms tend to use very large auditing firms. It is also argued that larger firms can defray fixed costs on the larger base of clients. Most important, however, large size is perceived as signaling greater capabilities and higher levels of expertise. One result has been a spate of mergers to create even larger size that may be perceived as allowing a better ability to serve clients effectively.

Esfahami (1991) explained low quality in developing countries by the high costs of establishing reputation. Such costs would be perceived as reasonable only if a firm would then gain a large market share in very large markets. Thus, size is not only an indicator of high quality and reputation, it is also needed to achieve that reputation.

Since past history conveys reputation, the age of a firm may be interpreted as an ability to survive or as an indicator of competitive advantage. Firms (or universities) have reputation because of their long history. Past customers are helping to certify to new clients the quality of the service. Persons often look at what others experienced as a major indicator of quality or its opposite (e.g. malpractice). The capabilities of top management are a powerful source of a competitive advantage (Pralahad and Doz 1987) that may explain differences in performance among firms (Thomas *et al.* 1991). Taylor (1975) found that factors such as age and knowledge cause differences in the level of impact of managers on their firms.

Other, more subjective, indicators may also be used. Since objective evidence is scarce, consumers must rely on these kinds of surrogates, at least for the first choice of a supplier. Needless to say, continuous customer loyalty is not based only on size or age. With time, such variables as satisfaction with the service provided may become crucial for the continuation of the relationships. Further, there is a considerable variation within professional business services in terms of the factors affecting reputation. Most research on the perception of customers and the process of generating loyalty was carried out on accounting and audit firms. In this profession, the level of standardization is high and the ability to create differentiation quite low. It is also a profession that moved quite early to foreign countries and became multinational long time ago. It may well be that expectations on service quality are less dependent on possible unique service of an individual then, say, when lawyers are concerned.

This chapter does not present a full model of the creation and maintenance of customers' loyalty nor does it enumerate the ways a firm may increase such a loyalty. It points to reputation as a possible explanation of the size differences among firms and mainly for the ability of some firms to become global operators. Clearly reputation signals quality of service, and certain factors are perceived as signalling reputation. To become large in a national setting and certainly to become a multinational, the reputation must be connected with the name of the firm, not with the competence of any specific individual.

Can suppliers influence customers loyalty?

Providers of professional business services can influence customers' initial choice and enhance customer's loyalty in a variety of ways. If the arguments presented in this chapter are correct, then loyalty can be enhanced not only by competent service, high level of integrity or proven expertise. Since reputation is so important it has to be established, nurtured, enhanced and protected. Firms make organized efforts to convey information that will enhance their reputation and also take steps to monitor quality internally. Clearly, performance evaluation is extremely subjective. Reputation may be judged by the 'track record' but also by word of mouth or indirectly by accepting such factors as large size or age of firm as indicating reputation. Nurturing and enhancing reputation has to do also with the inner working of the firm to assure quality control and indoctrination of the employees. It also has to do with public relations and other operations designed to build reputation in the eyes of prospective clients. This often means engaging in activities well beyond those needed to provide the service, in order to generate social approval. Thus, loyalty can be gained and nurtured also by increased size, by *pro bono* work, or by ensuring 'big name' customers.

Reputation and quality assurance

Two possible consequences of high information asymmetry and uncertainty may be hypothesized. The first is that under conditions of credence, firms have a strong incentive to sell a low-quality good or service at a high-quality price and reap higher returns. Another is that firms will be motivated to acquire and sustain reputation, since clients may be expected to use reputation as a surrogate to high quality. In professional business services, quality cannot be judged directly and timely; thus reputation is extremely important. Risk-averse clients would rather hire the services of the more reputable firms even at a much higher cost. Since long term relations are preferred, the short term possibility of cheating the customer is not very attractive. Firth (1990) has provided some empirical evidence by showing that auditors criticized by the UK Department of Trade incurred a small loss in market share and suffered economic losses as a result of the damage to their reputations. Firms would rather build reputations. A crucial assumption in both the theoretical models cited above or in Firth (1990) is that consumers learn fast and then disseminate information on any reduction of quality. In most professional service cases, however, consumers do not know whether the quality was superb even a long time after the service was provided. The customers cannot really assess the quality of service. Consequently, information about low-quality products does not spread quickly and widely. Customers must use some heuristic or simplified rule of thumb in choosing suppliers of services. Still, realization of the importance of reputation and the high costs of malpractice may create constraints on cheating; certainly cheating that is discovered has severe consequences. The negative repercussions of being caught cheating on quality or doing the wrong deed may be seen by considering the impact on firms in such cases as the *Exxon Valdez*, or the chip problems of Intel.

Conclusions

Major technological breakthroughs made it possible to globalize operations of service multinationals. These firms face somewhat different problems than producing firms. Yet clearly firm-specific advantages in any type of firm stem from expertise in services. With increasing globalization, more professional business service firms have attempted to offer global service. The large global service firms exist side by side with thousands of smaller, uni-national firms and are able to charge their clients much higher fees for their services mainly because the clients perceive these firms as able to offer higher quality service. This chapter proposes that multinational firms must possess global firm's reputation. Service quality is an abstract and complex construct, that cannot be measured objectively. Outside the firm, it is difficult for customers to enforce contingent contracts that are depending on the actual outcome of the services delivered. As a result, the importance of reputation as a criterion for choosing a supplier and as a means of signaling quality is enhanced. If clients believe the service of a certain firm is superb, this very belief in global excellence induces the client to employ the firm. The firm must build a firm's reputation for excellence that is independent of the competence and reputation of any individual professional employed by it. The cost of developing relationships with clients and tailoring the service to their needs are quite substantial. Therefore, firms are very keen to avoid losing major customers. The development and maintenance of the clients' loyalty is a major strategic objective. This loyalty must be leveraged to a wide variety of tasks in many national markets. Moreover, in most cases both the provider of the service and its recipient prefer long term relations. The switching costs are quite substantial to both sides. Clients look for providers with high level of professional competence, willing to supply them with high quality service. They may or may not believe that different providers are very different in the quality of the service they may provide. Clearly, they find it impossible to assess quality directly. Therefore they use peripheral or heuristic factors. Reputation is becoming a proxy for quality, and reputation itself is judged by such factors as the size of the firm, its age, its clients, or *pro bono* work done. If the reputation becomes a firm's characteristic, the firm has an important advantage.

The reasons for the differences in the magnitude of multinational operations of firms in different services are still not very clear. If reputation is important, why is it that distinguished universities did not become multinationals? Why do auditors and management consultants operate globally while many law firms and all dentists are local? More research on the ways customers choose professional business service suppliers, differentiate between the lackluster service provider and the excellent one and maintain loyalty to them will shed light on these important questions.

References

Aaker, D. A. and Myers, J.G. (1987) *Advertising Management* (3rd ed.), Englewood Cliffs, N.J.: Prentice Hall.

Aharoni, Y. (ed.) (1993) *Coalitions and Competition: the Globalization of Professional Business Services*, London: Routledge.

—— (1997) 'Management Consulting', in Y. Aharoni (ed.) *The Changing Role of State Intervention in Services in an Era of Open International Markets*, 153–79, New York: State University of New York Press.

Ajzen, I. and Fishbein, M. (1980) *Understanding Attitudes and Predicting Social Behavior*, Englewood Cliffs, NJ: Prentice-Hall.

Bitner, M.J. (1990) 'Evaluating Service Encounters: The Effects of Physical

Surroundings and Employee Responses', *Journal of Marketing* 54 (April): 69–82.

Bromley, D. B. (1993) *Reputation Image and Impression Management*, New York: Wiley.

Darby, M. and Karni, E. (1973) 'Free Competition and the Optimal Amount of Fraud', *Journal of Law and Economics* 16: 67–88.

Davis, M. (1992) 'Goodwill Accounting: Time for an Overhaul', *Journal of Accounting* 173: 75–86.

Day, E. and Barksdale, H. C. jr. (1992) 'How Firms Select Professional Services', *Industrial Marketing Management* 21: 85–91.

—— (1994) 'Organizational Purchasing of Professional Services: the Process of Selecting Providers', *Journal of Business and Industrial Marketing* 9 (3): 44–51.

DeAngelo, L. (1981) 'Audit Size and Audit Quality', *Journal of Accounting and Economics*, December, 183–99.

Doney, P. M. and Cannon, J. P, (1997) 'An Examination of the Nature of Trust in Buyer–Seller Relationships', *Journal of Marketing* 61 (2): 35–51.

Dunning, J. H. (1993) *The Globalization of Business*, London: Routledge.

—— (1993) *Alliance Capitalism and the Global Economy*, Reading, Mass.: Addison Wesley.

Eagly, A. H. and Chaiken, S. (1993) *The Psychology of Attitudes*, Fort Worth: Harcourt Brace Jovanovich.

Esfahani, H. S. (1991) 'Reputation and Uncertainty: Toward an Explanation of Quality Problems in Competitive LDC Markets', *Journal of Developmental Economics* 35: 1–32.

Firth, M. (1990) 'Auditor Reputation: the Impact of Critical Reports Issued by Government Inspectors', *Rand Journal of Economics* 21: 374–87.

Fombrun, C. J. and Shanley, M. (1990) 'What's in a Name? Reputation Building and Corporate Strategy', *Academy of Management Journal* 33: 233–58.

Goldberg, M. E. and Hartwick, J. (1990) 'The Effects of Advertiser Reputation and Extremity of Advertising Claim on Advertising Effectiveness', *Journal of Consumer Research* 17: 172–79.

Greenwood, R., Cooper, D. J., Hinings, C. R. and Brown, J. L. (1993) 'Biggest is Best? Strategic Assumptions and Actions in the Canadian Audit Industry', *University of Alberta*, working paper.

Gronroos, C. (1990) *Service Management and Marketing*, Lexington: Lexington Books.

Haas-Wilson, D. (1990) 'Consumer Information and Providers Reputations: an Empirical Test in the Market for Psychotherapy', *Journal of Health Economics* 9: 321–33.

Jones, E. (1981) *Accountancy and the British Economy 1940–1980: the Evolution of Ernst and Whinney*, London: Batsford.

Klein, B. and Leffler, K. B. (1981) 'The Role of Market Forces in Assuring Contractual Performance', *Journal of Political Economy* 89: 615–41.

Maister, D. H. (1986) 'The Three E's of Professional Life', *Journal of Management Consulting* 3 (2): 39–44.

Micheline, B. (1992) 'International Marketing of Professional Services', *Business Quarterly* 56 (3): 86–9.

Nachum, L. (1999) *The Origins of the International Competitiveness of Firms: the Impact of Location and Ownership in Professional Service Industries*, Cheltenham, UK: Edward Elgar.

Pallais, D. M. and Good, E. L. (1996) 'What do Clients Want?', Journal of *Accountancy* 182 (6): 75–7.

Palmer, R. E. (1989) 'Accounting as a "Mature Industry"', *Journal of Accountancy* 167 (5): 84–8.

Parasuraman, A., Berry, L. L. and Zeithaml, V. A. (1988) '*Servqual:* A Multiple-Item Scale for Measuring Consumer Perceptions of Service Quality', *Journal of Retailing* 64 (spring): 12–40.

Patterson, P. G., Johnson, L. W. and Spreng, R. A. (1997) 'Modelling the Determinants of Customer Satisfaction for Business-to-Business Professional Services', *Journal of the Academy of Marketing Science* 25 (1): 4–17.

Petty, R. E. and Cacioppo, J. T. (1980) 'Effects of Issue Involvement on Attitudes in an Advertising Context', in G. Gorn and M. Goldberg (eds) *Proceedings of the Division 23 Program*, 75–9, Montreal: American Psychological Association.

—— (1981) *Attitudes and Persuasion: Classic and Contemporary Approaches*, Dubuque, Ind.: Wm. C Brown.

—— (1986) 'The Elaboration Likelihood Model of Persuasion', *Advances in Experimental Social Psychology* 19: 123–205.

Pralahad, C. K. and Doz, Y. L. (1989) *The Multinational Mission: Balancing Local Demands and Global Vision*, New York: Free Press.

Previts G. J. and Merino, B. (1979) *The History of Accounting in America*, New York: John Wiley.

Richman, T. (1996) 'Service Industries: Why Customers Leave', *Harvard Business Review* 74 (1): 9–10.

Rogerson, W. P. (1983) 'Reputation and Product Quality', *Bell Journal of Economics* 14: 508–16.

Rowney, J. A. and Zenisek, T. J. (1980) 'Manuscript characteristics Influencing Reviewers Decisions', *Canadian Psychology* 21: 17–21.

Sprout, A. L. (1991) 'America's Most Admired Corporations', *Fortune International* 123 (3), 11 February: 38–55.

Strassman, W. P. and Wells, J. (eds) (1988) *The Global Construction Industry*, London: Unwin Hyman.

Taylor, R. N. (1975) 'Age and Experience as Determinants of Managerial Information Processing and Decision Making Performance', *Academy of Management Journal* 18: 74–81.

Thomas, A. S., Litschert, R. J. and Ramaswamy, K. (1991) 'The Performance Impact of Strategy–Manager Coalignment: an Empirical Examination', *Strategic Management Journal* 12: 509–22.

United Nations Center on Transnational Corporations (1990) *Transnational Corporations, Services and the Uruguay Round*, New York: United Nations.

Van-der-Walt, N. Scott, D. and Woodside, A. G. (1994) 'CPA Service Providers: a profile of Client Types and their Assessment of Performance', *Journal of Business Research* 31 (2–3): 225–33.

7 The globalization of professional business service firms

Fad or genuine source of competitive advantage?

Bente R. Løwendahl

Introduction

This chapter discusses the globalization of professional business service firms (PBSFs) contrasted with the globalization of more traditional manufacturing firms. The chapter builds primarily on the theoretical contributions of Michael Porter, particularly Porter (1986), where he discusses globalization in terms of market characteristics as well as in terms of the characteristics of the value creating activities taking place within the firm. I argue that due to the particular characteristics of professional services, most of the traditional arguments for globalization do not automatically apply, neither in terms of market characteristics nor in terms of internal value creating activities. In particular, many professional service firms do not compete on price and cost, and some do not even primarily maximize profits. Given these unique characteristics, it is absolutely crucial for professional service firms to analyse both costs and benefits carefully (economic as well as intangible) before a decision to go global is made. If not, internationalization or globalization may turn out not to be a formula for success; it may even reduce the probability of success in its most extreme sense, namely survival. Hence, professional service firm managers and owners should make sure a 'devil's advocate' has asked all the awkward questions and that they are capable of answering them well, before a global strategy is implemented. Even though globalization may be good for some companies, it may be disastrous for others!

This chapter starts with an overview of what PBSFs really are, and what distinguishes PBSFs from other (knowledge intensive) service firms. The following section discusses reasons for globalization in general, whereas the subsequent section applies and extends this theory to the globalization of PBSFs. The final section discusses implications and conclusions.

Knowledge intensive business services constituted the fastest growing sector in Western economies at the end of the twentieth century, and we see no signs of reduced growth in these sectors as we now enter the twenty-first century (see e.g. Aharoni 1993). Many factors contribute to such a development. One is the level of education of buyers and suppliers alike, raising the requirements for firms trying to achieve a knowledge-based competitive advantage substantially. Another is the trend for outsourcing, combined with the rapid diffusion of information leading to an increasingly globalized economy.

Most firms find that in this competitive context, given the fact that they also need a critical mass of knowledge workers in any area in order to stay ahead of competitors, specialized knowledge-based services are better outsourced and sought from expert firms. Firms in all industries outsource activities which are not core to their own competitive edge, and expert service firms typically are able to offer both better quality and lower cost than internalized staff. In addition, with the rapid development of new knowledge in all areas of society, small internalized staff units face an ever increasing danger of their knowledge being outdated. As a result, knowledge intensive service firms are found relating to all types of industries as well as to the public sector. These knowledge intensive service firms are different enough to challenge the industrial logic presently dominating most discussions of management and value creation, because they are fundamentally knowledge-based as opposed to capital-based. And they are different enough to warrant more research into their characteristics and their management practices, in order to achieve maximum value creation, not only in the knowledge intensive service firms themselves, but also in their client firms.

What is a professional service firm (PSF)?

Within the category of knowledge intensive service firms, one particular type of firm is beginning to receive more research interest in the late 1990s, and has been the core of my research for more than a decade. The professional service firm (PSF) (see e.g. Aharoni 1993; Greenwood *et al.* 1990; Løwendahl 1992, 1993, 1997; Maister 1993) constitutes an interesting and rapidly growing category of knowledge intensive firms, yet has received far less research interest than what its economic impact would suggest.

Today, most organizations say they are knowledge intensive, and most managers claim that knowledge or competence and human resources are their most important sources of competitive advantage. However, to those of us who study knowledge-intensive firms, it is clear that knowledge intensity is a relative concept, and that some firms are more knowledge-intensive than others. Hence, we need to have clear definitions of what kind of firms we are studying (or talking about, in a managerial context). Professional service firms constitute a distinctive and critically important sub-category of knowledge-intensive firms, and a further investigation into these distinctions is important before we draw conclusions about this group of firms in general, and about their globalization processes in particular. Even if most firms want to define themselves as knowledge-intensive, and a large proportion of these firms also want to been seen as professional firms, this attempt to build legitimacy and reputation through a generalization of concepts which were originally quite specific and meaningful, needs to be countered by students of business practice, academics and practitioners alike. When specialized concepts are used by everyone, they lose their definitional and specific content, and over time become void of meaning. We need to be able to discuss the fact that not all successful firms are highly knowledge-intensive, and that not all knowledge-intensive firms are professional firms. The distinctions help us analyse viable and less viable strategies, define success criteria, and so on. Lumping all firms into one category does not help anyone!

Banks offer an illustrative example, as they often claim to be both knowledge-intensive and professional, yet in my view most of their value creation does not result from delivering professional services to clients. The typical bank (at least in Norway), puts together a package of existing financial 'products' (their own expression) for their customers. There is no analysis of what the customer actually needs, there is no higher education and professional training required, and even more importantly: their pricing structure is based primarily on a fee per transaction framework, where profits depend on their ability to leverage the differential between the interest paid to investors and the interest charged to borrowers. PSFs, on the other hand, price their advice, their solutions, the hours required to develop a new solution or find the appropriate advice, or the hours required to diagnose and solve the problem at hand. I do not claim that banks cannot be professional service firms, or that banks cannot deliver professional services. Professional services typically constitute a (relatively small) part of a more traditional service portfolio in most banks, whereas the bank being set up as a professional service firm is more unusual. Still, there are examples of the latter as well, such as investment banks working primarily on a project basis (see e.g. Eccles and Crane 1988).

Professional service firms are, by definition, highly knowledge-intensive and service oriented, like most banks, but in addition they make a commitment to the delivery of client-tailored services based on a careful and ethically sound professional judgment. This is the number one factor which distinguishes the professional firm from other knowledge-intensive firms. In addition, another key characteristic of PSFs is that the bulk of the earnings is based on the professionals' application of their expertise, either in terms of a fixed fee for the service, sometimes on a 'no cure, no pay' basis, or in terms of a project contract stipulating payment at an agreed fee for the man-hours required to complete the task. Yet another major difference lies in the nature of potential opportunism. For the service selling bank, opportunism in the relationship is linked to the ability of the bank to withhold information about loans with lower interest rates, and this is also typical in many other types of broker or 'network' relationships (Stabell and Fjeldstad 1998). For the professional service firm, opportunism is typically linked to diagnosing a larger, more complex problem than necessary, thus increasing the number of man-hours required. Alternatively, the opportunistic professional service firm may involve more junior personnel than initially agreed, which may lead to both an increase in the number of hours required and possibly also a decrease in the quality of the solution delivered. Hence, an ethical requirement for professional service firms is that short term gains need to be given up in situations of conflicts of interest, in order to protect the professional reputation and client trust required for long term survival. One of the major challenges with the specialized knowledge typically constituting the foundation of professional value creation, is the fact that the client generally does not have sufficient knowledge to judge the quality of the service delivered. In other words, the information asymmetry is substantial (Normann 1984). Hence, high ethical standards enforced by a profession or by the firm itself are required, if a firm is rightly to be called a professional firm.

What then, are the unique characteristics of professional service firms; characteristics which may help us distinguish professional service firms from more traditional service firms which like to call themselves professional? Løwendahl's summary of characteristics (1992: 70; 1997: 20) builds on the vast literature on professions and professional organizations, in particular from sociology in the 1960s, including but not limited to Blau and Scott (1962), Etzioni (1964), Gouldner (1957–8), Higdon (1969), Hughes (1958), and Vollmer and Mills (1966). More recent debates about the same topic include Abott (1988), Raelin (1985/1991), and Schön (1983). The following characteristics are typical of professional service firms:

- their value creation centres around the delivery of highly knowledge-intensive services, delivered by highly educated employees, and frequently closely linked with research and scientific development within the area. The knowledge of the employees is frequently (though not always) certified by a professional organization and/or the authorities;
- the services are delivered based on a careful professional assessment or diagnosis carried out by experts in the field;
- the services are highly customized to each client's needs;
- delivery involves a high degree of discretion and personal judgment by the experts involved, and in many PSF industries partners are personally held legally responsible for any liability claim;
- delivery typically involves a high degree of interaction with the client representatives, both in the diagnosis and the delivery phase;
- services are constrained by professional norms of conduct, including setting client needs higher than profits and respecting the limits of professional expertise.

In addition, I limit my analysis to firms delivering services to business clients as opposed to consumers, and the implications of this distinction are further discussed in the section on globalization below.

By this rather pragmatic definition of professional service firms, we have avoided the much more 'touchy' debate of who is professional and who is not, as is frequently discussed in the literature. Since the term 'professional' also has a connotation of good quality, no knowledge worker or firm would like to be called 'non-professional'. In addition, the notion of a 'profession' also implies an organization with the right to include and exclude members based on both a set of entrance criteria determined by the profession itself, and a peer review of their behaviour. The medical profession, for instance, only gives access to doctors with a given set of qualifications, and excludes members who do not keep up to both medical and ethical standards. As a result, members restrict competition in the market for their services, and are able to charge a higher price than they would if competition had been perfect. On the other hand, society allows professions to 'monopolize' certain occupations, because we accept that the information asymmetry is so large, that only peers can truly evaluate the quality of what was delivered. Hence, when professions function well, they serve to guarantee that the quality standards agreed to are actually met by individual service providers.

Many occupations have tried to become professions, but few have been successful in the sense of being granted the exclusive right to license and police their members and to exclude applicants with alternative combinations of expertise and experience. In particular, management consultants, management consulting firms, and their organizations (e.g. ACME in the US and FEACO in Europe) have worked very hard to develop professional standards and ethical norms, in order to establish something similar to a profession (see e.g. Higdon 1969, Kubr 1996). Higdon (1969) is particularly critical of these efforts to create what he calls 'a blue ribbon society'. He addresses the negative implications of occupational monopolies, but does not really deal with the problems of the public in terms of distinguishing high quality from 'the charlatans in the trade'. When professions 'guarantee' the quality of what their members deliver in a highly asymmetric relationship, they serve an important purpose (Abbott 1988; Schön 1983). Where a profession exists, and where the firm adopts the standards and norms of the profession, it is easier for the firm to transfer its quality guarantees into future projects. Where no such profession exists, such as in management consulting, it becomes much more critical for the firm to develop and promote its own culture, norms, and reputation in such a way that the firm name can serve as the quality guarantee, rather than the profession. I will revert to the role of the profession in the subsequent sub-chapter on globalization of PSFs.

However, for the purposes of the strategic analysis of professional service firms, the debate about professions is not all that crucial. The issue at hand is not to decide whether or not the partners of a specific PSF are members of a profession or not, but rather to focus on how the firm creates value for/with its clients. All types of organizations may employ professionals, i.e. members of a professional organization such as lawyers, architects, engineers, medical doctors, and chartered accountants (see e.g. Raelin (1985/1991) for an in-depth discussion of the challenges involved when professionals are salaried employees in business firms). In addition, both firms and individuals may adhere to professional norms of conduct and behave professionally, even without membership in a profession. And finally, all types of service firms may deliver 'professional services', meaning founded on a highly knowledge based assessment or diagnosis in the best interest of the client. But only firms which fundamentally base their organization, their strategy, their hiring practices, and their managerial hierarchies on professional standards, and which deliver professional services (almost) all the time, rather than just occasionally, may rightfully be called professional service firms (see e.g. Etzioni 1964 for an extended discussion of professional versus non-professional organizations). Hence, in this framework a partnership with only professionals, such as a law firm, will not be considered a professional firm if it standardizes and pre-packages a number of services and sells them to clients regardless of their need or not. Similarly, firms offering professional advice as a small part of their portfolio, such as most banks in Norway, are not professional service firms, as the core of their value creation is not professional services. On the other hand, a management consulting firm with highly educated employees who are not members of any profession (e.g. MBAs), may be considered a professional service firm, as long as the diagnosis and the professional norms of the best interest of the client are core to the firm's ethical norms and actual value creation.

Why do firms globalize?

Before we discuss the globalization of professional service firms, we need to look at more general theory of globalization, and here I prefer to base my analysis on the well-established frameworks of Michael Porter. Porter (1986) discusses the evolution of global industries, as well as global strategies in response to industry (including market) characteristics. Central to Porter's theoretical framework is the discussion of the following issues:

- To what extent is the market global (as opposed to 'multi-domestic')?
- To what extent do the different activities (in the value chain) need to be centralized versus dispersed?
- Where should the centralized activities be located, in a global company, and in how many places?
- How should the different activities be co-ordinated across sites?

The first question to assess, then, regards the characteristics of the market (or industry). Porter states that:

> In multi-domestic industries, competition in each country (or small group of countries) is essentially independent of competition in other countries. A multi-domestic industry is one that is present in many countries (e.g. there is a consumer banking industry in Sri Lanka, one

in France, and one in the United States), but one in which competition occurs on a country-by-country basis. In a multi-domestic industry, a multinational firm may enjoy a competitive advantage from the one-time transfer of know-how from its home base to foreign countries. However, the firm modifies and adapts its intangible assets in order to employ them in each country, and the competitive outcome over time is then determined by conditions in each country. The competitive advantages of the firm, then, are largely specific to the country.

At the other end of the spectrum are what I term global industries. The term global – like the word 'strategy' – has become overused and perhaps misunderstood. The definition of a global industry employed here is an industry in which a firm's competitive position in one country is significantly affected by its position in other countries or vice versa. Therefore, the international industry is not merely a collection of domestic industries but a series of linked domestic industries in which the rivals compete against each other on a truly world-wide basis. Industries exhibiting or evolving toward the global pattern today include commercial aircraft, TV sets, semiconductors, copiers, automobiles, and watches.

(Porter 1986: 17–18)

Porter argues that in order to analyse the appropriate configuration of value creating activities in an international firm, we first need to disaggregate these activities. In global markets, he says, value creation is increased by organizing the activities in a global company, such that all activities are located where costs are lowest and value creation is greatest, yet taking into consideration the costs of transportation and co-ordination:

In international competition, a firm has to perform some functions in each of the countries in which it competes. Even though a global competitor must view its international activities as an overall system, it still has to maintain some country perspective. It is the balancing of these two perspectives that becomes one of the essential questions in global strategy.

(Porter 1986: 19)

Porter's logic of value creation and dis-aggregation of activities is fundamentally rooted in the value chain analysis, in which nine generic activities are identified and supposedly valid in all types of firms (Porter 1985, 1986: 21). Given the nine activities, it is clear that the underlying image of the firm is one of a manufacturing firm; a 'machine metaphor' (Morgan 1986) and a 'long-linked technology' (Thompson 1967; Stabell and Fjeldstad 1998). The nine activities included are, as most people now know, five primary activities: inbound logistics, operations (i.e., in most cases 'manufacturing'), outbound logistics, marketing and sales, and service, plus four support activities: firm infrastructure, human resource management, technology development, and procurement. The activities are further classified in terms of their relationship to the buyer: inbound logistics, operations, and part of outbound logistics, plus all support activities, are defined to be 'upstream activities', whereas the rest of outbound logistics, marketing and sales, and service are defined as 'downstream activities':

> A firm that competes internationally must decide how to spread the activities in the value chain among countries. A distinction immediately arises between the activities labeled downstream . . . and those labeled upstream activities and support activities. The location of downstream activities, those more related to the buyer, is usually tied to where the buyer is located.' 'Upstream activities and support activities, conversely, could conceptually be decoupled from where the buyer is located in most industries.
>
> This distinction carries some interesting implications. First, downstream activities create competitive advantages that are largely country specific: a firm's reputation, brand name, and service network in a country grow largely out of a firm's activities in that country and create entry/mobility barriers largely in that country alone. Competitive advantage in upstream and support activities often grows more out of the entire system of countries in which a firm competes than from its position in any one country.
>
> Second, in industries where downstream activities or other buyer-tied activities are vital to competitive advantage, there tends to be a more multi-domestic pattern of international competition. In many service industries, for example, not only downstream activities are tied to buyer location, and global strategies are comparatively less common. In industries where upstream and support activities such as technology development and operations are crucial to competitive advantage, global competition is more common.
>
> (Porter 1986: 23)

How does a professional service firm create value?

For professional service firms, the value chain does not represent an ideal tool for the analysis of costs and value creation. Even at first glance, the lack of fit of the five primary activities with the value creation processes of professional service firms becomes clear (Løwendahl 1992, 1997; Normann and Ramírez 1993; Stabell and Fjeldstad 1998). Yet, although the value chain is an inappropriate model for the analysis of the value creation in PSFs, an analysis of value creating activities and their appropriate configuration for potential competitive advantage is meaningful. Professional service firms do not create value through the transformation of (tangible) inputs into outputs with value added, as suggested in the value chain framework. With reference to management consulting,

Lorange and Løwendahl (see Løwendahl 1997: 42–3) suggested that there are three core processes involved in PSF value creation:

1   selling 'a credible promise';
2   delivering what has been promised;
3   learning from the selling and delivery processes, in order to improve both efficiency and effectiveness in future projects.

The first core process illustrates quite clearly one of the main differences between PSFs and manufacturing firms, namely that value creation starts with selling, or even convincing the client, of the firm's value creating capabilities. For some firms, this means diagnosing and solving a problem (e.g. engineering consultants and management consultants), for others it means designing or creating something for the client (e.g. architects and art directors in advertising), assisting the client in a process involving a third party (e.g. lawyers defending a client in court), or assessing and certifying the quality of the client's own processes (e.g. auditing). Rather than the traditional sequence of design–production–marketing and sales–delivery, the efforts to win the project itself comes before the design and delivery phases. As a result, the notion of 'upstream' and 'downstream' loses much of its original meaning, as the only activity which may be removed from the client/buyer is the final one; the internally focused learning process.

Stabell and Fjeldstad introduce an alternative model of value creating activities in problem solving firms, including but not limited to PSFs, namely the 'value shop'. The value shop builds on Thompson's (1967) 'intensive' (as opposed to 'long-linked') technology, which requires a high degree of interaction and mutual adjustment, both between the professionals delivering the service and between the professionals and the client representatives. The value shop contains five primary activities, like the value chain, but their content is very different: problem finding/acquisition, problem solving and generation of alternatives, choice of solution, 'execution' (implementation), and control/evaluation (Stabell and Fjeldstad 1998: pp. 424–5). This model is quite similar to the Lorange and Løwendahl model, since finding the right 'problem' to solve involves a lot of sales and bidding activities in most cases, and evaluation involves learning from the processes for further improvement. On the other hand, professional service delivery may extend beyond the identification and solution of problems, as explained above. 'A credible promise' may involve the solution to a problem, but it may also involve the certification of processes or solutions, the creation of something new, or acting as a supporting third party with particular expertise. If we accept such a broader definition of 'a problem', the processes of problem definition, diagnosis, and development and choice (or suggestion) of solution are clearly parts of 'delivering what you promised', and hence serve to refine the previous model.

Implementation is typically not part of the professional service delivery, as most professional service firms take an advisory role, but assistance in implementation is sometimes also included in the contract.

The distinction between primary and support activities and between upstream and downstream activities is much more difficult to clearly define in a PSF than in a manufacturing firm. The fundamental processes involved in the creation of value for – or even with – a client involve both the choice of the right models and tools to apply, the development of new models and tools, the 'mobilization' (Haanes 1997) of the right professionals to participate in the project (mostly internally, but often also external experts), and the 'procurement' of additional tools and materials to be used (handbooks, software, computers and printers, etc.). Most of the development of 'technology' as well as the generation of new knowledge and improved databases take place as a 'by-product' of operations (see e.g. Itami 1987), and is not delegated to separate functions or roles which can be defined as 'support functions'. However, there are a few functions which normally are pure support functions, such as the infrastructure (including accounting, secretarial services, desk-top publishing support, etc.). And some firms have begun to invest more in technology to improve the support functions, in particular in terms of database development and maintenance. These are 'upstream' activities in Porter's original sense; back-office activities which cannot be billed directly to the client project, but which are charged as part of total 'overhead'. When more professional time is allocated to such back-office functions, the nature of the firm changes somewhat and makes it more similar to the manufacturing firm than what it was originally. Implications for globalization will be discussed in the following section.

Why do professional service firms globalize?

As pointed out by Porter, global markets are less common in services than in manufacturing. Yet we do see a number of global PSFs, even though it is rather unclear whether the competition is truly global or rather multi-domestic. It seems that the character of such global competition may be both similar to and very different from that of more traditional manufacturing industries.

The underlying reasons for globalization in professional service firms probably depend on the nature of the industry, just like in manufacturing. However, there are a number of fundamental differences between professional business service firms and multinational manufacturing firms. The first challenge arises because the firms deliver to business firms, not to consumers, and this distinction alters some of the arguments in Porter's analysis above. This distinction is not, however, limited to service firms. Business-to-business marketing is different from consumer marketing, even in manufacturing industries. When a buyer is a person, the buyer is located somewhere. When a buyer is a firm, the buyer may be global, local, or multi-domestic ('polycentric'), and hence, even though the characteristics of the services and underlying technologies may be local in nature, the buying firm may want to deal with a single PSF world-wide. Many client firms demand consistent and common services globally (e.g. in terms of auditing and advertising), even though in both cases local expertise is critical, and 'production' cannot be centralized to one country.

The demand facing professional service firms varies substantially across industries as well as within industries. While consulting firms can 'create' a market if they develop a creative solution which is needed, but not yet demanded by their clients, the purchase of the basic services of auditors is mandated by law. Consultants may face both global and multi-domestic markets, depending on the kinds of solutions they offer, whereas law, auditing, and to a large extent advertising are constrained by local laws and consumer tastes. In Porter's terminology, the markets for these professional services are intrinsically 'multi-domestic' in nature, and as a result, as Perlmutter (1969) stated long before Porter, these firms are most likely to be 'polycentric'.

In manufacturing, the five primary activities of the value chain make sense, as well as their sequencing. Global competition in terms of actual delivery would mean either that the global presence would enable the firm to become more cost-efficient than local competitors, or that it would be able to deliver superior quality. Yet some professional service firms are able to deliver both higher quality and lower price, while other global firms deliver services at a much higher price, without being able to document a higher quality. And still they claim that globalization gives them a competitive advantage *vis-à-vis* local firms. How can this be possible?

The Lorange and Løwendahl model, focuses on much more than the 'primary activities' of the chain (the second process in our model), i.e. producing and delivering the 'product'. What the two additional processes of value creation add to the analysis, is first, that global presence may make it easier for the firm to sell a credible promise (and even charge a higher price, regardless of 'objective' level of quality), i.e. a 'reputation effect'. Here, the professional service firm may face a 'chicken and the egg' problem, as global presence may lead to a higher reputation, but on the other hand an excellent reputation may pull the firm into the global market, if the reputation transcends national borders. This is contrary to Porter's statement cited above, where reputation (connected to downstream activities) is considered to be local in nature. Second, global presence may enable the firm to develop broader and more sophisticated 'experience records' and shared knowledge, because of the access to a broader set of academic knowledge development sources. Again, this is the reverse of the knowledge transfer described by Porter above, where a temporary competitive advantage may result from a one-time transfer of know-how to the other country. In PSFs, the competitive advantage, if achieved, results from the ability of the firm to continuously tap into the knowledge developed in all relevant centres of the world, regardless of the local market potential in these knowledge centres. You may even gain competitive advantage from being located in a place where the market is not profitable at all, if the learning from these projects adds more value to other markets than what is lost locally. (See e.g. Bartlett and Ghoshal 1989 for an in-depth discussion of such organization forms.)

Since the markets for professional business services are different from the markets for (consumer) goods, we need to look at the three main categories of client firms which look to global PSFs for service provision: global clients, local clients with 'global problems', and finally local clients with local problems but who still prefer global PSFs. Each of these categories is explored in further detail below.

Global clients

Global clients may be divided into two fundamentally different sub-categories: firms which centralize the decision-making and/or the activities, and firms which demand consistent services globally.

Global clients with centralized decisions and/or activities

When a global client firm makes decisions about a specific category of professional service delivery at only one particular place in the world, firms which have a strong reputation in the country where the decisions are made and/or the activities are carried out, have an advantage. For example, if a large manufacturing firm with HQ in New York decides that all advertising should be run from New York, with an emphasis on globally renowned media such as CNN and National Geographic, firms with a strong reputation in New York will have an advantage even if the client is global. If the activities are centralized as well, the local advantage becomes even more obvious: if all customer databases of a global bank are managed from a central office in London, IT consultants located close to this activity centre are most likely to be considered for outsourced services as well as professional assistance. In both of these cases, the globalization of the PSF is likely to add to the costs of delivery, without adding much to the competitive position of the firm.

Global clients who demand consistent services at multiple sites

When a global client firm demands consistent services all over the world, the effects on the PSF may be very different depending on the types of services to be delivered as well as the actual delivery process. Here a number of possible options seem to be viable.

Consistent services delivered from a central pool of professional resources

If the services required are needed on an infrequent basis, the global firm as well as the PSF may agree to a contract where the professionals travel to the site where the services are needed, stay there for a limited period of time, then return to their own HQ. One example may be the maintenance of a particular type of machines, where e.g. the expert engineers may all be located in Boston, but they may travel to distant locations on a regular basis. Such PSFs, despite their global service delivery, are likely to remain 'ethnocentric' (Perlmutter 1969). Even if the client firm is global, the PSF delivers its services from one single knowledge centre, and does not need to worry about localization, configuration, and co-ordination across sites. The globalization of such a PSF would increase costs, and probably decrease quality, at least if the centre of new knowledge development was located in Boston.

Consistent services developed and distributed from a single 'hub' and a network of delivering units

If the services are required more frequently, the PSF may set up regional 'hubs' where professionals trained in the specific service delivery are located. From these hubs they travel to local sites. Knowledge development and training may still take place at one 'hub', such as Boston, but specialists are available closer to the client sites. As a result, the PSF is likely to turn 'regiocentric' (Perlmutter 1969). Yet, just like the 'ethnocentric' PSF above, the co-ordination requirements are minimal. The central hub develops the new knowledge and standards, and these are implemented through regional 'satellites' which know the local markets and the necessary translations, but which loyally accept the standards 'dictated' from the hub.

Consistent services developed and distributed from a global network of multiple 'hubs'

Just like manufacturing firms, PSFs with global clients may also develop a global matrix structure with multiple hubs and different 'centres of excellence', where knowledge generation and distribution is centralized. For a large management consulting firm, the knowledge centre for offshore oil companies may be located in Norway, whereas the financial knowledge centre may be located in New York, London, or Singapore. Each hub has a specific responsibility in terms of knowledge development and distribution throughout the entire network of local offices, and services delivered within that particular area of expertise are required to be consistent world-wide. Still, co-ordination across hubs is infrequent; there is one single authority per knowledge area. Such firms will benefit from being truly global, yet activities are still centralized (albeit at multiple centres, one per knowledge area), and co-ordination across sites is more one-way delivery and control than focused on mutual exchange processes.

Local clients with global 'problems'

Another typical category of professional service firms delivers to the local client with a global problem, such as the local municipality or government hiring the world's best architects after a bidding process. Public buildings may attract architects from all over the world, and as a result Norwegian architects could win a bid for a national library in Egypt, without any local representatives established. In engineering consulting, this is a well-known type of international activity as, for example, hydro-electric dams and power generators are more or less the same all over the world. Similarly, if you have the required local information about geological ground conditions, a sub-sea tunnel requires the same expertise whether it is located in Oslo or the English Channel or New York. These are mega-projects with international experts flown to the site for as long as their own *ad hoc* presence is required. Unless the problems are recurring, no local offices are likely to be established, and the PSF is most likely to remain 'ethnocentric'.

In this context, the existence of a global profession certainly helps. With a global professional knowledge base, local experts can easily judge the quality of colleague professionals from any country of the world, and international professionals can work with local professionals from any country of the world, provided they share the means of communication, be it mathematical symbols, drawings, or a common language (e.g. English). A global profession also means that world class professionals are known world-wide, and hence PSFs that employ such experts are also able to attract excellent young professionals from a global talent pool.

Local clients with local 'problems'

When local clients have local problems, the industry is multi-domestic, and Porter would not recommend the PSF to develop a global strategy. Still, some professional service firms globalize, even in industries which are fundamentally multi-domestic. Why? First of all, professional service firms seem to find size and globalization attractive because these two factors serve as proxies for high quality. When clients try to evaluate, before buying a service, the quality of a professional expert or a professional service firm, the client typically does not have the necessary expertise to evaluate the level of the person's or the firm's expertise. But as size and global presence is typically seen as signals of successful operations, particularly in manufacturing industries, size and global presence are also taken as indicators of high professional quality, and hence serve to enhance the reputation of the professional service firm. The following proposition may be presented:

> The more difficult the 'objective' judgment of professional service quality, the more likely it is that globalization and size will serve as a proxy for quality.

This is the opposite of Porter's argument about reputation being local in service industries, quoted above. And again, if a global profession exists, the assessment of quality locally is much easier than if no profession exists. Hence, where no profession exists, globalization is even more likely to serve as a proxy for quality.

Economies of scale are by definition very difficult to realize in PSFs, since the services are customized and heterogeneous. Still, they are not entirely absent, but they are most likely to be found in activities very different from the primary activities of Porter's value chain. Economies of scale seem to exist primarily in one area in professional services, namely in the only 'upstream' activity involved, i.e. what is often called 'knowledge management': a global information system, globally assigned responsibilities for knowledge gathering, creation and dissemination in specific areas, and centralized 'corporate universities' or development programs for all employees. Well known examples such as the education centre of Arthur Andersen/Andersen Consulting in Chicago, the global Knowledge Management system implemented by Ernst and Young, and the client industry databases developed by McKinsey and Co illustrate this type of competitive positioning. These activities sound like 'support activities' in Porter's framework; as a sub-set of 'human resource management'. But for professional service firms, these activities deal with the maintenance and development of their core resources: their professional competence, at the individual as well as at the collective levels. Knowledge management is not a support activity in professional service firms; it is core to value creation, and an activity with potential for competitive advantage. Another interesting characteristic of these activities is that they actually raise the quality of solutions while at the same time reducing the costs of gathering the necessary information for a client proposal, assessment or even report. The firm is able to deliver better quality, faster, and even at a lower cost.

In other words, in industries where traditional reasons for globalization do not apply, professional service firms may still choose global strategies, due to the potential impact of globalization on parts one and three of the Lorange and Løwendahl model described above, namely the credibility of the promise, and the ability to learn from a large number of diverse projects in order to further enhance the professional capabilities for future value creation. However, it is particularly in this category of client markets that the PSF needs to be very careful in its analysis of costs and benefits from globalization. The reputation and knowledge enhancement effects are not automatic, and the challenges and costs involved in co-ordination are substantial.

There are also examples of PSFs that are multinational without such operations enhancing value creation. The location of new local or regional offices is not always the result of rational analyses and strategic plans. Quite frequently local offices are established as the result of personal preferences of partners, such as when UK partner John Jones marries his Spanish fiancée, and sets up an office in Madrid. Depending on the nature of the market, this office may serve Europe, Africa, and the Middle East, or only the Mediterranean part of Europe. If Jones is successful and wants to expand, he may build a large office with many professionals, and add local clients to the portfolio. Such offices may turn into permanent parts of the infrastructure of the PSF. If Jones works mostly on his own, and develops new knowledge and solutions locally, the office is kept as long as it does not require support from HQ, it maintains an adequate quality, and it makes enough money to make Jones happy. Except for firm name and some information exchange, the local subsidiary is almost like an independent PSF. If John Jones leaves the firm and there is no other local partner ready to take over, the office is probably closed down.

Conclusions and implications

Whereas global manufacturing firms typically centralize a number of (upstream) activities in one or a few sites in order to exploit economies of scale, the economies of scale are less obvious in professional service firms, and the number of 'upstream' or equivalent activities is small. In fact, many professional service firms face a number of 'diseconomies of scale' if they try to centralize decisions, as the co-ordination across multiple sites, languages, cultures, and legal systems becomes extremely costly. However, the PSF organization depends fundamentally on the organization of the client firm activities it is supposed to support. If the professional service is tailored to support an upstream activity in a global client firm, the implications for the professional service firm depend on the organization of the client firm, including the number of places where the activity is located, and the extent to which it is co-ordinated across locations. If activities are centralized, the PSF may also centralize its service delivery. If the activities are dispersed but highly co-ordinated for consistency and efficiency, the PSF may also need to develop a structure of dispersed and co-ordinated efforts.

Porter's model (1986) focuses on key activities and where they should be located, and emphasizes the costs of co-ordination and transportation as important factors limiting the globalization of firms where global demand and economies of scale are not sufficient to offset these costs. In PSFs, the situation is different. Since there are no tangible raw-materials involved, no tangible products to be delivered to the client, and even no equipment required for the delivery of a high quality professional service, the question of location takes on a different meaning. Most of the activities involved in value creation are 'downstream', and take place in interaction with the client, typically at the client site. The professionals bring their lap-tops and their cellular phones, and hook up with colleagues regardless of whether they are at an office in the same country, at HQ far away, or even on an assignment for another client somewhere else. Hence, the costs involved in logistics and transportation are very different: in most cases all you need to do is transport the professionals to the client site. As a result, the key question is not the costs of setting up and maintaining permanent physical facilities where the activities can take place, but rather a question of duration and frequency of client demand. For *ad hoc* services such as bridges and tunnels and opera houses, there is no point in setting up a permanent local office, whereas for recurring 'problems' such as auditing, advertising, and legal counselling, local offices may be more cost-efficient than flying the experts in and out from HQ.

The challenge of co-ordination is also different when there are no tangible resources involved, but unless the professionals can work independently with each client, the problems are neither less important nor less complicated than in firms where the equipment or the raw materials force people to be present at the same place (if not the same time). Co-ordination involves the sharing of information, ideas, problems, methods for problem solving, knowledge about alternative solutions or sources of information, and so on. Such information can, with today's technology, be transported world-wide without costs, and hence the challenges are more important in terms of the content of information shared, than in terms of the costs of sharing it. On the other hand, there seem to be fundamental problems involved in the co-ordination of professionals, as the realized effects of seamless exchange of information are substantially smaller than the potential effects (Groth 1997, 1999). One such problem involves the professional need for autonomy, thereby reducing the willingness to abide by routines and procedures developed by the organization. What is individually rational does not always coincide with what is rational for the firm. The other problem is found at the other extreme: even if professionals want a substantial amount of autonomy, they also need and seek social interaction with peers. Professionals are motivated both by challenging tasks and by experienced and competent colleagues (Løwendahl 1992, 1997), and unless the firm is able to develop the appropriate learning arena for constructive exchange with other professionals, it risks losing the most competent people. In addition comes the challenges involved in co-ordination when client demand requires either consistent services at multiple sites or the joint efforts of numerous professionals simultaneously. On the one hand, services may be relatively repetitive and modularizable, such that it is possible to establish common standards to be applied simultaneously at all client sites. Here, the co-ordination problem involves the development of the best solution, the exchange of this information, and the obedience of the professionals to the standards set. On the other hand, services may be dependent on idiosyncratic inputs of several experts or unusually creative individuals simultaneously, and then the co-ordination problem may involve getting them all to meet in the same place at the same time, in order to develop a new solution. While the first type of co-ordination is amenable to globalization, the second is extremely costly to replicate, and I suggest that unless the individual experts who need to travel the globe are motivated by this travelling, they are not likely to accept it. If they are really world class professionals, they are not likely to have any spare time regardless of whether they work locally or in many countries. Similarly, the opportunity cost of their hours worked is likely to be determined by international fees (possibly minus costs of travelling, if that is seen as negative), regardless of whether they work at home or abroad. Hence, for 'guru-based' services where the individuals cannot be 'cloned' and personally need to be transported, globalization is only possible to the extent that these individuals prefer to travel and work globally.

PSFs show very clearly how the development of competitive advantage in a post-industrial context is going to require much more of management than what traditional manufacturing firms (and researchers of them) have been used to (Løwendahl and Revang 1998). Competition takes place in two arenas simultaneously: for demanding clients who are willing to pay a premium, and for expert employees who are able to develop the new solutions and sell new services to these demanding clients. The requirements on these two arenas are not always compatible. If globalization involves more subordination to routines and standards than what the best professionals are willing to accept, they will find another employer. Similarly, if globalization involves more individual sacrifices in terms of travelling and staying away from the family than what the best professionals want, again they are likely to leave. And finally, if individual experts are 'leveraged' to such an extent that the opportunities to learn more and develop the individual expertise further in collaboration with expert colleagues and demanding clients disappear, the firm is unlikely to be able to keep the best professionals for long, regardless of how much they pay them!

The differences between the manufacturing firm modelled by the value chain and the professional business service firm are fundamental. The PSF does not need much capital in order to undertake assignments in new countries, it does not need tangible resources, it does not need to set up an office, and it does not need to worry about the transportation of raw materials, intermediate products and final output from its production site to the customers. The entire value creation process may take place 'downstream', in close interaction with the client and at the client's site, and only involves 'transportation' of information and knowledge, once the professional experts are on site. Economies of scale do not result primarily from repeating solutions, but rather from 'upstream' or back-office modularization of partial solutions and methods for approaching assignments, and from meeting places which attract professionals to learning arenas which make the firm attractive to the best 'experts' in the industry.

As regards other types of service firms, there are numerous classifications which define typologies and differences. In short, the main dimensions making PSFs extreme even relative to other service firms is their lack of dependence on tangible equipment, their emphasis on delivering the service to the client site, and their emphasis on idiosyncratic and customized solutions for each individual client. PSFs differ, both within and across industries as regards their ability to modularize or reuse solutions from one assignment to another, but by definition they do not just sell one more 'package' of a generic solution. In terms of globalization, this means that the professionals have to be physically present and involved in direct interaction with each client to an extreme extent; the firm cannot assign some of the best professionals to an HQ R&D function and expect them to develop the solutions for the future unless they also transport these professionals to the client sites to see and feel the exact details of the 'problems' to be solved.

When it comes to globalization, it is very difficult to judge how global a professional service firm is, especially if we compare across industries. Counting number of offices or looking at the location of the firm's present assignments does not provide a solution. Engineering design firms, for instance, may have worked in every country around the world, without having established more than a single or a small number of offices. In this sense, these firms are very similar to manufacturing firms with *ad hoc* export contracts, who also rely on local contacts or agents and do not set up offices outside the home-country. Since the tools required are often minimal and carried in the heads of the professionals, maybe with the support of a computer and a cellular phone, operations may be carried out globally without a global infrastructure. And even the percentage of earnings from overseas operations, which is frequently used as an indicator in engineering design, may be a misleading figure in industries where contracts are large and *ad hoc*. The Norwegian Engineering design firm Norconsult was among the ten largest in the world in terms of foreign billings, during the years they were setting up the telecommunications infra-structure in Saudi Arabia. But after the project was completed, the 'size' of the firm was reduced substantially. However, even the term 'size' can be misleading, as the norm is to hire a large number of experts on a project-by-project basis. Hence, the size of the contracting firm often says very little about how large it may be when undertaking mega-projects. Norconsult was also among the very best in terms of percentage of revenues gained in international operations, but that was by definition, as the firm was owned by a number of local (Norwegian) engineering consulting firms, and was not allowed to compete with its owners in the domestic market. Today, one of the previous owners has taken over the entire operations, and as a result, Norconsult carries out a more typical portfolio of local as well as international projects. But does this shift in portfolio make the firm less global? The example of Norconsult illustrates how difficult it may be to apply the traditional criteria of globalization and global operations to PSFs, as operations are to a much lesser extent dependent on (permanent) physical location in a given market.

To conclude, then, it is not obvious that global clients require global PSFs, nor that the increased reputation effect from global operations adds more value than the costs involved in operations. In some cases the globalization adds value; in others, it does not. The most important conclusion regarding the globalization of professional service firms may be that it is important to look carefully at every expected cost and benefit from global operations.

Since most PSFs sell the expertise of their professional employees, these can be more easily transported to the local sites for *ad hoc* projects, than what is possible with heavy machinery in manufacturing. Hence, short term and temporary offices 'on location' are much more common in PSFs than in manufacturing. The costs of establishing a temporary local office do not need to be prohibitive, whereas the costs of running a permanent local office without a constant stream of new projects may threaten the survival of the entire global firm. On the other hand, for the PSF globalization may be profitable not only in terms of 'objective' quality and costs, but also in terms of enhanced reputation or improved learning for future quality assurance. Hence, the PSF may have fewer reasons to 'go global' in terms of a traditional 'Porterian' analysis, yet at the same time more options than manufacturing firms, when it comes to access to knowledge creation and the enhanced reputation of services delivered world-wide. Maybe it is true that being global is primarily a question of mindset, as the then president, Henry Michel, of the engineering design firm Parsons Brinckerhoff said in response to my questions in 1990. If a PSF is able to tap into knowledge development all over the world, is able to attract and work with professionals from any country of the world, and is able to undertake projects for clients anywhere in the world, isn't that firm a global firm? The danger of automatically adopting the industrial logic is obvious, and the questions need to be asked before PSF managers and owners invest their resources (e.g. time, money, key people, reputation) in local offices in far away locations. Even in the cases where clients do demand global presence, it is not automatically true that they are willing to pay the additional cost involved. Hence, it is extremely important for the PSF to pay attention to all the effects: both the costs, the potential benefits, and the risks involved.

Note

This chapter has benefitted from comments from Øystein Fjeldstad, Lars Groth and Norman Sheehan, as well as the two volume editors. Any remaining errors are my own responsibility.

References

Abbott, A. (1988) *The System of Professions: an Essay on the Division of Expert Labor*, Chicago: University of Chicago Press.

Aharoni, Y. (ed.) (1993) *Coalitions and Competition: the Globalisation of Professional Services*, London: Routledge.

Bartlett, C. A. and Ghoshal, S. (1989) *Managing Across Borders: The Transnational Solution*, Boston, Mass.: Harvard Business School Press.

Blau, P. M. and Scott, W. R. (1962) *Formal Organisations: a Comparative Approach*, San Francisco, Calif.: Chandler.

Eccles, R. G. and Crane, D. B. (1988) *Doing Deals: Investment banks at work*, Boston, Mass.: Harvard Business School Press.

Etzioni, A. (1964) *Modern Organisations*, Englewood Cliffs, N.J.: Prentice Hall.

Greenwood, R., Hinings, C. R. and Brown, J. (1990) '"P2-Form" Strategic Management: Corporate Practices in Professional Partnerships', *Academy of Management Journal* 33 (4): 725–55.

Gouldner, A. W. (1957–8) 'Cosmopolitans and Locals: Toward an Analysis of Latent Social Roles I–II', *Administrative Science Quarterly* 2 (3–4): 281–306, 444–80.

Groth, L. (1997) *Building Organisations with Information Technology: Opportunities and Constraints in the Search for New Organisation Forms*, Dr Oecon. dissertation, Norwegian School of Economics and Business Administration.

—— (1999) *Organizational Design: the Scope for the IT-based Enterprise*, Wiley UK.

Haanes, K. (1997) *Mobilizing Resources*, Ph.D. dissertation, Copenhagen Business School.

Higdon, H. (1969) *The Business Healers*, New York: Random House.

Hughes, E. C. (1958) *Men and their Work*, Glencoe Ill.: Free Press.

Itami, H. (1987) *Mobilizing Invisible Assets*, Cambridge, Mass. and London, UK: Harvard University Press.

Kubr, M. (ed.) (1996) *Management Consulting: A Guide to the Profession* (third, revised edition), Geneva: ILO.

Lowendahl, B. R. (1992) *Global Strategies for Professional Business Service Firms*, Ph.D. dissertation, University of Pennsylvania, The Wharton School, available from Ann Arbor, Michigan: UMI Dissertation Services.

—— (1993) 'Cooperative strategies for professional service firms: unique opportunities and challenges', in Y. Aharoni (ed.) *Coalitions and Competition: the Globalisation of Professional Services*, Chapter 11: 161–77, London: Routledge.

—— (1997) *Strategic Management of Professional Service Firms*, Copenhagen: Copenhagen Business School Press.

Løwendahl, B. R. and Revang, Ø. (1998) 'Challenges to Existing Strategy Theory in a Post-Industrial Society', *Strategic Management Journal* 19: 755–73.

Maister, D. (1993) *Managing the Professional Service Firm*, New York: Free Press.

Morgan, G. (1986) *Images of Organisation*, Beverly Hills, Calif.: Sage.

Normann, R. (1984) *Service Management*, New York: Wiley.

Normann, R. and Ramírez, R. (1993) 'From Value Chain to Value Constellation: Designing Interactive Strategy', *Harvard Business Review*, July–August: 65–77.

Perlmutter, H. (1969) 'The Tortuous Evolution of the Multinational Corporation', *Columbia Journal of World Business* 4: 9–18.

Porter, M. E. (1985) *Competitive Advantage*, New York: Free Press.

—— (1986) 'Competition in Global Industries: a Conceptual Framework',15–60, in M. E. Porter (ed.) *Competition in Global Industries*, Cambridge, Mass.: Harvard Business School Press.

Raelin, J. A. (1985/1991) *The Clash of Cultures: Managers Managing Professionals*, Boston, Mass.: Harvard Business School Press (paperback edition).

Schön, D. A. (1983) *The Reflective Practitioner: How Professionals Think in Action*, Basic Books.

Stabell, C. and Fjeldstad, Ø. (1998) 'Configuring Value for Competitive Advantage: on Chains, Shops, and Networks', *Strategic Management Journal* 413–37.

Thompson, J. D. (1967) *Organisations in Action*, New York: McGraw Hill.

Vollmer, H. M. and Mills, D. L. (eds) (1966) *Professionalization*, Englewood Cliffs, N.J.: Prentice Hall.

8 Enforcement and appropriation of music intellectual property rights in global markets

Martin Kretschmer, Charles Baden-Fuller,
George Michael Klimis and Roger Wallis

Introduction

There is a vast and diffuse literature on the increasing importance of knowledge and its applications to post-industrial economic growth and competitive advantage.[1] The shift from an economy of goods to an economy of ideas has fundamental theoretical implications, many still poorly understood. Information, ideas, knowledge have characteristics that make them unlike other resources or goods, in particular, they are not scarce but proliferate with usage.[2] These characteristics have been brought to the fore with the development of efficient, cheap, cross-border communication channels and the emergence of English as a *lingua franca:* two of the most cited drivers of globalization (Frank and Cook 1995).

Globalization has intensified the challenge to codify naturally proliferating 'intangibles' into tradable goods, and simultaneously to keep sensitive resources from the reach of the market by deeply embedding them into processes. The US-led push towards higher levels of international protection of intellectual property rights may be viewed as an attempt to expand what is tradable (Teece 1998). Under the TRIPs agreement (Trade-Related Aspects of Intellectual Property Rights), signed by more than 100 states in 1994 as part of the Uruguay round of the GATT, a minimum national protection of patents and copyrights has become a precondition for participation in the global free trade area.[3]

The music industry finds itself at the centre of these trends to globalization and propertization. On the one hand, music has become one of the first truly globalized businesses since music, as a product, is easily personalized, accessible and crosses cultural borders. On the other hand, music, as an industry, is heavily dependent on returns to intellectual property rights. In this article, we show that the global enforcement of intellectual property rights needs to be matched by effective mechanisms of governance. Much of the revenues from music intellectual property rights are generated downstream, from uses which may not have been foreseen, such as public performances and the integration of material into new contexts. The music industry has adopted sophisticated mechanisms for appropriating such downstream returns which should be of considerable interest to other knowledge-related businesses. Our study also shows the institutional fragility of the current regime of appropriation in the face of technological change and more integrated corporate structures.

Music is covered by complex intellectual property provisions. A right arises if an original musical idea is given a fixed expression, for example if a song is written down or recorded in some other form. By an act of legislation, the musical idea turns into a copyrighted work, owned by the creator who will have the power to prevent others from using it. Under the TRIPs agreement, this principle of exclusive usage shall last until fifty years after the author's death (seventy years in the European Union).

Although the copyright is first vested in the author, it rarely remains there for long. A composer might want to bring his/her work to the market. Thus he/she might turn to a publisher who might buy the work outright or, more typically, take on the work against a share of future income generated. The terms of these contracts vary greatly, but royalties are commonly split somewhere between 70:30 to 50:50 in favour of the composer over a term of ten to fifteen years. The publisher will promote the work by printing sheet music (until around 1900 the core publishing function), seeking performances and securing a recording contract.[4] If a work is recorded, a second set of rights is created: these so-called neighbouring rights are located in the performance of that particular work and are owned by the producer (e.g. broadcaster, record company) and the artists who perform the composition. Under the Rome Convention of 1961, these rights last for fifty years from the date of first broadcast or sale.

If the publisher and/or producer are independent firms of only local reach, the international rights might be subsequently assigned to a multinational company with world-wide distribution. Currently, the rights to the works and records accounting for 70–80 per cent of global music sales are appropriated by only five companies: EMI (UK), Bertelsmann (Germany), Warner (US), Sony (Japan) and Universal (owned by Canadian drinks group Seagram, which took over the world's largest music firm Polygram (Netherlands) in May 1998 in a $10.6 billion cash-and-stock deal).[5] One is tempted to conclude that the concept of the author underlying Western copyright legislation is perhaps no more than the 'functional principle' of a global music market exceeding $40 billion, although the multinational media groups claim that 20–30 per cent of music revenues will eventually flow back to composers and artists.[6]

In this article we describe and analyse the forces which determine the current appropriation of intellectual property rights in music, and ask whether this regime can last. Drawing on more than 100 interviews conducted between 1996 and 1999 in the US, Japan, Germany and the UK (the four largest music markets) we first report how the industry itself explains and justifies the dominance of multinational firms. Second, we describe the complex intellectual property revenue flows underpinning the global music business, and the role of so-called copyright collecting societies. Third, we identify recent challenges to the system posed by technological change, de-regulation and vertical integration. Fourth, we indicate the attitudes and likely responses by the main actors to these challenges. Finally, we claim that the current appropriation of intellectual property rights in music depends on a peculiar organizational division of publishing, production, distribution and revenue collection functions which cannot, and perhaps should not be upheld in the future. Thus we predict a radical restructuring of the global music industry.

Methodology

Semi-structured interviews (for full questionnaire, see end of chapter). Core sample (44):

- Five largest multinational music firms in Japan, Germany, UK.
- Copyright societies in Japan, Germany, UK.
- International organizations and trade bodies: European Commission, World Intellectual Property Organization (WIPO), International Federation of the Phonographic Industry (IFPI), British Phonographic Industry (BPI), Recording Industry Association of Japan (RIAJ), Music Publishers Association (MPA).

Context interviews (60) in Australia, Canada, Germany, Greece, Ireland, Japan, Korea, Sweden, UK and US with composers, artist management companies, independent labels and publishers, new media firms, telecommunications firms, and financial institutions.

Interviews conducted between 1996 and 1999 as part of a project 'Globalization, Technology and Creativity: Current Trends in the Music Industry' (grant no. L126251003) within the UK Economic and Social Research Council (ESRC) Media Economics and Media Culture Programme. Unless otherwise indicated, all direct quotations in this article are taken from these interviews.

The creation of value in the music industry

Over the last half-century, music has developed from a cultural fringe phenomenon into a commodity central to the developed national economies. Music is now an indispensable glue for many media offerings and pervades every level of society. Sport events, advertising, video games, shopping arcades, telephone calls have become inseparable from a constant stream of musical experiences. The industrialization of popular music took hold during the 1960s when the corporate model of divisional splits finally reached the music business (Frith 1993). A major music firm is organized into the following divisions:

- A&R (or Artist and Repertoire, the equivalent to the industrial Research and Development division): it is the function of A&R to discover, sign and develop new material and artists. According to industry sources, 'around 13 per cent of turnover is spent on Research and Development (more than in any other sector of the economy)'. A typical A&R executive 'gets two shots'. If neither of these signings takes off, the job will be lost.
- Production: recording and post-production costs of a 'master-tape' can rise past the £100,000 mark for a popular album. The costs of a parallel music video release mostly exceeds the costs of music production.
- Manufacturing: the pressing of CDs has become very cheap, with unit costs below £0.50.
- Marketing and Promotion: the working of outlets (advertising, broadcasting, retailing, cross-promotions) is now the major expenditure in 'breaking a new act', easily reaching £250,000 per album release in a national market like the UK.
- Distribution: the logistics of meeting sudden physical demand are complex. With high uncertainty and extremely short life cycles even for many successful products, there is little room for error. Capital intensive global operation.

In addition, there are two further functions:

- Publishing: publishers hold and administer the copyright to the work which is being recorded. Some publishers actively source, promote, commission, even produce new material, others are just passive accounting operations set up by media groups.
- Retailing: retailers can command a 30 per cent margin of the total sales price of a music carrier.

Figure 8.1 is a useful representation of how the cost buried in these different corporate activities are reflected in the retail price of a CD. Alternatively, in a chain model popularised by Michael Porter (Figure 8.2), each of the functional splits in the music business may be represented as adding value (Porter 1985).

Multinational companies are integrated across the value chain, with the exception of retailing. The multinationals' publishing arms often contract material to outside firms as well. Polygram Publishing (now part of Universal) was thought to control 50 per cent of the works recorded by Polygram Records, the highest percentage among the multinationals (*Financial Times*, Newsletter, 1996). By contrast, an independent label may not have its own publishing division, or manufacturing and distribution

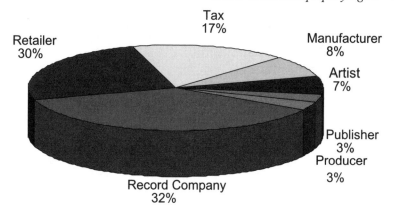

Figure 8.1 Cost for full-price CD, UK sample

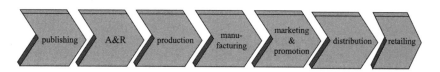

Figure 8.2 Value chain for music firms

network. Other organizational entities are best described as publisher-producers or as management-production companies.

Despite the conventions of corporate organization, there are peculiar characteristics of cultural goods setting the music industry apart: 'Music is unlike soap or socks. We deal in emotions. The goods we sell are not very price-sensitive. If people want Morrissey or 'Candle in the Wind' they buy it whatever the costs' (President, multinational).

Another gospel of the industry states that 'nobody knows the next hit', and that 'the hit/flop ratio of 1:10 has remained constant over the years', as many of our interviewees volunteered: 'If for every successful release there are eight-nine failures, we break roughly even' (CFO, multinational). Such claims have received some independent support from the application of network analysis to the dynamics of fashion (e.g. the endemic effects of word-of-mouth) and from the analysis of publicly available data on the income distribution of the copyright collecting societies (according to which 10 per cent of composers earn 90 per cent of revenues).[7]

If music is sold in such volatile markets, how can a few multinational firms dominate the global business? Over the last twenty years, the same five or six largest companies have consistently accounted for a total market share of 70 per cent to 80 per cent, although each individual firm experiences considerable year-to-year swings in turnover. Many within the industry glorify the market instincts of brilliant A&R people

Table 8.1 Value of world sales of recorded music and shares of major players, 1996

	Polygram[a] % share	Sony % share	Warner % share	EMI % share	BMG % share	Market Value US$ billions
US	13	14	22	10	12	12.1
Japan	13	18	7	14	8	7.6
Germany	23	12	13	22	15	3.3
UK	22	13	11	22	9	2.6
France	32	25	13	19	11	2.4
Canada	20	13	24	10	8	1.1
Netherlands	23	14	8	15	13	0.7
Australia	13	27	18	18	6	0.7
Italy	19	16	17	15	24	0.6
Korea	10	5	4	5	5	0.5
Sweden	20	19	13	26	22	0.3
Taiwan	17	5	14	6	5	0.3
World	17	16	15	11	14	35.5

Source: MBI, Music and Copyright, BPI

Note
a Universal's market share would total 23 per cent (Polygram and MCA's share combined)

who feel the pulse of time. '[W]hen the A&R department gets it right and discover the next Blur or Oasis, their success can bankroll the entire record company for years to come' (*The Times* 1999). Others emphasize a well-oiled marketing operation, 'a machinery of promotion and long-term rights' (Vice-President marketing, multinational), 'pressing products into the market' (CFO, multinational). 'Independent companies trade their international copyrights against our global market and distribution competence' (Chairman, multinational).

> Record companies provide artists with an 'entourage', a structure that understands the artist, the market, international contractual arrangements. How does an artist find a manager, once he has grown beyond the club circuit? How does he find a voice in the wider public? . . . The artist can't market himself directly because he does not understand direct marketing. Why doesn't Elton John go to Coca Cola? Because we integrate economic and artistic thinking, we know how to position an artist, and we understand the creative process.
>
> (Senior Counsel, multinational)

This still begs the question why so many long-term rights so consistently should have ended up in the hands of only a few firms. Independent labels are close to the market, they understand creative processes, they can buy in legal expertise. They excel in the competencies the multinationals claim. Why then have independent right holders found it so difficult to achieve organic growth? The trivial answer is: independents who tried to venture beyond their core territory have been bought; as in a landmark deal of 1992 under which EMI bought Virgin Records for close to $1 billion, at the time termed 'the end of the independents as a force in the music business' (Breen 1995).

At first sight, the situation appears quite similar for the global film business dominated by six major Hollywood studios which produce and distribute their own films, but also distribute independent movies: Walt Disney, Paramount (owned by Viacom), Twentieth Century Fox (owned by Rupert Murdoch's News Corporation), Warner Brothers (Time Warner) and Universal (Seagram). Economic explanations for the evolution of such oligopolistic industry structures often point to sizeable up-front capital investments, for example in steel or car manufacturing (Vogel 1997: 37ff).[8] In the case of the music business, the creation of an international distribution network is expensive and open to significant economies of scale and scope, yet the capital needs for music production itself are much lower than for movies and, as we shall see, shrinking.

Another argument might stress the peculiar nature of risk taking in cultural markets:

> One of our main functions – the artists know that well – is as financiers. Many indies can't do that. And telecoms or whoever would have to deliver that first. This is one of our big advantages. . . . There is not much venture capital in this area, and no bank will take the risk in a market with a flop rate of 98 per cent.
> (Director of Business Development, multinational)

From this perspective, the dominance of the multinationals will continue as long as they retain the financial clout to take over medium-sized independents, and remain the sole provider of risk finance to the music business.

In summary, we found executives defending almost every value creation function as responsible for the dominance of the multinational music firm: A&R and promotion (as market know-how), global distribution competence and the parallel provisions of finance. Economic explanations might stress high up-front capital investments in production and marketing, economies of scale in distribution, and financial portfolio management in high-risk, winner-take-all markets. Despite constant merger and acquisition activities, however, the consolidation processes of the music industry have not significantly increased the aggregate market share of multinational firms. The take-overs of substantial medium-sized enterprises, such as Virgin, Motown or A&M have typically only led to short-term gains. In the developed economies, a state of maximal horizontal consolidation may have been reached during the last decade. Scope for multinational expansion appears to remain only in underdeveloped markets, such as India, Korea or Brazil and in the vertical integration of music businesses into media conglomerates.

Table 8.2 Consolidation processes since 1985

Buyer	Target	Date	Price (US$ millions unless otherwise stated)
Chrysalis	Lasgo Exports Ltd (75%) (the other 25% in 1988 & 1989)	1985	n.a.
Virgin	Charisma Records	1985	£0.1mill.
Bertelsmann	RCA	1986	300
Warner	Chappell Publishing	1987	n.a.
Polygram	Go! Discs (49%)	1987	£0.75 mill.
Sony Corporation	CBS	1988	2,000
EMI	Chrysalis (50%)	1989	96.6
Polygram	Island	1989	322
Polygram	Big Life Records	1989	£ 1.05 mill.
Polygram	A&M	1989	500
Time Life	Warner Communications Inc. (includes WMG)	1990	14,000 (for the whole of Warner)
EMI	IRS Records	1990	£2.25 mill.
EMI	Filmtrax	1990	93.5
MCA	Geffen	1990	550
Matsushita	MCA	1990	6,600
Polygram	Really Useful Holdings Ltd (30%)	1990	£70 mill. and deferred payments paid on performance
Virgin	EG Records	1991	£3 mill.
EMI	Chrysalis (remaining 50%)	1991	£35 mill.
Carlton Comunications	Pickwick	1992	£71 mill.
Zomba Records	Embaro Ltd holding company for Conifer Records (76%)	1992	n.a.
Sony	Creation Records (49%)	1992	n.a.
EMI	Virgin	1992	957
Polygram	Big Life Records (outstanding 51%)	1993	n.a.
Polygram	Motown	1993	301
Bertelsmann	Ricordi Publishing	1994	n.a.
Seagram	MCA (80%)	1995	5,700
MCA	Interscope (50%)	1996	200
Seagram	Polygram	1998	10,400

Source: KPMG, Industry sources, MBI

Intellectual property revenue flows in the music business

Music copyright was first formally established in England following a court case in 1777. Johann Christian Bach (the youngest son of J. S. Bach, and London's leading composer of the day) had applied for an injunction against the unauthorised publication of one of his pieces. It was judged that music indeed fell under the Copyright Act of 1709 which protected 'books and other writings' for fourteen years from publication, renewable once. Treating music as literary work, however, missed its essence: music is not to be read but to be played, a more elusive legal concept. This dimension of music remained untapped until the pioneering introduction of a right to public performance into French Revolutionary law in 1791. In Paris, a bureau for collecting performance royalties for writers and composers of dramatic work was insti-gated by Pierre-Augustin Beaumarchais in the same year. However, there was no generally practicable way to turn the legal right to public performance into economic benefit until a further court case in 1847. Ernest Bourget, a composer of popular chansons, refused to pay his bill at the fashionable Paris café *Ambassadeur* where one of his pieces was being played. 'You consume my music, I consume your beverages', he argued. Although the *Tribunal de Commerce de la Seine* found in favour of the composer, Bourget realized that, as an individual, he would never be able to monitor general usage of his music. With the help of a publisher, a collective body was set up which, in 1851, became the *Société des auteurs, compositeurs et éditeurs de musique* (SACEM), the first modern collecting society (Melichar 1983; Kretschmer, forthcoming).

In many countries, publishers gradually became aware 'that eventually a composer's performing rights might be more valuable than his publishing rights' (Boosey 1931: 175).[9] Modern copyright institutions now seek to enforce a comprehensive 'Pay-for-play' principle, that is to monitor each and every usage of music in a given territory, and collect and distribute fees accordingly.

The Berne international copyright convention (1886) recognized for the first time this ambition across national boundaries. Rather than fully harmo-nizing national legislations, Berne required that each member country give the same protection to works created by nationals of (or published in) member countries as is afforded to works created by nationals of the country where protection is sought: the so-called principle of national treatment, subject to a minimum term of protection of fifty years *post mortem auctoris*.

During the early decades of the twentieth century, performing right soci-eties were founded in most major music markets (Germany 1903; Britain 1914; US 1914; Japan 1939).[10] They established links via reciprocal agree-ments under which each society collected royalties for the 'world repertoire' in its national territory, which were then passed back to the society of the respective country of origin, which again distributed the money to the original right holders. This Big Brother regime of global music usage is neither cheap nor unbureaucratic, but it generally works: if today a piece by a minor English song-writer is used in a Japanese advertising campaign, the original composer and publisher should receive, within a year, a sizeable remuneration for a usage they could never have anticipated when the song was first published. Senior collecting society executives have described the system as 'a miracle'.

Other crucial extensions of music copyright followed technological change. When music began to be recorded for gramophone, this too was judged to be an infringing reproduction of the copyrighted work. A French court first recognized such a 'mechanical' reproduction right in 1905. Mechanical royalties today are set at between 6 and 9.3 per cent of the 'published price to dealer' of a record.

When recordings began to be broadcast, composers and publishers again encountered resistance in collecting royalties. US broadcasters claimed that once they had bought a record, any further use was at their liberty: a puzzling confusion between work and copy. The argument escalated, and in 1939, the broadcasting industry decided to set up its own collecting society, BMI (Broadcast Music Inc.), to administer copyrighted material on more favourable terms. This was the birth of the radio licence formula of 2.75 per cent of a station's annual revenue which covered unlimited broadcasting of repertoire controlled by BMI. In 1941, the original US copyright society ASCAP finally settled on the same terms which since have been applied in most Western countries.

Compulsory licences set an important precedent in that they replaced in certain cases the older right to exclusive usage with a right to compensation. The music industry has since struggled to reclaim exclusive rights in as many domains as possible, most successfully with the WIPO (World Intellectual Property Organization) internet treaties of 1996, which framed any transmission of music via the internet within the exclusive right of 'a communication to the public' (Ficsor 1998).[11] Many in the music industry would like to extend this approach to all music usage:

> I give you figures for a typical private radio station: 93 per cent of programming is music from the charts, but only 2 per cent of total revenue goes to the music industry, equivalent to 3 per cent of net profit. A station's cost order is: 1. personnel, 2. telecom bill! The compulsory licence rates were set at a time when radio was the most important medium of promotion.
>
> (Senior Counsel, multinational)

> Only one thing can be a real danger to the established music industry: a breakdown of 'the system'. Schoolboys buy one CD and tape it for the whole class. This is the way back to an agrarian society, to barter, what the Greens want. WIPO is so important, because it allows the industry to say 'No' in the on-line environment. The compulsory license system for broadcasting should be revised too. Politicians appear to come around to

our view. It is not that we want to forbid broadcasting; but having the right to say 'No' would result in higher margins.

(President, multinational)

In this maximalist vision , the right holder (most likely not the author, certainly not the author after his/her death) would have the unilateral right to say 'No' for more than 120 years after publication if we take Stravinsky's *Sacre du Printemps* (composed in 1913) as a guide, or The Beatles' catalogue.[12]

For mechanical reproduction rights (that is rights involved in the pressing of records) and synchronization rights (that is rights to combine a work with a moving picture) a parallel scheme of collective licensing was developed (Germany, AMMRE, 1909; Scandinavia, NCB, 1915; UK, MCPS, 1924; US, Harry Fox Agency, 1927). The rationale for mechanical collecting societies is similar as for performing right societies. An individual right owner cannot effectively monitor all reproductions or other uses of his/her work. Conversely, users of music (record labels, broadcasters, night clubs, restaurants, supermarkets, etc.) find it more convenient to have one agreement covering all repertoire, rather than several with different artists representing different catalogues of works. Copyright societies remedy a market failure which arises from the high transaction costs involved in individual contracting (Kay 1993: 340; Towse 1997; Wallis *et al.* 1998).

With sophisticated modern monitoring technologies, the transaction cost argument for the collective administration of rights has come under scrutiny, in particular for 'mechanicals' which are now quite easy to identify and collect. The multinational companies, accounting for 70–80 per cent of global record sales and publishing revenues, mainly pay mechanical royalties to themselves, in many cases from the recording to the publishing arm of the same holding company. Multinationals have a clear economic incentive to by-pass the current copyright society structure. Polygram has reported potential annual savings of $2.5 million in Europe alone (*Financial Times*, Newsletter, 1996). In South-East Asia, where there is no established society structure, the multinationals have signed a Memorandum of Understanding under which they collect mechanical royalties themselves. In Europe too the collecting societies have been threatened with a withdrawal of repertoire in order to obtain better terms. An agreement reached in 1997 at the Cannes trade fair Midem, offers multinational firms a reduction on commission previously set at 8 per cent of received royalties to 6 per cent. By contrast, smaller right holders might now be charged a handling fee of 12 per cent or more.

Whether policy makers should allow this to happen is a different question. At another occasion we have supported the view that 'those who join a collective system, enjoying the accrued benefits of that system, cannot then undermine it by demanding different arrangements for handling parts of the activity where the transaction cost is low' (Petri 1997: 106–7).[13] A fixation on transaction costs may skew the music market towards bland, global products and erect entry barriers for new firms.

Current copyright society accounts show that, in most Western countries, revenues are roughly equally divided between income from 'mechanical' carriers and performance royalties. Table 8.3 offers details of royalty rates, institutional processes and total royalty revenues in a selection of countries.

Royalty rights for collective licensing through copyright societies are set in a complicated institutional process of bargaining, lobbying and statutory intervention. Terms and structures vary from country to country, in particular between the Anglo-American common law system and the civil law traditions of continental Europe. Under common law, protection resides as a transferable property right in the work, while civil law exempts some rights from the creator–user contract (i.e. they cannot be transferred from author to market intermediaries for exploitation).[14]

The UK mechanical copyright society MCPS was started by music publishers in 1924, who have a majority on the board. In 1997, a 'Music Alliance' joint venture was formed with the older performing right society PRS (founded in 1914) giving publishers a *de facto* overall control over both performance and mechanical rights collection (and distribution) in the UK. Germany's GEMA and Japan's JASRAC collect both mechanical and performance royalties, and are regarded as author dominated (with composers, lyricists and publishers each accounting for one-third of executive votes).

As *de facto* monopolies, author dominated societies took upon themselves some element of cultural and social responsibility, often encouraged by the State (for example in Germany, France, Japan and Sweden). Germany's GEMA defines itself as a '*Schutzorganization für den schöpferischen Menschen*', literally 'an organization for the protection of creative men', funding education, pensions and commissioning serious contemporary music. Similarly, Sweden's performing right society STIM uses cultural funds to promote local composers, run a Swedish MIC (Music Information Centre) and give stipends. An international agreement between collecting societies, under the umbrella of the *Confédération Internationale des Sociétés d'Auteurs et Compositeurs* (CISAC) situated in Paris, allows for the deduction of 'social and cultural funds', amounting to a maximum of 10 per cent of incomes generated in the home territory (i.e. excluding revenues transferred from other collecting societies for performances in other territories). Local societies can also apply their own brand of 'cultural policy' by introducing some subsidies into the way income is distributed (e.g. by paying more for some form of music when performed). The distribution formula tends to favour serious music over popular songs (even if performances of the latter generate most income for the societies). As might be expected, the multinationals are fiercely opposed to any cultural deductions which they view as 'expropriation'.

Despite their compelling rationales, collecting societies are extremely fragile constructions. They unite conflicting interests under one institutional roof in at least two respects. First, there is no harmony of interests between authors and publishers (contrary to the assumptions behind the standard economic analysis of copyright) (Landes and Posner 1989).[15]

Table 8.3 Global royalty collection in 1995 (US$ million)

Country	Net royalty (% of ppd)	Method of determining mechanical royalties	Phono-mechanical royalties	Performance-based total income[a]	Other income[b]	Grand total
Canada	6.16%[c]	collective bargaining	34.43	50.64	15.14	100.21
Japan	7.5%[d]	government regulations	378.53	231.73	170.21	780.47
USA	8%[e]	set by statute	471.07	594.96	263.26	1,329.29
UK	8.5%	government regulations	170.2	178.02	97.71	445.93
France	9.306%	BIEM-IFPI	163.42	329.51	239.1	732.03
Germany	9.306%	BIEM-IFPI	282.60	341.62	374.82	999.04
Italy	9.306%	BIEM-IFPI	57.22	261.23	73.12	391.57
Netherlands	9.306%	BIEM-IFPI	180.17	115.08	57.19	352.44
Spain	9.306%	BIEM-IFPI	50.35	64.44	40.18	154.97
Rest of Europe[f]	9.306%[g]	BIEM-IFPI	106.98	193.75	152.06	452.79
Rest of world	Various	Various	80.69	309.92	79.07	469.95
		Total	1,975.93	2,670.9	1,561.8	6,208.9

Sources: NMPA, IMRO, G. M. Klimis

Key:
IFPI: International Federation of the Phonogram Industries (represents the interests of the recording industry)
BIEM: *Bureau International des Sociétés Gerant les Droits d'Enregistrement et de Reproduction Mècanique* (represents the interests of collecting societies)
ppd: published price to dealers

Notes:
a Includes income from radio, TV/cable and satellite, live and recorded performances.
b Includes income from synchronization/transcription, private copy, reprint of printed music, sale of printed music, rental/public lending, interest investment income, and other miscellaneous income.
c Estimate based on the following assumptions: 10 tracks per CD, CD retail price $14, retailer's margin 25%. The official rate is 6.47 cents per work, 1.295 cents per minute.
d Estimate based on retailer's margin of 25%. Official rate is 5.6% of the rsp (retail sales price).
e Estimate based on the following assumptions: 10 tracks per CD, CD retail price $11, retailer's margin 25%. The official rate is 6.60 cents per work, 1.25 cents per minute.
f The countries included are Austria, Belgium, Denmark, Finland, Greece, Hungary, Iceland, Ireland, Norway, Poland, Portugal, and Sweden. Some of the countries have not reported performing income while Ireland's reproduction based income is included in the UK figures.
g Ireland's rate is 7.5% of ppd.

Under Common Law, everything is 'transferable', 'assignable', a total freedom of contract. For example, authors can sign away all their mechanical rights to their publishers. Civil Law legislation ensures that the publisher or producer does not get everything. If all claims are represented by the producer or publisher, the question is: do they really have an incentive to pass on the share of the author?

(Executive, international organization)

Second, collecting societies have to represent their members' interests against users, such as record companies or broadcasters, which might be part of the same multinational holding company as publishers on the society's board.

It is hard for the board of a collecting society which is planning a negotiating strategy against, say, the record industry as regards mechanical copyright rates, to have a smooth and open discussion if some of its members are from publishers which are owned by the same conglomerates which control the recording industry. EMI Music Publishing, for example, is on the board of both STIM (in Sweden), and PRS/MCPS (in the UK).

(Board Member, collecting society)

Collecting societies administer intellectual property rights in areas where right holders cannot individually exercise their rights. These rights are often called 'secondary rights', although they may be equally valuable to the 'primary rights' which are individually contracted between authors and intermediaries to the market. If an artist is first contracted to a record company, the distribution of primary rights is a reflection of their mutual bargaining power. 'What has always generated the main profits are newcomers on contracts favourable to the industry. Our industry is about finding new acts' (President, multinational). 'New artists are traditionally signed for seven album deals. This, in effect secures exclusivity for a label since the normal life cycle of an act is 2–4 albums' (Vice-President of Marketing, multinational). 'It is careless to allow management/production companies to retain the rights to the master tapes' (President, multinational label).

Often, sliding scales are used, paying a royalty rate on the price of each CD sold well below 10 per cent for the first 50,000 or 100,000 units, which then may move up to 15 per cent. If contracts of already successful artists come up for renewal, the bargaining power shifts dramatically. According to his 1991 Sony contract, Michael Jackson receives 22 per cent of the selling price of each CD. His sister Janet Jackson trumped him in 1996 when she negotiated a deal with Virgin (EMI) over 24 per cent royalties on sales, a $35 million signing-on fee, and a $5 million advance for each album while regaining the rights to the master-tapes after ten years. The largest advance of $10 million per album for six albums was reputedly paid to Prince, under the terms of his 1992 contract with Warner[16]. Still, TAFKAP (The Artist Formerly Known As Prince) soon wanted to get out of his contract, claiming violations to his artistic integrity: a case settled out of court.

Unsurprisingly, many now famous artists who are locked into long-term exclusive contracts try to re-negotiate terms, and sometimes take their record company to court for restraint of trade. George Michael versus Sony was such a headline case, lost by the artist in 1994 at the UK High Court.[17] It is now common sense within the industry, that the bidding war for the best known artists during the early 1990s has failed to produce economic return. 'I don't think this will repeat itself. We have become more sensible' (Director of Business Development, multinational).

Many of the best-known and lucrative artists are 'singer-songwriters', that is they hold rights covering both the music and the performance (e.g. The Beatles, David Bowie, Janet Jackson, Michael Jackson, Madonna, George Michael, Prince). The rights to the music are full copyrights, and have been discussed at length. The rights to the performance arise with the production of a mastertape. These so-called neighbouring rights are less strong. Under the Rome Convention of 1961, they are protected for fifty years from first release, and are often not exclusive rights (that is, they are entitlements to compensation rather than control). Among the right holders are the lead artists, backing musicians, the record producer, and the producing company. Performing artists and record producers may have individual contracts over royalties from sales of units ('primary rights'). We have seen above that they may range from 6 per cent to 24 per cent for the artist, while a producer may achieve a percentage between 1 per cent and 5 per cent of retail sales.

As with full copyrights, there are areas of ('secondary') exploitation of neighbouring rights where individual contracting is difficult (radio and TV stations, shops, hotels, airlines, etc.). In Europe, the record producers and performing artists have responded in the time-honoured way by setting up collecting societies to which they assign these specific rights. In the UK, production and artists rights are administered separately by PPL (owned by the record industry) and PAMRA (performing artists). In Germany, royalties are collected jointly by GVL, the world-wide biggest neighbouring rights society founded in 1959, with revenues of DM 185 million in 1995. In the US, which is a non-signatory of the Rome convention, performing artists are compensated via guilds: the American Federation of Television and Radio Artists (AFTRA) and the American Federation of Musicians (AFM).

We have given an exposition of the complex regime of intellectual property rights underpinning revenue flows in the global music business. At the end of this section, we should briefly focus on features of this system supporting exploitation processes as yet untried in much of the traditional economy.

- Intellectual property rights (IPRs) in music are located up-stream. They arise through the 'functional principle' of the author at the beginning of the chain of value creation.
- The main revenue streams from IPRs flow from exploitations far down-stream. In particular, they flow from uses which may not have been foreseen, and returns may be appropriated on a pay-per-use basis.

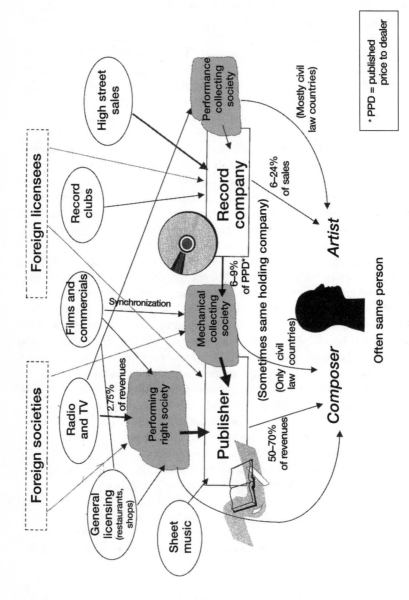

Figure 8.3 Music intellectual property revenue flows in the entertainment field

- Returns from intangible rights, such as the right to public performance, are comparatively immune from economic cycles and technological change. As long as music is used and media channels keep communicating, royalties will be due, regardless of fluctuating high street sales and the technological platform of delivery.
- Music which has entered a cultural back catalogue of classical works (e.g. Stravinsky, Elvis Presley, The Beatles) offers extremely secure returns, perhaps over more than 100 years. Not many artists have this potential but those who have are incomparable investments.
- Collective administration of intellectual property rights is a powerful concept but it poses tough regulatory questions, regarding the internal governance of these bodies, and regarding their ability to exert monopolistic control over certain markets.

Digitization, deregulation, convergence

Since the introduction of the Apple II personal computer in 1977, digital technology has been pervading more and more areas of life. This section follows the impact of technological and regulatory developments over the next two decades, culminating in a radical challenge to the current regime of intellectual property revenue flows in the music business.

Low-cost, high-speed computing could not have arrived at a more fortuitous moment for the music industry. Sales of vinyl records were stagnating at the end of the 1970s. The launch of the CD in 1983, the first mass market digital carrier, revitalised the business leading to a decade of strong growth, as consumers replaced their record collections and accepted a premium price for a glossier, surface-noise-reduced soundscape. At the same time, digital technology led to a revolution in music production with the introduction of the MIDI (musical instrument digital interface) standard in 1982, opening countless possibilities of sampling, manipulating and mixing sounds.

In a serendipitous parallel, Western governments began to de-regulate media and communication channels. New cable and satellite operators entered the market, commercial radio stations proliferated, music television was invented (MTV started broadcasting in 1981). A global youth culture began to spread carried by names such as Benetton, Coca-Cola, Disney, Michael Jackson and Madonna.

Researchers in mass communications and the sociology of culture soon identified such trends towards 'globalization', well before the inflationary impact of that term. They traced minutely the formal and informal integration within and between different sectors of the media industries (e.g. publishing, producing, broadcasting), and an increasing gap between local and global operations, leading to the demise of the medium-sized company. The 1980s saw the rise of Murdoch's News Corporation, Turner's creation of CNN, Disney's push into merchandise and themed marketing, Bertelsmann's entry into the US market, Warner's merger with Time Inc.,

Viacom's expansion in cable and music television. It is during this decade that multisector corporate media groups were formed with truly global ambitions, a message finally brought home by the arrival of Sony (1987) and Matsushita (1990, aborted 1995) in Hollywood.[18]

De-regulation and the new digital technologies changed the mission of the music business. The sudden multiplication of media channels combined with cheaper, more flexible means of producing, manipulating and integrating musical material into new contexts (such as music TV, video games and advertising) led to a shift in revenues from physical distribution to immaterial performance rights. A wider, simultaneous presence in global markets imposed further constraints to find instant 'synergies' across the activities of a media group. The image of the artist increasingly suppressed any musical aspirations (Qualen 1985; Roe and Wallis 1989; Rutten 1991).[19]

'The purpose of a major music company now is not to sell records but to develop artists. Developing artists means investing money to create a brand' (Director of New Media, multinational). 'Attitude is more important than music' (A&R Executive, multinational). 'Pop is anything that sells' (Chairman, multinational).[20]

Our interviewees were ambivalent about these developments. They complained about 'burn outs', 'an ever shorter life cycle of acts', 'a back catalogue that is not replenished'. 'There is greater pressure to suck money out of album one' (Vice-President of Marketing). 'Some products have an extremely short life cycle. A single, then quickly the album thrown in, and after two or three weeks, they have disappeared off the stage. This can't be the back catalogue of tomorrow' (Director of Business Development, multinational).

While the music industry partly drives this phenomenon, it may also be driven. A new threat is 'convergence': an acceleration of the factors of digitization and de-regulation. According to the visionaries of convergence, any content may soon reach any domestic appliance via any technological platform (US Patent and Trademark Office 1995; US Department of Commerce 1998; European Commission 1994; European Commission 1997). Thanks to the rapid adoption of internet technologies, the capital intensive logistics of global distribution can now be replicated by parties new to the music business.

> Hi-fi quality is already available over ordinary phone-lines, using compression techniques. Market research shows that music is high on the list of goods subscribers would buy on-line.
>
> (CFO, multinational)

> The topic, new media, is imposed on us from the outside: consultancy reports, questions from journalists, everybody is engaged with these issues. We don't set the debate ourselves. We react. We respond to tech-

nology, to the telecoms which are suddenly deregulated and look for new business areas, and the IT industry which, perhaps pushed by Microsoft, starts to look at consumer electronics. This is where the pressure comes from. They invent and develop clever new technical devices, and suddenly find they need content. The technical applications themselves are quite useless without content.

(Director of Business Development, multinational)

Growing access to decentralized digital production facilities and the rise of the internet as a global communication medium also have opened new possibilities for the independent players within the music industry. The trade of international copyrights against global distribution and market knowledge, which is at the heart of the current industry structure, suddenly looks less attractive.

There is now a vibrant underground scene of digital jukeboxes, such as IUMA and MP3.com in the US, which charge unsigned acts about $250 to post up their recordings. Consumers can hear the music on-line for free, or pay to download it. . . . Digital jukeboxes are the on-line version of independent labels but with such smaller cost bases that they may prove more resilient.

(Rawsthorne 1999)

How will the established music industry react to these technological and organizational possibilities? In the next section, we extract salient responses from our interview set.

Defensive postures

One common attitude among our interviewees was to play down the threat of on-line delivery, emphasizing instead the opportunity to appropriate the margins enjoyed at present by high street retailers:

Ten years from now, the music industry will look essentially the same. The resources of a major music company are difficult to develop. Many have tried it. It is a history of failures. Look at Dreamworks (bought former Warner people, no significant hit since its start) or Marlboro Records. New distribution technology is just that: a new form of distribution. It will not make a significant difference to the competencies of our industry which cannot be bought for money.

(President, multinational)

I don't see any change to the value chain. In the old environment, A&R to distribution was integrated. In the new environment, retailing will simply be added. We will keep A&R. Production will change because it is no longer physical production; it will be digitization, manipulation, compression: those elements make music transferable via networks. We will keep a close eye on that; we will not leave post-production to third parties. Perhaps now, in the pioneer phase, we might contract out to small software firms to develop specific tasks. But in the end, all the digitization will be in house. Manufacturing might disappear, it becomes database management. I think we will use the telco networks simply as pipes. Today, we have hauliers for transportation. These hauliers will be the telcos. I don't anticipate that the value chain will fundamentally change.

(Director of Business Development, multinational)

Music-on-demand will be simply one more way to use music. The digital environment will not shake the intellectual property regime. Three to four years ago, the idea of the information society was hyped. Even DG XV of the European Commission in Brussels [internal market and financial service directorate, home to the Copyright Unit] thought that every artist, from Michael Jackson to the local group, will simply put their offerings on a server, stating the conditions of usage. The copyright societies would become superfluous. Today, everybody accepts that it is much more difficult and costly to devise an alternative to the present system. Whatever happens in multimedia, we will be at the table.

(Vice-President, collecting society)

Market predictions have always been wrong. In 1979, I attended a direct marketing conference at the Algarve. There was a presentation on the CD: light, resilient. Boston Consulting argued that in ten years time, 50 per cent of record sales would be armchair shopping. Today, the figures are between 7 per cent and 9 per cent. And direct marketing people know their consumers very well!

(Senior Counsel, multinational)

Despite these assertions of confidence, the multinational music business has undertaken a number of steps to control the move towards new media channels. We encountered at least five (which could have been taken straight from a business strategy textbook):

'Don't force the issue'

It is always dangerous to open up a new market if it threatens you in the old.

In three to five years, demand might be there and we will be a fully active player. However, we will follow demand, not be proactive since our existing business produces very good margins, and we need to cultivate good relationships with retailers.

(CFO, multinational)

The major music firms should not encourage on-line distribution, since the margins are likely to be much smaller than for physical carriers. If networked distribution becomes inevitable (as it eventually will), the majors should do it themselves. But, customers also wish to own music, to have a visible, touchable library. This will not change.

(Chairman, multinational)

'Tighten up control of rights'

New template contracts are being issued by the multinational HQs, including on-line distribution and internet domain names.

If you control content, the form of distribution does not matter to you.

(President, multinational)

All new contracts are designed to cover any possible right the law allows in the multimedia environment. . . . There will be no watertight global IPR regime. For the Western markets, our strategy is to work within controlled environments, such as internet service providers, to avoid large scale piracy.

(CFO, multinational)

It is highly unlikely that servers in copyright free zones will become a major problem. The same 'no national boundaries' argument had been proposed when satellite broadcasting first took off. But 'Mercedes' will not buy advertising in an illegitimate environment.

(Vice-President, collecting society)

'Co-opt potential new entrants'

The most threatening competitors are network operators in the following order: Telcos, Microsoft, cable, Motorola (satellite network), utilities (the electricity operators reach every household). Retailers are no threat, nor is MTV. It is easy to build a broadcasting station (majors can do it: see Viva [German music channel]), but to create an infrastructure is beyond our clout.

(CFO, multinational)

Acting collectively, the industry has tried to seek control of the new means of distribution, by exploring strategic alliances in setting up a controlled infrastructure. Pilot schemes have been pursued with IBM in San Diego, BT in the UK, Deutsche Telekom in Germany, and under the umbrella of RIAJ in Japan. An extreme variation of this strategy would see record companies being transformed into distributors, licensing material from independent artists or production companies. As database management, this role may be occupied by network operators. Yet all our multinational interviewees were scathing about the prospects of third parties moving into the music business:

> The removal company wants to buy the furniture store. This is ridiculous. But the time has come to talk to each other, and gain a better mutual understanding between content producers, the telcos and consumer electronics. The contractual framework we agreed with Deutsche Telekom is far superior to the one operated by BT and the UK record industry during previous trials. The UK deal involved the transfer of some rights. In Germany, Deutsche Telekom merely operates an infrastructure and billing system. That's it. The infra-structure is open to all, but not very significant. Where the server is placed does not matter much. Key are the rights.
>
> (Senior Counsel, multinational)

'Develop own procedural competencies in the new technology'

Apart from pilot schemes in on-line delivery, the in-house creation and management of digital databases and websites has been advanced by all multinationals.

> New technologies, web-sites, narrowcasting may add to our market-knowledge. We start to own the consumer. We employ a new media task force mainly to this effect, not to explore distribution.
>
> (Chairman, multinational)

> To create and maintain a database of all content in digital parcels is both technologically and personally expensive. We are not yet prepared to throw big money at it but trials are being conducted. Under no circumstances would we allow such a database to be managed by a future network operator.
>
> (CFO, multinational)

'Create brand as the music navigator of the on-line environment.'

> The whole new media talk is an enormous hype. Sure, an increase in channels will make marketing more difficult. On the other hand, this will only increase the need for a gatekeeper. This will continue to be

the function of the record company. The internet must be seen mainly as a promotions medium and a mail order machine.

(President's office, multinational)

We already systematically build up our brand in the on-line environment. Labels will continue to be important to identify genres of music to customer groups, but the crucial brand will be [the record company], creating a trusted sales environment.

(CFO, multinational)

Branding, however, presents an obstacle for multinational companies. The consumer is interested in the artist, not the firm behind: "'Front line", it would be a disaster to market Bruce Springsteen, say, as Sony' (Vice-President of marketing, multinational). In music, typically, the artist is the brand.

The five defensive postures sketched here can be found among all multinationals and in all sample countries. There are some interfirm variations about the ways multimedia strategy is being formulated and implemented (Sony and Warner being the most centralized), and about the progress of the core markets (despite the second highest PC penetration in the world, Japanese internet usage and electronic commerce is somewhat lagging). The pattern of competitive responses, however, appears robust.

The future location of intellectual property rights

The location of intellectual property rights in music is dependent on the mutual bargaining power of the parties involved within a statutory frame vesting the copyright initially in the author. From this perspective, the current dominance of multinational record companies is the outcome of contingent circumstances which are about to change. We identified the technological revolution of digitization and the de-regulation of media and communication channels as the main factors affecting the power balance.

Four negotiations are at the heart of the music business:

Commodification

The author wants to bring music to the market. Because he/she often lacks the necessary resources, he/she will assign the copyright to an intermediary who commodifies the musical work into a product. This first intermediary is traditionally the publisher. It might also be a management or production company. The trade is essentially copyright against some specific commodification competence (e.g. music production, market knowledge).

Globalization

The first intermediary often lacks the resources for multi-purposing and international exploitation of the rights acquired. Independent companies then trade their international intellectual property rights against a global, multi-purpose competence (chiefly marketing and distribution). This is the deal cementing the role of the multinational record company.

Delivery

The third intermediary finally delivers the product to the consumer. This might be a high-street retailer or a media channel. Normally, this trans-action does not involve any transfer of intellectual property rights.

Royalty management

After the product has been brought to the market, no individual player (author, first intermediary, second intermediary, third intermediary) has the resources to monitor secondary usage (performances on the media and in public places). Author and/or intermediaries therefore assign these specific rights to collective bodies, the copyright societies.

Intellectual property rights are located up-stream with the fixation of an original musical idea by the author. For each down-stream intermediating function, questions need to be asked:

- why is there pressure to assign intellectual property rights further down the chain?
- why don't first or second intermediaries buy the copyrights outright, rather than splitting royalties?
- why does the retailer or media channel normally not hold any rights to the music products they sell?

We have shown in some detail, in the section on Intellectual Property Revenue Flows in the Music Business, that the allocation of intellectual property rights is essentially a result of bargaining power in the process of bringing music to the market. We have also argued that the functional splits of the music business are the result of historical accidents (e.g. printing sheet music) rather than reflecting the negotiation process in bringing music to the market. A change in technology and regulation should lead to a different allocation of intellectual property rights around the value adding functions of

1   commodification
2   globalization
3   delivery
4   royalty management.

Following our analysis, these functions do not match the prevalent organizational entities in the global music business.

An example from the Japanese market may illustrate the dynamics of IPR allocation. In Japan, the media are essential to 'breaking an act'.

> Many sales are tied to TV and radio. Japanese stations exert a far greater independence. It is like Britain twenty years ago. 'Pluggers' which today dominate the British radio scene don't find easy access to the Japanese media. The record companies cannot control promotion in the same way as in Europe where a 'big push' virtually guarantees sales. This partly explains the unsuspected success foreign acts can experience in Japan. They may be virtually unknown in their own country, not heavily promoted by their Japanese label and sell three million copies.
>
> (Marketing Director, multinational)

> Record companies are the weakest player. The media are all powerful. . . . One problem with the new media is: how do you find out about a new act. We have to introduce new artists. In Japan, everything goes through TV. Nine out of ten hits are hooked up to television.
>
> (Director of International Pop, multinational)

This leads to a situation in which intellectual property rights are assigned further down the value chain to the third intermediary:

> What is never talked about is that in return for exposure on television, record companies have to sign over some rights to the broadcaster. Many TV stations, even radio, have started to set up their own publishing company solely for this purpose. These publishers are not involved in any publishing activity, they are a vehicle for receiving money. If we want to tie-in a new act to a drama series on [broadcaster's name], for example, they will ask us to sign over some of our publishing rights. If we don't own the publishing rights, they ask for a share of the royalties from record sales. In other countries, of course, this might be out-lawed as anti-competitive practices. But this is how the Japanese system operates.
>
> (Director of International Pop, multinational)

Another example from Japan indicates that similar pressures operate up-stream, at the beginning of value creation.

> In recent years, the contracting structure in the music industry has changed. Record companies now rarely sign and develop new artists directly. They contract with management/production companies who use changing artists as commodities and even dictate sudden changes in style.
>
> (Marketing Director, multinational)

In 70 per cent of contracts, the management/production company now owns the mastertape. In terms of sales, the situation is much more dramatic since only the best-selling artists can negotiate these terms.

(Legal Consultant, multinational)[21]

It is imperative that we reverse this trend. This is why it is so important to develop our own artists.

(President, multinational label)

In the Japanese market, IPRs are stretched between the first intermediary (management/production company) and the third intermediary (media channel) appropriating returns down stream. These developments may anticipate some of the dynamics of digitization and de-regulation in the Western markets. In our concluding discussion we shall briefly summarize possible future roles for the main organizational entities in the global music business.

Artists

Most artists are still unlikely to command the resources required to bring music to the market. If they already enjoy the benefits of a local fan base, access to cheap production and distribution points may enable some artists to retain their intellectual property rights while growing the market. Digital technology facilitates that option. More entrepreneurial spirits may try to set up their own commodification intermediary, such as a publishing company, a label or a strong management team. Alternatively, they may be forced to contract to an established third party. This would involve the transfer of substantial IPRs. Since supply in cultural markets far exceeds demand, the commodification intermediary retains a strong position.

Artists who become famous, are often locked into long-term contracts with intermediaries. When such contracts come up for renewal, 'superstars' are in an extremely strong position to recover and retain their IPRs. Such artists are commodified products in themselves, they have increasingly access to alternative means of finance, and they may use new distribution technologies to control globalization and delivery processes.[22] This scenario is the great fear of the multinational companies.

Publishers

Publishers have developed into two entirely different types of organizations. The first continues the traditional intermediating role of sheet publishers. They seek to provide a commodification platform for attractive new material and have developed a specific promotional competence. The second type of organization is an accounting subsidiary of a larger media group, occupying either the second or third intermediating function: A record company may sign a new act, and 'encourage' the transfer of publishing rights to its subsidiary; a broadcaster or producer may commission a piece of music and 'encourage' the transfer of publishing rights to its subsidiary.

This second type of publisher does not appear to add any independent value to the product. The location of IPRs in such subsidiaries depends on the bargaining power of the parent company. Competition authorities are well advised to study this grey and rapidly growing area of transfer practices. Another dubious practice is to channel foreign publishing earnings through so-called 'sub-publishers'. In some European countries, these subsidiaries can take a 50 per cent slice of all revenues before the remainder is passed back to the original publisher which then takes its negotiated percentage of between 30 per cent and 50 per cent. This double cut can hardly be justified by a passive accounting operation.

Using technological advances, publishers may further venture either into other commodification functions (such as music production) or into full-scale royalty management.

> In a world of digital water marking and comprehensive automated monitoring of electronic channels, I can even see publishers bringing royalty collecting in house for mechanicals, broadcasting and internet, leaving only general licensing to third parties.
>
> (President, collecting society)

Record labels

In a multi-channel environment, physical carriers will be only one form of music licensing, and perhaps not the central one. As indicated previously, in the section on Defensive postures, multinational record companies may be re-positioned as branded media gateways, as digital distributors or providers of risk finance. In all these areas, they are open to increased competitive pressure from independents within the music industry (publishers, labels, artist management), from network operators (telcos, IT firms) and from financial institutions (venture capitalists, investment banks specializing in securitization).

Retailers

The generous high street margin of 30 per cent of cover price may be under threat from direct-mailing operations or digital delivery. New entrants (CD Now; Music Boulevard; Amazon.com) and major retailers (Barnes and Noble; HMV; Tower) are already moving into internet retailing, as have record companies (BMG, Sony and Warner). Traditional retailing intermediaries have the advantage of offering a complete selection of music (unlike the web sites of multinational record companies promoting only own brand goods). Specialist niche retailers may succeed in widening their client base with a global service. However, pure retailing intermediaries are unlikely to appropriate IPRs.

Media groups

If media groups control the main communication channels through which new acts are promoted, they may command commodification, global-ization and delivery functions, and thus substantial transfers of intellectual property rights. Universal, Time Warner, Sony and Bertelsmann all appear to treat their music divisions increasingly as part of global corporate strategies. Music contents may be cross-promoted and customized across many different media channels.

Collecting societies

The collecting societies are in a precarious situation, as the transaction cost argument from the cost of individual contracting loses its persuasion. In many lucrative areas, multinational right holders are now in a technological position to monitor music usage and collect royalties themselves, rather than assigning rights to a collecting society. From this position of strength, the multinationals now try to force the copyright societies into offering special, discounted terms. In countries influenced by the civil law tradition of conti-nental Europe this has been met with great hostility. There is a growing argument that the collective administration of music copyrights should be restyled as a 'universal service' provided for all right holders under statutory guarantees. Major right holders may be required to contribute to the financing of that system, even if they don't want to use it.

In countries such as the US with its competition between three collective bodies (ASCAP, BMI, SESAC), copyright societies have all but abandoned areas where royalties are expensive to collect. These societies try to secure their survival by adding A&R functions (i.e. signing new talents early in their career) and offering individual deals to high turnover superstars. The current uncertainty in the field of collective licensing may have detrimental effects on the aggregate returns to global music copyrights.

Conclusions

In this article, we have examined the current, and likely future location of intellectual property rights in the global music business. Music is one of the most deeply rooted human activities. It is accessible, easily personalized and permeates as commodified good every level of society. Yet it is complex to produce, difficult to trace and forever swayed by the waves of fashion. The global music industry is significant in its own right but we also suggest that a greater understanding of the music industry may illuminate the subtle processes of appropriating returns to intellectual property rights in a knowledge-based economy. Intellectual property may be viewed as one system for managing knowledge. The legal recognition of intellectual property rights (much advanced under the GATT process) is only one constraint on this system. To be sure, without statutory protection of a intellectual property right vested in the author, the global music market would shape up in very different ways. But the granting and enforcement of that right does not determine how it is filtered down in a heterogeneous process of value creation, and how the appropriation of returns is governed. We have shown that complex institutional processes of bargaining and governance have led to a regime that is at once powerful and fragile. Through concepts of pay-per-use, royalty management technologies and the collective administration of intellectual property rights, returns from down-stream applications of knowledge products become possible. This may have far-reaching theoretical implications for how we think about the knowledge economy. The music industry offers itself as a prime site for studying these themes.

Appendix: the questionnaire

1   Which are the parties in the music industry that can/can't appropriate value in a multimedia environment? Why?

2   Which are the parties in the music industry that will appropriate value in a multimedia environment? Why?

3   Which are the parties outside of the music industry that can/can't appropriate value in a multimedia environment? Why?

4   Which are the parties outside of the music industry that will appropriate value in a multimedia environment? Why?

5   Which part of the old value chain will all of the above try to appropriate? (Show model old value chain)

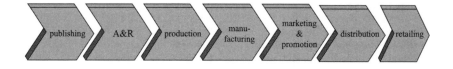

6   What part of the new value chain will all of the above try to appropriate? (Show model new value chain)

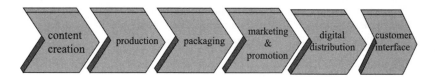

7　What will be the relationship of those parties (both in the physical and in the multimedia environment) with:

　　i　　*Artists*
　　ii　　*Publishers*
　　iii　　*Labels*
　　iv　　*Retailers*
　　v　　*Other media (music TV, radio, etc.)*
　　vi　　*New digital distributors of music*
　　vii　　*Telcos*
　　viii　　*IT firms*
　　ix　　*Collecting societies*

8　What will your relationship be (both in the physical and in the multimedia environment) with:

　　i　　*Artists*
　　ii　　*Publishers*
　　iii　　*Labels*
　　iv　　*Retailers*
　　v　　*Other media (music TV, radio, etc.)*
　　vi　　*New digital distributors of music*
　　vii　　*Telcos*
　　viii　　*IT firms*
　　ix　　*Collecting societies*

9　What will your relationship be with the parties that can and will claim a stake in the multimedia environment?

Notes

We are grateful to Anne Barron (London School of Economics), Peter Drahos (Queen Mary Intellectual Property Research Institute, University of London), Simon Frith (Sterling University) and the editors of this volume for helpful comments. We acknowledge financial assistance from the ESRC, grant nos L126251003 ('Globalisation, technology and creativity') and L325253009 ('Intellectual property and knowledge transfer'). Substantial parts of this article have first appeared in *Prometheus* (vol. 17, no. 2, 1999); they are used with kind permission of CARFAX publishing.

1　In the field of economics, evolutionary economics and the so-called 'new growth' theories have become influential (Nelson and Winter 1982; Romer 1989), while management theorists have adopted knowledge and resource-based views of the firm (Grant 1991; Spender 1996). These references are only pointers to some seminal theoretical streams in a burgeoning literature.

2　Kenneth Arrow has pointed out the public good characteristics of knowledge many years ago (Arrow 1962). For a review of the development of information economics, see Lamberton (1996).

3　On the implications of linking intellectual property to trade issues, see Drahos (1995, 1998).

4 In many cases, a new act may first sign with a record company before contracting to a publisher.
5 Universal's offer for Polygram was reduced to $10.4 billion in June 1998. The deal was completed in December 1998.
6 The figure of 20–30 per cent was given by the CFO of one multinational company. We have been unable to verify this claim. On the author as functional principle, compare Michel Foucault's notorious diagnosis:

> the author is not an indefinite source of significations which fill a work; the author does not precede the works; he is a certain functional principle by which, in our culture, one limits, excludes, and chooses; in short by which one impedes the free circulation, the free manipulation, the free composition, decomposition, and recomposition of fiction.
>
> (Foucault 1984, p. 101)

7 The role of network effects for the fashion dynamics of cultural markets are examined in Kretschmer *et al.* (1999); the income distribution of the British copyright society PRS is analysed in a Monopolies and Mergers Commission (MMC) report (1996: 65–6). The various articulations of success as '1:10 hit/flop ratio', '10 per cent of composers/90 per cent of revenues', '98 per cent flop rate', 'one successful release/8–9 failures' are not consistent but point to winner-take-all dynamics.
8 Since 1995, Dreamworks (led by Spielberg, Katzenberg and Geffen) had some success in establishing a new major studio.
9 William Boosey (heir to the publishing dynasty).
10 Japan started to collect royalties for foreign repertoire only with the Copyright Law of 1971.
11 The US congress implemented these terms with the Digital Millennium Copyright Act, passed on 8 October 1998; the European Commission has proposed a directive to the same effect.
12 The topical debate between copyright maximalists and minimalists is well covered in Hugenholtz (1996). See also Samuelson (1996).
13 For a conflicting analysis, accusing the collecting societies of charging excessive rates and handling fees, see Temple Lang (1997: 51ff).
14 This 'inalienability' is prominent in civil law conceptions of a creator's *droit moral*, the right to claim authorship of a work, and to protect its integrity (Sarraute 1968; Durie 1991).
15 For a critique, see Towse (1997: 34) who casts the relationship of author to publisher as a principal-agent problem.
16 Contract terms are never officially revealed by the industry. The above figures are regarded as reliable, and are often repeated in the trade press (e.g. *Rolling Stone; Hollywood Reporter; Billboard; Music Week*).
17 George Michael's original deal with CBS (as part of the group Wham!) was signed in 1983 and was to last until 2005. After the battle won in the UK High Court, Michael's record company (now Sony) agreed to release the artist from his contract only against a 3 per cent royalty on Michael's next two albums (with Dreamworks and Virgin), while retaining the rights to his valuable back catalogue and a Greatest Hit compilation (*Music Business International*, August 1995).
18 Instructive material on this decade can be found in Hirsch 1992; Malm and Wallis 1992; Wallis 1990.
19 According to one multinational record company, one-eighth of revenues are now royalty earnings.
20 Nick Phillips, Chairman, Warner Music UK quoted in *The Times*, Saturday Magazine, 6 February 1999: 34.

21 Sony Music Japan contradicted this claim. They appear to control 70 per cent of mastertapes by holding systematic talent spotting competitions all over Japan, signing promising acts early.
22 In 1997, David Bowie issued bonds secured against future royalties from his back catalogue of rights, raising $55million. Rod Steward and heavy metal band Iron Maiden have followed suit (*Financial Times* 7 February 1998, 'Superstars give you their bond'; *Evening Standard* 26 January 1999, 'Iron Maiden to tune in with bond package'). Already twenty years ago, Frank Zappa proved the income potential of mail order operations controlled by the artist. The internet is increasingly used for this purpose.

References

Arrow, K. J. (1962) 'The Economic Implications of Learning by Doing', *Review of Economic Studies* 29: 155–73.

Boosey, W. (1931) *Fifty Years of Music*, London.

Breen, M. (1995) 'The End of the World as we Know it: Popular Music's Cultural Mobility', *Cultural Studies* 9: 486–504.

Drahos, P. (1995) 'Global Property Rights in Information: the Story of TRIPS at the GATT', *Prometheus* 13 (1): 6–19.

—— (ed.) (1998) 'Trade and Intellectual Property', *Prometheus* (special issue) 16 (3).

Durie, R. (1991) 'Moral Rights and the English Business Community', *Entertainment Law Review* 2: 40–9.

European Commission, *Europe and the Global Information Society*, Bangemann Report, May 1994 (http://www.ispo.cec.be/infosoc/backg/bangeman.html).

European Commission, Green Paper (1997) *Convergence of the Telecommunications, Media and Information Technology Sectors, and the Implications for Regulation: Towards an Information Society Approach*, COM(97) 623.

Ficsor, M. (1998) 'Copyright for the Digital Era: the WIPO "Internet" Treaties', *Columbia – VLA Journal of Law and the Arts* 21 (3–4): 197–223.

Financial Times, Newsletter, *Music and Copyright* no. 94, 17 July 1996.

Foucault, M. (1984) 'What is an Author?', in P. Rabinow (ed.) *The Foucault Reader*, New York: Pantheon Books.

Frank, R. H. and Cook, P. J. (1995) *The Winner-Take-All Society*, New York: Free Press.

Frith, S. (1993) 'The Industrialisation of Popular Music', in J. Lull (ed.) *Popular Music and Communication* (second edn.), Beverley Hills: Sage.

Grant, R. M. (1991) 'The Resource-based Theory of Competitive Advantage: Implications for Strategy Formulation', *California Management Review* 33 (spring): 114–35.

Hirsch, P. M. (ed.) (1992) Special Issue: 'Globalization of Mass Media Ownership', *Communication Research* 19, 6 (December).

Hugenholtz, P. B. (ed.) (1996) *The Future of Copyright in a Digital Environment*, The Hague: Kluwer.

Kay, J. (1993) 'The Economics of Intellectual Property Rights', *International Review of Law and Economics* 13: 337–48.

Kretschmer, M. (forthcoming 2000) 'Intellectual Property in Music: a Historical Analysis of Rhetoric and Institutional Practices', *Studies in Cultures, Organizations and Societies* 6 (2).

Kretschmer, M., Klimis, G. M. and Choi, C. J. (1999) 'Increasing Returns and Social Contagion in Cultural Industries' [most innovative paper award British Academy of Management (BAM1998)], *British Journal of Management* 10: S61-S72.

Lamberton, D. M. (ed.) (1996) *The Economics of Communication and Information*, Cheltenham: Edward Elgar.

Landes, W. M. and Posner, R. A. (1989) 'An Economic Analysis of Copyright Law', *Journal of Legal Studies* 18: 325–66.

Malm, K. and Wallis, R. (1992) *Media Policy and Music Activity*, London: Routledge.

Melichar, F. (1983) *Die Wahrnehmung von Urheberrechten durch Verwertungsgesellschaften*, Munich.

Monopolies and Mergers Commission (MMC) (1996) *Performing Rights*, Cm 3147, London: HMSO.

Music Business International (MBI) (August 1995) London: Miller Freeman.

Nelson, R. R. and Winter, S. G. (1982) *An Evolutionary Theory of Economic Change*, Cambridge, Mass.: Belknap Press.

Petri, G. (1997) 'Copyright: the Right to Ownership', in Roger Wallis (ed.) *The Big Picture: the Global Entertainment and Telecommunications Forecast*, London: American Chamber of Commerce (UK).

Porter, M. E. (1985) *Competitive Advantage: Creating and Sustaining Superior Performance*, New York: Free Press.

Qualen, J. (1985) *The Music Industry: the End of Vinyl*, London: Comedia.

Rawsthorne, A. (1999) 'Big Five Shudder at Digital Jukeboxes', *Financial Times*, 13 January

Roe, K. and Wallis, R. (1989) 'One Planet – One Music: the Development of Music Television in Europe', *Nordicom Review.* 35–41.

Romer, P. (1989) 'What Determines the Rate of Growth and Technological Change', *World Bank Working Papers* WPS 279.

Rutten, P. (1991) 'Local Popular Music on the National and International Markets', *Cultural Studies* 5: 294–305.

Samuelson, P. (1996) 'A Prohibition Law Glides Over the Internet', International UNESCO Symposium on the Effects of New Technology on Cultural Information, Transmission and Dissemination, the Protection of Authors' Rights and Other Holders of Rights, Cultural Developments and Trends in Social Life, Madrid, March 11–14 (available at http://negocios.com/tendencias/artic11.htm).

Sarraute, R. (1968) 'Current Theory on the Moral Right of Authors and Artists under French Law', *American Journal of Comparative Law* 16: 465–86.

Spender, J.-C. (1996) 'Making knowledge the basis of a dynamic theory of the firm', *Strategic Management Journal* 17 (winter special issue): 45–62.

Teece, D. (1998) 'Capturing Value from Knowledge Assets: the New Economy, Markets for Know-how, and Intangible Assets', *California Management Review* 40 (spring): 55–79.

Temple Lang, J. (1997) 'Media, Multimedia and European Community Antitrust Law', Competition Directorate of the European Commission (DGIV) working paper.

Times (1999) *Saturday Magazine*, 6 February: 37.

Towse, R. (1997) 'Copyright as an Economic Incentive', in H. L. MacQueen (ed.) Special Issue: 'Innovation, Incentive and Reward: Intellectual Property Law and Policy', *David Hume Papers on Public Policy* 5 (1): 31–45.

US Department of Commerce (1998) *The Emerging Digital Economy*, (available at www.ecommerce.gov).

US Patent and Trademark Office (1995) *Intellectual Property and the National*

Information Infrastructure: the Report of the Working Group on Intellectual Property (chaired by Bruce Lehman).

Vogel, H. L. (1994) *Entertainment Industry Economics* (third edn.), Cambridge: Cambridge University Press.

Wallis, R. (1990) 'Internationalisation, Localisation and Integration: the Changing Structure of the Music Industry', Dept. of Mass Communication, University of Gothenburg, working paper.

Wallis, R., Baden-Fuller, C., Klimis, G. M. and Kretschmer, M. (1998) 'Capturing Rents from Intellectual Property Rights', London: City University Business School, mimeo, October.

Wallis, R., Baden-Fuller, C., Kretschmer, M. and Klimis, G. M. 'Contested Collective Administration of Intellectual Property Rights in Music: the Challenge to the Principles of Reciprocity and Solidarity', *European Journal of Communication* 14 (1): 5–35.

9   International franchising

A network approach to FDI

Karin Fladmoe-Lindquist

Introduction

Franchising has become an important mechanism for many service firms to enter foreign markets. A 1998 survey conducted by the International Franchise Association indicated that of 578 franchisors, 41 per cent had some type of international operations (IFA 1999). Although many of these units are currently limited to Canada, the trend is towards greater overall international expansion. In addition, the pace of international investment by individual franchisors is also increasing. For example, by 1994, one quick service food franchisor had expanded its operations to sixty-five countries with over 4,000 franchised outlets, even though it only began international operations in 1967 (Sadi 1994).

Consequently, global franchising has become a significant form of foreign direct investment in services. Its structure of control systems and mix of corporate and contractual arrangements (Bradach 1998) create a complex web of relationships that are central to its foreign direct investment efforts. Typically, these relationships are examined as market-based dyadic franchisor–franchisee agreements. However, the increasing use of multi-unit agreements and the system of franchisees in other countries raises the level of interdependence among franchise system participants and creates a network of formal and informal relationships. Although a network perspective has been applied to understanding the globalization of professional services (Aharoni 1993), it has not been used to understand FDI in franchising.

Because of the complexity of relationships involved in international franchising, this paper moves beyond the decision of whether or not to franchise in a foreign market entry decision (Contractor 1985; Root 1994). It proposes that international franchising may be examined through a network view that suggests FDI performs an important resource seeking activity through the creation of linkages and network relationships (Johanson and Mattson 1988). This does not suggest that other FDI explanations (such as Hymer's (1960) firm-specific advantage) are not applicable to international franchising. However, an alternate relationship-based approach may enhance our understanding of the drive to pursue foreign investment by international franchisors. This relationship-based approach is particularly valuable in examining the service sector where the separation of customer and provider is less distinct and linkages among actors are central to achieving and maintaining competitive advantage.

To address this gap, this paper examines how a network perspective on FDI informs our understanding of international franchising. Furthermore, it describes the four key dimensions of network theory that are central to franchising FDI. These are: a shared sense of identity, collective learning, franchise partner status, and the role of franchise network culture. Ultimately, it argues that FDI through international franchising provides an important collective resource access and learning mechanism that would be more limited under corporate-ownership.

Characteristics of international franchising

Most of the international growth in franchising over the last twenty years has been in the specific area of business format franchising. In this type of franchise arrangement, the owner of a business concept (franchisor) enters into a contract with an independent actor (franchisee) to use a specific 'model' to sell services or goods under the franchisor's trademark. This approach to franchising involves a set of procedures, designs, management approaches, and services that are to be delivered exactly as specified by the franchisor. For example, McDonald's French fries use a specific potato (Idaho russet) and are cut to precise sizes, regardless of the country that they are served in. The importance of the type of potato to its business format led McDonald's to develop the production of Idaho russets in Russia and Eastern Europe with local contract farmers.

International franchising is frequently associated with service firms, such as hotels, retail outlets, and quick service restaurants. These firms often have strongly identifiable trademarks and try to guarantee the customer a uniform and consistent level of service and product quality across different locations and over time. However, the high degree of standardized operations makes the replication of the format across diverse markets difficult. Differences in things such as key ingredients, labour, and physical space can force significant modifications to the service formula. In Japan, the smaller space of the Tokyo outlets forced KFC to reconfigure its cooking equipment from a wide, horizontal design that worked in the free-standing US style of restaurant to a narrower, more vertical design that saved space (Bartlett and Rangan 1987). Consequently, in international franchising, the fundamental service may be similar to that of the home country, but details in the delivery of the service are often altered. The challenge is to adapt the format in response to the local market without affecting the overall image and service of the franchise.

The use of contracts in international franchising also varies from the standard approaches used in domestic operations. Because of the importance of consistency across outlets (both franchised and corporate-owned), the primary research focus of franchising has been on understanding how best to ensure that the franchisee delivers the business format service as specified by the franchisor. Typically, it is believed that this can be achieved through well-designed contract mechanisms such as fees and royalties (LaFontaine 1992; LaFontaine and Kaufmann 1994). However, contracts become more difficult to monitor and enforce in the international environment as a result of time and distance (Fladmoe-Lindquist and Jacque 1994). The use of standard contracts that is common in the domestic setting (Shane 1998) is less common internationally where contracts are usually modified for host country laws and cultural differences. Even the use of a contract often takes on a different meaning in the diverse cultural and legal environments of international business (Trompenaars and Hampden-Turner 1998).

Finally, the importance of the foreign franchisee to overall operations relative to that of most individual domestic franchisees is often greater as well. First, in international franchising, the foreign franchisees are often major multinational firms rather than small, independent entrepreneurs. This may be a result of greater awareness by the larger host country firms regarding the franchisor's business concept. Such firms also are attractive franchisees due to their strong financial position and longevity in business making them less 'risky' partners in an unfamiliar business environment. In Japan, Burger King's franchise partner is Japan Tobacco, one of Japan's largest firms and reflects JT's efforts to diversify its business portfolio (CNNfn 1996). Many of the international agreements also involve either a joint venture or a strategic alliance, as in the case of Japan Tobacco and Burger King. This type of relationship typically is more extensive in its contract terms than a simple franchise agreement and places additional responsibilities on both the franchisee and the franchisor.

Second, the importance of the foreign franchisee is also increased because of the number of units for which it may hold development rights. International franchising often makes extensive use of different types of multi-unit franchising agreements. Generally, multi-unit franchising refers to either master franchise arrangements or area development agreements (IFA 1995; Bradach 1998). In these agreements, franchisees are assigned the rights to larger blocks of units covering a specific geographic area. Additionally, the master franchise agreement allows the franchisee to recruit and enter into contracts with additional sub-franchisees. The use of multi-unit franchising internationally has been an important method for franchisors to be able to expand their operations without the need to monitor and evaluate numerous distant franchisees. The popularity of this approach is reflected in the findings by the 1995 IFA survey of 169 international franchisors who indicated that they heavily used master franchise agreements (81 per cent) for their international operations (IFA 1995: 33). The use of area development agreements had also increased and was used by 71 per cent of the surveyed franchisors. The implication of this expansion approach, however, is that a single franchisee may hold the rights to all development for several countries and can become a powerful actor in the franchise system.

Taken together, these differences regarding partner size, contract type and quantity of units in international franchising fundamentally affect the relationship between the franchisor and the franchisee. The bargaining power between the two parties becomes more equal than has been true domestically. Franchisees are in a position to demand a greater role in the local decision-making and are also more interested in receiving information from and sharing information with the franchisor. Franchisees become more than simply a method to run distant outlets and can provide important access to resources and contacts in foreign markets.

International franchising research

Generally, the research on international franchising has pursued four major approaches. First, early research examined the impact of key country variables and concluded that host government policies and monetary uncertainties such as royalty repatriation requirements were major concerns that discouraged some franchisors from pursuing international expansion (Hackett 1976). Although this initial work was helpful in identifying early franchisor concerns, most of it was atheoretical and did not incorporate a clear conceptual grounding. Additionally, key cultural and regulatory differences were not directly integrated into the research. Such differences have been important in many businesses, not just franchising, in choosing market entry approaches and pursuing FDI (Root 1994; Dunning 1993a).

The second key stream has focused primarily on the franchisors' general interest in foreign markets or their reasons for not entering international markets. For example, Aydin and Kacker (1990) investigated US-based franchisors' international expansion intentions. They concluded that the primary reasons that firms remained domestic were adequacy of opportunities in the US and lack of international knowledge and competencies. Kedia et al. (1994) alternatively suggest that the attitudes of a firm's managers are better indicators of the likelihood for a firm to franchise internationally. The two managerial attitudes that were found most important were a strong desire to expand and to increase profits. Although each of these studies provided helpful insights into the interests and motivations of franchisors, neither investigated directly the impact of the host country context on issues of agent monitoring and risk.

The third research stream extends the work that examined the franchise decision in the domestic context from an administrative efficiency perspective (Brickley and Dark 1987; Brickley and Weisbach 1991). This approach integrates agency and transaction cost analysis to examine principal/agent risk and monitoring issues. Here, Fladmoe-Lindquist and Jacque (1994) examined the likelihood of using franchising in several service industries world-wide. They found that similar to the domestic context, distance and monitoring were important factors. In addition, the extent of cultural differences and years of international experience were also relevant. This research, however, did not integrate key elements of the system of relationships into the franchise decision.

Finally, a fourth approach examines the key franchisor capabilities that are central for successful international franchising. Huszagh *et al.* (1992) identified core competencies that allow franchisors to expand internationally, and concluded that experience and size were important factors in the expansion decision. Shane (1996a) builds upon this perspective and suggests that a superior capability for reducing opportunism is central to international expansion. He concludes that the specific characteristics that explain international franchising, such as monitoring management, differ from those important in domestic franchising. Finally, Fladmoe-Lindquist (1996) applies dynamic capabilities theory to propose a framework that distinguishes among different types of international franchisors. She suggests that franchisors will fall into four broad groups depending on their ability to manage their international franchise relationships and operate in a foreign context. Although the capabilities perspective begins to expand the thinking on alternate explanations for international franchising and FDI, it still does not address the set of relationships that are created by the system of franchisor and franchisees.

Clearly, research suggests that franchising can and does provide a very efficient and effective approach to business expansion (Martin 1988; LaFontaine and Kaufmann 1994; Brickley and Dark 1987; Oxenfeldt and Kelly 1969; Shane 1996a, 1996b). While research on the international aspects of franchising is expanding, more needs to be understood regarding the system of relationships among the franchise participants. International franchisors are more typically described in a rather static and dyadic context that does not address the complexity of the set of network relationships that are central in the internationalization process.

Foreign direct investment and franchising

Traditionally, it is suggested that a firm-specific advantage was a key element to understanding why a firm would invest in another country (Hymer 1960, 1976). A firm needed a substantial advantage over host country firms in order to compensate for the time, distance, and cost incurred through foreign market investment. This firm-specific advantage might include a specific resource as well as the capabilities to more efficiently organize transactions (Dunning 1993b; Hennart 1982; Buckley and Casson 1976). For example, McDonald's extensive experience and marketing has built a global brand name and operational system which results in a substantial firm-specific advantage over the lesser known Bob's Hamburgers of Rio de Janeiro.

A second explanation for FDI focuses on a more evolutionary perspective in which firms were expected to follow a progression of increasing commitment and involvement. Over time, the firms' products matured and they gained experience of the complexities of conducting business over long distances in cultures different from that of the home country (Aharoni 1966; Johanson and Valne 1977; Perlmutter 1969; Vernon 1966). This explanation can also be applied to franchisors such as McDonald's Corporation. As awareness of foreign opportunities increased and home markets became more competitive, McDonald's has expanded its world-wide operations to include more than 8,500 foreign franchised and affiliated outlets (McDonald's Corporation 1999).

Together, these two approaches to FDI are powerful explanations of why a franchisor would choose to expand its general operations to a foreign country. However, they only provide part of the story because they do not address the network of relationships among the franchisor, franchisees, buyers and suppliers that can be critical to maintaining an integrated franchise image and system. It is this system that is a fundamental ingredient of the firm-specific advantage as well as the increased awareness of opportunities and host country resources. Consequently, a third, less common approach to FDI is important to address: the network approach to FDI (Johanson and Mattson 1988). This explanation of FDI suggests that a key purpose for FDI is to gain access to critical resources and relationships in foreign countries (Chen and Chen 1998). This may be achieved through extension into an entirely new national network, expanding a current position, or co-ordinating and integrating a position among several national networks (Johanson and Mattson 1988). The critical element of this approach, however, is the perspective that FDI involves a system of relationships that are needed to attain specific resources that are not otherwise available. This explanation captures the final, critical element of international franchising as a method for foreign direct investment. It involves the complete system of relationships among the franchisor and franchisees that are crucial for developing and transferring resources, including ideas for new products and services, and technologies for improved service delivery. The system of relationships also serves as an important mechanism for gathering information regarding new opportunities or partners for outlet expansion and development. For example, the ideas for the original Egg McMuffin and the Big Mac came from franchisees in the McDonald's network and now are two of the best selling items on the system's menu.

Network approach to international franchising and FDI

Although previous research has focused on the franchisor–franchisee relationship as a dyad, a franchise system is a much more extensive set of firms that includes the franchisor and all of the different franchisee firms. Because of the fundamental business contract, the primary relationship is clearly between the franchisor and each franchisee firm. In practice, all of the franchisees are connected and interdependent, both informally and formally. The 'informal' ties occur through participation in the franchise business in which the reputation and success of each franchisee has the potential to impact the reputation and success of all the other franchisees. Poor performance by one franchisee can sour customers on the general business and discourage them from purchasing from another unit, regardless of ownership. For example, in December 1998, a Dunkin' Donut franchisee in New York City was discovered to have mice on its shelves of doughnuts (*New York Post* 1998). The franchisor has sued the franchisee for termination of the franchise contract for degradation of the franchise concept and failure to uphold standards. Although the franchisee only operated in that geographical area, the resulting publicity can affect the reputation and sales of other outlets as well. Not only was the offense on the front page of the *Post*, but it was also broadcast on national network news as well as discussed on syndicated shows such as David Letterman.

The formal relationships often emerge through membership in franchisee associations. As a result of the their mutual dependence on the business format and their relationship with the franchisor, many franchisee systems have developed franchisor independent organizations. These groups sometimes act as a negotiator with the franchisor, create a forum for advancing ideas, and provide an environment for airing complaints. Both Burger King and McDonald's Restaurants have large franchisee associations that have been active in discussions with the respective corporate franchisors regarding changes and innovations to the franchise system. In fact, a major impetus for some of the current changes in the McDonald's system has come from the franchisees who see the market stagnating in the US (Barboza 1999). Consequently, franchising can be conceptualised as a complex network of formal and informal interdependent relationships and contracts among the franchisees and franchisor.

Network theory's primary concern with examining relationships among actors (Nohria 1992) makes it particularly appropriate for franchising. Broadly, network theory focuses on understanding the set of ties between parties and the role that such linkages play in the actions and decisions of particular groups. The general proposition is that the connections between parties provide an important mechanism for understanding several key issues. These include:

- the relationship patterns within organizations as well as between organizations and their external environments;
- the positions of actors and their actions;
- the constraints that such networks impose on actions;
- the comparative effects of different organization's networks.

(Nohria 1992)

Within this broad agenda of the network perspective, research has tried to more finely examine different aspects of network relationships under various conditions. Different features that have been investigated include the density of the ties (Powell *et al.* 1996), collaborative routines (Powell and Brantley 1992), structural embeddedness (Uzzi 1997), and social capital (Nahapiet and Ghoshal 1998). In addition, collective identity (Saxenian 1994), collective learning (Powell *et al.* 1996), partner status (Podolny 1994), and network culture (Jones *et al.* 1997) have received substantial attention.

It is proposed here that these last four particular elements of network systems are especially important to understanding international franchising as a form of FDI. These dimensions – shared identity, collective learning, franchise partner status and franchise network culture – contribute to the ability of franchisors to access distant resources in the global expansion and internationalization process. These four are discussed separately in greater detail below.

Shared identities

One of the important observations by Saxenian (1990, 1994) regarding her research on high technology firms in Silicon Valley is the sense of 'community' among the firms and participants in the high technology region. The members of the region have a shared sense of a common identity and purpose that has contributed significantly to the advancement of the members both individually and as a group. Along the same lines, Kogut and Zander (1996) discuss the important role that shared identity plays in the definition of the firm. Fundamentally, shared identity is thought to reduce communication costs as well as perform an important role in the ability to co-ordinate activities (Kogut and Zander 1996), and to learn through combining and exchanging knowledge among various parties (Nahapiet and Ghoshal 1998).

Although a franchise system is not geographically based in the same sense as addressed by these researchers, it requires a shared identity among the franchisor and the various franchisee units for the system to be successful (Bradach 1998; Caves and Murphy 1976). The identity that binds the system is a unique combination of the brand name, the service, and the operational system. The requirements of a business format system demand that this shared identity be carefully cultivated and guarded. Deviations from the standards of the identity are grounds for franchise contract termination. Classic symbols of this identity that are recognized world-wide include the golden arches of McDonald's and KFC's Colonel Sanders.

The franchise system's shared identity facilitates the pursuit of FDI by a franchisor. The image and reputation that result from the shared identity serves to attract potential franchisee inquiries regarding business and partnership opportunities. This 'pull' approach to franchisee search can reduce search time and costs when a franchisor is considering an initial expansion into different markets. For example, the European quick food service firm, Autogrill, has considered expanding its restaurant line to include hamburgers. In this case, Autogrill initiated the search process and discussions with Burger King regarding the possibility of including Burger King in its facilities (*Wall Street Journal* 1999). This process is consistent with the evidence that much of international franchising is actually initiated by requests from prospective franchisees rather than by franchisors looking for new places to expand the business (IFA 1995). The 1995 IFA study indicated that of the 169 international franchisors, 68 per cent expanded in response to unsolicited prospective franchisee inquiries. Only 18 per cent of the respondents actually pursued expansion through a proactive strategic plan that involved franchisor initiated searches (IFA 1995). It is Burger King's name and reputation through its shared identity that allowed Autogrill to identify it as a potential partner in the first place and gives BK the possibility of alternative retail outlets that it may not have considered.

Shared identity, therefore, is an important network property that facilitates access (Saxenian 1990) to restricted resources which may not be otherwise available because of close ties and pre-existing relationships (Jones *et al.* 1997). Fundamentally, it facilitates the extension of the franchise business into an entirely new national network or market and reduces information costs associated with the search process. For example, KFC was able to gain access, and achieved a major market position in Japan as a result of the efforts by Mitsubishi to find an outlet for its chicken operations (Bartlett and Rangan 1987).

Collective learning

A second important aspect of international franchising is the potential ability of the system to engage in 'collective' learning. The network can serve as an important mechanism for innovation and learning when there is a broad distribution of knowledge (Powell *et al.*1996). In addition, collective learning is closely related to the concept of shared identity. One of the important benefits of shared identity is that it also facilitates collective learning because of the sense of community (Kogut and Zander 1996).

Within international franchising, this sense of collective learning may be an important, yet often under-utilized feature of the system. The franchisor needs to transfer important knowledge and changes throughout the entire system of both corporate-owned and franchisee-owned units. Yet, depending on the contract and relationships, it may be difficult to impose certain changes on the franchised units. In fact, one of the key management challenges identified by Bradach (1998) is that of system-wide adaptation in which all parties must adopt new products, services and technologies. This process is complex because any change must be appropriate for the wide variety of markets (both domestic and international) in which the franchise system operates, yet it must also be simple enough that the required business format uniformity can be maintained. Ultimately, the process of system-wide adaptation involves both mandate and persuasion. Franchisors are able to implement such changes by order in corporate outlets, but must rely on persuasion with the franchisees (Bradach 1998).

Historically, most franchisors have used an 'international' approach (Bartlett and Ghoshal 1989) to foreign direct investment. In this approach, the firm transfers its knowledge and expertise to foreign locations without much modification or effort to transfer learning from the host country to home. There has been minimal concern for either global efficiency or local responsiveness. Essentially, this has emphasized a corporate centred approach to development and diffusion of innovation that assumed that the original business format was transferable to most host country environments. Within franchising, this meant that the franchisee was given limited permission to make changes to the format within a narrow permitted 'band' of modifications. Despite such restrictions, most foreign franchisees typically have been given more latitude in local adaptation that has been true for domestic franchisees. In quick service restaurants, some international franchisees may make specific menu additions to cater to local tastes (e.g. beer in Europe). The ability to understand local culture and make appropriate changes has been viewed as one of the major contributions of a foreign franchisee to franchise operations (Abell 1990).

The 'international approach' to FDI is beginning to be reconsidered in franchising, as it already is being re-evaluated in other industries such as machinery and opticals (Bartlett and Ghoshal 1989). For international franchising to be successful as more firms develop expertise and enter the market, there will be increased need to engage in some form of system-wide collective learning by all members in a franchise system (Bradach 1998). Collective learning allows the franchisor and franchisee firms to adapt to changing circumstances and also allows them to develop more efficient means or routines for co-ordination.

Interestingly, McDonald's is an example of a franchisor that has been successful with its collective learning in its international operations, but has only recently begun to apply it to its domestic operations. Part of its international success has come from recognizing the value of its foreign franchise network and allowing learning, knowledge transfer, and appropriate modification to flow. In addition to menu modification, it has also allowed host country franchisees systems to create local supply infrastructures as well. It is now attempting to integrate this more decentralized approach into its domestic operations and relationships as it attempts to re-establish its position in the US market (Barboza 1999). As part of this agenda, it intends to create five management zones in the US that will have the authority to make major changes (Horowitz 1999).

Franchise collective learning also becomes important for FDI because of its information sensing benefits. The national franchisees can play an important role in collecting and diffusing information regarding new opportunities and issues regarding competitors. Fundamentally, it allows the franchisor and its franchisees to collect information regarding potential opportunities, synergies, and new franchise partners through indirect relationships (Gulati 1995). Such information is nearly impossible to gain through direct franchisor experience. The impact of time, distance, and different cultural systems with remote outlets makes it much more difficult to acquire such critical information. Consequently, the remote sensing resource that is created by the large franchise network helps not only increase awareness of opportunities and threats, but can also identify potential franchisees that will be more successful partners. Unfortunately, franchisors do not always take advantage of such information sensing opportunities. In the case of Arby's in Mexico, the American franchisor failed to take advantage of the information that its subfranchisee tried to communicate regarding the adverse impacts of exchange rate fluctuation and economic instability. The result was a significant loss of capital and time for both the subfranchisee and franchisor (Hoy and Hoy Echegaray 1994).

The collective learning function of international franchising is an important element of network FDI. Ultimately, this collective learning may be considered a network resource (Gulati 1999) that may be used to access additional resources and future network partners. The information and know-how that can be gained through the network will ultimately provide ideas on new technologies, services and products that may be offered both locally and at home. Furthermore, the experiences of other international franchisees in some less developed markets may be more helpful in understanding the application of the franchise business format than the experience of the corporate franchisor whose own experience may be limited to more sophisticated markets. In other words, the solutions of a Brazilian franchisee to unstable markets may be more valuable to the Indonesian or Mexican franchisees than those of the American corporate office. These franchisees will have a more intimate understanding of local values, technologies, and economics that may affect modifications to the business format. Finally, the collective learning aspect will be particularly important in expanding a current position in a national network (Johanson and Mattson 1988). Without a clear understanding of the existing network resources and the local supporting infrastructure, such expansion can be hampered.

Franchisee partner status

The status of the franchisee, as well as its broad set of relationships and social capital within its own national network, also affects international franchising. In network research, the concept of status refers to a superior position within a specific social group based on prestige or economic and political power (Jones *et al.* 1998). Affiliation with such a partner is often an important mechanism for improving one's own position (Podolny 1994). Within international business, the status of a local partner in its national network can have a major effect on the foreign direct investment efforts of a firm. Partners with greater status can provide significant access to political and business systems that might otherwise be difficult to enter. This is broadly supported by the finding that partner status is an important element in the creation of successful strategic alliances and joint ventures (Contractor and Lorange 1988).

The ability of a foreign partner to access resources derives from the larger set of relationships and social capital that it holds. In network analysis, social capital involves the complete set of existing and possible resources that result from the relationships among the actors within the network (Nahapiet and Ghoshal 1998). These relationships have the potential to provide important sources of suppliers, customers, and ideas that can greatly facilitate the management of the business from remote locations.

In domestic franchising, partner status and social capital are of less importance because the franchisor already has significant knowledge of key markets and industry participants. The international arena is a very different matter, however. The political, market, and cultural systems may vary significantly from the domestic context. Well-positioned and connected franchise partners can make the difference between success and failure for franchise FDI.

Two firms, KFC and Burger King, are good examples of the use of partner status in franchise FDI. In Japan, KFC's franchise partner is Mitsubishi. The size and position of Mitsubishi in its industrial group (i.e. *keiretsu*) has allowed KFC better access to resources than if it had tried to enter Japan alone, or with a less influential company. Also in Japan, Burger King has developed a franchise joint venture with Japan Tobacco (CNNfn 1996). The ample resources of Japan Tobacco are important for Burger King due to its late entry into the Japanese market where McDonald's has been operating for more than twenty years. Consequently, Burger King needs a partner that has both substantial financial and network resources to help it rapidly increase its presence in the Japanese market.

Status and social capital are important to international franchisors for several reasons. First, they can provide access to a national network that may otherwise be difficult to enter (Johanson and Mattson 1988). In many countries, FDI is an involved process that requires many different governmental agencies and local firms. High status partners with significant social capital can help facilitate the approval process.

Second, international franchisors may also use high status partners to increase their own standing within a national network. For example, in Bolivia, Burger King is owned and operated by an individual who is also the largest shareholder of a major cement manufacturing firm (Burger King 1999). In Bolivia, the cement industry is among the five most important industries in the national economy. Consequently, the local franchisee holds a significant position in the Bolivian market through his broader business connections. In countries where relationships can be as or more important than the actual contract (Trompenaars and Hampden-Turner 1998), a franchisee with such status may confer legitimacy and status to the franchisor by association.

Finally, the social capital that results from such high status relationships may be valuable in ensuring that the business format and reputation of the franchise is maintained. A major managerial challenge in franchising is trying to uphold an 'identical' and integrated image and service regardless of the different business contexts (Bradach 1998). As a result, a reliable supplier infrastructure is a requirement and the importance of these suppliers to the franchise system cannot be overstated. These actors provide the basic ingredients of the franchise system's format and are essential to achieve the needed consistency, uniformity, and quality. In Russia, McDonald's has constructed its own supplier network to ensure both the quality and quantity of key ingredients, such as beef. High status franchisees can reduce the need for a franchisor to create its own network by helping to identify and providing access to the secondary network of more reliable, higher status suppliers. At the same time, the cost of non-compliance and failure by a supplier may be increased because of the already embedded system of relationships among the participants. Essentially, the failure to perform in one arena may have adverse, long-term effects in other relationships, as well.

In sum, franchise partners can provide access to host country resources that may not be as easily available if a franchisor pursues FDI with a lower status, less connected partner. In terms of the three approaches of network FDI (Johanson and Mattson 1988), partner status will be particularly relevant when entering into an unfamiliar national network. Not only is the initial partner important, but so is the network infrastructure of suppliers that such partners may have in their constellation of relationships (Jones *et al.*1998).

Franchise network culture

Business format franchising involves the adherence to a system of business practices, norms and values that are central to its implementation (Bradach 1998). Taken together, this system constitutes an organizational culture that exerts control over its members (Ouchi 1980; Wilkins and Ouchi 1983) and facilitates the replication of the franchise format across many different and diverse locations. By its nature, however, franchising involves a more extensive set of relationships than just that of the core organization of the franchisor. As a result, concepts of network culture are helpful to understand the last element of franchising FDI. Network culture may be viewed as a subset of social capital and includes a set of shared beliefs, norms, and language (Jones *et al.* 1997; Nahapiet and Ghoshal 1998). The development of a shared identity (discussed previously) is a key element in the formation of a network culture (Kogut and Zander 1996; Saxenian 1994).

Franchise network culture is essential to creating common norms and shared values concerning the mutual expectations (both explicit and implicit) that are basic to both franchise co-ordination and the successful replication of its service concept. The complexity of delivering outwardly identical services in varied environments requires not only explicit routines and standards (Nelson and Winter 1982), but also a willingness not to free-ride on the performance of other members in the franchise system. A major concern in franchising is the possibility that a franchisee may take advantage of the lack of immediate oversight by the franchisor and under-invest his or her efforts in a particular franchise unit (Brickely and Dark 1987; Rubin 1978). The overall performance of the complete system and the adherance to the standards and values by the other system members effectively allows such under-performing franchisees to do well without complying with the franchise system's expectations. Although contracts, royalties and fees attempt to control such behaviours, without a shared culture, the problem of franchisee free-riding can be further exacerbated. The more that franchisees believe in the culture of the franchise format concept, the more likely they are to try to maintain the image and the standards of the franchise system.

Given this concern for free riding, the use of a shared language within franchise network culture is important for both technical and relational reasons. Although important domestically, shared language takes on even more importance internationally where time and distance can interfere with the technical aspects of the implementation process. Common definitions and specifications of products, services and routines ensure that the delivery of core items will be nearly identical from one outlet to another. In order to achieve the common identity of image, product and service, it is essential to transfer the central elements of the business format franchise without error. Otherwise, misunderstandings and mistakes may occur that can adversely affect the implementation and extension of the common franchise format.

From a relational standpoint, shared language also helps maintain the sense of a collective agenda and identity in delivering consistent, uniform services over long distances. As discussed above, one of the difficulties with distant franchisees is the possibility of free-riding behaviour on the reputation of the overall franchise network. The further away the franchisee is located from the corporate offices, the more important communication becomes in an effort to moderate potential free-riding behaviour. Communication through the use of a common, shared language both creates and supports the set of norms and values that form a basis of network franchise culture. Thus, the use of shared language serves as an important relational tool to encourage adherence to franchise standards and the control of the systems members (Jones *et al.* 1997).

Lastly, the franchise culture has the potential to allow the franchisor access to resources that might not be otherwise available. An important aspect of network culture is that it can help identify potential opportunities, formulate agreements, and co-ordinate and adapt actions (Jones, Hesterly and Borgatti 1997). This allows both opportunities and threats to be more quickly and easily identified because there is a common language along with a set of norms and beliefs that allows both information and knowledge to be transferred (Uzzi 1997). Fundamentally, franchise network culture is necessary to create the linkages that allow access to international resources. This would be particularly important in pursuing the integration aspect of FDI that focuses on the co-ordination of positions in different national networks (Johanson and Mattson 1988) and will be critical as franchisors move from an 'international' to more of a 'transnational' type of strategy (Bartlett and Ghoshal 1989).

Conclusions and recommendations

This paper develops an alternative explanation for FDI in franchising. It proposes that a network approach to FDI in international franchising enhances our understanding of the collective advantages of using franchise agreements for resource access. It also suggests that four key aspects of network theory are central to franchising FDI. These are a shared sense of identity, collective learning, franchise partner status, and the role of franchise network culture. These four dimensions facilitate access to resources, ideas and partners (both formal and informal) that might otherwise be difficult to gain.

Implications for research

For researchers in international business, this framework supports the contention that it is important to understand an organization's network in examining international co-operative interfirm relationships (Walker 1988). Although these network dimensions are important even in the domestic context, they take on additional value in the international environment due to differences in social and political–legal systems that are compounded by the impact of time and distance. In many countries, the system of relationships is much more important than is the fundamental contract (Trompenaars and Hampden-Turner 1998). This suggests that an important aspect of international success in franchising may depend on the franchisor's ability to transfer its collective culture, learning, and identity through its organizational systems. Furthermore, the value of identifying partners with position and status in the national network may be a fundamental requirement for long-term success. This is particularly true given that most franchise agreements run for a minimum of ten years, and an inadequate partner could adversely affect the franchise's development for a long time as well as adversely impact other franchisees.

For researchers within the franchise literature, it is important to begin to examine alternative theories such as the network perspective. While administrative efficiency and contracts are still important issues in franchising, the broader set of relationships also merits attention. Even within the domestic context, major franchisors such as McDonald's and KFC are moving toward cultivating close connections with groups of key franchisees.

This discussion should be viewed as a first step toward integrating network concepts into understanding international franchise FDI. Future research should examine other network characteristics such as collective routines and reputation for their impact on franchise investment and expansion decisions. Also, successful relationships and partners are not always selected the first time even under the best of circumstances. Consequently, it would be useful to examine the shift in networks and the pattern of relationships among the franchisor and its franchisees and how such shifts affect franchise success.

Implications for practice

The inclusion of network variables in this discussion should help international franchisors understand that FDI should also be treated as an important source of resources, both tangible and intangible. This may facilitate a shift from looking at the expansion of franchising as an international strategy to one that moves it closer to a transnational approach (Bartlett and Ghoshal 1989). Just as many of the larger manufacturing multinationals have discovered that the network of relationships provides important sources of information and know-how, so too may the franchisors (Barboza 1999). As a result, it is important to not only develop a set of relationships, but also to develop the routines that support and integrate ongoing collective learning, identity, and culture. Such systems will be necessary to retain a competitive position at home and abroad.

References

Abell, M. (1990) *The International Franchise Option*, London: Waterlow.

Aharoni, Y. (1966) *The Foreign Investment Decision Process*, Boston: Harvard Business School.

Aharoni, Y. (1993) 'Ownerships, Networks and Coalitions', in Y. Aharoni (ed.) *Coalitions and competition: the globalization of professional business services*, 121–42, Routledge: London.

Aydin, N. and Kacker, M. (1990) 'International outlook of US based franchisers', *International Marketing Review* 7 (2): 43–53.

Barboza, D. (1999) 'Pluralism under the golden arches', *New York Times*, 21 February 1999: C1,C7

Bartlett, C. A. and Ghoshal, S. (1989) *Managing across Borders: the Transnational Solution*, Boston: Harvard Business School Press.

Bartlett, C. A. and Rangan, U. (1987) 'Kentucky Fried Chicken (Japan) Limited', Harvard Business School, case no. #9-387-043, Boston: Harvard Business School Press.

Bradach, J. (1998) *Franchise Organizations*, Cambridge, Mass.: Harvard Business School Press.

Brickley, J. A. and Dark, F. H. (1987) 'The Choice of Organizational Form: the Case of Franchising', *Journal of Financial Economics* 18(2): 401–420.

Brickley, J. A. and Weisbach, M. S. (1991) 'An Agency Perspective on Franchising', *Financial Management* 20 (1): 27–35.

Buckley, P. and Casson, M. (1976) *The Future of the Multinational Enterprise*, London: Macmillan.

Burger King. (1999) 'Burger King Enters Bolivia', Corporate press release, 12 March.

Caves, R. E. and Murphy, W. F. (1976) 'Franchising: Firms, Markets, and Intangible Assets', *Southern Economic Journal* 42 (4): 572–86.

Chen, H. and Chen, T.-J. (1998) 'Network Linkages and Location Choice in Foreign Direct Investment', *Journal of International Business Studies* 29 (3): 445–68.

Combs, J. G. and Castrogiovanni, G. J. (1994) 'Franchisor Strategy: a Proposed Model and Empirical Test of Franchise Versus Company Ownership', *Journal of Small Business Management* 32 (2): 37–48.

Contractor, F. (1985) *Licensing in International Strategy*, Westport, Conn.: Quorum.

Contractor, F. and Lorange, P. (1988) *Cooperative Strategies in International Business*, New York: Lexington.

CNNfn (1996) 'BK to Storm Tokyo', Cable News Network Financial News, 14 November.

Dunning, J. (1993a) *The Globalization of Business*, London and New York: Routledge.
—— (1993b) *Multinational Enterprises and the Global Economy*, Reading, Mass.: Addison-Wesley.

Dyer, J. and Singh, H. (1998) 'The Relational View: Cooperative Strategy and Sources of Interorganizational Competitive Advantage', *Academy of Management Review* 23 (4): 660–79.

Fladmoe-Lindquist, K. and Jacque, L. L. (1994) 'Control Modes in International Service Operations: Explaining the Propensity to Franchise', *Management Science* 41 (7): 1238–49.

Fladmoe-Lindquist, K. (1996) 'International Franchising: Capabilities and Development', *Journal of Business Venturing* 11 (5): 419–38.

Gulati, R. (1995) 'Social Structure and Alliance Formation Patterns: a Longitudinal Analysis', *Administrative Science Quarterly* 40: 619–52.

—— (1999) 'Network Location and Learning: the Influence of Network Resources and Firm Capabilities on Alliance Formation', *Strategic Management Journal* 20 (5): 397–421.

Hackett, D.W. (1976) 'The International Expansion of US Franchise Systems: Status and Strategies', *Journal of International Business Studies* 7: 65–75.

Hennart, J-F. (1982) *A Theory of Multinational Enterprise*, Ann Arbor: University of Michigan Press.

Horowitz, B. (1999) 'Restoring the Golden-arch Shine', *USA Today*, 16 June: 3B

Hoy, F. and Hoy Echegaray, M. (1994) 'Double your Trouble through International Franchising: Arby's Goes to Mexico', conference paper, Babson Entrepreneurship Research Conference, June.

Huszagh, S.M., Huszagh, F. W. and McIntyre, F. (1992) 'International Franchising in the Context of Competitive Strategy and the Theory of the Firm', *International Marketing Review* 9 (5): 5–18.

Hymer, S. (1960, 1976) *The International Operations of National Firms*, Cambridge, Mass.: MIT Press.

IFA (International Franchise Association) (1995) *International Expansion by US Franchisors*, Washington D.C.: IFA Educational Foundation.

—— (1999) 'IFA Member International Operations Survey', *Franchising World*, January/ February: 12

Johanson, J. and Mattson, L.-G. (1988) 'Internationalization in Industrial Systems: a Network Approach', in N. Hood and J.-E. Valne (eds) *Strategies in Global Competition*, London: Routledge.

Johanson, J. K. and Vahlne, J.-E. (1977) 'The Internationalization Process of the Firm: a Model of Knowledge Development and Increasing Foreign Market Commitments', *Journal of International Business Studies* 8 (spring/summer): 23–32.

Jones, C., Hesterly, W. and Borgatti, S. (1997) 'A General Theory of Network Governance: Exchange Conditions and Social Mechanisms', *Academy of Management Review* 22 (4): 911–45.

Jones, C., Hesterly, W., Fladmoe-Lindquist, K. and Borgatti, S. (1998) 'Professional Service Constellations: How Strategies and Capabilities Influence Collaborative Stability and Change', *Organization Science* 9 (3): 396–410.

Kedia, B. L., Ackerman, D., Bush, D. and Justis, R. (1994) 'Determinants of Internationalization of Franchise Operations by US Franchisors: a Study Note', *International Marketing Review* 11 (4): 56–69.

Kogut, B. and Zander, U. (1996) 'What Firms Do? Coordination, Identity and Learning', *Organization Science* 7 (5): 502–18.

LaFontaine, F. (1992) 'Agency Theory and Franchising: Some Empirical Results', *Rand Journal of Economics* 23 (2): 263–83.

LaFontaine, F. and Kaufmann, P. (1994) 'The Evolution of Ownership Patterns in Franchise Systems', *Journal of Retailing* 70 (2): 97–114.

Martin, R. E. (1988) 'Franchising and Risk Management', *The American Economic Review* 78 (5): 954–68.

McDonald's Corporation. (1999) 'McDonald's Announces Strong Global Results, 2–for–1 Stock Split and Dividend', McDonald's press release, 26 January.

Nahapiet, J. and Ghoshal, S. (1998) 'Social Capital, Intellectual Capital, and Organizational Advantage', *Academy of Management Review* 23 (2): 242–66.

Nelson, R. and Winter, S. (1982) *An Evolutionary Theory of Economic Change*, Cambridge, Mass.: Harvard University Press.

New York Post (1998) 'Under Mouse Arrest', 31 December: 1.

Nohria, N. (1992) 'Introduction: Is a Network Perspective a Useful Way of Studying Organizations?', in N. Nohria and R. G. Eccles (eds) *Networks and Organizations: Structure, Form, and Action*, 1–22, Boston: Harvard Business School Press.

Ouchi, W. (1980) 'Markets, Bureaucracies, and Clans', *Administrative Science Quarterly* 25: 129–41.

Oxenfeldt, A. R. and Kelly, A. (1969) 'Will Successful Franchise Systems Ultimately Become Wholly-owned Chains?', *Journal of Retailing* 44: 69–87.

Perlmutter, H. (1969) 'The Tortuous Evolution of the Multinational Enterprise', *Columbia Journal of World Business* 4 (1): 9–18.

Podolny, J. (1993) 'A Status-based Model of Market Competition', *American Journal of Sociology* 98: 829–72.

—— (1994) 'Market Uncertainty and the Social Character of Economic Exchange', *Administrative Science Quarterly* 39: 458–83.

Powell, W. W. and Brantley, P. (1992) 'Competitive Cooperation in Biotechnology: Learning through Networks?', in N. Nohria and R. G. Eccles (eds) *Networks and Organizations: Structure, Form, and Action*, 366–94, Boston: Harvard Business School Press.

Powell, W., Koput, K. and Smith-Doerr, L. (1996) 'Inter-organizational Collaboration and the Locus of Innovation: Networks of Learning in Biotechnology', *Administrative Science Quarterly* 41 (1): 116–45.

Root, F. (1994) *Entry strategies for international business*, New York: Lexington.

Rubin, P. (1978) 'The Theory of the Firm and the Structure of the Franchise Contract', *Journal of Law and Economics* 21: 223–33.

Sadi, M. A. (1994) 'International Business Expansion through Franchising: the Case of Fast-food Industry', unpublished dissertation, Virginia Polytechnical Institute and State University, Blacksburg, Virginia.

Saxenian, A.-L. (1990) 'Regional Networks and the Resurgence of Silicon Valley', *California Management Review*, fall: 89–112.

—— (1994) *Regional advantage: Culture and competition in Silicon Valley and Route 128*. Cambridge, Mass.: Harvard University Press.

Scott, J. L. (1990) 'Fastframe in America', in M. Abell, (ed.) *The International Franchise Option*, 248–56, London: Waterlow.

Shane, S. (1996a) 'Why Franchises Expand Overseas', *Journal of Business Venturing* 11 (2): 73–88.

—— (1996b) 'Hybrid Organizational Arrangements and their Implications for Firm Growth and Survival', *Academy of Management Journal* 39 (1): 216–34.

—— (1998) 'Making New Franchise Systems Work', *Strategic Management Journal* 19 (7): 697–707.

Shook, C. and Shook, R. (1993) *Franchising: The Business Strategy that Changed the World*, Englewood Cliffs, N.J.: Prentice-Hall.

Stopford, J. and Wells, L. (1972) *Managing the Multinational Enterprise*, New York: Basic.

Trompenaars, F. and Hampden-Turner, C. (1998) *Riding the Waves of Culture: Understanding Cultural Diversity in Global Business*, New York: McGraw-Hill.

Uzzi, B. (1997) 'Social Structure and Competition in Interfirm Networks: the Paradox of Embeddedness', *Administrative Science Quarterly* 42: 35–67.

Vernon, R. (1966) *Sovereignty at Bay*, New York: Basic.

Walker, G. (1988) 'Network Analysis for Cooperative Interfirm Relationships', in F. Contractor and P. Lorange, eds., *Cooperative Strategies in International Business*, 227–40, New York: Lexington.

Wall Street Journal (1999) 'Burger King, Autogrill Mull Food Sale Deal', *Wall Street Journal*, European edition, 22 February: 9.

Wilkins, A. and Ouchi, W. (1983) 'Efficient Cultures: Exploring the Relationship Between Culture and Organizational Performance', *Administrative Science Quarterly* 28: 468–81.

10 Knowledge creation and transfer in global service firms

Robert Grosse

Introduction

The globalization and even the viability of service firms at the beginning of the twenty-first century clearly depends on the ability of these firms to produce, transfer, and guard knowledge that they use in providing services to clients. From the simplest financial services that a bank provides to a foreign client or a foreign affiliate of a domestic client, to the most complex management consulting project that involves extensive interaction between the service provider and the client firm, each of these situations requires the service provider to take specialized knowledge and apply it to a client's needs, while trying to retain the relevant skills, structures, and other appropriable aspects of that knowledge. In short, the service firms rely fundamentally on their ability to produce the knowledge that they sell to clients, and equally on their ability to utilize and protect that knowledge from competitors. Knowledge is the key competitive advantage in the service sector.

This may not seem like a particularly striking statement, with all of the emphasis being placed on knowledge management in recent years (Nonaka and Takeuchi 1995; Stewart 1997). Even so, it is quite remarkable that this one dimension is the key to competitiveness time and again in the services sector. In other sectors such as manufacturing or extractive industries, such issues as natural resource availability and production scale economies often play very large roles in creating competitive advantage, along with knowledge such as patentable products or production processes. In services, knowledge is *the* critical element, and frequently it cannot be protected by patents, trademarks, or copyrights.

The present chapter takes a somewhat narrow view of the services industry, focusing on business or producer services. These sectors include all kinds of support offered to businesses by service providers, from trash removal to internet access. They include management consulting, advertising, transportation, travel, banking, accounting, legal advising, and many more. Each of these sectors provides some kind of assistance to the client firm, including an intangible 'product' such as advice, data manipulation, or transfer to other locations. How can service firms build defensible organizations and strategies for competing in the twenty-first century? And how can service firms build global competitiveness?

This chapter explores producer services, describing the kinds of service provided and constructing a perspective on how firms in such sectors can develop global strategies. The emphasis is on knowledge management, given that this resource is the key competitive force in the industry.

To keep the discussion clear and focused, examples are taken concerning the generation and transfer of key knowledge that enables global firms in three service sectors – management consulting, commercial banking, and advertising – to establish competitive advantages and compete successfully in multiple markets. The intent is to generalize to the degree possible about service sectors overall, but certainly the evidence about these three sectors may not be applicable to services as a whole. In considering the transfer of knowledge, the paper also examines the organizational forms that service firms have used to enter and operate in foreign markets, including their relationships with client firms.

The analysis does not compare services with manufacturing industries in great detail. Still, many comparisons can be made as to the kinds of knowledge that are central to multinational service firms versus their manufacturing counterparts, and the ways in which that knowledge is moved across borders within the firms (or between alliance partners).

The key difference between service firms and their manufacturing and extractive counterparts is that services are generally intangible, while manufacturing and extractive outputs are generally physical products. In simplest terms, a service is an intangible item that depends to some extent on interaction between the buyer and the seller for its provision. Despite this key difference, the globalization of service firms looks a lot like the same process in the case of manufacturing firms.

The particular services considered in this analysis are producer services, whose target clients are other businesses rather than consumers. Clearly, management consulting firms and ad agencies seek corporate clients rather than individual clients in most instances. In the commercial banking sector, our focus is on the corporate market, rather than on retail banking. Overall, then, this study looks at the strategies and characteristics of service firms in the context of providing services to other businesses.

Driving forces in competitiveness in services

How can management consulting firms establish themselves and keep clients coming back? How can an ad agency continue to satisfy a corporate client? How can a bank offer differentiated service to clients that likewise keeps them satisfied and coming back? One can imagine that the answer to these questions is that they have to offer better service than the competitors. But what is 'better'?

Certainly one aspect of the answer is to provide service that enables the client firm to succeed in its business. So if a service firm can contribute to its client's success, it has achieved an initial step forward. If one service provider offers this contribution and charges less than a competitor, then that would be better service. If one service provider offers a contribution that gains the client greater sales or greater cost reduction, then this would be better. If one service provider offers more accessible contact points, this would be better. There is not much different here than for any kind of business.

Another way to examine the issue is to look more closely at the value-added chain in a producer service, to see the various levels of interaction with the client. Figure 10.1 depicts the chain for an advertising agency.

Notice that the ad agency purchases inputs like any other firm, and that it produces the basic product (an ad campaign) through typically extensive interaction with the client. Here is where the differentiated quality can be

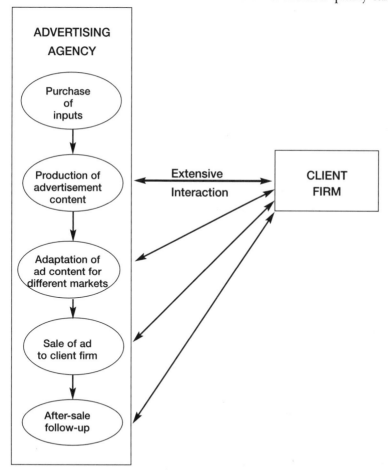

Figure 10.1 The value-added chain in advertising

built. Also, moving further down the chain, additional interaction occurs when the ad may be adapted for use in other countries where the client operates, and where the ad must be sold to the client. As with any sector, after-sale service requires yet more interaction with the client.

The result of viewing this value-added chain is that there appears to be a great deal of interaction between client and provider at the production stage as well as at the usual sale and after-sale service stages. That is, much more than with manufacturing firms, the value-added chain here seems to imply a greater degree of interaction. Is this a result of conceptualizing the sector, or does it have real roots in the ad agency or other service provider's business? Some empirical evidence can help with this question.

A sample of service multinationals

To better answer the above question, and others posed further along, two surveys of service providers were undertaken during 1991 and 1996–8. A team of six graduate student assistants plus the author carried out personal interviews at seventy-two affiliates of multinational service firms in Latin America in 1991, and four other graduate students carried out interviews at thirty-eight affiliates in industrial countries (France, Germany, Japan, Spain, and the United Kingdom) during 1996–8. The firms were all among the twenty-five largest in their industries world-wide. In each case a set of closed-ended questions were asked about the firm's competitive advantages, its knowledge transfer process, and other basic questions about structure and strategy.

The main clients of the firms studied tend to be large multinationals that use the service firms' assistance in multiple countries. In almost every case the service firms explained that more than half of their business in any country (outside of the home country) was with multinational firms rather than purely local ones. In this context, issues such as global relationship management, global brand management, and global strategy generally are crucial issues.

In answer to the previous question, the largest numbers of firms in the sample declared the following capabilities to be key to their competitiveness:

- knowledge of clients and relationships with them
- global scope of the service firm's affiliate network
- methodologies for producing services
- knowledge of the market for the services
- management skills
- technical/specialized information.

This is quite a striking list, if one compares it with the traditional kinds of competitive advantages of manufacturing firms. The key competitive advantages here clearly focus on knowledge (plus the geographic scope of service-providing locations). We are not looking at high-tech sectors, in which hundreds of millions of dollars must be invested to develop new products such as computer chips, or genetically engineered wheat, or a new satellite system. The 'products' may be high-tech, in the sense of a proprietary methodology for evaluating a possible business acquisition, but the capital requirements to develop and produce these products are dramatically lower-tech.

The implications of this difference remain to be fully understood. Some elements are clear. Since the service firms depend so heavily on interactions with clients, as well as on the brain-power of their employees, then guarding against employee raiding and other turnover must be a very high priority. Since the capital requirements are relatively low, the service firms can more easily establish 'production' affiliates overseas, though this begs the question of staffing with high-quality people in the overseas location. The present analysis helps to advance understanding of the service firms' global expansion, though there are still many implications left to explore.

Kinds of knowledge

When looking at the key knowledge advantages identified above, it can be seen that they tend to relate more to products than to processes or management. In the traditional view of technology management, three kinds of technology are considered: product, process, and managerial. In the present case, the knowledge that seems to dominate in importance is that which refers to understanding of clients' needs and ability to deliver services (products) that meet those needs. It does not seem to lie in management of the service firm, or in operating a service provision process that is superior to other firms, although the identification of proprietary methodologies for service provision is one exception. A methodology for designing a strategic plan or an advertising campaign clearly is a kind of process knowledge.

Service firms tend to view relationships with clients as the single most important kind of knowledge that gives them competitive advantage. This specific knowledge may fall outside of all three traditional categories. The knowledge has to do with delivering products that best serve client needs, but it also has perhaps more to do with knowing the clients and their needs. It is knowledge of the market rather than of the product. Since many of the service-sector products are easily copied (for example, bank products such as deposits or loans), it may be the ability to understand the client's needs and to thus offer products that best serve those needs that is the key.

Client relationships present an opportunity for service providers to protect their investment in knowledge. In all three of the sectors under study, client relationships involve more than one person from the service provider and from the client. In the case of an advertising agency, a team from the agency typically interacts with the client to define the scope of a campaign, the content, the timing, etc. At the agency there are business managers, creators of the ads, marketing people, and perhaps others involved with counterparts at the client firm. In international ad campaigns, often ad agency people from more than one country are part of the team that deals with the client. The net result is that the relationship is not at all dependent on one person, but rather on a group of people. No doubt, one key person who defects from the team or causes bad relations with the client could subvert the business, but the service provider generally has a broader, less-limited relation with the client than just a dealing between two people.

Another aspect of the relationship that gives the service provider a competitive edge over rivals exists with long-term clients. With a relationship that lasts for some years, the service provider develops a history of successful interaction with the client. While this does not protect completely against a client defection, it does provide more insulation for the provider against problems that may occur with individual relationships of people in the two firms. For example, when a disagreement arises between a key member of the client firm and someone at the service provider, it is much more common to see that difference resolved by other members of the two teams, given the levels of mutual trust and satisfaction developed over the years.

Thus, there appear to be three levels of client relationship that contribute to the service provider's competitive advantage: dealings between individuals at each firm; dealings between the provider's team and the client's team; and long-term, historical dealings that develop client–provider trust and satisfaction in maintaining the relationship.

The second type of key competitive advantage that was identified by service multinationals was knowledge of the business. This is interpreted to be knowledge of the market in which clients operate, knowing how to deal with clients in general, and knowledge of how to produce the service. Much of this knowledge is embodied in the people of the firm, again highlighting the fragility of the firm's competitive advantage, since individuals can be lured away to other firms.

Knowledge of the business was particularly important in the banking sector, where fewer opportunities exist for developing proprietary, team-based skills. Individual, skilled bankers were at once the source of competitive advantage and the asset most at risk to attacks by competitors. Curiously, banks seem to have simply accepted this situation and resigned themselves to dealing with a high degree of turnover of executives, rather than pursuing the strategies of the ad agencies and consulting firms that build teams of interlinked personnel.

The third type of key knowledge-based competitive advantage identified by service multinationals was a proprietary methodology for producing the service. This methodology ranged from a management information system to deal with client accounts at banks to a full-scale process for designing and implementing ad campaigns, to a consulting firm's template structure for doing project analysis or strategic planning for clients.

This last example illustrates at once the people-dependent nature of the advantage and the ways that service firms are moving to make it proprietary. A management consulting firm may have a method for designing corporate strategy: Boston Consulting Group's experience curve; Monitor's industry cluster and five forces; McKinsey's MECE (mutually-exclusive, collectively exhaustive) approach to problem definition and solving. The template is developed initially and used by one or more teams of the firm. With experience in applying it to client needs, the methodology is developed to the point that it can be used as an overall structure for analysing client situations and designing strategies everywhere. If the methodology is sufficiently robust to different applications, it can be applied to clients generally, as with the methods noted. (Obviously, there will be occasions when the general model does not apply, and it requires that the consulting firm be sufficiently agile as to see those circumstances and react to design a strategy based on the different situation.)

The only noteworthy competitive advantage that was not knowledge-based among these service firms was the possession of a global network of affiliates. This geographic spread of points of contact with clients was seen as a substantial competitive advantage, largely in comparison with local competitors in the major markets. In both management consulting and advertising, these locations were consistently owned affiliates (e.g. subsidiaries). In the case of banks, the global network included not only owned affiliates but also contractual relations with local financial service providers. From sharing automatic teller machines among banks, to correspondent relationships with dozens of partners, to joint lending business, the banks were far more prone to utilize other banks to help provide the full range of services to clients around the world.

Internationalization of service firms

As in the case of manufacturing and extractive industries, service firms' expansion to overseas markets and sources of inputs may be characterized as market-seeking and resource-seeking. In this case the resource-seeking motivation is primarily based on seeking technological resources, though some low-cost production of services such as computer software has followed the classic pursuit of low-cost labour. None of the service sectors reviewed here has significant natural resource needs, so pursuit of those resources is not presented as a factor in services globalization.

Service firms tend to go overseas in search of new markets and to follow existing clients who have moved overseas, just as manufacturing firms do. The forms of expansion for service firms tend to be parallel to those of manufacturers, though the cost of establishing a full-service presence overseas tends to be much smaller (much less capital intensive) for the service firms. There are certainly exceptions, such as hotel service, which requires huge capital costs for construction and operation of a new property. But this is the exception, far from the rule.

The service firms tend to prefer first to explore overseas opportunities through the export of their services, rather than to jump into owned 'production' of the services in the foreign markets. This is more feasible when the client is a multinational firm, where contact can occur with the client's home office in the service firm's home country, as well as with a local affiliate overseas. In this situation, the service firm may be able to provide occasional contacts with the local affiliate, while maintaining strong and frequent contacts with the home office. When dealing with local clients overseas, the export strategy is much more difficult to operate.

While the capital costs of overseas expansion are generally much lower than for manufacturing firms, the corporate resources costs may still be very high. Since the establishment of an overseas operation typically means reproducing a large part of the activity carried out in an existing operation, scale economies in terms of facilities are not likely to be important. Some sharing of personnel is possible, indeed, this is the idea of using teams from multiple locations to deal with client needs anywhere. Nevertheless, the firm needs to have essentially a full-service operation in each location where it operates, so it has to replicate the existing structure in each affiliate. Probably the greatest complication with this reality is that the firm has to find qualified personnel to staff each operation, since home-office people cannot carry out day-to-day interaction with clients in each foreign market.

The relationships between service provider and clients may be visualized better with a graphic representation. If one pictures the business services industry as a producer and seller of services to corporations, then the buyer/supplier structure might be pictured as in Figure 10.2 (page 225). This figure demonstrates that the service firms operate as do many multinationals, with local offices serving some clients, exports serving others, and clients themselves having uni-national and multinational presence. As with manufacturing companies, the service multinationals tend to have fewer offices in emerging markets. This is especially true since they are not pursuing low-cost raw materials or product assembly, as is sometimes the case in manufacturing in low-cost countries.

Service firms in the three sectors under study here have moved abroad much as their manufacturing counterparts did in earlier decades of this century. That is, they have formed alliances with local firms to offer their services overseas, they have exported their services to clients in other countries, and they have set up their own affiliates abroad. Nevertheless, it is clear that the services firms are much more recent arrivals to globalization than their counterparts in manufacturing and raw materials industries. Other than Citibank, ITT (telephone service), Sheraton, Pan Am (airline), Arthur Andersen, and a handful of other service providers, the service multinationals have expanded overseas mostly in the period of the 1980s and 1990s.

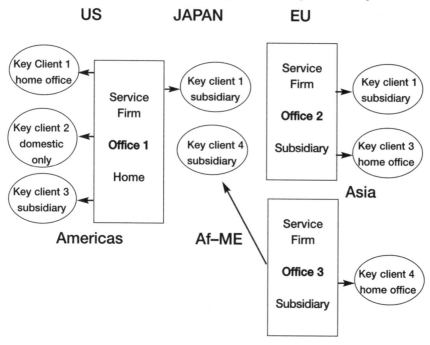

Figure 10.2 A global services company configuration

One interesting strategic move was uncovered in a global ad agency that may be indicative of the agencies' efforts to build relationships with multi-national clients. This agency had been dealing with a large pharmaceuticals company, and was its agency world-wide. The ad agency was reacting to the client's requests for campaigns tailored to each of its major markets, when the company decided that it wanted to pursue a globally-standardized corporate strategy, including its advertising. The ad agency had not come to that conclusion, but it was quick to jump to the client's request. The resulting strategic shift produced lower costs for the ad agency, a stronger relationship with the client, and a decision to look for other opportunities to introduce globally standardized campaigns.

Organizational structures

The legal structures used by the ad agencies and management consulting firms is often the partnership form, but with the past decade's growth of truly global competitors in these sectors, the move is toward publicly traded firms. That is, to compete in raising funds and obtaining other scale economies, the ad agencies and consulting firms are finding that bringing in equity capital has become very valuable if not necessary. In banking this has been a reality for many years. The commercial banks generally used branches overseas, or representative offices that are permitted only to refer business to full-service locations of the bank elsewhere.

In examining the fifty-eight firms with affiliates in industrial countries, the most common organizational form was the wholly-owned subsidiary, with about 55 per cent of the cases using this structure. In emerging markets the same result held. Figure 10.3 shows the distribution of ownership structures found in the sector.

In banking, the 'exporting' of services through alliance partners rather than direct investment or contracting (licensing) was common. That is, banks use correspondents with which they maintain parallel (corresponding) balances of deposits and offer services to each other's clients in each country. Large banks tend to have many such relationships around the world, in addition to any overseas affiliates they may operate.

In addition, banks tend to operate several more kinds of strategic alliances. They use multiple-bank alliances to provide automatic teller machine access to their clients in many locations. They operate credit-card alliances through Visa and MasterCard to offer such services globally to their clients. Both of these types of arrangements involve links with actual or potential competitors. Banks also often contract out parts of their activities to alliance partners in a vertical de-integration context. For example, many banks contract out their mortgage loan servicing activity to specialist firms, or they even sell off their mortgages to intermediaries that create mortgage-backed bonds in a secondary market. Banks also frequently

	% Owned by Parent Firm	Fre-quency	%	Method of Operation
				Newly created, wholly-owned subsidiary (31%)
1	100%	25	71	
2	80%	1	3	
3	70%	1	3	Partnership (22%)
4	62%	1	3	
5	60%	2	6	Whole acquisition of another
6	0%	1	3	firm (17%)
7	Not Applicable / No Response	4	11	Majority joint venture (14%)
				Other (16%)
	Total	35		

Figure 10.3 Ownership of affiliate

Note:
These 35 responses comprise:
    8 Ad agencies
    13 Commercial / investment banking / securities companies
    14 Management consultants

contract out activities such as cheque processing and other specific, repetitive functions for which specialist companies can offer low costs by achieving economies of very large scale.

The ad agencies and consulting firms essentially never operated through alliances with other firms in their same sector. A management consulting firm might co-operate with an accounting firm or a computer information systems firm, but in no case did two management consulting firms, or two ad agencies, work together for a common client. Presumably this is because their capabilities are so overlapping, but it may also be due to the firms' unwillingness to expose their people and their methodologies to rivals.

This situation is curious, because just as with the banking examples listed above, there are surely situations in which alliances would make sense. The more obvious area would be repetitive activities in management consulting and advertising that could be contracted out. This vertical de-integration does happen to some extent, with farming out activities such as bill paying or cash management. However, horizontal alliances are non-existent.

The above discussion had to do with legal structure and external alliances. As far as internal organizational structures are concerned, it is common for service firms to invest heavily in the use of teams of people to carry out key activities such as maintaining client relationships, as well as in producing their services. This team structure is often project-specific, with a team potentially consisting of people from several locations of the consulting firm, for example, depending on their experience with the client and/or the issue.

This structure helps to create a joint production of knowledge in the firm, since a team of people and often software is needed to operate the project. For a management consulting firm working on a strategic plan for a client, the team may consist of two or three local partners, who deal frequently directly with the client. In addition, an expert on the industry with experience in another country may be put on the team. Also, a person from another country office with experience dealing with the same client may be on the team. And finally, perhaps a computer expert who can operate an expert system or a complex program for the project may be brought in. The result is that no one person possesses the entire knowledge base, but rather the team does. The provider firm is reasonably protected from losing its team-based knowledge, unless the entire team deserts it!

The frequent use of project teams is probably the most common feature of ad agencies and management consulting firms that differentiate them from manufacturing firms or those in other industries. Instead of alliances with outside partners, the firms use inside alliances of people from different divisions and locations. Conceptually, this should be easier to control than external alliances, but little evidence has been compiled to explore this idea.

A paper by Moore and Birkinshaw (1998) looks at the team structure employed by consulting and other producer services firms in Europe. They find that a key structural component of these firms is the 'centre of excellence' in which teams that are invented for a project or activity are then leveraged to be reused in other contexts that the firm encounters. This may be for the same client in another country, another client in the same situation, or another setting entirely where the same team can be applied. They cite applications such as a multimedia centre of excellence at Andersen Consulting, which involves a small team of people who have worked on multimedia technology projects, and who know the current technology as well as knowing the firm's experience in the field. At McKinsey they found a business-to-business marketing centre of excellence, which is used to help McKinsey offices develop marketing efforts with clients in many countries. The experts in both of these cases have been moved to single locations, for the rest of the firm to be able to call on them efficiently. In principle, the centres could be groups of people who are geographically dispersed, but who have the requisite knowledge (skills and experience).

Knowledge protection

Given that relationships are the key knowledge category in most situations for these firms, it is quite interesting to see how they try to protect that knowledge: meaning largely how they try to retain their employees. The banks were mostly unable to hold onto key employees when raided, and they tended to have less of their key knowledge bound up in team-based structures or implicit forms. The consulting firms and ad agencies had much greater loyalty of employees (lower turnover), and simultaneously made much greater use of team-based projects and methodologies, as well as implicit (uncodified) knowledge.

One of the intended outcomes of creating teams for building knowledge leadership is to overcome some of the problems of the uncodified nature of much of the knowledge. That is, teams force the members to share their knowledge with each other, spreading it beyond the initial possessor. Thus, the team structure produces some sharing of personal knowledge, though the knowledge does not necessarily become codified. If the team can put some of the knowledge into written, video, or some other codified form, it can be transferred even more widely through the organization. Logically, the firms should investigate the value of the knowledge, the cost of making it codified, and then the calculation of codifying when it would add value.

Knowledge transfer methods

The ways that these firms move knowledge among affiliates are numerous, beginning with the relatively costly transfer of experts to foreign assignments, and perhaps ending with low-cost, frequent streams of electronic mail (e-mail). Since the key knowledge has been found to be relationships with clients and knowledge of the industry, these things are particularly hard to transfer, except when the client is a multinational with which the service firm deals in another country (or other countries). Since the service firms generally had more than half of their business with multinational clients, the possibility to utilize knowledge of these clients is very real.

In addition the firms often have proprietary methodologies for producing their services. These methodologies can be transferred along more traditional lines, namely through manuals, training programs, and various telecommunications means.

The main methods used for transferring knowledge are shown in Figure 10.4.

The figure shows that electronic means now dominate the knowledge transfer process, with an important role remaining for the interpersonal transfers through training programs and team interaction. Interestingly, the survey done in Latin America in the early 1990s showed much more use of training programs and transfers of people, with virtually no e-mail. Telephone and FAX communications were more frequently cited at that time as well. Today, service firms use similar knowledge transfer methods with affiliates in industrial countries (Europe and Japan) as they do in emerging markets (Latin America).

Global strategies to build on service-sector strengths

This section suggests some strategic directions that are consistent with the management of key knowledge and the problems of operating a highly skill-based organization in multiple locations.

A first step may be to consider organizational form, assuming that the firm wants to sell the same services world-wide as it does in the home country. It is clear for ad agencies and management consulting firms

	Methods of Knowledge Transfer	Frequency	%
1	Electronic mail (e.g. Lotus notes)	9	36
2	Telephone/conference calls	4	16
3	Local training	4	16
4	Team interaction	2	8
5	FAX	2	8
6	Edit	1	4
7	Post	1	4
8	Periodicals/newsletters	1	4
9	On-the-job experience	1	4
	Total	25	

Figure 10.4 Methods of transferring knowledge to affiliates

that export of services cannot be used in most cases. Even with the advent of widespread availability of video conferencing, there still remains a need for personal contact with clients. Some key relationship managers from the service firm will have to be located in the target market, at least for the next few years until some other technological advance may make such presence less critical.

An intermediate step may be feasible in regional country blocs, where transportation is rapid enough that a person living in one city can realistically visit clients in several countries on a regular, frequent basis. This would certainly work for multiple countries in Europe, if not for the whole European Union, and also for multiple countries in Latin America (or at least the Southern Cone, the Andean countries, and Central America/Mexico.

The more the firm can identify themes for which project teams can be created and used in different applications, the less the need will be for full staffing in every location. In principle, one or two relationship managers could be present in a given location, and all of the experts on the industry, the client multinational company, and the theme, could communicate by video conferencing and other telecommunications methods on a daily basis. This would allow for scale economies in the use of key personnel.

In terms of the types of clients to pursue, it probably depends on the size of the market as much as the service firm's own capabilities. In smaller markets it may make more sense to pursue multinational firms' affiliates, since it may be easier to link them to services offered to the same firms elsewhere. Local firms large enough to need or want the services offered by the multinational ad agency or consulting firm will be relatively few and perhaps more difficult to develop relationships with.

To protect its proprietary knowledge, the service firm must find ways to keep key employees and to make the knowledge either codified (and thus able to be copied by people other than the original possessor) or team-specific, so that no one person can take it with him/her to a rival firm.

Conclusions

Given that knowledge is the key competitive advantage in the producer services sector, firms need to find ways to build their knowledge resources, share that knowledge among affiliates, and protect it against incursions by rivals. Since the knowledge ordinarily resides in people, other than that which has been codified into some kind of medium such as a document or a computer program, the firm faces the need to find and hire high-quality people, to train them in the business, and to retain them over time.

One general strategy that has emerged, in particularly the advertising and consulting industries, is the use of teams of people to provide the services to clients. By creating and using teams, the firm is able to take the offensive in developing new knowledge from the co-operation among team members, and take the defensive in making sure that team knowledge is not able to be 'stolen' by a defecting team member. Both of these attributes enable the firm to build a stronger competitive advantage.

The kind of knowledge that seems to produce key competitive advantages is relationships with clients. This knowledge includes person-based knowledge of key individuals at the client firm; team-based knowledge of the client firm's people involved in the overall relationship; and historical 'knowledge' embedded in the supplier/client relationship that has built up over time. The latter two types of knowledge are more appropriable by the firm, since no individual can capture the full relationships. Firms should aim to build up those kinds of knowledge, since they can provide the most durable competitive advantages.

In pragmatic terms this means always looking for ways to ensure that services are provided by multi-person teams. It means building relationships with clients that last for years, and that thus build up the historical trust and willingness to co-operate of long-term relationships.

In a defensive manner the firm can not only look to build teams and avoid placing too great dependence on individuals, but it can also look to codify knowledge that is possessed by key individuals, so that it can be shared more widely in the firm. This certainly will be difficult in many instances, but even when codifying is costly, it may be possible to share the knowledge through operation of the teams.

When extending their strategies to the global level, service firms find lower entry barriers for setting up full-service operations overseas than typically occurs for manufacturing firms (that is, lower capital costs), but significant costs to reproducing the home-office knowledge base. To deal with this reality, the service multinationals have frequently set up international teams of experts to deal with clients, applying the key knowledge to projects in multiple countries rather than just one. Teams may be temporary or permanent, but they give the firm the ability to leverage individual knowledge into more applications, and to some extent to transfer it to other members of the team across countries.

References

Davenport, T., Jarvenpaa, S. and Beers, M. (1996) 'Improving Knowledge Work Processes', *Sloan Management Review*, summer: 53–65.

Davenport, T., De Long, D. and Beers, M. (1998) 'Successful Knowledge Management Projects', *Sloan Management Review*, winter: 43–57.

Edvinsson, L. and Malone, M. (1997) *Intellectual Capital*, New York: Harper Business.

Glazer, R. (1998) 'Measuring the Knower: Towards a Theory of Knowledge Equity', *California Management Review*, spring: 175–94.

Grosse, R. (1996) 'International Technology Transfer in Services', *Journal of International Business Studies*, fourth quarter: 781–800.

Hedlund, G. (1994) 'A Model of Knowledge Management and the N-form Corporation', *Strategic Management Journal*, summer: 73–94.

Moore, K. and Birkinshaw, J. (1998) 'Managing Knowledge in Global Service Firms: Center of Excellence', *Academy of Management Executive*, vol.12, no. 4: 81–92.

Nonaka, I. (1994) 'The Dynamic Theory of Organizational Knowledge Creation', *Organization Science*, February: 38–50.

Nonaka, I. and Takeuchi, H. (1995) *The Knowledge-Creating Company*, Oxford: Oxford University Press.

Quinn, J. B., Anderson, P. and Finkelstein, S. (1996) 'Managing Professional Intellect: Making the Most of the Best', *Harvard Business Review*, March–April: 71–80.

Ruggles, R. (1998) 'The State of the Notion: Knowledge Management in Practice', *California Management Review*, spring: 80–9.

Stewart, T. (1997) *Intellectual Capital*, New York: Doubleday/Currency.

Teece, D, (1998) 'Capturing Value from Knowledge Assets', *California Management Review*, spring: 55–79.

Ulrich, D. (1998) 'Intellectual Capital = Competence x Commitment', *Sloan Management Review*, winter: 15–26.

Part III
Case studies

11 Global competition in industrial services

An analysis of aircraft maintenance, repair and overhaul services

Tan Kim Seng and Peter Enderwick

Introduction

The nature of a number of services means that many of the activities in a service firm's value chain must be performed at or near the buyer. As a result, many service industries are highly fragmented, with numerous small firms providing services on a localized basis. However, globalization of markets and the introduction of new technology are causing major changes in industry structures and the sources of competitive advantage in many service industries. An increasingly global market, efficient logistics and telecommunications systems, combined with new generation information technology, mean that many service industries are rapidly consolidating and large, multi-unit firms are emerging. This, in turn, has accelerated the internationalization of service competition.

These tendencies are well illustrated in the increasingly global aircraft maintenance, repair and overhaul (MRO) industry which is the subject of this chapter. This industrial services industry, which highlights a number of insights in the pursuit of global strategies, has been subject to very little academic research.

We present, in the following section a discussion of the precursors to globalization in the industry. This is followed by an overview of the industry and the major competitive players. In the following three sections brief outlines of the strategic thrust of representatives of the three major competitor types: airlines, independent shops, and original equipment manufacturers (OEMs), are presented. The section on competitive restructuring and globalization provides an analysis of these cases in an attempt to identify similarities and differences. This analysis reveals predictable changes in an increasingly mature and global service industry – a shift from technology to customer and market-orientation – as well as continuing pressures to contain costs and improve performance. Four waves of competitive response are evident: rapid globalization, intense price competition, consolidation and collaboration. Global restructuring is being led by the aggressive expansion of OEMs who are responding to the growing tendency of airlines to focus on their areas of core competency: passenger and cargo transport. Their expansion appears to be at the expense of the independent sector. The final section provides concluding thoughts from the discussion.

Precursors to globalization

Like many services, the aircraft maintenance, repair and overhaul industry has in part globalized in response to the demands of its primary client group, the airline companies. As airlines have increasingly globalized operations, they have demanded a similar response from maintenance suppliers.

By its very nature the airline industry has long been international. However, the growth of multinational manufacturing and the globalization of financial markets, with an accompanying increase in air travel and cargo shipments, has brought greater international integration of airlines and the development of cross-national ownership.

The conditions for this process can be found in the 1970s and 1980s. The massive changes brought by deregulation of the US airline industry in 1978 were replicated in other countries with privatization of former state-owned airlines and the relaxation of national regulations and controls on routing, pricing, gateway access and passenger and cargo limits. The crises faced by US airlines in the 1980s prompted a reconsideration of company strategy and government support. Early in the 1980s US airlines posted combined losses of some US$8 billion and more recently have suffered from economic recession, a period of high oil prices, severe price competition and a downturn in air travel during the Gulf War. There were forty-three airlines in the US in 1978, by 1998 there were fifteen.

To assist their airlines in entering new growth markets the US government pushed hard to overcome national regulations. The Bush administration negotiated the first 'Open Skies' agreement with the Netherlands in 1992, enabling unrestricted air service by airlines of the two countries between and beyond the other's territory. This enabled the first transatlantic partnership in 1993 between US carrier Northwest and KLM Royal Dutch Airlines. The Clinton administration has negotiated thirty more 'Open Skies' agreements encompassing Europe, the Middle East, Asia and Central America. Bilateral agreements have also been reached with Japan, France, and Canada. Furthermore, the US Department of Transportation has provided anti-trust immunity to major carriers involved in global alliances.

At present there are two dominant global alliances, the Star Alliance and Oneworld. Alliances appear to be particularly attractive to airlines as they enable carriers to vastly increase their offerings to customers and to discourage them from using competitors. Companies in an alliance can create a global service network that is much more capable of providing superior service than the sum of its parts. This is of particular importance in an industry subject to severe competition and where major competitors enjoy limited opportunities for differentiation on other bases. Airlines tend to face similar costs (fuel, operating, and staffing costs), they use similar technology and face similar levels of regulation. Alliances also offer an attractive alternative to mergers in the pursuit of scale economies and enhanced service provision. There have been twenty-two mergers in the US airline in the past decade, none of which have been particularly successful.

The global alliances which exist today illustrate the extent to which the client industry has globalized. The Oneworld alliance (American Airlines, British Airways, Canadian Airlines, Cathay Pacific, Quantas, Iberia and Finnair) carries 206 million passengers a year on a fleet of 1,783 aircraft to more than 680 destinations in 143 countries. This alliance flies nearly seven million miles, equivalent to 280 times around the world, every day.

The Star Alliance also has massive reach with a membership that includes Air Canada, Air New Zealand, Ansett Australia, Lufthansa, SAS, Thai, United Airlines, Varig and, from late 1999, All Nippon Airways. Together they service 720 destinations in 110 countries.

The purpose and expected benefits of such alliances are of considerable interest. Members of the Star Alliance have stated that it is not their intention to merge the airlines or to create identical product offerings. Rather, diversity is seen as a strength. This suggests that such alliances will be compatible with a strategy of product or brand differentiation. Equally, the maintenance, repair and overhaul service is not likely to form part of that differentiation. Airlines do not compete on the basis of their commitment to MRO or on their safety records. Rather, consumers take for granted that appropriate maintenance and safety commitments will be made. For this reason, MRO activities can be outsourced with no tangible effect on marketing strategies. It is this context which is driving the MRO industry, the need for global service provision and at the same time, the demise of MRO as a core element of airline service.

Industry analysis: commercial aircraft engine overhaul services

As indicated in the preceding section the commercial airline industry has experienced significant change. The business environment has seen a shift from controlled competition to liberalized markets, scale achieved through internal growth to growth achieved through strategic alliances, and a shift in focus from technology to the economics of the business. In common with many other industries, management is increasingly focusing on asset utilization, cost reduction, network management, core competence and outsourcing, partnerships and alliances.

Increasingly, engine maintenance is not seen as a core airline activity. Cost pressures are causing airlines to consider outsourcing if the activity is not a source of competitive advantage and the current scale does not justify internal capability. Outsourcing maintenance work enables an airline, especially a new entrant airline, to eliminate the need for the complex infrastructure that is required for maintenance.

Commercial aircraft engine overhaul market

Despite considerable over-capacity world-wide, global opportunities in the maintenance, repair and overhaul business are increasing. As airlines restructure, some are divesting their maintenance assets to reduce costs and others seek to increase their MRO share. Maintenance companies are experimenting with new strategies to cut costs in an already crowded field as original equipment manufacturers (OEMs) looking for growth, enter the market. Global over-capacity is intensifying already stiff competition, encouraging the formation of maintenance alliances and the pooling of spare parts to reduce costs.

Thorne finds the maintenance industry for large aircraft and engines in a state of internal conflict:

> On one hand is overcapacity in the third-party segment. Many competent facilities are beating the bushes in search of a level of business that will ensure survival. Contributing to this situation is the sound business decision of many airlines to seek work to fill out the schedules of their in-house facilities spun off into either separate profit centers or independent subsidiaries.
>
> On the other hand, the airlines' continuing drift towards outsourcing of facility-intensive jobs such as heavy maintenance gives those already in the field a reason to hope. Unfortunately, it also lures new operators into the field. Engine-overhaul shops, meanwhile, are threatened on two fronts: the increasing reliability of modern engines reduces shop visits, while aggressive manufacturer moves into the maintenance/overhaul sector mean more competition for what business remains.
>
> (Thorne 1996: 75)

The MRO industry is a significant one. The market for heavy airframe, engine and component overhaul, as well as line maintenance is valued at nearly US$24 billion (McKenna and Scott 1997). Some 30 per cent of this is outsourced. The engine overhaul market is about US$6.6 billion and almost half of the engine overhaul business is contracted out to third party suppliers (Todhunter 1997).

There are three major types of player in the MRO market: original equipment manufacturers (OEMs), large airlines, and independents. It is the OEMs, particularly the engine manufacturers such as General Electric, Pratt and Whitney, and Rolls Royce, who are driving globalization and change in the MRO industry. The OEMs have always provided overhaul work, it is becoming a bigger part of their business. The business strategies of OEMs are changing significantly. The airline recession has meant stiff competition for new engine orders. With greater reliability rates, OEMs are experiencing fewer orders for spares.

In 1993, Rolls Royce formed Rolls Royce Aero Engines Services Limited as a separate company to handle engine maintenance, repair and overhaul work. Two years later the venture was contributing about 10 per cent of the entire company's annual revenues. Pratt and Whitney increased overhaul revenues from about US$250 million in 1995 to more than US$1 billion in 1998. In the period 1993–5 General Electric put eight airlines under contracts ranging from five to twenty years that were valued at US$1 billion. Three-quarters of General Electric's aircraft engine business net income in 1994 was generated by engine service (Smith 1997). The increased interest in this market segment by the OEMs as a source of additional revenue and as a means of helping their airline customers control costs, poses the threat of even more competition to long-established third-party maintenance organizations.

While many airlines seek to outsource MRO activities, it is important to understand that the outsourcing relationship is unlikely to be an arm's length one. The paramount demands for safety in the airline industry mean that airlines are likely to take considerable oversight of their maintenance activities. A trend in maintenance contracting is for 'right-sourcing', whereby an airline will not just seek to outsource to the lowest bidder, but will examine the quality of the work that will be performed. While it may not contribute as much to cutting costs directly, rightsourcing can improve aviation safety and boost the public's confidence in the industry.

The ValuJet crash incident provides valuable but painful lessons:

> ValuJet took a tested strategy and extended it farther and faster than any other carrier had done. It proudly said it was a 'virtual' airline, concentrating on the core activity of transporting passengers, leaving the rest of the business to others. . . . All of this came crashing down in the aftermath of the Everglades crash, when FAA decided the carrier had been far too loose in its oversight of maintenance. FAA now has codified the actions an airline must take in outsourcing maintenance. . . . Airlines must bear the ultimate responsibility for their product. Outsourcing is an essential tool but care must be taken when jobs are outsourced, responsibility is not outsourced as well'.
>
> (Donoghue 1996: 7)

When viewed in this way, outsourcing is not simply a contract or a job, but a partnership with a service provider that transcends earlier relationships, with each getting involved in the other's business to suggest better ways to complete the work. Maintenance service providers must aim at positioning themselves based on service quality and reliability. They must achieve operational excellence. This means improving competitiveness through a focused strategy of improving quality, reducing costs and improving service in all areas. New approaches to providing products and services will be required. New kinds of competitors will emerge.

> The formation of partnerships and alliances will become indispensable. Airlines, on the one hand, require low-cost, flexible, and responsive suppliers to reach their objectives in a competitive and rapidly changing world. On the other hand, the stronger supplier partners best suited to meet airlines' needs will be large and broad-based. This dichotomy – large yet responsive, broad-based yet low-cost – will require most specialized suppliers to form strategic partnerships that create seamless, 'virtual' companies with the requisite combination of scale and efficiency.
>
> (The Canaan Group 1996: 22)

Airlines which seek to retain their MRO capability are increasingly adopting a business unit approach for their maintenance operations, one which emphasizes a task-oriented structure designed to meet rapidly changing market demands. Independent entities provide more accurate cost information and they can be made fully accountable financially. A decentralized structure may also be more efficient in generating third party income. It also opens up new possibilities in terms of asset sales and joint ventures, once the profit centre has become a legally separate subsidiary.

In summary, the future will bring significant changes in the participants' share of the commercial engine overhaul market. Airlines' share of the total market will decline with small airlines outsourcing, large ones having more focused capability, and those with large third party business spinning off their maintenance functions into separate business entities. OEMs are likely to become stronger as they increase their aftermarket focus. As most of the engine overhaul market growth will be in new technology engines, the share of OEMs will be greatest for these engines. Independents' share will grow with increased outsourcing but they face considerable uncertainty. As participants become more economically driven, there will be some consolidations and exits, but fewer new entrants because of the high barriers to entry including heavy investment, strong technical capability and customer acceptance.

The following sections provide examples of the various competitors and examine the strategic imperatives driving these changes.

Airline restructuring: the case of SIA Engineering

The organization considered in this section is SIA Engineering Company (SIAEC) which was formed in April 1992 as a wholly-owned subsidiary of Singapore Airlines, merging its maintenance and overhaul activity with that of an existing subsidiary, Singapore Engine Overhaul Centre (SEOC). It is built on the client base of SEOC and Singapore Airlines' Engineering

Division, which includes sixty airlines and twenty-nine aviation companies.

With a wealth of human and technical resources built up over the years, SIAEC is equipped to provide customers with a comprehensive range of MRO services including aircraft servicing, aircraft maintenance and overhaul, component maintenance and overhaul and engine maintenance and overhaul (including auxiliary power units). SIAEC is well placed to provide MRO services for the new generation engines as it has to meet the fleet upgrading needs of its parent company, Singapore Airlines. To increase capacity and capability, it embarked on further expansion of its facilities and upgrading in high technology equipment together with staff training.

Being accustomed to providing services only to its own parent company since its initial set-up in 1977, the company has made changes both to its corporate thinking towards customers and its systems to cope with the increased workload as a result of introducing third-party work. The demand for accurate accountability of engine parts and material used, and labour charges becomes critical. However, the greatest constraint on its future growth is its heavy reliance on the parent company for management initiative in business development. Business development in catering for an engine type not operated by SIA will pose a considerable challenge.

In organizing SIAEC as a subsidiary, a number of advantages were anticipated:

- Awareness of value added: as a subsidiary, the company is fully accountable for its own performance, including financial aspects.
- Control and accountability: being a subsidiary, the company is fully accountable for its own performance, including financial performance.
- Decision-making and implementation processes: due to fewer management levels and more autonomy, decision-making and implementation processes should be faster.
- Entrepreneurship and innovation: since its business goals are more clearly defined, with definite targets, the company has to be innovative in doing business, raising the level of entrepreneurship (one example is the plan to diversify its capability to overhaul other makes of engine besides those operated by SIA).
- Acceptance by third-party customers: as a separate entity, third-party customers expect and accept that they will be given equal priority with SIA.
- New possibilities in terms of joint ventures and asset sales: such a structure also opens up new possibilities in terms of joint ventures and asset sales, once the profit centre has become a legally separate subsidiary.

From 1992 SIAEC moved aggressively into joint ventures in the aviation industry, both locally and overseas to support its core business of providing aviation engineering services. In July 1997 Pratt and Whitney (P&W)

bought into SIAEC's existing engine overhaul division, acquiring 51 per cent of the venture with SIAEC owning the remaining 49 per cent. The joint venture company is Pratt and Whitney's exclusive Center of Excellence facility in the Asia–Pacific and Indian sub-continent. They direct all their work in this part of the world to this joint venture.

There are also a number of joint ventures in Singapore. One of these is a 49 per cent stake in a venture with Pratt and Whitney to set up Combustor Airmotive Services Private Limited to refurbish combustion-chamber liners so that these need no longer be shipped to the USA to be repaired. A second joint venture is a 29 per cent stake in Asian Surface Technologies Limited with Pratt and Whitney and Praxair to provide engine fan blade repair. The third local joint venture is with Rolls-Royce Aero Engine Services Limited to form a new component services company. The new company, International Engine Component Overhaul Private Limited (IECO), is owned equally by the two partners. IECO will initially refurbish high technology nozzle guide vanes and compression stators. It will serve the growing number of customers in the Asia–Pacific region who operate aircraft powered by Rolls-Royce Trent and RB211 engines.

In Taiwan, SIAEC has formed a joint venture company with China Airlines and Pratt and Whitney to repair and overhaul PW4000 compressor vanes. The company, Asian Compressor Technology Services, in which SIAEC has a 24.5 per cent stake, commenced operations in June 1997. SIAEC has a number of other joint ventures under consideration. Such ventures provide an effective means of technology transfer. Certain proprietary processes, which are otherwise unobtainable from the engine manufacturer and are of value-added benefit to SIAEC, are now available through the various joint ventures. The local joint ventures fit very well with the Singapore Economic Development Board's aim to develop Singapore into a regional aerospace repair and overhaul centre and could benefit from the attractive incentives offered, such as tax relief for the first ten years, and assistance in securing industrial land or factory premises.

An independent MRO operator: Greenwich Air Services

Greenwich Air Services (GAS) was created from the acquisition of a Miami-based engine overhaul company and became operational in 1988 as a US$20 million a year company, then limited to the JT3D and LM 1500 indus-trial/marine powerplant capabilities. By 1994, a string of acquisitions of comparatively small companies, overhaul shops and assets led to annual sales of US$200 million. GAS acquired idle Eastern Airlines' engine overhaul assets and subsequently moved into the facilities in August 1992. Then in 1994, GAS acquired Chromalloy's Gas Turbine Corporation, more than doubling sales.

In the past, there was no independent overhauler of high thrust, high by-pass ratio aero-engines in North America. The overhaul of engines such as the CF6, JT9D and RB211 was either accomplished in-house by US-based airlines, subcontracted to the OEMs, or carried out by European engine overhaul shops. Greenwich Air Services' expansion represents the first independent shop in North America to offer the overhaul of large engines. Airbus Industrie placing five ex-Eastern CF6-50 engines into Miami in 1993, was the start for GAS in the large turbofan sector. In the same year, the Rolls-Royce RB211–22B engine overhaul capability was added, an engine that was easily accommodated in the former Eastern Airlines engine overhaul facilities. As a significant advance in overhauling large engines, the acquisition of Gas Turbine Corporation (GTC), a division of Chromalloy, in 1994, is entirely consistent with Greenwich's strategy to expand into JT9D work.

Through its acquisition strategy (see Table 11.2) Greenwich Air Services has strengthened its capability (Table 11.1) and its position in the aviation aftermarket and became the dominant independent player in the aircraft maintenance services business.

Greenwich has continued to seek acquisitions since early 1996 when it bought the engine overhaul business of Aviall for US$231.5 million. This expanded its turbofan overhaul capability to cover the IAE V2500, CFM56 and PW100.

As GAS grew with new engine services and customers, work from the Asia–Pacific region marked the path for international expansion and diversification. GAS has the capability to repair and overhaul a broad range of aircraft engines, as well as service the related engine accessories and components under one roof. This gives GAS a decided competitive advantage in areas such as turn time and cost control. The simplicity and

Table 11.1 The growth of capability at Greenwich

Greenwich's capability	Introduced in
JT3D	1988
JT8D-7 through -17	1990
CF6-6/-50	1993
RB211-22B	1993
JT8D-200	1994
JT9D-7A through J	1994
JT9D-7Q	1995

Table 11.2 Principal acquisitions by Greenwich

Greenwich's acquisitions	Acquired in
Eastern Airlines' facility	1992
GTC (Chromalloy)	1994
Aviall (Commercial engine services division)	1996
UNC	1997

reliability that comes with one-stop shopping of maintenance has made GAS a value-added provider of services to the aviation industry.

As in the case of GAS, the independents tend to rely on a high level of customer support, offering a value for money repair service and customized workscopes to meet individual customer requirements including a customer support package for accessories and components repair and overhaul. As different OEM's engines can often be repaired in the one facility, independents can offer significant advantages to airlines with mixed fleets. However, independents are vulnerable. Some two weeks after the proposed GAS/UNC merger was announced, GAS was acquired by General Electric, one of the major OEMs.

Engine manufacturers in the aftermarket business

Better engine reliability has encouraged the major engine manufacturers to consider greater involvement in the MRO business and spares inventory management to replace earnings once generated through spare parts. General Electric Aircraft Engines, Pratt and Whitney, and Rolls-Royce have each made strategic moves in recent times to enhance their revenue streams by aggressive expansion into the overhaul and maintenance field. Because of the proprietary technological advantage that each OEM enjoys in the overhaul of their own engines, expansion to undertake work on competitors engines is unlikely. This section will outline the strategies each of the original equipment manufacturers (OEMs) have undertaken in their after-market focus and their impacts on the engine overhaul market.

General Electric Aircraft Engines

Engine overhaul has long been a core part of General Electric (GE) Aircraft Engines' business, and is viewed as having significant growth opportunities. GE bought its first overhaul shop outside the US in December 1991 from British Airways. The facility (formerly known as EMMS) located near Cardiff, became GE Engine Services: Wales. Retaining much of its work-force and product line, it continues to have airline expertise and management influence besides the OEM influence. The OEM having designed and built the engine will greatly influence the overhaul process, especially in speeding up the development of repair processes.

In September 1996, GE Engine Services was organized as a separate company. Since then it has aggressively expanded in international markets. It has moved to form a joint venture with Malaysia Airlines in engine overhaul at the Malaysia Airlines AERO facility in Subang, Malaysia. This became fully operational in early 1997 and performs engine maintenance on CFM International, CFM56, and Pratt and Whitney PW4000 series engines, as well as the APS Auxiliary Power Units.

GE's acquisition of Greenwich Air Services can be seen as part of a wider strategy on the part of GE to expand its engine servicing capabilities to include more non-GE engines. The purchase of the combined GAS/UNC entity brought over 100 new types of engine to GE's already large overhaul capabilities, making it the largest engine overhaul concern in the world and allowing the company to substantially expand the services it can offer on competitors' engines. With the closing of the deal, independent companies essentially became an insignificant component of the aircraft engine MRO services market. Because a sizeable number of independent players have been eliminated, Pratt and Whitney and Rolls-Royce are forced to turn to MRO operations of airlines to improve their competitive position relative to the new GE Engine services.

Internationally, GE has invested in the Taipei-based Evergreen Aviation Technologies Corporation with a 20 per cent stake, with the remaining 80 per cent stake held by Eva Airways. GE is also discussing joint venture agreements with both Philippine Airlines and Varig. Positioned as the world's most experienced provider of aircraft engine management services and a key part of one of the largest engine manufacturers, GE Engine Services has strategically located facilities world-wide; a network of resources it has continued to acquire or build up through joint ventures to be a truly global aircraft engine MRO service organization. It has integrated parts business into its operation to ensure optimum coordination when replacement – rather than repair – serves the best interests of the customer. GE combined its parts business to make sales possible through putting together spares with used serviceable parts. It has also enhanced fleet management services and asset management programme support including maintenance cost per hour (MCPH), on-wing support, and aircraft leasing company support; teaming with aircraft and engine leasing companies to offer maintenance as part of the lease package.

Pratt and Whitney

Pratt and Whitney has refocused its engine overhaul and repair business since 1990 towards providing a full range of services for airline customers, rather than just carrying out warranty work as was previously the case. Briefly, the company has mapped out and implemented the following strategies in an attempt to achieve enhanced competitiveness:

- Decentralization of responsibility and authority: 'small' and highly focused business units are set up within the overall larger structure of Pratt and Whitney. They are run as individual profit centres which are accountable for customer satisfaction by implementing process-driven engine repair programmes aimed at providing customers with the lowest cost of engine ownership.
- Global expansion: Pratt and Whitney has recognized the global nature

of the engine after-market, resulting in a world-wide expansion of engine support facilities by creating specialized joint venture companies. Such examples include P&W Airmotive International, Ireland; Turbine Overhaul Services, Singapore; Combustor Airmotive Services, Singapore; Asian Surface Technologies, Singapore; Asian Compressor Technology Services, Taiwan; and P&W Overhaul and Repair Center, Europe, in the Netherlands.

- Provision of additional support organizations: Pratt and Whitney further focuses its activities in several other engine after-market areas through dedicated specialist organizations. These include a maintenance tool unit, a serviceable material management organization, and an inventory management group.
- Re-engineering: repair process effectiveness is evaluated· on a continuous basis which will result in significant repair cost savings as well as elimination of excess inventory.
- Continuous improvement: plans for continuous improvement are in place to reduce cost and turn times.

Pratt and Whitney and SIA Engineering Company (SIAEC) have formed a joint venture to overhaul aircraft engines in Singapore. SIAEC is to provide the bulk of the initial workforce and management staff and Pratt and Whitney will provide the general management and specialist support. It is Pratt and Whitney's first engine overhaul facility outside the US and is part of the effort to establish a network of bases to tap a growing market. A major and key joint venture, the partnership will enable both Pratt and Whitney and SIAEC to expand their respective service businesses. Pratt and Whitney's approach is to work with airline customers on their engines, even if they do include those made by rivals. Partnerships with airlines provides a surety of input of work and, at the same time, helps the customers to reduce their cost of ownership.

Rolls-Royce

In 1993 Rolls-Royce established a separate company, Rolls-Royce Aero Engine Services, to focus solely on overhaul and repair. In line with Rolls-Royce's stated goal of supplying one-third of the world's commercial aircraft engines, the overhaul facility has distinct growth objectives and is designed to provide a very high quality of service.

In a highly competitive market where there is over-capacity, one solution is the type of teaming agreement that Rolls-Royce has with Hong Kong Aircraft Engineering Company (HAECO). In November 1995, HAECO entered into a 50/50 joint venture with Rolls-Royce Aero Engine services, to form a commercial aero engine overhaul company, Hong Kong Aero Engine Services Limited (HAESL). Rolls-Royce has committed its commercial engine overhaul interests in the region to HAESL.

In the area of engine component repair, Rolls-Royce Aero Engine Services has formed a new component services company with SIA Engineering Company. The new company, International Engine Component Overhaul Private Limited (IECO), is equally owned by the two partners. It specializes in the refurbishment of high-technology aero-engine nozzle guide vanes and compressor stators and has begun work at the Loyang Industrial Park in Singapore which will serve the growing number of Rolls-Royce Trent and RB211 operators in the region.

As a further development, since Rolls-Royce has already committed to HAECO in their joint venture, HAESL a new joint venture with SIA Engineering Company (SIAEC) to undertake Trent engine overhaul and maintenance in the Asia–Pacific region, will be a three company venture. The new venture is expected to be launched formally in 1999 and to be fully operational in 2000 following the commissioning of a new facility to be sited near Changi Airport.

Rolls-Royce is also set to gain a significant footing in the US engine overhaul market with its tie-up with American Airlines' Alliance maintenance base in Fort Worth, Texas, initially for the overhaul of engines, including the RB211–535, Tay, and ultimately the Trent. The engine maker has also recently boosted its US presence with the signing of a US$17 million maintenance agreement with Gulfstream Aerospace for Spey, Tay, and BR710s.

From the above cases it is apparent that a subtle change has occurred across the aero-engine industry, with a shift in strategic emphasis among the major engine manufacturers. It is a shift from the traditional role of providing warranty repair and sales support services to a more aggressive expansion into the maintenance, repair and overhaul (MRO) business.

Competitive restructuring and globalization of MRO Services

The five case studies discussed above are representative of the main players in the aircraft engine overhaul business and provide a perspective on the development of each sector. The purpose of this section is to identify the distinctive characteristics, and to compare and contrast structural differences and strategies, of the different types of competitors. A summary of the results of a cross-case analysis is provided in Table 11.3 (page 248–9) and a more detailed analysis of each factor follows.

Competitive advantages of airline-owned services

Airline-owned services have many distinctive characteristics which can provide the competitive advantages to expand the firm's business horizons. One advantage is the operational knowledge it has gained from its fleet experience. These insights on engine maintenance problems relating to

Table 11.3 A comparative analysis of the different types of competitors

Type of competitor	Competitive advantages	Core activities in strategic management
Airline-owned	Operational knowledge from fleet experience; large inventory of spares; economies of scale from captive market; OEM leverage as their customer.	Redefining its core business and its strategies to fulfill its mission/objectives; pursuing strategic growth by joint ventures; building customer-oriented, market-driven organization.
Independent	Entrepreneurship and speed in decision-making and implementation processes; innovation with unique skills and capabilities; flexibility and ability to tailor to customers' needs.	Strengthening its core business and realigning its strategy to fulfill its mission/objectives; pursuing strategic growth by mergers and acquisitions; building customer-oriented, market-driven organization.
OEM	Technical knowledge of an engine designer; ability to provide engine performance warranty; technological and financial resources for development of new and proprietary repairs and processes; availability of spare parts and inventory management programme; points-of-sale leverage; after-sale support to lower the cost of ownership.	Redefining its core business and strategies; identifying key areas of focus; pursuing strategic growth by joint ventures; building customer-oriented, market-driven organization.

airline operation are unavailable to others, including the engine manufacturers who rely heavily on the feedback only airlines can provide.

Historically, airlines have stocked for 'just in case' rather than today's preferred practice of 'just in time'. This concept, widely practised by airlines, has resulted in a large inventory of spares held by them. This may reduce the risk, and the resulting cost, of having an aircraft-on-ground situation, but the cost of holding such a vast amount of inventory is increasingly difficult to justify. However, this surplus inventory can be an asset to the airline owned service, putting it in a commanding position to market its engine services with adequate spare part support.

An international reputation for reliability enjoyed by an airline, based on technological and engineering excellence, could be extended to any of its customers. With the parent airline providing the bulk of the work, the facility would be well-equipped and experienced, and have the

Table 11.3 (continued)

Core activities in service management	*Core activities in business development*
Restructuring engineering division/ department as a subsidiary; redesigning its service concept, redefining its operating strategy; creating an excellent service delivery system.	Developing global markets; shifting from an airline requirement to an extended business focus; decentralizing; serving captive and third party markets; marketing total aircraft maintenance services; proving single source procurement.
Enhancing its service concept; realigning its operating strategy; improving its service delivery system for increased efficiency.	Developing global markets; increasing scale in its primary business; linking specific core competencies; serving third party markets; providing innovative customer service to attract niche markets.
Restructuring service division/department as a subsidiary; redesigning its service concept; redefining its operating strategy; creating an excellent service delivery system	Pursuing globalization; shifting from a secondary after-sale support to a primary business focus; integrating vertically; serving third party markets; securing business on long-term, cost-per-hour contracts at point of sale; providing integrated engine services including fleet management programmes.

economies of scale to undertake any project required by customers. Additional support such as logistic support in transportation of engines with preferential rates and availability of cargo space, one stop comprehensive maintenance services, easily accessible and round the clock technical support and quick deployment of manpower, will ensure less disruption to the customer's operation if the maintenance centre is an airline owned facility. Large airline shops that do third party work can provide total aircraft maintenance services, providing single source procurement.

As a customer to the OEM, the airline-owned service enjoys the full support of the OEM technical representative office, especially in terms of obtaining original engineering data and evaluation of repair development, trouble-shooting assistance, and priority in the allocation of critical spares. Thus, the OEM leverage – having access to the OEM's technical support – is an added competitive advantage that airline- owned services have over independents.

Competitive advantages of independent services

Recent market trends such as the continued decline of the mature engine overhaul market coupled with the larger overhaul interval of the new generation engines, tighter OEM control of their after-market, and more demanding customers have adversely affected independents and mean that they are likely to lose market share. With their entrepreneurship and speed, some independents may survive through internal growth by increasing their customer base and external growth through mergers and acquisitions. The key challenge for them is to improve cost competitiveness while establishing or expanding their position in new generation engines.

Alternatively, innovation in customer service to develop niche markets, such as tailoring flexible work packages to meet diverse customer requirements, providing on-wing repair services, providing engine management and record keeping services, and providing inventory management and warranty administration, could become increasingly important to independents and it seems that this is where their strengths lie. Their unique skills and capabilities will be the competitive advantages they must rely upon. With the engine overhaul services as their primary business focus, independents have the flexibility and ability to tailor their services as solutions to customer needs. These unique characteristics of the independents and the broad customer base that accompanies this have greatly attracted the OEMs in their acquisition trail.

Competitive advantages of OEM services

As global over-capacity of engine overhaul services leads to consolidation, OEMs looking for a growth market will be the largest beneficiaries from changes in the market. The business strategies of OEMs are changing swiftly, aggressively moving into the after-market of their products and those of their competitors. One of the principal drivers for the OEMs is to ensure that their products continue to be low cost to operate, lowering the cost of ownership, which is necessary for continued industry viability.

It is noted from the case discussion that the technical knowledge OEMs have as designers is the greatest competitive advantage they have over others. Their thorough technical knowledge of the engine enables them to provide extensive engine performance warranty for work done by them according to their specific engine workscope. They also have the technological as well as financial resources necessary to invest in the development of new and proprietary repairs. Thus, in increasing their share and control of the repair market, they are able to establish a strong position in the new technology repair market. Another competitive advantage of the OEMs is the availability of spare parts, since they are the manufacturers of those parts. This assurance is critical to the operator in keeping the fleet flying and maintaining an on-time record.

Point-of-sale leverage of OEMs has given them an edge over others. Long term, competitive maintenance packages which are contractually integrated into the sale of new powerplants have enabled, for example, CFM International partners, General Electric and Snecma, to capture one-third of the available CFM56 engine overhaul market. An added advantage is the global after-sale product support of the OEMs that is in place for their customers world-wide. After-market support partnerships have been pursued and developed by the OEMs to achieve vertical integration up the supply chain through the different levels: support services, parts supply, component repair, engine overhaul and, ultimately, fleet management. In forming strategic linkages of core competencies through partnerships, the OEMs will be able to achieve long-term competitive advantage for global dominance.

Strategic activities of competitors

From the industry analysis and case presentations, it is clear that there has been a rethinking on the ways of doing business. As airlines are redefining their core business, independents are realigning their strategies to form linkages of specific competencies and the OEMs are integrating vertically.

As airlines recognize the need to focus their resources on core business, only high value-added activities are certain to be retained, outsourcing those activities that are not a source of competitive advantage. Many prefer to restructure their engineering departments into separate entities or sell them off to third parties. The airlines owned services who are seeking strategic growth, do so through joint ventures with partners, especially OEMs who have complementary competitive advantages to offer (Table 11.4, page 252). The technical knowledge of the OEM as an engine designer will complement the airline-owned services' lack of engineering design expertise and through spare parts pooling with the OEM, the high holding cost of inventories experienced by airline-owned services can be reduced. As an engine designer, the OEM will also be in a position to contribute to a better understanding of engine performance in evaluating performance warranty and to develop new extensive repairs. Added advantages of OEMs that are important to airline-owned services are market access through point of sale leverage and after-sale support network.

As airlines rationalize their supplier base to lower their procurement costs, some small independents are forced to merge in search of economies of scale to be competitive while others look for niche acquisitions that can strengthen their market positions and supplement internal product development effort.

Engine OEMs have redefined their objectives to seek a financial return and recoup the development cost of new generation engines from the sale

Table 11.4 Competitive strengths/weaknesses of airline-owned services and complementary strengths of OEM services

Strengths of airline-owned services	Weaknesses of airline-owned services	Complementary strengths of OEM services
Operational knowledge from fleet experience	Lack of engineering expertise	Technical knowledge of an engine designer
Large inventory of spares	High holding cost of inventories due to 'just-in-case' mentality	Ability to provide engine performance warranty
Economies of scale from captive market		Technological and financial resources for development of new and proprietary repairs and processes
	Lack of entrepreneurial drive	
OEM leverage as their customer		
	Lack of flexibility due to most systems designed to cater specifically for the parent airline	
		Availability of spare parts and inventory management programme
	Dependency on the parent airline for captive works and management initiatives	Point-of-sale leverage
		After-sale support to lower the cost of ownership

of parts and the accomplishment of repair and overhaul of engines. They are seeking and achieving dominance in the after-market through vertical integration by acquiring independent parts repair and engine overhaul facilities, and partnering with airlines in joint ventures. In the past, large airlines have been leaders in the full service arena. As airlines de-emphasize maintenance as a core activity, competition from large airlines is likely to diminish. While independents do not have the breadth of resources – either technical or financial – the engine OEMs have taken the opportunity to rapidly consolidate the engine after-market. Thus, OEMs will emerge to provide one stop services: a role previously reserved for large airlines.

In the reorganization efforts of all the organizations studied, a number of key tendencies were apparent. The first is the importance of responding to the increasing globalization of airlines, the principal client group for MRO services. Strategies of consolidation, alliance formation and global coverage are apparent in both sectors. Consolidation and alliances are encouraged by overcapacity, a problem apparent in both the airline and MRO industries. Furthermore, both industries have been characterised by new entrants and competitive expansion. New entrants have been a significant force in the airline industry as widespread deregulation and liberalization have lowered barriers to entry. Within the MRO industry, barriers to entry (investment, technical capability and reputation) remain considerable and the competitive expansion has been achieved by established players, primarily airline companies and engine manufacturers.

Second, there has been a shift from a technology focus to a customer focus, and towards achieving customer satisfaction based on the marketing philosophy of orienting the whole business to identify and satisfy customers' needs. Customers' needs have been identified and continuous performance improvement programmes are being implemented to achieve customer satisfaction. For both the airline-owned and OEM services, restructuring into a profit centre and, eventually, a subsidiary, has proved to be effective in improving overall customer satisfaction, eliminating unnecessary bureaucracy and creating a flatter, more responsive organizational structure.

Third, all engine overhaulers are seeking improved efficiencies to create the competitive edge required to outperform their rivals. A key focus has been on providing high quality, value-added service to customers.

However, despite these similarities, there are clear differences in the strategies pursued by particular types of competitor. These differences can be explained in terms of the characteristics of service industries and the differing competitive advantages of firms (Tables 11.3 and 11.4). Two characteristics of industrial services, their 'experience' nature and the importance of economies of scale and scope, are particularly relevant to the MRO industry. Clearly, airline maintenance is an industry where safety and reliability is paramount. This means that airlines subcontracting their maintenance functions must have the utmost confidence in their suppliers. The experience nature of such services (the quality of which can only be fully assessed in practice) is a major problem in the aviation business where the cost of such learning is prohibitive. For this reason, new entrants face considerable barriers to entry and, equally, established contractors enjoy considerable advantages. This demand for demonstrated capability also encourages high levels of specialization (since it is easier for customers to evaluate a narrow range of services) (Enderwick 1989). It also encourages in-house provision, or at least contractual arrangements, that make quality monitoring and evaluation relatively cheap and efficient. For this reason MRO services have traditionally been supplied in-house by major airlines (e.g. SIA) or by well established specialist independent servicing firms (e.g. GAS). This characteristic also helps to explain the ease with which OEMs have been able to expand into the after-sales market. They have both the technical capability and the reputation for high quality production. Indeed, their success in improving the reliability of their engines and reduced servicing intervals has meant that further growth has necessitated them moving aggressively into the service market. While they possess considerable resources and technical knowledge, OEMs do not have the operating experience that airlines enjoy. The OEMs' development of partnerships with major airlines has provided them with access to this knowledge.

Globalization of airline services has increased the importance of economies of scale and scope in the MRO industry. As airlines have combined to more fully utilize their assets, including aircraft, their geographical coverage has also increased considerably. This is the result of reduced regulation and the growth of both 'Open Sky' agreements and competitor alliances. Competitive pressures in the airline industry have put considerable pressure on the goal of cost minimization and, in turn, this pressure has been applied to the MRO industry. The achievement of considerable economies of scale contributes to such cost containment. Growing pressures on economies of scope result from the increasing mix of airline fleets, the growing longevity of engines and the amalgamation of engine types within global alliances. The various competitors within the MRO industry have sought to increase the scope of their service coverage in a number of ways. Independent shops have expanded their coverage through acquisition. In turn, they have become attractive targets for OEMs seeking to extend their scope beyond their own engine types. Airlines providing servicing functions have found it attractive to decentralize these activities in an attempt to obtain third party business. In each of these cases, acquisition or strategic alliance are the preferred strategies; this is, in part, a reflection of the need to rapidly acquire such expertise and, in part, the advantage of acquiring proven suppliers who enjoy market recognition. This reflects the vulnerability of smaller independents who are an attractive target for both OEMs (seeking new types of expertise and diverse locations) and airlines (seeking third-party customers).

Restructuring activities of competitors

From the industry analysis and case studies, it is apparent that the intense competition has caused four major waves to sweep through the industry: globalization, price competition, consolidation and collaboration.

Globalization

Globalization of the airline industry, the principal buyers of MRO services, has accelerated markedly since deregulation in the late 1970s. The emergence of two dominant global airline alliances has brought considerable consolidation and global reach. At the same time, airlines have increasingly focused on their core competencies: transporting passengers and cargo. The airline maintenance, repair and overhaul industry has faced considerable pressure to match this globalization. The original equipment manufacturers with their existing global after-sales support are best placed to respond to this pressure to globalize. They have achieved this through partnerships with their customers (airlines). Airlines providing MRO services have restructured their operations to provide greater independence, and the ability to service outside clients and new engine configurations. They have formed partnerships to enhance their geographical coverage and to ensure representation in at least the Triad blocs of Europe, North America and East Asia.

Price competition

As MRO transforms into an increasingly mature and global industry, there is intense pressure to contain costs. One of the effects of international competition has been to establish product (including service) quality as the primary basis for competition. This has led to a new concept of the relationship between price and quality. Fierce price competition has been combined with the demand for high and continuing quality standards, and this has eroded profit margins. To remain competitive MRO service suppliers will have to strive to cut costs further, boost productivity through flexible work practices and more clearly define their technical objectives in order to improve reliability and maximize financial returns. The more successful companies are moving toward flexible pricing structures, longer term contracts, participating in spare parts pooling programmes, and setting and keeping to 'target costing'.

Consolidation

Following price competition, consolidation has been the most obvious response to try to gain a balance between service providers and market opportunities.

As airlines rationalize their supplier base to lower their procurement costs, vendors are pressurized to merge so that they can be robust enough, in terms of capability, capacity and revenues, to be competitive. Another driver of consolidation is the on-going search for niche acquisitions that can strengthen market positions and supplement internal product development effort. One of the most compelling reasons for mergers and acquisitions is to improve the ability to deliver greater value to customers.

Further consolidation will define the structure as well as the dynamics of the industry. It will determine the number of players, the competitiveness of many companies and the level of vertical integration. For the survivors, consolidation also will yield a financially healthier industry, with greater market share concentrated among fewer competitors. However, some airlines, such as Lufthansa, are concerned that the OEMs could eventually monopolize and control the whole aftermarket, and in the long run price could increase. One of the dilemmas of globalization is that economic power can fall increasingly into fewer hands. Airlines who decide to subcontract MRO services prefer to have a choice in the market-place. Similarly, they fear that as OEMs increasingly acquire a greater share of the MRO market, their control over spare parts and the technical processes of repair, will bestow them with unwarranted power. However, the growth of airline alliances and the bargaining leverage they will enjoy represents a considerable countervailing force.

Collaboration

Although consolidation of the industry has improved the market outlook, it is not a 'cure all' solution. As airlines increasingly restructure their operations through alliances, MRO service providers are seeking ways to use such partnerships to improve their competitive position. Companies are forming alliances with suppliers, customers, other contractors, and sometimes even competitors in an attempt to make business relationships more efficient, costs more predictable, and financial investment more palatable.

In many industries, including aviation, established corporate advantages and predictable firm behaviour have been replaced by continuous innovation, co-operative agreements and other forms of collaboration. Within these networks, strategic alliances are of particular importance in bringing large and otherwise competing firms together to achieve specific objectives. The move to complex integration strategies is now influencing the MRO industry, integrating the value-added chain within the aviation industry. The OEMs are aggressively collaborating to compete to ensure that their products continue to be low cost to operate, lowering the cost of ownership which is necessary for continued industry viability.

Overall, our findings suggest that the most successful competitors in the new decade will be those engine overhaul shops that can buy market shares or secure all services to sustain the value of the engines at reduced cost of ownership for their customers. A priority is to build up a network of strategically located facilities and resources world-wide as the market consolidates and globalization becomes a reality. Active consolidation is currently taking place in the aircraft engine overhaul markets and it appears that the OEMs will emerge as truly global MRO organizations.

To facilitate local market penetration, service providers are moving closer to customers in order to identify and meet their needs. As a result, more co-operation and collaboration in the form of joint ventures and strategic alliances are being established in an attempt to spread risk, capture significant market share, and create more stable and efficient relationships with suppliers, customers and partners.

Conclusions

Our discussion of the aircraft maintenance, repair and overhaul industry highlights a number of tendencies which are likely to be found in a mature, and increasingly global industry characterised by globalization, over-capacity and technological change. Like many other intermediate service industries, MRO services are globalizing in part in response to the globalization strategies pursued by their major client group, the world's airlines. The globalization of both airline carriers and service providers appear to be intimately related.

The strategic changes characteristic of the MRO industry appear to be representative of many other increasingly global industrial service industries: increased interdependency, a growing customer- and market-focus, high quality value-added service provision combined with strict cost containment and growing consolidation. The major players in the MRO industry are pursuing distinctive strategies, strategies based on a combination of their resources, capabilities and expectations. Airlines are restructuring their MRO activities as separate businesses forced to seek third-party work as their parent organizations increasingly focus on their core business of transportation. Airline-owned services grow by joint ventures in line with their decentralizing effort. Independent shops have pursued growth in an attempt to achieve either a global presence or to develop a specialist niche market position. They have done this through mergers and acquisitions in forming strategic linkages of specific core competencies. However, the growing globalization of airline services and the increasingly mixed fleets being operated mean that specialization by region or engine type is unlikely to occur. Any specialization is likely to be along the lines of add-on services such as on-wing repair, engine management and record keeping, inventory management and warranty administration. The most aggressive competitors, OEMs, have shifted their strategic orientation from the provision of warranties to managing the cost of engine ownership through acquisitions and joint ventures and strategies of vertical integration. The engine OEMs who have the technological and financial resources are actively pursuing globalization of their engine services and appear likely to achieve world-wide domination. OEMs seem likely to emerge as the dominant industry players as they acquire independents and exploit asset complementarity through partnerships with airlines.

References

Donoghue, J. A. (1996) 'Outsourcing and the Cycle', *Air Transport World,* September: 7.

Enderwick, P. (1989) 'Some Economics of Service-Sector Multinational Enterprises', in P. Enderwick (ed.) *Multinational Service Firms*, 3–34, London: Routledge.

McKenna, J. T. and Scott, W. B. (1997) 'MRO's Challenge: Quality vs Cost', *Aviation Week and Space Technology*, 14 April: 44–5.

Smith, B. A. (1997) 'Engine Makers Develop New Service Strategies', *Aviation Week and Space Technology*, 17 March: 59–62.

The Canaan Group (1996) 'Airline Outsourcing: Implications for Airline Suppliers', *Overhaul and Maintenance*, March–April: 19–22.

Thorne, V. A. (1996) 'Heavy Maintenance: Around the World' *Air Transport World,* July: 75–103.

Todhunter, A. (1997) 'Outlook for the Engine Aftermarket', *The Fifth Annual AeroEngine Cost Management Conference*, Aviation Industry Conferences.

12 International alliances in service business

The case of the airline industry

Hannu Seristö

Introduction

The 1990s appear to have become the decade of alliances, just as the 1980s were the decade of mergers and acquisitions. Already in the 1980s it was suggested that strategic alliances are essential for firms to survive and prosper in the intensifying global competition (e.g. Ohmae 1989). The growth of alliances in the 1990s has been rather phenomenal; studies suggest annual growth rates above 100 per cent in the number of business alliances (see e.g. Pekar and Allio 1994; Luo 1996). Strategic alliances have been found to be unstable and they generally speaking have a poor record of success (see e.g. Gant 1995; Brouthers *et al.* 1995). Strategic alliances have been studied from various perspectives; these include that of alliances' characteristics (Borys and Jemison 1989), complexity of alliances (Killing 1988), rationale of alliances (Contractor and Lorange 1988), transaction costs (Parkhe 1993), alliances between competitors (Hamel *et al.* 1989; Hamel 1991; Doz 1996), trust and contractual arrangements in alliances (Gulati 1995), learning from alliances (Parkhe 1991; Lei *et al.* 1997; Inkpen 1998), value creation through alliances (Chan *et al.* 1997; Doz and Hamel 1998), and the assessment of alliance performance (Dussauge and Garrette 1995; Gleister and Buckley 1998). Very often studies have included transnational partnerships, but what is common for most of the studies is that they mainly focus on manufacturing industries, service sector less often being the object of research. However, it appears that alliances are becoming popular in the service sector, too, and therefore the dynamics of strategic alliances in the service industries deserve a closer look. Within the service sector it is the airline industry that is currently the main theatre for alliances, partly because mergers and acquisitions in this industry are often not possible due to authority regulation and government ownership. Consequently, this chapter will focus on the international alliances in service industries using the airline industry as an example, and sets out to seek answers to the following questions:

- what are the drivers of international airline alliances?
- what are the objectives of international alliances?

The main objective of this study is to present a model which depicts drivers and key variables of international airline alliances in the framework of airline strategies. Also, generalizability of the findings to other service industries will be assessed; even if the airline industry can be seen as an industry of rather unique features, the basic problem is rather similar to those in, for example, telecommunications. Finally, the dynamics in this service industry are compared to those in manufacturing industries and suggestions for areas of further studies are made.

Earlier studies on airline alliances from specific perspectives, different from the one here, include those by Youssef (1992), Ott and Sparaco (1997), Park and Cho (1997), and Park and Zhang (1997, 1998).

A brief history of airline alliances

The world airline industry has seen very strong growth during the last decades. For example, the volume of scheduled services, measured in the number of passenger-kilometres flown, more than doubled from 1980 to 1998. As for the future, most forecasters see an annual growth rate of traffic volume in the region of 4–5 per cent, meaning that the traffic volumes would again double in about fifteen years.

The airline industry has experienced major changes in the operational environment during the last two decades. Liberalization, or deregulation, has changed the rules of competition drastically in most major markets of the world. The industry experienced a severe recession in the early 1990s, sparked by the Persian Gulf crisis, but with the recovery of major economies and the very strong growth in air transport demand it has improved performance significantly towards the end of the decade. In fact, in 1997 the 100 largest airlines of the world had combined sales of US$ 288 billion, operating profit of 18.6 billion, and net profit of 9.5 billion. In 1992, the worst financial year of the industry history, the corresponding net result was a loss of US$ 8 billion. Still, the financial performance leaves room for improvement: the net margin for the top 100 carriers in 1997 was only 3.3 per cent (Gallacher 1998).

A great majority of the existing alliances in the airline industry have been formed in the 1990s, but there are alliances the origins of which can be traced as far back as to the 1940s. For example Air France has helped to set up the operations of many African airlines – such as Air Afrique, Royal Air Maroc and Tunisair – and still have equity stakes in those carriers. Similarly, Iberia had already invested in 1948 in Aviaco in South America. However, there was very little alliance activity until the late 1980s when a number of equity-based arrangements took place.

In the 1990s the number of alliances grew steadily each year, and the scene became very unstable. In 1990 the industry sources listed 172 alliances, of which eighty-two involved equity investment (Airline Business 1990). The latest survey by Air Transport Intelligence (1998) reported that there were a total of 513 airline alliances among 204 airlines in mid-1999, with an increase of 40 per cent over the year 1997. Most airline alliances are between two partners, but recently arrangements of more than two participants have emerged. It appears that world airlines are in the process of forming groups in their preparation for stiffer global competition: the largest groups – Star Alliance and Oneworld – now each have about 20 per cent of the world international passenger markets. Most alliances are between airlines from different countries, but there are alliances between carriers of the same nationality, too. Most airlines have several alliances, including domestic and international alliances; the largest number of alliances in 1999 was by Air France with thirty-three arrangements, out of which all but one were with foreign partners.

Out of the total of 513 alliances in 1998 only fifty-three (10 per cent) involved equity. It appears that equity-based arrangements were rather popular in the early 1990s, but lost some of their appeal after the mid-1990s. Here it must be mentioned that government authorities play a crucial role in determining the conditions for equity-based arrangements; this will be discussed in more detail later.

In 2000 there are four major alliance groups in the global airline industry. They all are constantly evolving, and some of them have not even been given a clearance by the competition authorities to proceed with concerted operations. In all of the alliances there are partners in at least two tiers: there are the core partners and associate partners. Again, it seems that the division into core and associate partners is also in constant flux. Only the Star Alliance, formed by United Airlines, Lufthansa, SAS, Air Canada, Thai Airways, and Varig, can be considered a truly multilateral alliance, where each partner has alliances with each and every other partner. The biggest of the alliances in 1999 was the Oneworld alliance built around the partnership between American Airlines and British Airways.

On the nature of airline alliances

There have been very few mergers and acquisitions in the world airline industry as a whole. There was quite a lot of merger and acquisition activity in the United States in the 1980s, but overall, particularly international mergers and acquisitions are almost non-existent. The reason for this is the prohibitive stand by regulatory authorities world-wide. Consequently airlines have been forced to use other ways than mergers and acquisitions in their search for more competitiveness. There is a strong need to consolidate the industry but, largely due to government control, airlines can only go halfway along the consolidation path.

As the number of alliance arrangements in an airline grows, conflicts of interests may arise and the justification for a certain alliance becomes less straight-forward. Consequently the alliance scenario appears to be in a flux: alliances are broken and new ones formed very frequently. The alliance frenzy in the late 1990s developed into a situation where it sometimes is difficult to categorize another airline either as a competitor or a partner.

Another interesting dimension is the role that authorities play in the airline business. As has been mentioned, the airline industry has been very tightly regulated for most of its history. Liberalization really started only in 1978 with the US airline industry deregulation. Even after the European Union reached the final stage of its airline industry liberalization in 1997 there are many types of regulations and limitations that government authorities set on airline operations and competition. In fact the situation has reached a somewhat schizophrenic point: on the one hand authorities press for more competition through less regulation, but on the other hand, when stronger airlines try to rationalize operations in the name of better competitiveness, then authorities intervene and set limits on or even deny such efforts. Consequently it is the authorities, primarily those of the United States and the European Union, that may decide whether the airline industry can develop into one of efficient global players, global quality service and, perhaps, low fares for consumers. Overall it appears that this particular service industry is watched much more closely by authorities than are most manufacturing sectors.

Challenges and open questions

Airline alliances, just like strategic alliances in most other industries, have had a rather poor record of success. It has been suggested that fewer than 30 per cent of international alliances in the airline industry have been successful (Lindquist 1996).

Simply put, airlines seek international competitiveness through alliances. Even if in general it is the economies – be they those of scale, scope or density – that motivate airlines, it is not quite clear what are the different types of drivers that are behind alliance formation. Also, the consequent objectives of alliances are not necessarily clear. Moreover, it appears that there are not very good models available that could be used as tools when assessing the value and performance of alliances.

As to the drivers of international airline alliances, the starting point is that quite evidently there are drivers of different level. Some alliances are driven by mere cost savings in operations, like through rationalizing ground handling at airports operated by both or all partners. Others are more of a market power issue, for example through code-sharing and pooled frequent-flyer programs. Yet others may be more of a strategic nature, aiming at the mere survival of the airline. Concerning the objectives of international airline alliances, the immediate objectives can naturally be drawn from the drivers; so, the objective of a block seat arrangement with another airline would be to secure or increase sales. However, the longer-term, more strategic level objectives of, say, growth, market expansion, image enhancement, learning, and so on are less clear.

This study is based on prior research on competition in the airline industry and on strategic alliances. The core of the study is a longitudinal analysis of the alliances reported in the industry, using firms' own and third-party material as sources of information. Key sources of information are annual reports between 1988 to 1997/8 from the following airlines: Air Canada, American Airlines, British Airways, Canadian Airlines (PWA Corp.), Delta Air Lines, Finnair, KLM, Lufthansa, Qantas Airways, SAS, Swissair, Thai Airways International, and United Airlines.

Features of the airline industry

Before going into the discussion on the MNCs in the airline business, a brief mention of the ownership arrangements in airlines is in order. In Europe, in most Asian countries, in Africa, and in South America major carriers have until recently been mostly government-owned, and flag carriers of nation states. However, in the United States, the world's largest air transport market, airlines have been private enterprises from the very beginning of the industry. In Europe the first major airline to be fully privatized was British Airways in the 1980s, with the rest seeming to follow with different schedules.

The airline industry is in many ways one of the most international of service industries. International traffic forms a major portion of all air traffic, and even domestic traffic is most often dependent on, or at least tightly linked to, international services. Then, do multinational enterprises dominate in this highly international business, as they do in most other industries?

In this very international business there are no dominant, truly global players. A question has often been asked whether there are true multinational companies (MNC) among airlines. By definition MNCs should conform to the criteria (see Bartlett and Ghoshal 1995) of, first, having substantial direct investments in foreign countries. Second, they should be engaged in the active management of their offshore assets, rather than simply holding them in a passive portfolio. The management criteria would appear to be fulfilled by most internationally operating carriers. However, concerning investments, airlines rarely have significant tangible investment in foreign countries, but typically hold only rather small marketing subsidiaries abroad. However, as Bartlett and Ghoshal (1995) define these investments not only as production facilities but also as financial, legal and contractual relationships with foreign affiliates – in addition they emphasize the management integration of operations in different countries as the key differentiating characteristic of an MNC – it is fair to say that many internationally operating large airlines are MNCs. Then, whether airlines are transnational companies can be questioned too. The term transnational has often been used rather loosely, but the more specific definition of the term used by Bartlett and Ghoshal refers to firms being locally responsive in various national markets while retaining their global efficiency. This definition suggests specialized but dispersed resources and activities, realized in the form of an interdependent network of world-wide operations, producing both efficiency and flexibility at the same time. Now, whether airlines operate as suggested by the transnational criteria is rather difficult to determine. Perhaps the best answer today is that some do, most do not.

The role of governments and unions

International air traffic has been strongly affected by bilateral agreements between governments, regulating traffic rights and traffic volumes. The so-called 'Five Freedoms' have been used to determine the traffic rights, ranging from the right to fly over another country without landing (first freedom) to the right of an airline from country A to carry revenue traffic between country B and other non-A countries (fifth freedom). These five rights have been amended by further two rights, the seventh one being the right of an airline of country A to carry revenue traffic between two points in country B; this is also called cabotage right. The process towards more liberal bilaterals, extensive multilateral arrangements, and so-called 'Open-Skies' agreements has been long and is still far from completed. Bilateral agreements have been a barrier to organic international growth for many airlines, and they could be considered tools of protectionism by nation states. The bilateral agreements have been an important variable when foreign ownership of airlines has been discussed; the system has historically built on the assumption that an airline based in and operating mainly from one country is also owned by parties of that country.

In general terms, authorities have eased their regulation of the airline industry since the late 1970s, but they still play an important role. The liberalization, or deregulation if you like, of the industry has aimed at bringing competition to the market place, compelling airlines to better efficiency, and bringing benefits to consumers in the form of better offering of services at a lower price. The same rationale is seen in many other industries, where eventual consolidation of the industry has often followed, mostly through mergers and acquisitions. In the airline industry, however, authorities have been very strict about allowing particularly transnational mergers or acquisitions, something that puts airline management in a rather perplexing position. It seems that governments are very careful and protective of their national airlines, no matter whether the government has an equity stake in the airline or not.

A major argument from the authorities – and a very understandable and valid one – is that the consolidation of the airline industry would spell dangers particularly to the consumers: division of markets between a few very large carriers, less competition, less choice, higher fares, and poorer service. In other words exactly those problems that were tackled through the deregulation process started in the US in the late 1970s. While the arguments of the authorities make sense, they could lead to a re-regulated airline industry, where the competitive pressure would not drive airlines to rationalized operations and efficiency.

Another interested party in the issue of international airline industry consolidation is the labour unions. Interestingly it is the pilot unions that are working on transnational labour movement to protect the interests of their members. It appears that unions have opposed mergers and acquisitions – and appear to oppose large-scale alliances, too – because they might lead to more efficient organization and thus lower demand for personnel. However, it appears that in the light of the 4–5 per cent forecasted annual growth of demand for air transport, the fear that jobs would be lost in the industry as a whole has been unwarranted. It would perhaps be more correct to speak of the need for personnel only increasing more slowly.

Drivers of international alliances

In general terms, earlier research has categorized the reasons for alliances as, for example:

- risk sharing
- scale economies
- access to markets
- access to technology
- market convergence.

As to airline alliances, it has been suggested (see e.g. Alamdari and Morrell 1997) that there are two main drivers: the search for more market power, and the search for lower operating costs. These broad categories cover the two basic reasons for airlines' alliance arrangements, but it would seem that there is room for further elaboration.

Studying airline industry alliances of the past suggests that the role of authority control is an area which in itself deserves to be discussed as a reason for alliances. The following factors can be found among the reasons for alliances in the industry:

- mergers and acquisitions in general have been tightly controlled in the airline industry;
- foreign ownership in airlines has been restricted by governments;
- bilateral agreements between countries make foreign ownership of airlines problematic.

Examples of control concerning mergers and acquisitions are numerous; in the US there have been several domestic cases where authorities have intervened in planned mergers and acquisitions. In the international arena examples include the attempt by SAS to acquire one-quarter of British Caledonian in 1987; this attempt was blocked partly by the opposition from the UK Government. (British Caledonian was eventually taken over by British Airways.)

As to restrictions on foreign ownership in airlines, it appears to be the control that worries authorities. For example, the US has set a 25 per cent limit to the share of foreign ownership and voting rights in US airlines, so that KLM of the Netherlands and British Airways could not go above that limit in the early 1990s when investing in Northwest Airlines and USAir, respectively. Control by a foreign investor in an airline has been restricted by other means than ownership limitations, too, such as the number of members to be appointed in the board of the airline.

Considering their need for reaching the assumed economies of scale, scope or density, airlines have been left with very few options other than slow organic growth or alliances. In pursuing alliances airlines have, again due to government control, had limited options, leading mostly to code-sharing arrangements. However, even code-sharing arrangements are seen by some officials as being *de facto* mergers and are considered only a way around anti-trust laws.

Objectives of alliances

Earlier research on strategic alliances – typically dealing with manufacturing industries – has pointed to two primary categories of objectives in alliance arrangements: product objectives and knowledge objectives. In the area of product objectives there appears to have been two primary goals: either the enhancement of product offering or the reduction of production costs. As to knowledge objectives, the goal has typically been to learn some specific new technology or process from a partner; it appears that the goals as to knowledge transfer have often been rather specified and particular.

Concerning airline alliances earlier research has listed several objectives for the co-operative arrangements. These objectives represent different levels in terms of being tactical or strategic in nature. This study is not discussing the tactical, operative objectives such as shared lounges or streamlined check-in procedures but focuses on the objectives of a more strategic nature. It is hoped that such a new way to determine or classify alliance objectives could be used as an additional tool by airline management to assess and develop alliances in airlines.

Evidence on airline alliance drivers and objectives

This study examined the alliance history of the major airlines of the world using several sources of information such as general news services, industry press, and the airlines' own publications. In order to illustrate the alliance development in the industry in more detail and to provide background for the industry-level analysis later in this chapter, summaries of alliance development in a few key airlines are presented. As the purpose of the chapter is to determine drivers and objectives of international airline alliances, the summary below is limited to the international alliance activities of the airlines in question, leaving domestic arrangements aside. Moreover, the summaries illustrate the development during the last decade, from 1988 to 1998, because that is when most of the alliance activity has taken place.

The summaries present quotations from one type of information source only: airline annual reports. This selection is made in order to enhance the comparability of company views; namely, for each airline the annual report is a key medium for delivering messages to the investors, authorities and the general public, and the messages need to be informative and truthful. Of course a lot is left unsaid in annual reports – for instance comments concerning some particular competitors – but that is likely to apply to any contemporary published material. The airlines presented here are American Airlines, Delta Airlines, KLM, and SAS. They are all key partners in today's big multilateral alliances and have played in their own way important roles in the development towards large airline groupings. These cases also reveal somewhat different drivers and objectives of alliance arrangements in airlines.

Scandinavian Airlines System (SAS)

SAS has been perhaps the trailblazer of the industry in developing alliances. Already in 1985 SAS's CEO Carlzon predicted that there would be only five major airlines in Europe by the year 1995 and declared that SAS wanted to be 'One of Five in 1995'. During the latter part of the 1980s SAS tried to build alliances of various type with other carriers but was unable to raise sufficient interest; in SAS's words the 'long-term visions were shadowed by thriving economies'. Carlzon wrote in 1987 for the Annual Report of 1986:

> We base our efforts on two main strategies: broadening our passenger base through co-operation in Europe, and establishing new gateways on other continents. By establishing alliances with local airlines in these foreign locations, we can extend our fully integrated system to our passengers in their continued travel.

In the late 1980s SAS fought to acquire a part of British Caledonian, but eventually lost it to British Airways. Co-operation in the USA was started with Continental Airlines in 1988. In the early 1990s SAS stepped up its drive for alliances. In the 1992 Annual Report Carlzon wrote:

> SAS's goal in its search for partners has been to join a constellation which can operate a profitable global traffic system with strong hubs in

Europe and which meets our basic task of developing services to, from, via and within Scandinavia. The best alternative is an extensive strategic co-operation with at least two of the medium-sized companies or one of the giants. In our opinion it is more advantageous for our shareholders and our home market for SAS to be an equal partner in a 'fourth force' in Europe rather than a small part of one of the three major carriers.

The urgent need for defensive strategic moves was echoed in the same message by Carlzon:

> In the future companies which obstinately uphold national interests and allow them to stand in the way of essential restructuring will have chosen the route towards elimination. At best they can expect to be a regional air transport operator which feeds traffic to one of the industry's giants.

Further, the same annual report stated:

> But long-term survival requires stable platforms. It can only be achieved with cross-ownership, viable mergers or other forms which allow fundamental structural, financial and commercial integration.

The backbone for SAS's international co-operation for a long time was the European Quality Alliance (EQA) formed in 1990 with Austrian Airlines and Swissair, later joined and again left by Finnair. In addition to market presence aspect, within the EQA SAS emphasized strongly the great potential to reduce costs through co-operation in, for instance, aircraft maintenance. SAS along with other EQA partners started talks with KLM in 1991 about extensive strategic co-operation, called Alcazar, but this project collapsed in 1993. By 1992 SAS had built co-operation agreements also with All Nippon Airways, LanChile, Qantas, Varig, and Thai International.

The recession of the early 1990s forced SAS to reconsider its strategies. In 1995 the new CEO, Stenberg, wrote in the Annual Report:

> Scandinavia has been given greater prominence in SAS's strategy. It is the task of SAS as an independent company to serve the home market with an effective and in every way attractive air transport product. Reliable co-operation partners, with good traffic systems which complement SAS, will be an important part of what we have to offer. But we no longer regard the partners issue as a matter of survival.

As to the strategic alliance built with Lufthansa, Thai Airways International, and United Airlines in 1995, SAS aimed in 1996 at a 5 per cent improvement in operating revenue in five years thanks to the alliance.

In 1997 SAS estimated that it had benefited by some US\$ 20 million in the form of additional revenues from the Lufthansa alliance alone. The new, more extensive Star Alliance, formally established in 1997, included Air Canada and Varig, and went much further than mere code-sharing. In 1998 it was estimated at SAS that the Star Alliance had provided an earnings contribution of nearly US\$ 50 million for SAS in 1997.

SAS started in the 1980s with a strategy of building alliances with airlines that were either smaller or of the same size as SAS itself. In the 1990s, under new leadership, the alliance strategy was refocused on partnering with large airlines. Also, SAS experience had taught that equity-based arrangements are very difficult to manage, and therefore further alliances would be pursued without ownership. Moreover, the emphasis in its own operations was pulled back from one of global reach to one that concentrated on being a dominant player in the markets of its home region. It appears that the Star Alliance has been seen to produce significant benefits in the short and medium-term in the area of marketing, while in the longer term additional benefits are expected from operational cost savings in maintenance, sourcing, handling, and so on.

KLM

In its 1989 Annual Report KLM emphasized the liberalization of the European aviation as a motive to strive for co-operative links with other carriers. These links were seen to provide additional opportunities in both passenger and cargo markets to safeguard KLM's market position. The criteria for the co-operative links were determined, among other things, as:

- increased market penetration and geographical coverage of the KLM network;
- securing or expanding the position of Schiphol (Amsterdam) airport as the gateway to Europe;
- expansion of regional European feeder lines and intra-European traffic;
- enhancement of intercontinental supply lines.

In addition to its several smaller partnerships, KLM's investment in 1989 in Wings Holdings, Inc. brought it a partial control of Northwest Airlines, the fourth largest American carrier, and was meant to strengthen KLM's position on the North Atlantic market. Partnership with Garuda Indonesia was to strengthen presence in the South-East Asian market. Moreover, KLM wanted to invest in Sabena World Airways of Belgium to 'open up new opportunities in intra-European air transport', but these attempts were frustrated. In 1991 the company saw strengthening its European market base as the key task. In 1992 KLM intensified its partnership with Northwest Airlines, following the Netherlands–US 'Open-Skies' agreement; the alliance was granted anti-trust immunity in the US in the same year. However, due to the losses at Northwest Airlines KLM wrote down the book value of its investment (initially US$ 400 million) in 1993. In 1994 KLM reported:

> KLM continues to consider alliances also in Europe as desirable at some stage in the future, to achieve the economies of scale needed to strengthen KLM's competitive position. Following the termination of the Alcazar alliance negotiations with Austrian Airlines, SAS and Swissair, we have focused mainly on strengthening KLM's position as a global carrier.

The proposed Alcazar alliance failed in late 1993 as its partners were unable to agree on the positioning of the alliance in the US and the consequent choice of the American partner. In 1995 KLM stated in its Annual Report:

> KLM has committed itself to developing a global airline system jointly with partners. It aims at the creation of a strong, globally competitive position, which can be defended even in less favourable economic circumstances. . . . KLM must, in alliance with its partners, further strengthen its market base in Europe and further reduce the cost of its European operations.

Moreover, in 1995 it was seen that KLM needed more than one partner in the rapidly growing Asian market.

In 1995 KLM expanded its alliance with Northwest Airlines to include – in addition to operating joint flight services – such areas as ground handling, reservation co-ordination, aircraft maintenance, and sales. In its 1996 mission statement KLM gave, as one of its four commitments, to 'strengthen its market presence, in part through alliances with other carriers'. In 1997 there was a slight refocus in the KLM strategy, as stated in its Annual Report:

> Our strategy is based on the development of an efficient, world-wide network, together with partners. . . . We have chosen a more focused approach to growth. We will continue to strengthen our network but will seek depth rather than further spread.

In 1997 KLM made a distinction between different types of alliances by putting its partners into five categories: global partner, network partners, route partners, leisure flight partners, and cargo partners. In the same year the partnership with Northwest Airlines was reorganized; in 1998 the two partners rationalized their sales and handling organizations both in North America and Europe, thus reducing overlap.

In 1998 KLM reported its ambition 'to be a key player in a strong global alliance that develops and operates a world-wide airline system spanning the world's three major trading blocs: America, Europe and Asia'. In addition, the company reported in 1998:

Our growth strategy is underpinned by belief in KLM's future as an independent airline and strong partner in a global alliance. The intended increase in scale will reduce unit cost and structurally raise profitability. . . . The alliance with Northwest Airlines – the first step towards a Global Airline System – will provide the leverage required to realize this target.

In 1998 KLM negotiated with Alitalia and Continental Airlines about joining the KLM–Northwest alliance; the companies also had an objective of finding another Asian partner in the near future.

Overall, KLM's approach to alliances appears to represent a rather common way of seeing alliances. First of all, air traffic politics and the regulation by government authorities are both a major motivator and a limitation to the pursuit of alliances. Second, it appears that the relative significance of market presence and more efficient resource utilization varies according to changes in the economy: in good times market expansion appears as a key driver, but in harder times the need to reduce costs is emphasized. Company reports do not mention specific actions against any competition nor learning as a particular motivator for alliance pursuits.

American Airlines

American Airlines – the world's largest airline in 1997 by many measures such as revenue, operating profit, and the number of employees – has built its international operations quite slowly, operating first and foremost within the USA. The strong areas for American Airlines outside the USA have traditionally been the Caribbean and Central and South America. Even in 1990 the company operated to only eight countries in Europe, but during the 1990s international expansion has been significant. The international growth has been primarily internal, although American Airlines has acquired international routes from other airlines such as Eastern and TWA. It has been perhaps the most active airline to participate in the international air politics debate and has demanded more opportunities to operate internationally on a competitive basis. American Airlines' alliance arrangements were sped up in 1990 when it established code-sharing with Air New Zealand, the Hungarian Malev and the Hong Kong based-Cathay Pacific. The recession of the early 1990s had an effect on American Airline's strategic thinking. Its Annual Report for 1991 stated:

We will be less growth oriented in the '90s and will aggressively seek alternative approaches to controlling costs, enhancing productivity and increasing revenues.

However, in 1991 the company made a code-sharing agreement with

Lufthansa. In 1994 American Airlines made a long-term services and marketing agreement with Canadian Airlines, and began co-ordinating services with British Midland Airways, Qantas, South African Airways and Gulf Air, and made marketing alliance agreements with Alitalia and Japan Airlines. In 1996 the company announced a number of code-sharing agreements and a broader alliance with British Airways. The full realization of the alliance with British Airways has, then, been delayed for years. In 1997 American Airlines' CEO, Crandall, wrote in the Annual Report:

> Because the airline industry is increasingly global, remaining competitive requires us to serve the largest possible number of origin-destination markets world-wide. The most important international development of 1996 was the announcement of our alliance with British Airways, which will, once implemented, position American to compete in thousands of new markets and make us fully competitive with the existing global alliances of other major US carriers. The American–British Airways alliance is the centrepiece of a pattern of alliances we have been building as we adjust to the changing nature of international competition.

In 1997 alliance agreements were made, or plans for such announced, with Iberia, Aerolineas Argentinas, Japan Airlines, LanChile, Aero California of Mexico, Asiana of South Korea, China Eastern of mainland China, and Philippine Airlines.

The 1998 American Airlines Annual Report stated:

> By granting antitrust immunity to alliances between US and foreign carriers, the US has made international alliances a virtual necessity. American has reacted to the changing environment by setting out to create the industry's premier set of alliances.

Delta Air Lines

Delta purchased nearly all of the collapsed Pan Am's transatlantic routes, shifting its focus from being a predominantly US domestic carrier to that of being a global airline. In the early 1990s Delta stated that a part of its international strategy was to use code-sharing with other quality airlines to support Delta's international service. The reasoning was that this enabled Delta to remain in markets that would be unprofitable to fly alone, and to offer service in new markets without major capital expenditures. Delta's 1995 Annual Report stated:

> codesharing arrangements allow Delta to establish, maintain or increase its presence in key international markets, while more efficiently managing its resources.

In 1996 there were thirteen code-sharing partners, and with three of them Delta received approval of anti-trust immunity from the US Department of Transportation to pursue a global marketing alliance. This marketing alliance, called Atlantic Excellence, between Delta, Austrian Airlines, Sabena, and Swissair included – in addition to code-sharing – pricing, scheduling and other operational co-ordination; joint sales and marketing were still seen as 'opportunities'. In 1997 Delta announced code-sharing arrangements with Air France, China Southern and Transbrasil. In 1998 Delta and United Airlines agreed on a broad marketing relationship; however, due to opposition from the pilots' union Delta was not able to proceed with a code-sharing arrangement with United Airlines, but had to continue their co-operation through a recip-rocal frequent-flyer program only. In their Annual Report for 1998 Delta underlined the role of strategic alliances:

> Delta will proceed aggressively with world-wide alliance discussions in the future, not just because alliances are desirable from a business standpoint – although they are – but also because we must. Airline alliances are revolutionising the nature of world-wide competition, and Delta intends to be a leader as these changes occur.

In about seven years Delta has grown from a domestic carrier to a signif-icant global player, thanks mainly to alliance arrangements, particularly in Europe. For example, Delta has been since 1997 the largest operator on the North Atlantic market, the largest and most competitive international market in the world. In Delta's history of international alliances the roles of market power and evasion of regulations as drivers appear to stand out, and the resource utilization improvement seems to be primarily Delta's internal effort.

Model for international airline alliance dynamics

Based on the study within the airline industry, a model (Figure 12.1) is presented here on the dynamics of international alliances, depicting factors that have been the drivers of alliance efforts. The model is set in a framework where the relevant recent changes in the airline industry are shown, as well as the consequent basic strategic choices, and the alternative strategies for airlines. The model builds on a strategy framework presented earlier (Seristö 1993).

There are numerous factors, many of which have been touched upon in this chapter, that effectively limit the basic strategy choices of airlines into three: growth strategy, focus strategy and lowest cost strategy. Growth can be sought either internally (organic growth) or externally. As internal growth is often slow, it may be preferable under the present circumstances for many airlines to seek growth externally; then the options are mergers

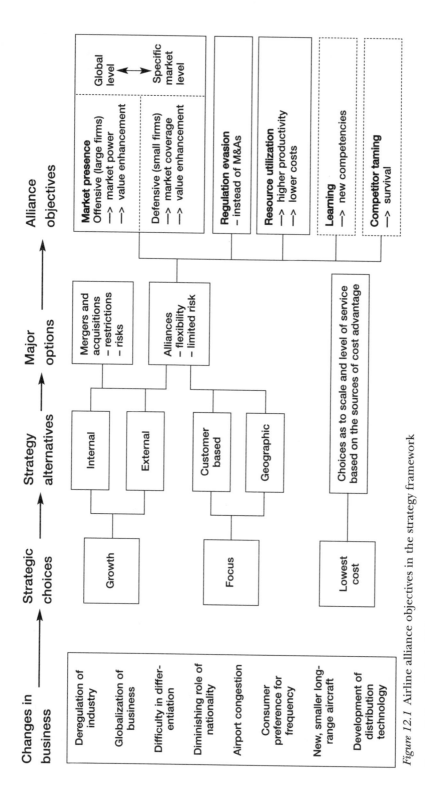

Figure 12.1 Airline alliance objectives in the strategy framework

Source: © Hannu Seristö, 1999

and acquisitions, or alliances. As there are many limitations to airline mergers and acquisitions, alliances often provide a less complicated route for growth. Alliances provide more flexibility than outright mergers and acquisition, and they are likely to carry less risks than do the latter.

Even if an airline chooses focus as its basic strategy, there are pressures in the competitive environment suggesting the utilization of alliances. Whether the airline bases its strategy on different customer groups (e.g. business travellers) or on certain geographic area (e.g. traffic between Europe and South America), it is nevertheless likely to benefit from some sort of partnership with suitable airlines. The simple rationale is that no matter what the niche or specific geographic market is, an airline is likely to benefit from a larger catchment area and better connections.

As to airlines choosing the lowest cost strategy, alliances may be of lesser importance, at least in the light of today's experiences, because of the nature of operations by low-cost carriers. In Europe the low-cost airlines, in practice charter carriers, typically cater for tourist traffic in and out of holiday destinations, and in this type of traffic connecting flights provide only limited added value. Elsewhere in the world, primarily in the USA, low-cost carriers serve the business traveller segment too, but so far a major part of the business has been on domestic point-to-point markets where the value-added provided by good connections is not necessarily essential. Here it is necessary to make a distinction between low-cost carriers such as Southwest Airlines and the feeder carriers, such as American Eagle, which typically operate relatively small aircraft on short routes with the primary objective of providing connections to the networks of larger carriers. However, the fact that today alliances for low-cost carriers are rare should by no means be interpreted as meaning that there is no potential in building an international alliance of low-cost carriers for the ever-more important leisure-travel segment; in fact, that might provide interesting opportunities in the global tourist market of the future.

As to the drivers of international alliances, it appears that, first, the changes in the industry have made it essential for most carriers to seek growth and to secure presence in a larger market; second, the many types of regulation in the industry make alliances the only feasible way to grow and seek presence in a larger market; and third, there is a pressure to utilize resources better, i.e. to reduce operating costs.

Securing market presence can be seen either as an offensive objective of alliances, typical for large airlines, or as an defensive objective, typical for medium-sized and small airlines. Larger airlines seek market power and consequent enhanced value for customers by pursuing larger network coverage, higher frequencies, more extensive loyalty programs and dominance of so-called hub airports through alliance arrangements. Medium-sized and small carriers appear to seek more market coverage rather than outright market power in order to respond to the challenge by expanding larger airlines; smaller carriers seem to consider participation in alliances essential in trying to avoid shrinking into mere regional operators, which, of course, might be the destiny of small carriers even with alliance arrangements. In the market presence objective of airline alliances it is necessary to distinguish the global level and the specific market level, which may require arrangements of conflicting interests. For example, for many reasons it is valuable for SAS to co-ordinate closely its operations on a global level with its Star Alliance partners, but in the specific markets of the Nordic countries SAS may need to deviate from the ideal Star Alliance strategy because it needs to respond decisively to the challenges from Finnair, a key rival in SAS's home market.

Getting around various forms of regulation in the airline industry is another motivator for alliances. For one thing, the fact that governments are still notable owners in many internationally operating airlines makes acquisitions of and mergers with airlines somewhat problematic in general: national flag carriers are still considered in many countries a part of the national property and the country's image, and therefore foreign ownership is not viewed favourably. Second, governments have often set specific limitations on the share of foreign ownership in the airlines of their nationality; for example in the USA there is a limit of a maximum 25 per cent on the shares and voting rights that a foreign firm can control in a US airline. Third, anti-trust legislation makes mergers and acquisitions problematic in many countries because these often would lead to a dominant, if not monopoly, position of the united firm, at least in some markets. The background for this is that for historic regulatory reasons there are very many markets where a duopoly exists. Finally, the fact that bilateral agreements between countries still form much of the basis for international air transportation causes some problems.

The third motivator for alliances is the need to utilize resources better. This can be pursued either through higher productivity or simply by lowering costs. Higher productivity is sought, for example, through sharing aircraft and air crew capacity, using partner's ground handling and airport passenger services at foreign stations instead of providing them by the airline itself, and making better use of possible excess aircraft maintenance capacity by servicing partner airlines' aircraft. Capacity sharing arrangements can often be complemented by specialization, for example in engine maintenance. As to direct cost savings, for example joint sourcing of fuel, catering, aircraft, spare parts, or information and marketing services may produce significantly lower costs than sourcing alone by each partner.

As to the relative role of the three alliance motivators it appears that it is the pursuit of stronger market presence that clearly has been more apparent and dominant, the need for better resource utilization being clearly secondary, and also more of a longer-term nature. Concerning the role of regulation and the need to circumvent it, the assessment is somewhat difficult. It seems very often to be a factor in alliance building, but very rarely it is seen as the primary reason: it could be seen as a common factor, part of the environment for nearly all airlines of the world.

It appears that different drivers have a different nature, or perhaps justification, in different kind of airlines. In this respect airlines can be grouped roughly into large and small firms, and the relevant dimensions for the nature of drivers can be determined as tactical-versus-strategic and defensive-versus-offensive. Figure 12.2 illustrates the positioning of drivers along these dimensions for large airlines.

Markedly different from many manufacturing industries, where the ability to learn from a more experienced or otherwise better partner is often given as a reason for building alliances, the learning factor hardly ever came up in this study. Even if it is understandable that airlines are not very willing to publicly shout about their needs to learn from other airlines, thereby indicating their own possible deficiencies, it still appears that airlines generally speaking do not make sufficient use of the opportunity to learn better practices. My earlier research (e.g. Seristö 1995; Seristö and Vepsäläinen 1997) has shown that there are big differences in the performance levels of airlines in various functions, indicating great improvement potential in some firms.

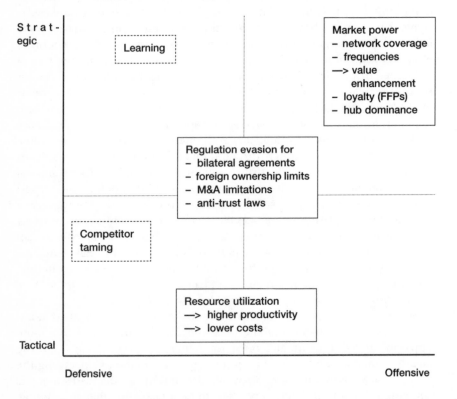

Figure 12.2 Drivers of international alliances in the airline industry: large carriers

Source: © Hannu Seristö, 1999

Finally, making competitor airlines partners rather than rivals would appear to be a very valid motivator in today's airline business. This, however, hardly ever came up specifically during the study. Certainly it is true that firms are not eager to pinpoint their arch-rivals in an industry of such turmoil – where today's rival can be tomorrow's partner and vice versa – but nevertheless it was something of a surprise that what is here called 'competitor taming' was never really suggested by the airlines. Earlier research, mainly concerning manufacturing industries, has suggested that making friends out of foes would be a motivation for many alliances. 'Competitor taming', in the sense of the term used here, is very close to what Doz and Hamel (1998) have termed 'co-option'. Again, just as with regulation evasion, the airlines' rush, primarily for market presence, and secondarily for resource utilization, perhaps just over-shadows competitor taming as a motivator for alliances, but presumably is a hidden factor in many alliance cases.

One outcome of the study is the evidence of the essential role that market presence plays in airlines' strategic planning for survival and pros-perity: having global reach appears to be a must in most airlines' strategic plan. Also, it appears that resource utilization is a factor often acknowl-edged but actively pursued quite slowly. One explanation for this slow action is, of course, the rigidity that airline management face due to both very strong labour unions and regulation by authorities. However, overall it appears that the firms are rushing so hard to secure positions as to their market reach that they are paying perhaps too little attention to the longer term factor of learning from alliances. Maybe the history of airlines as national icons, at least in Europe, have created corporate cultures that are not the best environments for absorbing new practices. It would seem that the crisis of the industry in the early 1990s has brought some more flexi-bility in many airlines, but a comparison to other industries would indicate that there is still quite a way to go, but a way with great potential.

Managerial challenges

It appears that alliance building is so much a part of evolution in the airline industry that most airlines need to participate in it: the opportunity cost of not participating might prove too high. Management in airlines face consid-erable challenges in making alliances work: there is the pressure from authorities, demands by unions, perhaps mixed ownership by government and private parties, and the normal challenges of different cultures in different countries and firms, differing organizational arrangements in airlines, and strong personalities among airline executives.

As to making alliances work it has been suggested (e.g. Phatak 1997: 296) that firms should build trust in small steps, select partners that are compatible, and create and maintain alliances where power is rather more equally distributed. All this would apply to the airline industry, too, but the turmoil in the industry is such that, in the airline management's view, there is simply no time to follow the ideal path.

It seems that the area where airline management face their hardest challenges and where there appears to be much potential for improvement is that of learning. Earlier research (Inkpen 1998: 225) has emphasized the role of trust between the partners as a contributor to successful learning. It is the very notion of trust that makes airline alliances different from those in many other industries: so far alliances in the airline industry have been either very short lived or limited in scope, or both, and therefore the trust has not been developed between the partners. As there is no trust, partners are very cautious in managing the alliances, and consequently there is no real opportunity for learning to take place. It seems that the learning aspect of alliance management should be given much more emphasis, which would in practice require, first, strong and specific initiative from the highest management, and second, allocation of sufficient capacity and perhaps the best talent into the management of key alliances.

Summary and conclusions

Changes in the industry have made it essential for most airlines to seek growth and to secure presence in a larger market. Also, the many types of regulation in the industry make alliances the only feasible way to grow and seek presence in a larger market. Finally, there is again pressure to reduce operational costs in airlines through better utilization of resources, which is the third major driver of international alliances in the industry.

Market presence appears to play an essential role in airlines' strategic planning for survival and prosperity: having global reach appears to be a must in most airlines' strategic plan. Therefore the primary motivation for international alliances so far has been the need to secure an extensive catchment area or a large onward connection network.

Airlines appear rather frustrated by the fact that the natural evolution towards transnational companies in this industry is effectively blocked by authorities. This frustration is echoed in the comment by Paul Moore, spokesman for Virgin Atlantic, concerning US limitations for foreign airlines on acquiring or setting up a US subsidiary: 'It's blatant protectionism. Alliances are an artificial solution to an artificial problem. There is no reason why the rules should not be different now' (*Airline Business*, October 1998: 76).

As to governments' role in regulating the formation of truly transnational airlines, it appears to be a question of finding the right balance between enough freedom to allow efficiency in the global airline industry to develop, but sufficient regulation to make sure that there is competition between the alliance groups, at least in most markets.

Overall it appears that the pursuit of stronger market presence has been the most apparent and dominant factor, the need for better resource utilization being clearly secondary, and also more of a longer-term nature. The role of regulation and the need to circumvent it is rather difficult to assess. It seems very often to be a factor in alliance building, but very rarely is it seen as the primary reason.

It seems that resource utilization is a factor that is very often acknowledged in international airline alliance arrangements. However, airlines have in fact been rather slow in pursuing higher productivity or outright lower costs through concerted efforts with partners; there seems to be rigidity in airlines in operationalizing the changes and therefore the resource utilization has so far not been as significant a motivator as market presence.

As to other drivers of alliances, it appears that airlines generally speaking do not make sufficient use of the opportunity to learn better practices from partners: the industry could pay heed to experiences from other industries, mainly in the manufacturing sector. Concerning 'competitor taming' it would appear to be a possible hidden driver in some alliances, but certainly not in an expressed way. Also, in the manufacturing sector it has been perhaps better realized that global competitiveness requires co-operation, where one has to give up something in order to gain something. This authentic marriage-type of approach to strategic alliances is yet to establish itself in the airline business.

Validity of the findings to other industries

The assessment of the validity of the findings from this study to other industries can be made by comparing the key features of the airline industry competition with those of other industries. The key features are the following:

Nature of competition in the industry

Airline industry has been strongly regulated, but has experienced extensive liberalization during the last decade. However, even if more competition is made possible through deregulation, the markets are still primarily in the individual city-pairs (e.g. Hamburg–Paris), where a duopoly exists. Sometimes there are monopoly situations, and sometimes – particularly between major cities – there may exist an oligopolistic competitive situation. Never is there a situation that comes even close to perfect competition.

Differentiation possibilities in the competition

The core of air transport product is getting a person or cargo from point A to point B. The possibilities to differentiate the product are very scarce; the connections and the extent of network, the level of service, and the corporate or product image are the areas of differentiation, but with very limited scope. As an example, most of the aircraft today come from two manufacturers, and are thus very much similar in every airline's fleet.

Moreover, airports are a key component in the air travel product, and there the possibilities of airlines to differentiate are very much limited. However, it is in the ability to provide extensive service in a large route network where the alliances come to play a major role in airlines' ability to differentiate.

Cost structure in the operations

The share of fixed costs is very high in the airline operations. Major operative cost items are personnel (some 30 per cent), fuel (some 10 per cent), and capital costs (typically about 10 per cent). Alliance arrangements may have a cost effect, primarily in the area of personnel and secondarily in the area of capital costs, in other words the efficiency of aircraft utilization.

Critical success factors

In the airline business it is possible to name certain critical factors of success, of which the most important ones appear to be schedules, geographical coverage, dependability, safety, fares, and service level.

In order to assess the validity of the findings from this study to other industries, it will be useful to build a matrix (Figure 12.3) where the above listed key features are compared between various industries, which have some common features to the airline industry. The industries selected for illustrative purposes are other service sectors: telecommunication,

Key industry features

	Nature of competition	Differentiation possibilities	Cost structure	Key success factors
Airlines	Oligopolistic	Small	High fixed	Network, service quality, distribution
Shipping	Often oligopolistic	Small	High fixed	Network, service package, low costs
Hotels	Varies strongly by market	Extensive	High fixed	Location, service quality, distribution
Telecomm- unications	Oligopolistic	Small	High fixed	Network coverage, account volume
Car rentals	Often oligopolistic	Small	High fixed	Service quality, distribution

Figure 12.3 Key feature comparison for generalizability assessment, selected service industries

Source: © Hannu Seristö, 1999

shipping, hotel, and car rental industries. The purpose of the matrix here is merely to present a tentative and simple framework for the generalizability assessment: the actual assessment of whether there is strong analogy between the airline industry alliances and alliances in other sectors, particularly service industries, is a topic worthy of study of its own.

While the characterization of service industry sectors in this matrix is arguable, it would appear that the findings from this study might be applicable to the telecommunications and car rental industries and other service industries sharing the same sort of features. Further research should look into these industries in more detail from the alliance perspective.

Overall it appears that the dynamics of international co-operative operations in the service sector are so much different from the manufacturing industries that there is perhaps a need to modify existing models to better take the services into account. It seems that particularly the roles of knowledge, know-how and learning in the service industries deserve vigorous research in the future.

References

Air Transport Intelligence (1998) Survey on Airline Alliances, reported in *Airline Business*, June: 42–81.

Airline Business (1990) 'Strategic Illusions': 24–30.

Alamdari, F. and Morrell, P. (1997) 'Airline Alliances: a Catalyst for Regulatory Change in Key Markets?', *Journal of Air Transport Management* 3 (1): 1–2.

Annual Reports for 1988–97/98 from the following airlines: Air Canada, American Airlines, British Airways, Canadian Airlines (PWA Corp.), Delta Air Lines, Finnair, KLM, Lufthansa, Qantas Airways, SAS, Swissair, Thai Airways International, and United Airlines.

Antoniou, A. (1998) 'The Status of the core in the Airline Industry: the Case of the European Market', *Managerial and Decision Economics* 19: 43–54.

Bartlett, A. and Ghoshal, S. (1995) *Transnational Management: Texts, Cases, and Readings in Cross-border Management*, second edn, Chicago: Irwin.

Bissessur, A. (1996) 'The Identification and Analysis of the Critical Success Factors of Strategic Airline Alliances', Ph.D. dissertation, Cranfield University.

Borys, B. and Jemison, D. (1989) 'Hybrid Arrangements as Strategic Alliances: Theoretical Issues in Organisational Combinations', *Academy of Management Review* 14 (2): 234–49.

Brouthers, K., Brouthers, L. and Wilkinson, T. (1995) 'Strategic Alliances: Choose Your Alliances', *Long Range Planning* 28 (3): 18–25.

Chan, S., Kensinger, J., Keown, A. and Martin, J. (1997) 'Do Strategic Alliances Really Create Value?' *Journal of Financial Economics* 46: 199–221.

Contractor, F. and Lorange, P. (eds) (1988) *Co-operative Strategies and International Business*, Lexington, Mass.: Lexington Books.

Doz, Y. (1996) 'The Evolution of Co-operation in Strategic Alliances: Initial Conditions or Learning Processes?' *Strategic Management Journal*, special issue 17, summer: 55–84.

Doz, Y. and Hamel, G. (1998) *Alliance Advantage: the Art of Creating Value through Partnering*, Boston: Harvard Business School Press.

Dussauge, P. and Garrette, B. (1995) 'Determinants of Success in International Strategic Alliances: Evidence from the Global Aerospace Industry', *Journal of International Business* 26 (3): 505–30.

Gallacher, J. (1998) 'A Time for Celebration', *Airline Business*, September: 29–58.

Gant, J. (1995) 'The Science of Alliance', *Euro Business*, September: 70–3.

Gleister, K. and Buckley, P. (1998) 'Measures of Performance in UK International Alliances', *Organization Studies* 19 (1): 89–118.

Gulati, R. (1995) 'Does Familiarity Breed Trust? The Implications of Repeated Ties for Contractual Choice in Alliances', *Academy of Management Journal* 38: 85–112.

Hamel, G. (1991) 'Competition for Competence and Interpartner Learning within International Strategic Alliances', *Strategic Management Journal* 12: 83–103.

Hamel, G., Doz, Y. and Prahalad, C. (1989) 'Collaborate with your Competitors – and Win', *Harvard Business Review* 67: 133–139.

Inkpen, A. (1998) 'Learning, Knowledge Acquisition, and Strategic Alliances', *European Management Journal* 16 (2) April: 223–9.

Killing, J. (1988) 'Understanding Alliances: the Role of Task and Organizational Complexity', in Contractor, F. and Lorange, P. (eds), *Co-operative Strategies and International Business*, 55–67, Lexington, Mass: Lexington Books.

Lei, D., Slocum. J. and Pitts, R. (1997) 'Building Cooperative Advantage: Managing Strategic Alliances to Promote Organisational Learning', *Journal of World Business* 32 (3): 203–23.

Lindquist, J. (1996) 'Marriages Made in Heaven?' *The Avmark Aviation Economist* 13 (1): 12–13.

Luo, Y. (1996) 'Evaluating Performance of Strategic Alliances in China', *Long Range Planning* 29 (4): 534–42.

Ohmae, K. (1989) 'The Global Logic of Strategic Alliances', *Harvard Business Review*, March/April 1989.

Ott, J. and Sparaco, P. (1997) 'Unique Industry Facets Shape Europe's Alliances', *Aviation Week and Space Technology*, 17 November: 63–5.

Park, J. and Zhang, A. (1997) Effects of Intercontinental Alliances: Cases in the North Atlantic Market, conference proceedings of the 1997 Air Transport Research Group of the WCTR Society, vol. 3, no. 1, University of Nebraska at Omaha.

—— (1998) 'Strategic Alliance and Firm Value: a Case Study of the British Airways/USAir Alliance', paper presented at the 1998 Air Transport Research Group of the WCTR Society Conference.

Park, N. and Cho, D. (1997) 'The Effect of Strategic Alliance on Performance: a Study of International Airline Performance', conference proceedings of the 1997 Air Transport Research Group of the WCTR Society, vol. 1, no. 1, University of Nebraska at Omaha.

Parkhe, A. (1991) 'Interfirm Diversity, Organizational Learning and Longevity in Global Strategic Alliances', *Journal of International Business Studies* 22 (5): 579–601.

—— (1993) 'Strategic Alliance Structuring: a Game Theoretic and Transaction Cost Examination of Interfirm Cooperation', *Academy of Management Journal* 36 (4): 794–829.

Pekar, P. and Allio, R. (1994) 'Making Alliances Work: Guidelines for Success', *Long Range Planning* 27 (4): 54–65.

Phatak, A. (1997) *International Management*, Cincinnati: South-Western College Publishing.

Seristö, H. (1993) *Strategies of Airlines in the Deregulated European Competitive Environment*, Helsinki School of Economics and Business Administration Press, B–136, 213 pp.

—— (1995) 'Airline Performance and Costs: an Analysis of Performance Measurement and Cost Reduction in Major Airlines', doctorate thesis, Helsinki School of Economics and Business Administration Press, A–107, 254 pp.

—— (1996) 'An Executive View on the Cost Problem of European Airlines', *European Business Review* 96 (4): 14–17.

Seristö, H. and Vepsäläinen, A. (1997) 'Airline Cost Drivers: Cost Implications of Fleet, Routes, and Personnel Policies', *Journal of Air Transport Management* 3 (1): 11–22.

Youssef, W. (1992) 'Causes and Effects of International Airline Equity Alliances', Ph.D. dissertation, series UCB–ITS–DS–92–1, Institute of Transportation Studies, University of California, Berkeley.

13 DHL Worldwide Express

Providing just-in-time delivery services across customs borders in Central and Eastern Europe

Michel Kostecki

The DHL services and customs

Few companies have better knowledge of customs rules and procedures, 'red tape' and other mis-functionings in customs controls than international courier companies. This case presents DHL's account of difficulties in serving its clients across customs borders with special emphasis on Central and Eastern Europe. Among problems encountered by trading firms, inefficiencies and irregularities in functioning of customs far outweigh other hindrances to trade (such as currency fluctuations or tariffs), and unhelpful, old-fashioned and ill-managed customs signify increasingly high costs in a trading environment where just-in-time supplies, electronic trading and globalization are gaining grounds.

DHL is the world's largest international express carrier generating about 40 per cent of the world supply of such services. The company was founded in 1969 and has expanded rapidly, establishing over 2,300 service centres in more than 220 countries and territories and employing more than 55,000 people world-wide. That expansion was favoured by rapid growth of international trade and the increasing importance of time management in logistics and world-wide supply networks.

Speed and a reliable delivery system are essential in today's international trade business since time became a major factor of competitiveness. The way in which the leading trading firms manage time in their supply chains extending beyond national borders represents a powerful source of competitive advantage (Kostecki 1996). Dealing effectively with customs and putting pressure to encourage rational and efficient customs operations is an integral part of managerial skills of time management in major trading firms.

DHL delivers more than 100 million shipments per year. In addition to transporting documents, it also handles significant quantities of parcels and heavier weight shipments, with tailored products to ensure swift and efficient delivery. DHL's renowned 'hub and spoke' network of planes, trucks and facilities is an example of a physical network in which the IT network assumes the role of a nervous system. To supplement its core product range, all of which is supported by state-of-the-art technology, DHL offers customers bespoke logistic solutions on a global scale to meet even the most demanding distribution requirements (DHL 1997).

Speed and reliability are of critical importance for DHL. To maintain its lead in a very competitive market-place the company focused on quality and speed of delivery. In the recent ranking of courier firms established by the British Market Research Institute 'Data + Decision' DHL was on the first position as far as the speed of delivery was concerned.

The DHL courier service is generated by a complex process. The range of core and supplementary services which constitute the DHL service chain comprises: order taking, pickup, documentation, tracing of the supplies when information is needed, billing, packaging, transportation and delivery, and problem solving, as well as advice and information to the clients and partners.

DHL's objective is to ensure on-time delivery and to reduce the level of irritation that customers experience with different types of possible failures. There is, obviously, a time sequence of problems which have to be dealt with by a courier: failures such as abandoned calls and missed pickups lead (sometimes) to complaints; over-goods and late aircraft lead to late deliveries, which lead in turn to traces, invoice adjustment requests and additional complaints. Damaged packages and missing documentation may also lead to supplementary complaints.

DHL monitor closely their performance in order to improve it and better respond to clients' demands. Percentage failure rates concerning delivery look minuscule but become large in absolute numbers if the number of transactions is large. Note that for a courier carrying 0.8–1.5 million packages a day, even 99.9 per cent on-time delivery still signifies that 800–1,500 packages would be delivered late each day.

Certain failures are worse than others in terms of customer aggravation. A thirty minutes delay in delivery may not even be noticed by the customer, whereas a one-day delay is serious failure for a firm promising on-time delivery (especially 'next day' service). Sometimes important construction work has to be stopped and/or chain production delayed if an essential chemical component or spare part for the working equipment cannot be delivered on time. For a fraction of cases the delay signifies high costs and the impossibility to practice the just-in-time delivery, which is one of the leading elements of competitive edge in today's international business.

The most critical internal failures at DHL world-wide comprise transportation delays and over-goods (packages that get left behind at hub or station). However, number one on the list of external reasons for late delivery are inefficient customs controls and procedures.

Few companies are better placed than DHL to monitor and analyse the issue of customs controls and their impact on a wide range of client firms.

An important element of the DHL's service chain is getting the parcels through the border controls and ensuring the necessary documentation. DHL's strategic advantage of speed is directly dependent on the efficiency of the customs administration, and the DHL skills in fulfilling the customs requirements are essential for the courier's success. It is for that reason that the company closely monitors customs difficulties that prevent its clients from doing business world-wide, or increase the cost of such operations, and is deeply concerned by the efficiency of customs services world-wide.

A motivated and well-trained work force is the most critical element for maintaining a competitive advantage that a courier services firm, such as DHL, possesses. Leadership is needed at both the corporate level, and at the level of individual national subsidiaries or even groups. Both front stage and backstage teams must work together to ensure that parcels get through customs controls on time. An appropriate corporate organization is essential to deal with that task.

DHL has a local customs service department in every major country. These local departments are headed by an international customs service department at the company's headquarters in Brussels. The mission of every local department is to get the cargo through customs at the right time, by-passing whatever obstacles are standing in the way. The DHL customs services are equally responsible for tracking and tracing of packages and should be able to pinpoint the exact location of every parcel at all times. The local departments are implementing the company's pro- and reactive strategies *vis-à-vis* the customs or trade control authorities, and are responsible for daily reports, providing detailed information about customs trouble-spots, which are distributed world-wide via the international headquarters in Brussels (Lorange 1998).

To minimize the hassle at customs, DHL makes sure that all paperwork is carefully checked and cleared in the sender's country before shipments leave. As explained by Mr Svikovsky, one of DHL's managers of a local customs service department, the basic approach at the operational level is 'just to follow the customs rules and procedures, however crazy they may look, otherwise no package will ever get anywhere'. DHL's management is well aware of the fact that a personalized approach to customs may be highly important in certain countries. It is particularly true of countries in which shipments are subject to numerous authorizations that may be more or less easy to obtain depending on who is at the customs. Customs officers frequently have different attitudes towards the DHL personnel in charge, towards DHL as a company, or the country of shipment's origin.

Public relations work is performed by the DHL customs service departments both at a grass roots level (customs officials), and on the macro level of national, regional, or international bodies. At the grass roots level it is important to forge a lasting relationship of confidence and trust with the customs authorities. Companies that have a good reputation for honesty and employees' integrity generally do better at customs. A lasting relationship with local customs is also built on the understanding that it is hardly possible in any country to implement perfectly all the customs rules and regulations to the letter. A full application of the regulation in force would shut down all trade, as happens when customs officials 'work to rule' in order to manifest their dissatisfaction.

Courier service gap in Central and Eastern Europe

There were no air express services in the former state-trading countries of Central and Eastern Europe prior to 1989. Such services were not only neglected under central planning, but they were actually discriminated against. During the Communist area postal offices had a monopoly for delivery of letters and packages and there was no need for international courier services. (Even if such needs had existed, they could not be satisfied due to rigid border controls and censorship of printed materials, films, cassettes or letters.)

During the 'first wave' of transformation in the countries of Central and Eastern Europe – the transition economies – services such as telecommunications, financial services, accountancy and numerous other business services have been at the forefront of economic change. The 'services gap' had to be narrowed rapidly if the economies were to develop. Neglected distribution systems had to be modernized, and trading companies had to grow to open up autarchic economic systems. The privatization and restructuring of state-owned assets urgently required business services, such as management consulting, private banking or financial reporting. International courier services were needed to move documents, publications, computer disquettes or spare parts rapidly, across customs borders.

DHL was the first express delivery company that entered Eastern Europe and the CIS, where the existing transportation infrastructure was poor, and demand for a fast and efficient service was on the increase. It was also among the first service companies to manifest a long term commitment to business development in Eastern Europe.

The company's management was fully aware that the successful undertaking of services operations in the post-Communist countries required fundamental changes and improvements across a spectrum of activities, ranking from technical to managerial. Organizational forms, as well as management styles and mentalities had to adjust progressively to the requirements of a modern service-based market economy. DHL's commitment to the region was well-illustrated by the firm's programme to progressively replace expatriate country managers in Central and Eastern European with local employees. Local managers now run DHL's operations in Romania, Bulgaria, the Czech Republic, Hungary, Slovenia, Croatia, Serbia and Montenegro, Albania, and Bosnia-Herzegovina, as well as in the Ukraine, and the Central Asian republics in the CIS.

As services tend to be management-intensive rather than equipment-intensive, and management skills were clearly behind technical skills in Central and Eastern Europe, the upgrading of service operations was best accelerated through foreign direct investments (FDI). Involvement of foreign investors such as DHL favoured incubation (through access to the necessary capital and expertise abroad and careful nursing when things went badly wrong), quality leadership and access to a world-wide network that was a condition *sine qua non* of success. Since 1989, $50 million has been invested in the Central and Eastern Europe region as recognition of the growing part logistics has started to play. Half of this amount has been used to develop and invest in aircraft, vehicles, staff training and state of the art computer technology.

In 1995, Prague, Warsaw and Budapest saw a significant upgrade and improvement in capacity because of the growth of volumes, and a new dedicated line haul to Bucharest, Romania and Sofia in Bulgaria was introduced. DHL has clearly led the way forward in developing an effective air express network for the fast growing economies of Eastern Europe and the Western businesses that have chosen to invest there. By 1998 DHL was the express distribution market leader in every single country in Central and Eastern Europe. It operates flights every night out of forty-one gateways in the region and its customer base includes both developed market companies such as IBM, Microsoft, Smithkline Beecham and Citibank, as well as local firms such as Skoda, Bata, or Bank Handlowy.

DHL currently operates 165 stations manned by 3,000 people throughout Eastern and Central Europe alone, and the company continues to open new offices and add to its infrastructure in the region. For example, in 1997 it opened a new Gateway in Katowice providing service direct to southern Poland, enabling business in the region to be more competitive. It also reopened the Sarajevo office after four years, a new gateway in Zagreb and a ground distribution centre in Budapest.

The rate of change in transformation economies, such as the Czech Republic, Hungary, or Poland is impressive indeed. Banks and well-stocked shops, new distribution chains and business services, garages and restaurants, trading companies and travel agencies were rapidly created where people once had trouble finding a place to have a meal or buy a pair of shoes. However, these dynamic developments in private service sector contrasted with the continuous inefficiencies of public services and administration in most transformation economies.

Customs are just one example of a public service that is often criticized. There have been improvements over the past three years in the form of easier document requirement and faster processing of shipments. However, given the important increase in traffic and trade flows, more marked improvements are still required. Many of those improvements are not only needed in Central and East European countries but are necessary world-wide in most trading nations.

DHL's business in Poland

DHL Worldwide Express (Poland) was created in 1990 as a joint venture with a majority participation (85 per cent) of DHL and 15 per cent local investment. The Polish company is thus part of a near world-wide express package pickup, transport and delivery service of DHL. In 1997 DHL Poland employed some 300 people and had seventeen branches and eight representations. By and large the lesson of the DHL's expansion strategy in Poland has been that fortune favours the brave. Demand for express courier services was growing at an annual rate of 50 per cent, DHL's turnover in 1996 reached $24 million, and prospects for growth and business development in Poland are good given the rapid growth of the country's economy.

The prices for courier services from Poland to Western Europe and the United States are about 50 per cent lower than the prices charged by DHL in the West for return. This is due to the cost structure and the company's pricing policy. Operating costs for courier services in the West are clearly higher than in Poland. The DHL's pricing strategy in Poland also aims at the promotion of courier services among the Polish business community and is aimed at increasing generic demand and the company's share of Poland's market

Delivery services of DHL Poland are dominated by such destinations as Western Europe and the United States. Nevertheless, some 15–20 per cent of deliveries are destined for markets of the CIS or other transition economies. In is particularly in that area that DHL clients experience frequent difficulties with customs 'red tape' hampering rapid deliveries, and other regulatory problems.

DHL clients and customs administrations

Problems with customs rules and regulations is by far the biggest problem that large and small firms from advanced countries seem to face when doing business with Central and Eastern European countries, as well as most developing countries. The results of a recent survey conducted by DHL show that almost nine out of ten multinational companies had experienced customs clearance problems in Central and Eastern Europe and that customs difficulties are rated as the most important problems to trade with that region (DHL 1997).

Let's start at the beginning: business dislikes customs, says Mr Krzysztof Goralski, Vice-President of DHL Poland. There is obviously an intrinsic conflict of interest between a firm that is required to pay fees or import charges and a customs officer who is expected to promote and apply national legislation which is not always in business firms' interest.

The border entry into a customs territory has traditionally been considered the best place to raise import duties and to effect controls required for the administration of quotas and licences, prohibitions, or health and safety standards, and so on. From a social perspective, such controls and procedures are usually seen as an effort to collect government revenue, implement trade policies, and reduce malpractice and irregularities. From a business perspective, however, the controls and procedures associated with the customs' work are considered to be at best inconvenient and at worst onerous, bureaucratic, or even corrupt. The criticism of customs by business firms concern two major claims:

- the *modus operandi* of today's customs tends to be archaic, incompatible with the modern trading methods and ill-adjusted to the requirements of a global economy;
- customs administrations, both in the high-income and low-income countries, often suffer from inefficiencies, irregularities and corruption that raise transaction costs in international trade business.

Group discussions conducted with the DHL managers and a recent questionnaire by the RED Consultancy in London – administered to the managers of Western European multinationals operating in Central and Eastern Europe – identifies several categories of concerns at customs.

Diversity of national requirements concerning packages and documentation

Countries maintain various limitations concerning the size and weight of packages that may be shipped by courier services. Such diversity of norms concerning packaging and documentation are not only typical for Eastern Europe or developing countries. For example, the requirements maintained by the United States differ from those in force in the European Union, meaning that particularly large portions of international trade flows are affected by such diversity of rules and procedures. Nevertheless, the diversity of requirements in the area of packaging and documentation is often quoted as a managerial concern in Central and Eastern Europe and it results in substantial additional marketing costs to DHL clients.

One wine exporting company reported that shipments of wine were refused because the corks in the bottles commonly used in the European Union were considered not to conform with the technical requirements in Russia. In another case, date indications on the packaging of chocolates differed from those given on the larger boxes by two days, and shipments were held back for three weeks. One British company recalled that its supplies of cider to Eastern Europe were delayed because customs didn't have a product code for it and refused to label it as an apple drink (DHL 1997).

Customs requirements concerning documentation that has to accompany the package also differ between countries. Such diversity is not a major difficulty for DHL because the company is well aware of various legal requirements, but it creates frequent problems for DHL clients.

A 1997 DHL internal report referring to Russia contained, for example, the following passage:

> 100 per cent reconciliation audits by customs of shipments, paperwork and manifest information, as advised in OPS UPDATE Ref. 13.08.97–1 have been completed and clearance performance has returned to previous level; however, the poor quality of origin paperwork and discrepancies require extensive additional steps to be taken in clearance process. WPX coded to MOW continue to require an additional copy of AWB and invoice in the window attached to the shipment.
>
> Conflicting information between AWB, invoice and manifest data continue to threaten operations. Special attention to these points and adhering to the following instructions for invoices can prevent delays.
>
> Invoices should be original and on company letterhead with original stamp and signature. State the exact description, ('spare parts', 'soft ware', 'stationery', 'personal effects' are insufficient) of goods, catalogue reference numbers, with the unit and total value per commodity. State the currency, the INCO term and reason for export. Commercial invoices should have invoice number and reference to contract number and date: for non-commercial transactions, *pro forma* invoices should state 'Free of Charge to Consignee, of No Commercial Value – Declared Value for Customs Purposes Only'. State realistic value: understatement will always result in delay. For media carriers (developed film, tapes, diskettes, etc.), always state value for material versus program/data separately. Invoices in languages other than English can often result in delay. For formal clearance, consignee paperwork is always required, so please state consignee contact and telephone number.
>
> (DHL Internal Operations Update Document,
> REF: 08.09.97–2)

Such updates on the Russian Federation in the DHL operations document might send a shiver down the spine of even the most hardened export manager.

Red tape

In numerous transformation economies including Hungary, Poland and Slovakia, courier services do not benefit from any simplification of customs procedures or documentation requirements. The same documentation is required from a DHL package shipment as from a lorry or a ship entering the customs territory. Dealing with such complexities is burdensome and costly. Moreover, certified photocopies are often refused even though their use is a standard operating procedure in advanced country customs.

But red tape in the customs administration seldom exists as a stand-alone factor in a country. It tends to manifest itself and flourish, in particular in those countries where the economic and political environment is tainted. Such an environment favours controls and procedures, which despite the objectives of the World Customs Organization 'Kyoto Convention,' are both inconsistent and unpredictable. Perhaps the major factors are the paper-based and outdated procedures which allow for easy manipulation or arbitrary decision-making by the customs officers. Even in those countries where computerization of customs procedures has been introduced (for example, the UNCTAD 'ASYCUDA/SIDONIA' system), the opportunities offered by the use of such a system are seldom taken advantage of. Invariable the old paper-based system remains in use and inefficient paper-based practices continue to exist. Several countries of the CIS are perceived by Western European business firms as leaders with respect to red tape at customs.

Customs of certain countries refused documents because they had been signed in black rather than blue ink (the latter ink was viewed as an indication that a document was an original), or because rubber stamps on documents were not pressed on hard enough or put in wrong place. In such circumstances, argues one of the experienced forwarding agents – 'speed money' is the order of the day – anything (that pays) goes. Customs have many ways to put pressure on business firms. They may, for example, threaten to delay the release of the goods, or threaten to call for higher customs fees and charges than are really due on the consignment.

Moreover, customs authorities in Central and Eastern Europe often take a negative attitude towards businessmen, or do not understand the way business works. They tend to see themselves as policemen and often lack the necessary flexibility to assist trade operators in accomplishing their standard tasks in the area of logistics, storage, or preparing goods for inspection. The countries which are first in line for European Union membership such the Czech Republic, Hungary or Poland have much better customs than countries such as Bulgaria, Kazakhstan, Romania, Ukraine, Moldavia or Russia.

Vague customs regulations

It is a frequent occurrence in Eastern and Central Europe that customs regulations lack precision. Such equivocal application of the customs rules signifies that the officials in charge of customs controls may give contradictory instructions, that the requirements may change overnight, or that different customs officials have different rules, or distinct interpretations of those rules. In numerous cases customs procedures are reported to be non-tariff barriers to trade when officials assign goods to an incorrect classification to which a higher tariff applies, or assign goods a value greater than appropriate. Such arbitrary customs procedures can then be used to ensure that a government (or customs officials) collect as much revenue as desired, independently of the formally announced tariff schedule.

The problem is particularly acute in Russia and the Asian republics of the former Soviet Union. The least difficulties at customs in Central and Eastern Europe are met in the Czech Republic, Hungary, Poland and Slovenia (DHL 1997).

Most large corporations doing business across national borders in Central and Eastern Europe consider that the customs delays, harassment, or red tape had resulted in substantial losses of revenue to their businesses. In some cases the very contracts were lost because of delayed delivery, in other cases reparations had to be paid to the clients expecting just-in-time delivery, or business relations were negatively affected resulting in worsened relationships with the clients or client's perception of poor quality.

'Facilitation fees' and corruption

An important reason for inefficiencies in the operations of customs and irregular practices are low salaries of the officers and little funding available for investment in the up-grading of the customs administration and training. In several countries of Eastern Europe the basic wage of a middle ranking officer is hardly sufficient to cover the cost of the monthly rent of his family's apartment in the capital and basic bills for heating and electricity. Bearing in mind that the customs officer has to feed and clothe his family, he has little option but to join his fellow officer in extracting a 'living wage' by imposing a facilitation fee. When this state of affairs exists, it is a short step to even more serious corruption.

How to turn customs into a modern institution?

What is the solution to these problems in Central and Eastern Europe or elsewhere? A number of DHL managers and experts have given some thought to the problem. But will things move fast enough?

Traditionally, international trade was conditioned by customs and business firms accepting the customs controls and procedures without question. In the rapidly changing trading environment, however, there is a growing perception that customs controls and procedures have, in the majority of countries, not kept pace with the changes. Although international in their presence, customs remain essentially national bodies (Black 1997). It is today a generalized view in the world business community that customs administrations show little concern for the wider international trade issues, development in technologies, or management techniques and approaches (e.g. just-in-time delivery) which call for new customs clearance procedures and the integration of customs controls into the export management chains. To put it in the words of one of the leading spokesmen of the express couriers community, Mr John Raven: 'customs administration is a nineteenth-century institution in the twenty-first-century world' (Raven 1997).

One of the reasons for this situation, DHL managers see is the fact that customs' powers are limited to their sovereign territories and that in such a structure national needs and concerns take priority over global preferences, or the interests of companies operating in global markets. Another is that traders apply new technologies in the international trade environment at a greater pace than customs.

Technology provides traders with the facilities to develop cost effective international systems using a 'one stop' data capture facility. The electronic transfer of transaction data between parties in trade transactions such as banks, insurance firms, transportation companies, importers and exporters, forwarders, and so on permit the creation of a comprehensive transaction data file. Such files can be easily consulted and provide new opportunities for reviewing traditional customs controls and procedures. Technology-driven trading systems render conventional paper-based export and import declarations redundant. They also render redundant, traditional customs control points, at least as far as revenue assessment and collection of data is concerned.

In the words of one of the leading customs experts of Société Générale de Surveillance (SGS), modern customs will become increasingly a preventive and enforcement body. Access to advanced consignment data enable customs to use 'profiling ' techniques (i.e. ones that permit the identification of 'high risk' consignments) and concentrate on problem-solving rather than routine border point controls.

There is also a steady growth in the incidence of fraud and malpractice in developed and low-income countries alike. Note, for example, that the EU anti-fraud group UNCLAF has increased its staff from some twenty people in the early 1990s to some 300 members in 1999. Customs attempt to co-operate internationally in the World Customs Organization (WCO), previously known as the Customs Co-operation Council. The WCO is concerned by the growing problem of malpractice, inefficiency, and corruption, and it dealt with that issue in its Arusha Declaration of 1993. Substantial efforts have been made to fight customs malpractice, but there is an emerging view of the international business community that only an in-depth reform and a complete rethinking of the role of customs in international trade may provide a remedy to the problem. DHL shares this view.

Note

The support of the Swiss National Science Foundation (grant no.: PLPJO48243) and of the World Trade Organization (WTO) is gratefully acknowledged. Published with the permission of the WTO and the SNSF.

References

Black, R. (1997) *Business Concerns with Customs Controls and Procedures*, presentation at the Fifth International Conference on Marketing Strategies, University of Neuchâtel, Switzerland, 20 May.

DHL (1997) *Customs Report for Central and Eastern Europe*, London, prepared by D. Singer and R. Kanareck of the RED Consultancy.

Kim Kyung Won (1998) *Regulatory Barriers to Exports: a Marketing Analysis*, Neuchâtel, the Enterprise Institute of the University of Neuchâtel (manuscript of a diploma thesis).

Kostecki, M. (1995) 'Business Options in the Service Sector of the Transition Economies: a Framework for Inquiry', in M. Kostecki and A. Fehérvary, (eds), *Services in the Transition Economies*, 3–27, Oxford: Pergamon Press.

Kostecki, M. (1996) 'Waiting Line as a Marketing Issues', *European Management Journal*, 14 (3): 295–303.

Lorange, C. (1998) *Corporate Structure, Procedures and Responses Relating to Trade Policy: Case Studies of Four Multinational Corporations*, Neuchâtel: the Enterprise Institute of the University of Neuchâtel (manuscript of a diploma thesis).

Raven, J. (1997) *Managerial views of the Customs*, paper presented at the Fifth International Conference on Marketing Strategies, University of Neuchâtel, Switzerland, 20 May.

14   Globalization of hotel services

An examination of ownership and alliance patterns in a maturing service sector

Farok J. Contractor and Sumit K. Kundu

The objectives of this study

The present study examines three issues:

1   Why are some firms more internationalized than others? Since the degree of internationalization is often held to be an indicator of competitive success, it is worth asking why firms within the same service sector exhibit such a wide variation on this attribute?

2   Why do different organizational forms (modal choices) co-exist? Hotels conducting international business have deployed several organizational forms, including fully-owned, joint-venture, franchising, and management service agreements. Not only do these exist from one company to another, but they may co-exist even within the same firm's operations in different countries. What determines the optimum choice of organization mode for a particular international hotel property?

3   What facilitates franchising and explains its global coverage? The proliferation of non-equity based international entry modes has generated a lot of interest both among academia and among practitioners. We ask, 'Given a choice between a company-run and a franchised operation, what factors will tip the strategic selection toward franchising for a particular hotel property?'

An overview of the international hotel sector

The international hotel industry may be very concentrated in terms of the numbers of global chains. The *International Hotels Group Directory, 1992*, said to be a comprehensive compilation covering more than 90 per cent of all hotel rooms associated with multinational firms, showed only 110 companies as having a managerial or equity association with one or more hotels outside the home nation of the firm. (Of course, if domestic firms were included, the number would be far larger).

Table 14.1 (page 298–9) shows the distribution of the foreign operations (only) of these 110 firms, headquartered in fifteen principal home nations. The US, UK, and France are by far the leading home or source countries where the multinational hotel firms are headquartered, accounting for 55 per cent of the world total. One noteworthy change is the increase in the share for Asia as a source region, from 7.4 per cent in the Dunning and McQueen (1981) study to 17.28 per cent in 1991.

These 110 companies managed 1,913,081 rooms world-wide as shown in Table 14.1. However, the focus of this study is only on operations outside the home country of the firm. These account for 540,224 rooms. The remaining columns of Table 14.1 show the distribution of these 540,224 rooms by destination region outside the home nation of each firm. By destination region Europe and Asia lead, followed by North America. The hotel companies based in Europe account for 46 per cent of the non-home-country rooms. By comparison 55.45 per cent of the 110 companies are headquartered in a European nation.

The data and sample

Data were drawn from a questionnaire sent to all 110 companies in the *International Hotels Group Directory, 1992* (i.e. those that had at least one foreign property listed). The response rate was 31 per cent, or thirty-four firms in all. However, these covered 1,131 foreign hotel properties located in 112 nations with 306,810 rooms (outside the home nation of the firm), and comprised slightly over 60 per cent of the statistical universe (of non-home-country hotel properties). The data were collected by a questionnaire mailed to all hotel firms having an international operation. The distribution of the sample is broadly representative of that of the statistical universe, except for a large firm bias. Out of the fifteen principal countries originating hotel multinationals (Table 14.1), thirteen home countries are included in the sample. The 110 firms in the population had 540,224 rooms outside their home country; of which 203,311 rooms (37.63 per cent) were located in North America; 249,282 rooms (46.14 per cent) in Europe; and 82,200 rooms in Asia (15.21 per cent).

The sample matches the statistical universe closely in the proportion of rooms in the home nation of the firm versus rooms outside the home country. By source country, approximately three-quarters originate in developed nations while one-quarter originate in developing countries.

Distinctiveness of the global hotel industry

The hotel business appears to be different from other service sectors in terms of the attributes summarized below, although since there are no comparable studies of other sectors these can only be treated as possibilities and hypotheses for further investigation:

Table 14.1 Characteristics of 110 hotel multinational firms: universe of all 110 firms

Source countries	Destination by rooms outside the home country, 1991				
	% by firms	North America	Europe	Middle East	Africa
North America					
USA	22.73%	43,333	34,104	3,095	10,532
Canada	2.72%	7,477	228		
	25.45%	50,810	34,332	3,095	10,532
Europe					
UK	21.82%	18,954	39,650	775	9,738
France	10.90%	8,763	32,707	863	14,225
Germany	7.27%	1,613	6,673		
Italy	1.82%	314	2,953		
Spain	2.73%	6,192	10,369		508
Sweden	2.73%	1,241	12,166		
Switzerland	2.73%	2,640	3,530		965
Others	5.44%		7,452		
	55.45%	39,717	115,500	1,638	25,436
Oceania					
Australia	1.82%				
	1.82%				
Asia					
Japan	4.55%	6,418	1,567		
Hong Kong	7.27%	16,405	6,461	125	171
Singapore	1.82%				
India	1.82%	1,850	600	1,310	1,189
Malaysia	0.91%				
Others	0.91%	164			
	17.28%	24,837	8,628	1,435	1,360
Totals	100.00%	115,364 (21.36%)	158,460 (29.33%)	6,168 (1.14%)	37,328 (6.91%)

Source: *International Hotel Directory*, 1992.

Note: Universe comprises only international hotels and excludes purely domestic hotels or chains

- A longer history of global expansion. Cross-border investments in this sector go back over a hundred years. This may also have resulted in a greater degree of concentration than is found in other global services.
- A greater global coverage by chains in terms of the number of foreign markets covered by each company.
- Mature global brands, many with world-wide recognition.
- A greater degree of standardization globally compared to most other services, in terms of designs, operating procedures, codification of knowledge, brands, reservation systems, and economies of scale.
- A high level of capital investment risk. The provision of hotel services

Table 14.1 (continued)

Asia	Oceania	South America	Caribbean	Global Total
57,057	12,793	20,431	13,842	195,187
			419	8,124
57,057	12,793	20,431	14,261	203,311
21,178	3,130	6,692	3,520	103,637
12,896	742	3,071	2,011	75,278
1,718		313	1,270	11,587
				3,267
3,344		777	997	22,187
900				14,307
4,432				11,567
				7,452
44,468	3,872	11,053	7,798	249,282
873	4,558			5,431
873	4,558			5,431
6,246	1,566		1,571	17,368
24,496	1,951	395	2,805	52,809
3,431				3,431
1,761	200			6,910
600				600
			918	1,082
36,534	3,717	395	5,294	82,200
138,932	24,940	31,679	27,353	540,224
(25.72%)	(4.62%)	(5.86%)	(5.06%)	(100%)

is accompanied by a substantial level of capital investment in real estate that may exceed $100 million in a few resort properties.

- High incidence of international alliances. Fully-owned foreign operations are in a distinct minority, with franchising and management service agreements ubiquitous. Many alliance strategies are predicated on the attempt to separate the investment risk from management operations, and are enabled by a relatively high degree of standardization.
- Almost no studies. Apart from Dunning and McQueen (1981) there are virtually no other studies with comprehensive global coverage.

We first describe the three research questions tackled in this chapter, and then follow with analysis and discussion.

First research question:

Why are some firms more internationalized than others?
The unit of analysis is each firm

The first research question asks why some firms have far more international operations than others? In several industries, one can find a wide variation in the proportion of 'foreign over worldwide total business'. But for the hotel industry, the range of the foreign propensity ratio measured in terms of the proportion of rooms outside the home country to the global total is very wide (from a mere 3 per cent to as large as 96 per cent) in our sample of firms, depicted in Table 14.2. (This is the dependent variable named GLOBAL.) This is a striking degree of variation that we seek to explain statistically.

Second research question:

Modal choice and the propensity to use alliance modes
The unit of analysis is (the modal choice for) each property

The second research question examines the issue of different organizational forms or modal choices in the international hotel operations. The hotel business is a graphic illustration of the fact that competitive advantages can equally well be derived from inter-firm co-operation in non-equity based agreements such as management service contracts and franchising, as from equity-based operations. This is especially true in service sectors such as hotels, where the capital-intensive elements (such as real estate) can be separated from the knowledge-based or managerial expertise elements of competitiveness. In the hotels sector, management service contracts (between the owners of the physical capital or real estate and the global hotel company which supplies managerial expertise) appear to be the single most common governance mode.

As seen in Table 14.3 (page 302), non-equity modes account world-wide for 65.4 per cent of foreign operation properties, and arrangements involving two companies account for as much as 81.2 per cent of the total number of hotels world-wide. Overall, the hotels business has a large number of alliances (joint ventures, franchising, management contract) world-wide. Table 14.3 shows that for the world as a whole, 37 per cent of foreign properties were under management service contract, making this

Table 14.2 Characteristics of thirty-four hotels included in sample

	Total rooms outside home country	% in developed countries	% in developing countries	Foreign propensity ratio (global)
Radisson	6,313	41	59	.14
Hyatt	21,866	32	68	.24
Sheraton	47,500	43	57	.35
Choice	13,892	78	22	.07
Holiday Inn	54,104	55	45	.24
Small Luxury	526	38	62	.36
Nendels	120	100	—	.03
Wyndhams	1,566	—	100	.17
Westin	11,514	28	72	.36
Journeys End	1,595	100		.13
Delta	923	76	24	.53
Four Seasons	5,606	100	—	.76
Hilton In'l	40,210	50	50	.92
Friendly	90	100	—	.06
European	54	100	—	.47
Steigenberger	1,421	65	35	.24
Kempinski	2,364	34	66	.66
Ciga	2,227	100	—	.42
Le Meridian	15,892	50	50	.87
Movenpick	3,971	38	62	.66
Iberotel	1,648	—	100	.23
Southern Pac.	5,038	61	39	.50
Nikko	8,633	51	49	.75
ANA Hotels	3,006	54	46	.30
Ming Court	600	—	100	.37
Oberois	3,194	6	94	.58
Taj Group	3,716	66	34	.42
Regent Int'l	4,258	35	65	.88
Ramada Int'l	26,322	69	31	.96
Mandarin	2,432	7	93	.63
Peninsula Group	1,553	29	71	.62
Lee Gardens	2,632	—	100	.78
Shrangi La	4,376	5	95	.86
New World Hotel	7,648	6	94	.69
Total	306,810			

Source: questionnaire

the single most common organizational modality in the international hotel business. The percentage of properties for the fully- and partially-owned taken together was 35.6, and for franchising was 28.4.

Inter-firm co-operation in the hotels business is not peripheral, but central to global strategy. Global hotels may have a higher incidence than other service sectors, in terms of the prevalence of alliances and non-equity modes of doing business. By covering many foreign markets, our

Table 14.3 Distribution of hotel properties and rooms outside the home country of
the firm, by modal type (number and %)

Modal choice	Number of properties	Number of rooms
Equity		
– Fully-owned (m=4)	213 (19.8%)	60,376 (17.0%)
– Partially-owned (m=3)		
(joint ventures)	179 (15.8%)	62,202 (17.5%)
Non-equity		
– Management services (m=2)		
contract	418 (37.0%)	135,660 (38.2%)
– Franchise agreement (m=1)	321 (28.4%)	96,924 (27.3%)
Total	1,131 (100.0%)	355,162 (100.0%)

Distribution of modal types across major regions of destination (%)

Modal choice	by major destination (host market) region		
	North America	Europe	Asia
Fully-owned	9.46	28.60	22.40
Partly-owned	11.46	6.20	22.93
Franchise agreement	38.31	28.66	12.45
Management service contract	40.76	36.53	42.21

Source: *International Hotels Groups Directory* and questionnaire

data enable us to examine the extent to which environmental (i.e. market
or country-specific) variables, as opposed to firm-specific variables, affect
the choice of organizational mode.

Since the focus of the second research question is the determinants of
foreign strategy, the data again relate only to hotel properties outside the
home nation of each firm, and include the organizational mode chosen
for each hotel property. Each property is the unit of analysis. Explanatory
variables are based on the global hotel companies involved, as well as characteristics of the host nation where the hotel property is located.

There appear to be variations in equity ownership and franchising by
region, while the prevalence of management service contracts is high across
all major regions. (See Table 14.3). Equity ownership is lower, and franchising is more frequent in North America. In Asia, by comparison,
franchising is less common and equity ownership modes are most common.

Third research question:

Explaining the propensity to use franchising
The unit of analysis is each hotel property

The third research question examines the reasons for the substantial growth in franchising in the international hotel business. In expanding internationally, a firm may replicate its organization in a foreign nation by using its own personnel and equity investment in an affiliate. Alternatively, for other locations, it may contract with local investors to franchise its brand name, corporate image, and business systems to them, collecting fees and royalties from the franchisees, instead of the returns on equity that it might have earned if it had made a foreign direct investment. Under what circumstances would a firm prefer to franchise its capability rather than run the operation itself? This is the focus of the third research question.

The rapid growth in international franchising over the past twenty years, documented in several studies (Fladmoe-Lindquist and Jacque 1995; Shane 1996; Kedia *et al.* 1994; Huszagh *et al.* 1992) suggest conditions which favour franchising over company-run operations. Though international franchising of services started in developed countries and are dominant there, based on geographic proximity, language and cultural similarity (Steinberg 1991; Aydin and Kacker 1989), it is now spreading rapidly into emerging markets such as Indonesia, the Philippines, Thailand and Mexico. Recent literature on services acknowledges the fact that different service sectors can exhibit very different characteristics in terms of prevalance of organizational types and strategies (Lovelock and Yip 1996; Domke 1997).

To explain the growth of international franchising in the hotel industry, we identify the internal (company characteristics and strategy) as well as external (country or location) factors that lead to the choice of this organizational form over company-owned operations. The three influences combine to determine whether, for a particular property located in a foreign country, the global hotel firm will decide to franchise or own the hotel. Earlier works by Dunning (1980), Hill *et al.* (1990), Contractor (1990), and Erramilli and Rao (1993) demonstrate the usefulness of a unified or eclectic approach to the modal choice question.

Transaction cost and agency theory has been used to develop hypotheses explaining the propensity to franchise, based on the country-specific and hotel firm-specific factors. While several of the hypotheses could relate to different service sectors, some relate only to the hotel and lodging business.

Do the characteristics of the country where the hotel is located affect the global hotel firm's propensity to franchise (as opposed to running the hotel itself)? Four factors were identified:

1 country risk
2 cultural distance between the home nation of the hotel firm and the nation where the hotel property is located
3 level of economic development of the nation in question
4 and the country's openness to international business.

The propensity to franchise also varies across firms in an industry or service sector, depending on each company's global strategy and internal capabilities. In developing firm-specific hypotheses, we combined transaction cost and agency theory concepts with the literature on strategic behaviour and organizational capability. Hotel companies possess internalized knowledge that can be exploited in a new foreign location by either company run operations or franchising. Franchising will tend to be used if transaction costs are low; if knowledge – despite its tacit nature – can be transferred at not too high an incremental cost (Winter 1987; Contractor 1985), and if returns under franchising are acceptable (or even better than equity investments on a risk adjusted basis).

As a world-wide average, as many as 28.38 per cent of the total foreign properties were franchised. There is a large variation in the relative use of franchising based on the region of origin of the global hotel firm as shown in Table 14.4. North American firms are the clear leaders in international franchising, with Asian firms next, followed by European hotel companies.

Explanatory variables used in this study

For the three research questions examined in this study, we have used three groups of variables, namely, firm specific, country specific, and perceptual strategy-related factors. The last group of factors has been tested for the modal choice question. Table 14.5 summarizes the explanatory variables used for the three research questions. The data collected for this study was a combination of primary (questionnaire) and secondary (published data from a variety of sources). We list and discuss briefly the independent variables used in this study.

For the first research question, the list of independent variables includes, eight firm- and country-specific factors. Four of the explanatory variables relate to the firm characteristics alone, namely its

Table 14.4 Distribution of franchised hotel properties

By region of origin of hotel firm	By destination (host market) region			
	North America	Europe	Asia	Other
North America	33.95	24.61	8.09	17.45
Europe	1.56	0.62	1.56	0.93
Asia	2.80	3.43	2.80	1.25
Other				0.93
World-wide average of hotel properties under franchise mode				28.38%

Table 14.5: List of explanatory variables used in the research study

	Explanatory variable (EV)	Definition	EV#	Research question 1	2	3
Country specific factors	Firm size or SIZE	World-wide revenue in US $	EV1	✓		✓
	Reservation system	Percentage of sales attributable to reservation or referral system	EV2	✓		
	International experience or IEX_j	Number of years since initial foreign direct investment	EV3	✓	✓	✓
	Investment in training	Expenditure on training as a percentage of world-wide sales	EV4	✓		
	Geographic proximity	Indicator variable: if more than 50% of rooms outside of home country are in the same region as home country, variable = 1, otherwise 0.	EV5	✓		
	Trade to GDP ratio	(Exports + imports) divided by GDP *2 ~	EV6	✓		
	FDI to GFCF ratio	[(Inward + outward investment)/2] divided by gross fixed capital formation	EV7	✓		
	Cultural distance[a]	Cultural distance from home country of firm, weighted by proportion of rooms in each host nation hotel(s)	EV8	✓		
Structural	CRI_I[b]	Composite Risk Index for country i where property is located (Highest risk =0, lowest risk =100)	EV9	—	✓	✓
	CUL_{IJ}	$CUL_{IJ} = [(I_{ih} - I_{ihk})^2/v_h]^{1/3}$, where I_h, h =1-4, equals the four cultural indices from Hofstede (1980) and V_h is the variance of the hth index as per Kogut and Singh (1988).	EV10			
	$GDPCAP_I$	GDP per capita of country i of hotel property	EV11	✓	✓	✓
	$FDITOGDP_I$	FDI/GDP ratio of country I	EV12	✓	✓	✓
Firm specific factors	$SIZE_j$	World wide revenues of Firm j in US $	EV13	—	✓	✓
	IEX_j	Number of years since Firm j's first FDI	EV14		✓	✓
	$GLOP_j$	Ratio of the number of properties the firm has outside of home country divided by the total number of properties world-wide	EV15	—	✓	✓
Strategy/control	(P)FS[d]	The need for size in global operations	EV16	✓	✓	✓
	(P)RES	Reservation system and brand	EV17	✓	✓	✓
	(P)INV	Investment in training	EV18	✓	✓	✓
	(P)SCA	Economies of scale	EV19	✓	✓	✓
	CQ	Firm's ability to exercise management control and maintain quality	EV20	✓	✓	✓

Notes to table 14.5:

a

$$CD_j = \frac{\sum\limits_{k=1}^{k=m_j} [(r_{jhk}) * (1/4 \sum\limits_{i-1}^{j=4} (I_{ih} - I_{ihk})^2/v]}{\sum\limits_{k=1}^{k=m_j} S\, r_{jhk}}$$

Where I_{ih} = Index for the ith cultural dimension in home country.

i = 1, . . ., 4 cultural attributes.

I_{ik} = Index for the ith cultural dimension in host country k.

V_i = Variance of the ith cultural dimension, $i = 1,2,3,4$.

m_j = Number of host nations for firm j.

r_{jhk} = Number of rooms in country k associated with company j located in host nation h.

CD = Weighted Average Cultural Distance Index for company j

j = 1 . . . 34 firms.

Source: Hofstede (1980)

b Frost and Sullivan, International Country Risk Guide 1991.
c Perceived importance of strategy factors where 5 equals very important . . . 1 equals not important.
d (P) prefix for strategy factors used in second and third research questions.

size, international experience, the level of proprietary knowledge and training in the firm, and the firm's extent of dependence on a global reservation system. All the above were collected from the questionnaire. The remaining variables pertain to the firm's cultural distance and geographic proximity to target markets, trade to gross domestic product ratio, and foreign direct investment to gross fixed capital formation ratio, were collected from several published sources.

In order to specify independent variables for the second research question, we undertook a syncretic approach combining transaction cost and agency theory reasoning, as well as country-specific and firm-specific factors, as pointed out by Contractor (1990). This eclectic or syncretic approach is echoed in earlier studies by several scholars such as Kim and Hwang (1992), and Erramilli and Rao (1993). Firm size, international experience, and foreign propensity ratio captures the company level characteristics. The country specific factors used were country risk, cultural distance, gross domestic product per capita, and the ratio for foreign direct investment to gross domestic product. Finally, perceived importance of strategy was captured through multiple variables as listed and defined in Table 14.5.

The explanatory variables used for the third research question are similar to the previous research question, though, as depicted in the next table, the expected sign in relation to the dependent variable differed in six cases.

A list of the dependent variables and their relation to the explanatory variables used in this study

In the international business literature, the degree of internationalization of firms is operationalized in many ways, in cross-sectional studies. While this may be too many, ten alternative measures of internationalization of the firm (our dependent variable) were created for the first research question. Testing with multiple constructs is usually a good check on the stability and robustness of data and results. Data were drawn from the questionnaire responses as well as the hotel directory.

The dependent variable for the second research question was the modal choice for each property. Table 14.6 (pages 308–9) shows the dependent variable M as a polytomous measure depicting rising levels of equity ownership and overall control:

- Franchise M = 1
- Management service contract M = 2
- Partially owned (joint venture) M = 3
- Fully owned M = 4.

In the third research question for each hotel property the analysis statistically distinguished between a franchise (F=1) mode versus a company-run operation (F=0) as the definition of the dependent variable.

Discussion of results

In order to examine the first research question, a stepwise regression using a forward procedure was implemented to explain the cross-sectional variation in the internationalization of hotel firms. The R^2 ranged from 0.22 to 0.68, as depicted in Table 14.7 (page 310–11). Overall, the size, international experience, and geographic proximity to foreign markets were the most frequently entered, suggesting these variables as the most relevant overall. Despite the fact that ten different indexes were used for the dependent variable, the subset of the eight independent variables chosen by the procedure is reasonably congruent. The negative sign for the coefficient for size was contrary to expectation and since this happens in several analyses, some explanation may be offered as hypotheses for further research. Possibly, the negative sign may have to do with hotel firms having large domestic markets, such as the United States and Canada. The absolute number of properties is much larger in the above mentioned countries as compared to the smaller European nations. On the other hand, firms from United Kingdom, France, Italy, the Netherlands, and Spain as source nations may have focused on international markets due to the small size of their domestic markets. Results for the geographic proximity show a consistent negative sign, suggesting that in the early stages of

Table 14.6 List of all dependent variables and their expected relation to explanatory variables

Research question	Dependent variable		Explanatory variables and expected sign																			
	Title	Definition	1	2	3	4	5	6	7	8	9	10	11	12	13	14	15	16	17	18	19	20
One	GLOBAL	Foreign propensity ratio measured by number of rooms outside home county divided by total number of rooms world-wide	+	+	+	+	-	+	+	-													
	GLOBAP	Foreign propensity ratio measured by number of properties outside home country divided by total number of properties world-wide	+	+	+	+	-	+	+	-													
	COUNTRIES	Number of foreign countries in which the firm has property																					
	FSALES	Foreign Sales to total world-wide sales (in US $)	+	+	+	+	-	+	+	-													
	GLOBAPFD	Number of properties abroad divided by number of properties in home country	+	+	+	+	-	+	+	-													
	GLOBALFD	Number of rooms abroad divided by number of rooms in home country	+	+	+	+	-	+	+	-													
	FSALESFD	Foreign sales divided by domestic sales (in US $)	+	+	+	+	-	+	+	-													
	SMI	Geographic dispersion index by sales[a]	+	+	+	+	-	+	+	-													
	RMI	Geographic dispersion index by rooms[b]	+	+	+	+	-	+	+	-													
	PMI	Geographic dispersion index by properties[c]	+	+	+	+	-	+	+	-													

| Two | M | M is a polytomous measure depicting rising levels of equity ownership and control: franchise $M=1$; management service contract $M=2$; partially owned (joint venture) $M=3$; and fully owned $M=4$ | + | - | - | + | + | + | + | - | + | + | + |
| Three | F | Propensity to franchise ($F=1$ if hotel property is under franchise, or 0 if property) is company run | - | + | + | + | - | + | - | - | + | + | + |

Notes:

a Measured by $\dfrac{a_1 m_1 + a_2 m_2 + \ldots\ldots\ldots\ldots + a_0 m_0}{a_1 + a_2 + \ldots\ldots\ldots\ldots + a_0}$

Where a_i is sales and m_i is miles from headquarters to country i

b Measured by $\dfrac{a_1 m_1 + a_2 m_2 + \ldots\ldots\ldots\ldots + a_0 m_0}{a_1 + a_2 + \ldots\ldots\ldots\ldots + a_0}$

Where a_i is rooms and m_i is miles from headquarters to country i.

c Measured by $\dfrac{a_1 m_1 + a_2 m_2 + \ldots\ldots\ldots\ldots + a_0 m_0}{a_1 + a_2 + \ldots\ldots\ldots\ldots + a_0}$

Where a_i is properties and m_i is miles from headquarters to country i

Table 14.7 Regression results explaining differences in internationalization among hotel multinationals

Dependent variable	Intercept	Size	International experience	Reservation system	Investment in Training
GLOBAL	0.29728	-0.00019 (0.0011) [3]+++	0.01879 (0.0008) [2]+++	**	**
GLOBAP	0.3396	-0.00021 (0.0004) [3]+++	0.01893 (0.0008) [2]+++	**	**
CNTRYS	-3.1868	0.00938 (0.0001) [1]+++	**	**	728.7028 (0.0913) [2]+
FSALES	0.0342	-0.00009 (0.0841) [3]+	0.01511 (0.0205) [2]++	**	**
GLOBAPFD	1.0721	**	**	**	**
GLOBALFD	-0.2883	-0.00119 (0.0562) [3]+	0.14921 (0.0131) [2]++	**	**
FSALESFD	-1.99320	**	0.08846 (0.0511) [2]	**	**

Regressions with seven independent variables (geographic proximity removed)

SMI	-14142.4	**	16103.618 (0.0001) [1]+++	**	**
RMI	198.29	-0.4340 (0.0995) [1]+	80.736 (0.007) [2]+++	**	**
PMI	-1760.569	**	217.434 (0.0002) [1]+++	**	**

Notes:
( )   Prob F Value; two-tailed test
+++   Significant better than .01
 ++   Significant better than .05
  +   Significant better than .10
 **   Indicates the variable was not loaded for lack of significance

internationalization the firm first expands in its own geographic region. This supports the gradualist model of international expansion, at least as far as geographic proximity is concerned, that companies exhibiting a relatively lower degree of internationalization are more likely to internationalize within their own geographic region, *ceteris paribus.*

The international experience variable was entered in eight of ten equations, and is strongly significant, with signs in the hypothesized direction. Companies which went abroad earlier in the past were found to have a higher proportion of their business outside their home nation. Overall,

Table 14.7 (continued)

Geographic proximity	Trade to GDP	FDI to GFCF	Cultural distance	Overall F	R2
-0.24511 (0.0187) [4]+++	0.00508 (0.1613) {3}	**	**	7.97 +++	0.6392
-2.27508 (0.0097) [4]+++	0.00470 (0.1947) [3]	**	**	8.65 +++	0.6578
**	**	**	**	21.83 +++	0.6858
**	**	**	0.11758 (0.0462) [1]++	4.76 ++	0.4289
-2.73179 (0.0808) [1] +	0.10004 (0.1290) [2]	**	**	2.86 +	0.2221
-2.0024 (0.0844) [4]+	-.0676 (0.1103) [1]	**	**	4.66 ++	0.5087
**	**	0.28121 (0.0485) [1]++	**	4.67 ++	0.3181
	**	**	**	24.00 +++	0.5332
	**	**	**	5.18 ++	0.3419
	**	**	**	20.02 +++	0.4880

the hypothesis for cultural distance variable was not supported. The cultural distance variable was significant in only one out of ten equations. Our non-significant results do not necessarily imply that cultural learning is unimportant. First, this may be due to data insufficiency problem for the cultural distance variable. Second, it may simply be that in a cross-sectional study where most firms are already internationally mature (i.e. most of the sample already has long-standing and substantial international cultural experience), that this variable then is not statistically significant in explaining cross-sectional variance. In our sample, the mean length of international experience is a fairly long: 17.44 years.

Dunning and McQueen (1981) placed considerable emphasis on ownership or firm-specific factors, such as global reservation system, or investment in training, as explanations for the international competitiveness of hotel firms, but these did not show strong statistical association in explaining cross-sectional variation in the degree of internationalization of firms. (They did have significant association with other dependent variables, as we shall see later.) It may be that these competitive factors which did serve to discriminate between companies twelve years ago in the Dunning and McQueen study, no longer do so in a maturing business. In the early stages what may distinguish some companies, may not do so later as competitors catch up and match the former leaders in training and information management. Then what distinguishes some companies may be environmental or contextual factors such as the firm's location and source country characteristics. Lack of statistical significance may also simply be a quirk of the data, as the size of the sample was limited to thirty-four firms only.

A logistic regression using a generalized logit model, under the assumption of a common slope parameter for the predictor variable (also known as the 'proportional-odds' model) was used for the second research question. The results in Table 14.8 show a strongly significant overall chi-square value of 380.27, and a Somers D' of 0.61. For the overall model, concordant probabilities were a fairly high 79.6 per cent.

Seven out of the eleven independent variables are significant at better than 0.05, and of these, five are significant at better than 0.01 level.

Country independent variables CRI (Country Political and Economic Risk), and GDPCAP (GDP per capita) both had results congruent with the hypotheses. The negative sign for the GDPCAP variable confirms the hypothesis that non-equity modes are preferred in high-income nations, and equity investment in low income nations, *ceteris paribus*. The positive sign for the CRI coefficient confirms that, with higher political and economic risk, non-equity modes, such as franchising and management service contracts are preferred in higher risk environments.

Hypotheses for CUL (Cultural Distance) and FDITOGDP (FDI to GDP ratio in the host nation) were not supported. In the case of the cultural distance variable, missing data may be the problem causing lack of significance, because while Hofstede's (1980) data cover less than fifty nations, the number of nations in our sample is 112.

The objective firm variables IEX (International Experience) and GLOP (Proportion of hotels outside the home nation) yielded strong support for the hypotheses, that equity-based modes will be preferred by companies with considerable experience and existing geographic reach. The results for the Management and Quality Control (CQ), support the hypothesis that the organizational mode for the property would be influenced towards more equity ownership, *ceteris paribus*, in firms whose executives place a higher importance on control over daily management and quality. The sign for the

Table 14.8 Ordinal logistic regression using a generalized LOGIT model explaining the entry modes of hotel multinationals

Variable	Description	Parameter estimate	Standard error	Wald Chi-square	Signi- p > Chi-square
Intercept 1		-1.633	1.188	1.892	0.17
Intercept 2		-0.979	1.186	0.681	0.41
Intercept 3		1.515	1.187	1.628	0.20
CRI	Country risk index	0.027	0.014	3.722**	0.05
CUL	Cultural distance	-0.049	0.078	0.390	0.53
GDPCAP	Per capita GDP	-0.068	0.020	11.277*	0.0008
FDITOGDP	Foreign property ratio	-0.000	0.001	0.453	0.50
IEX	International experience	0.046	0.009	28.180*	0.0001
GLOP	Foreign property ratio	2.867	0.402	51.002*	0.0001
PSCA	Economies of scale	0.168	0.188	0.806	0.37
CQ	Management and quality control	0.189	0.049	14.742*	0.0001
PFS	Importance of size	-0.695	0.166	17.543*	0.0001
PRES	Reservation system and brand	-0.334	0.131	6.460**	0.01
PINV	Investment in training	-0.185	0.208	0.791	0.37

* Better than .01.
** Better than .05.

Log L	Chi-Square	d.f.	P	C-Index	Somers' D
-2	380.27	11	0.0001	0.81	0.61

Predicted probabilities		The dependent variable M			
Concordant	79.6%	M-1	M-2	M-3	M-4
Discordant	18.4%	Franchise	Management	Partly-	Fully-
Tied	2.0%		service	owned	owned
			contract		

PFS (Importance of Size) variable is opposite to the hypotheses (and highly significant). This suggests that the expressed importance of size, as a strategic factor, is not necessarily correlated to the propensity to use high ownership modes. The sign for PRES (Importance of Reservation System and Brand) is congruent with the hypothesis. The results suggest that a global reservation system and brand name are crucial strategic assets that enable a global hotel company to build and control a network of contractual alliances. Finally, the results for the PSCA (Importance of Scale) and PINV (Importance of Investment in Training) variables were not significant.

The second research question examined three groups of explanatory variables, namely, country-specific, firm-structural, and perceptual strategy variables, which were shown to influence the modal choice. The results suggest the significance of all the three categories of explanatory variables. In particular, country risk index and GDP per capita were significant for the country specific category; international experience and foreign propensity ratio were significant in the firm-specific category; and management and quality control, perceived importance of size and reservation system were significant in the strategy-related factors.

In the final research question, a binary logistic regression model was used to examine the propensity of firms to use franchising for their international operations (F = 1 or 0). The statistical findings in Table 14.9 suggest that the propensity to franchise is at least as strongly influenced by firm characteristics and global strategy as by market conditions. Overall, both logistic regression equations are very strong, with highly significant values for the Goodness of Fit statistics, and -2 Log L, at better than .01 level, as well as a high value for Somers' D.

Among the country-specific variables, the only one that had statistical significance was GDP per capita, confirming that franchising propensity rises with level of economic development. In the objective firm characteristics category, greater international experience and greater degree of international expansion (ratio of foreign to total properties) are negatively associated with the likelihood of franchising, suggesting a greater use of company-run operations with greater international experience. In perceptual firm factors, a greater emphasis on quality is negatively correlated with franchising likelihood, while franchising is positively associated with the perceived need for global size, investment in training and the use of global brand as a control tool to keep franchisees in line.

All in all, with seven of the twelve hypotheses unequivocally supported, with weaker support for some others, Somers' D values of 0.75, and high goodness to fit statistics for the regression equations, the overall results appear quite satisfactory.

The old presumption on the part of managers that company-run operations make for a superior global strategy is being overturned. Franchising is a 'lower return/considerably lower risk' strategy compared with equity investments in hotel abroad. Each franchise typically provides a lower return. But a network of global franchises can possibly, in the aggregate, provide the firm with as high a total global return as an equity based strategy, by enabling faster international expansion and greater territorial coverage world-wide. In the past few years, a large number of international hotel chains have aggressively moved into the non-equity segment of the global hotel business. Firms such as Hyatt Hotels Corp. (Morris 1994), and Holiday Inn Worldwide are moving away from a dominant equity-based ownership strategy to franchise-based strategies, thus creating a spin-off advantage for themselves.

Conclusions

This chapter examined the global spread, strategies, and foreign operational modes of hotel firms. As observed in the discussion for each of the three research questions, there is a considerable amount of overlap and synergy amongst the firm-specific, country-specific, and strategic

Table 14.9 Logistic regression explaining the propensity to franchise of hotel
multinationals

	Model 1	*Model 2*
Total number of cases (N)	517	721
Of which franchising used in	227	320
Degrees of freedom	11	10
Intercept	-8.21	-10.04`
	(***)	(***)
Explanatory variables:		
Size	—	—
International experience	-0.09	-0.13
	(***)	(***)
Foreign to total properties	-5.02	-6.60
	(***)	(***)
Firm size	1.17	1.50
	(***)	(***)
Economies of scale	-0.25	0.73
Control over quality	0.01	0.18
		(***)
Reservation system	1.18	1.28
	(***)	(***)
Investment in training	.87	1.35
	(***)	(***)
GDP per capita	.10	0.06
	(***)	(***)
FDI to GDP	-0.00	0.00
Composite risk index	-0.03	
Cultural distance	0.058	-0.06
-2 Log L	275.01	407.60
	(***)	(***)
Somers' D	0.75	0.76

Note:
*** Significant at 0.01
** Significant at 0.05
* Significant at 0.10

factors in explaining the variation in the degree of internationalization,
organizational forms, and location patterns for the global hotel
business. The international business literature has only just begun to
address the question of the globalization of service industries, compared
to studies in manufacturing. Further special attention should be given
to explain the phenomenal growth of services in both industrialized and
emerging countries.

An interesting aspect of this study and its data is the considerable variation across firms in the degree of internationalization, and the incidence of alliances, and their types. Franchising is more likely with higher levels of national income (which may be for market size reasons as well as considerations of legally-enforceable property rights).

A salient conclusion that emerged from this research project was the overall very high incidence of alliance modes. (The term 'alliance' here is used broadly, to include any arrangement that uses local partners, be they as equity investment partners, or real estate owners of the local hotel property, or be they franchisees.) Alliance-based modes account for the large majority of international hotel chain operations. The hotel sector thus exemplifies an advanced trend in the propensity to use alliances because of the ability of the business to separate key strategic assets and reduce risks by:

- codification and international replicability of knowledge (be it via franchises or via management service contracts) in terms of designs, operating procedures, and setup;
- maintaining control over global brand names (hence reducing the fear of opportunism and retaining leverage over alliance partners);
- maintaining control over (and earning incremental revenues from) a global reservation system;
- separating real estate or country risk versus commercial risk over the partners involved, in management service contracts, as well as in other modes by royalty provisions;
- network scale advantages, not just in transfer of knowledge in the chain, but in the logistics of global supply.

One general conclusion that can also apply to other sectors is that contractual relationships can effectively substitute for equity ownership, when key strategic variables can be codified, and the fear of partner opportunism is reduced by the global company's ongoing control over key strategic assets.

One of the crucial tasks facing managers is how to choose the right organizational type, or entry mode choice, from the variety of organizational forms now available. The general modal choice set now includes varying levels of equity ownership, as well as several alliances of various descriptions. The manager can increasingly choose from a large set of options, as illustrated by the hotel business.

Note

This chapter is partially based on material drawn from the following articles: 'Explaining Variation In The Degree of Internationalization of Firms: the Case of the Hotel Industry', *Journal of International Management*, spring 1995; 'Modal

Choice in a World of Alliances: Analyzing Organizational Forms in the International Hotel Sector', *Journal of International Business Studies*, second quarter 1998; and 'Franchising versus Company-Run Operations: Modal Choice in the Global Hotel Sector', *Journal of International Marketing*, Volume 6, No.2 , 1998. In preparing this manuscript, assistance was provided by Mary Aita, Ph.D. student in International Business at St Louis University, USA.

References

Agarwal, J. P. (1980) 'Determinants of Foreign Direct Investment: a survey', *Weltwirtschaftliches Archiv* 4: 733–39.

Andersen, O. (1993) 'On the Internationalization Process of Firms: a Critical Analysis', *Journal of International Business Studies* 24 (2): 209–32.

Aydin, N. and Kacker, M. (1989) 'International outlook of US based franchisers', *International Marketing Review* 7 (2): 43–53.

Ball, C. A. and Tschoegl, A. E. (1982) 'The Decision to Establish a Foreign Bank Branch or Subsidiary', *Journal of Financial and Quantitative Analysis*, September: 411–24.

Contractor, F. J. (1985) 'A Generalized Theorem for Joint Venture and Licensing Negotiations', *Journal of International Business Studies* 16 (3): 23–50.

—— (1990) 'Contractual and Cooperative Forms of International Business: Towards a Unified Theory of Modal Choice', *Management International Review* 30: 31–54.

Culem, C. G. (1988) 'The Locational Determinants of Direct Investments among Industrialized Countries', *European Economic Review* 32: 885–904.

Davidson, W. H. (1980) *Experience Effects in International Investment and Technology Transfer*, Ann Arbor: UMI.

Domke, D. J. (1997) 'International Entry Mode Choice for Service Firms: the Role of International Strategy and Service Throughput Technology', paper presented at the Academy of Management, Boston, August.

Dunning, J. H. (1977) 'Trade Location of Economic Activity and MNE: a Search for an Eclectic Approach', in B. Ohlin, P. O. Hesselborn, and P. J. Wijkman (eds) *The International Allocation of Economic Activity*, London: Macmillan.

—— (1980) 'Towards an Eclectic Theory of International Production: Some Empirical Tests', *Journal of International Business Studies* 11 (1): 9–31.

—— (1981) *International Production and the Multinational Enterprise*, London: Allen and Unwin.

—— (1988) *Explaining International Production*, London: Unwin and Hyman.

Dunning, J. H. and McQueen, M. (1981) *Transnational Corporations in International Tourism*, New York: UNCTC.

Dunning, J. H. and Norman, G. (1983) 'The Theory of the Multinational Enterprise: an Application to Multinational Office Location', *Environment and Planning* 15: 675–92.

Erramilli, M. K. and Rao, C. P. (1990) 'Choice of Foreign Market Entry Modes by Service Firms: Role of Market Knowledge', *Management International Review* 30 (2): 135–50.

—— (1993) 'Service Firms' International Entry Mode Choice: a Modified Transaction Cost Analysis Approach', *Journal of Marketing* 57: 19–38.

Fladmoe-Lindquist, K. and Jacque, L. L. (1995) 'Control Modes in International Service Operations: the Propensity to Franchise', *Management Science* 41 (7): 1238–49.

Goldberg, L. G. and Johnson, D. (1990) 'The Determinants of US Banking Activity Abroad', *Journal of International Money and Finance* 9: 123–37.

Goldberg, L. G., Johnson, D. and Saunders, A. (1980) 'The Causes of US Bank Expansion Overseas', *Journal of Money, Credit and Banking*, November: 630–43.

Grubaugh, S. G. (1987) 'Determinants of Direct Foreign Investment', *The Review of Economics and Statistics* 69 (1): 149–52.

Hill, C. W., Hwang, P. and Kim, W. C. (1990) 'An Eclectic Theory of the Choice of International Entry Mode', *Strategic Management Journal* 11 (2): 117–28.

Hirsch, S. (1967) *The Location of Industry and International Competitiveness*, Oxford: Oxford University Press.

Hofstede, G. (1980) *Cultures Consequences: International Differences in Work-related Values*, Beverly Hills, Calif.: Sage.

Hollander, A. (1984) 'Foreign Location Decision by US Transnational Firms: an Empirical Study', *Managerial and Decision Economics* 5 (1): 7–18.

Huszagh, S. M., Huszagh, F. W. and McIntyre, F. S. (1992) 'International Franchising in the Context of Competitive Strategy and Theory of the Firm', *International Marketing Review* 9 (5): 5–18.

Johanson, J. and J.E. Vahlne (1977) 'The Internationalization Process of the Firm', *Journal of International Business Studies*, spring.

Kim, W. C. and Hwang, P. (1992) 'Global Strategy and Multinationals Entry Mode Choice', *Journal of International Business Studies* 23 (1): 29–53.

Kedia, B. L., Ackerman, D. J., Bush, D. E. and Justis, R. T. (1994) 'Determinants of Internationalization of Franchsing Operations by US Franchisors', *International Marketing Review* 11 (4): 56–68.

Khoury, S. J. (1979) 'International Banking: a Special Look at Foreign Banks in the United States', *Journal of International Business Studies* 10 (4): 36–52.

Li, J. and Guisinger, S. (1992) 'The Globalization of Service Multinationals in the "Triad" Regions: Japan, Western Europe and North America', *Journal of International Business Studies* 23 (4): 675–96.

Lovelock, C. H. and Yip, G. S. (1996) 'Developing Global Strategies for Service Business', *California Management Review* 38 (2): 64–86.

Morris, Steven. (1994) 'Hyatt is Opening the Door for Hotel Franchising', *Chicago Tribune*, 25 June.

Morrison, A. J. (1990) *Strategies in Global Industries*, Westport, Conn.: Quorum.

Nigh, D., Cho, K. R., and S. Krishnan (1986) 'The Role of Location-related Factors in US Banking Involvement Abroad', *Journal of International Business Studies* 17 (3): 59–72.

Pearce, R. D. (1991) *The Determinants of Foreign Direct Investment: a Survey of the Evidence*, New York: United Nations.

Schollhammer, H. (1974) *Locational Strategies of International Firms*, Studies in International Economics and Business, no. 1, Los Angeles: Center for International Business, Pepperdine University.

Shane, S. A. (1996) 'Explaining why Franchise Companies Expand Overseas', *Journal of Business Venturing* 11 (2): 73–88.

Steinberg, C. (1991) 'Franchising: in our own Backyard', *World Trade* 4 (3): 52–59.

Terpstra, V. and Yu, C. M. (1988) 'Determinants of foreign investment of United States advertising agencies', *Journal of International Business Studies* 19 (2): 33—47.

Weinstein, A. K. (1974) 'The International Expansion of US Multinational Advertising Agencies', *MSU Business Topics* 10 (3): 29–35.

—— (1977) 'Foreign Investments by Service Firms: the Case of the Multinational Advertising Agency', *Journal of International Business Studies*: 83–92.

Winter, S. (1987) 'Knowledge and Competence as Strategic Assets', in David Teece (ed.), *The Competitive Challenge: Strategies for Industrial Innovation and Renewal*, 159–84, Cambridge, Mass.: Ballinger.

World Bank (1992) *World Development Report*, Oxford: Oxford University Press.

Yip, G. (1989) 'Global Strategy. . . . in a World of Nations?', *Sloan Management Review* fall: 29–41.

15 The search for core competencies in a service multinational

A case study of the French hotel Novotel

Susan Segal-Horn

Introduction

Within strategic management the resource-based view of the firm has emerged as an approach to strategy which sees strategy as formulated on the basis of the resources and competencies of the firm (Prahalad and Hamel 1990; Grant 1991; Peteraf 1993). This may be contrasted with the market positioning view which sees strategy as formulated on the basis of the structure of the industry in which the firm competes and its market positioning within that industry (Porter 1980). Competencies may be distinctive to a firm and form the basis of its positioning and performance. In management terms, it is an approach that emphasizes the quality of management thinking and implementation in identifying, building, and nurturing resources and competencies over time. This chapter explores the nature of the competencies critical to competitiveness for multinational service firms.

Core competence management

Within the resource-based theory of the firm internal resources are viewed as the key to determining strategy formation and choice, and to explaining economic performance (Penrose 1959; Wernerfelt 1984; Barney 1991; Peteraf 1993). Resources include both physical and intangible skills, including human skills such as management skills. Within each firm, an idiosyncratic bundle of resources will exist, some of which will be the basis for core competencies, which may in turn then provide the basis for competitive advantage. Core competencies are made up of combinations of each firm's resources. Such combinations are themselves idiosyncratic and specific to each firm. They may therefore be difficult to imitate and thus valuable, since competencies or capabilities are the outcome of using groups of resources in particular ways (Barney 1991; Amit and Schoemaker 1993). Thus firms may have the same or similar resources, but different competencies or capabilities. Given the diffusion of innovation, knowledge, skill, and other aspects of competition that eventually occurs in any industry, investment in the continuous nurturing of existing competencies and the identification and building of new competencies becomes critical to performance and long-term survival. Novotel provides an illustration of such a process of 'identification and building of new competencies' to keep pace with continuous industry development.

Although competencies may reside in the mind of a single individual or be shared within a group, they must be cultivated and managed both formally and informally. In understanding core competence management, it is useful to use Bogaert *et al.*'s (1994) distinction between 'having' and 'doing'. While resources are about 'having', competencies are about 'doing'. Resources are tangible; competencies are intangible and depend for their development on internal management processes. 'Productive activity requires the co-operation and co-ordination of teams of resources' (Grant 1991: 118). The Novotel case discusses 'doing' in the hotel chain and how the processes of 'doing' have evolved over different periods of its history within different competitive contexts.

Core competence management involves processes of building, enabling and continual development within an organization. Building and continuing development of competencies can only occur through processes of integration and co-ordination to enable the knowledge held by individuals to be shared within the firm. Core competence management is about the processes within a firm, which transfer and interpret knowledge within the organization about the business context, the industry, and its own internal functioning. For Novotel, the external business and industry contexts had changed considerably during the 1980s and 1990s. This in turn changed the bases of competition within the international hotel sector requiring in response both revolutionary and evolutionary developments within the organization.

Application to service multinationals

Service firms provide a particularly fruitful context in which to test some of the aspects of core competencies. Service firms typically have a different balance of resources and competencies to manufacturing firms (Zeithaml and Bitner 1996). The distinctive features of a service business are located around what is usually referred to in the service management literature as 'the service encounter' (Normann 1984; Czepiel *et al.* 1985; Bowen *et al.* 1990), that is, the employee/customer interaction typical of service businesses. It is not whether a particular service business is capital-intensive or labour-intensive (and services may be either or both) which is the significant factor, it is the fact, as Normann (1984) has cogently argued, that services are 'personality-intensive'. Thus, the service experience for the customer is essentially a result of how people carry out their responsibilities at work, irrespective of whether they have high or low levels of information technology or other supporting infrastructure. This intensifies the need for a robust core competence management process to mediate between strategy, operations and service delivery. Effective service delivery requires management interpretation of both the external environment and customer needs, together with internal learning from and with the employees.

The role of competence management processes in multinational service firms is particularly demanding, especially for complex services with a high intangibility content because of the difficulties of delivering such assets across national, cultural and linguistic borders with consistent quality. Service industries span an array of different types between 'hard' and 'soft' services, each with its different mix of tangibles and intangibles (Erramilli 1990). The 'hard' tangible elements are increasingly identical to those of a manufacturing business. The 'soft' (service encounter) elements retain the distinctive needs of service management and service delivery. This 'hard'/'soft' distinction can be illustrated with reference to the hotel industry. 'Hardware' (such as beds or televisions) is relatively more straightforward to co-ordinate and deliver across national borders than 'software' (such as the style and atmosphere of a hotel, or how staff conduct themselves in their dealings with guests). The selection and supply of beds or televisions to hotels around the world, are fairly standardized tasks. However, the shared values and tacit knowledge underpinning the delivery of service encounter 'software' are far more problematic in terms of international management processes. The management task of service MNCs has thus become one combining hard and soft into effective organizational routines.

The French hotel chain Novotel provides an opportunity to analyse such management processes in a service MNC and to illustrate the processes of competence-building as a basic component of the internationalization of a service firm or a service concept.

The case of Novotel

The first Novotel hotel opened in 1967, near Lille Airport in France. The first Novotel outside France was opened in 1973. By 1998 the chain had grown to 280 hotels in forty-six countries around the world. The hotels provide 43,000 rooms and employ 33,000 people. Novotel is just one of the hotel chains belonging to the Accor Group of France of which Novotel's two founders are the co-chairmen. Accor operates more than 2,000 hotels world-wide, offering more than two million rooms at different ratings and service levels. Other chains in the Accor Group include Sofitel, Mercure, Ibis, Formule 1. These range from 4-star (Sofitel) to 1-star (Formule 1).

The Novotel business concept: 1973–87

Novotel was the first international 3-star hotel chain. Prior to this strategic innovation, international hotel chains were to be found in the 4 and 5-star rank only. The business idea behind the Novotel hotel concept was of international standardization of the offering at the 3-star level. To achieve such standardization, consistency of the service offered was required in every location in which it was available. Standardization is one of the elements of internationalization of a service that is especially problematic. It means putting in place a service delivery system that is robust enough to survive transferability across borders and generate consistent service standards to satisfy customer expectations, irrespective of local conditions, local culture or local infrastructure. Therefore at the early stage in its development, the core competencies Novotel needed and valued for implementation of its international strategy were those that delivered international standardization of both the tangible and the intangible elements of the hotel service.

The tangible elements of standardization were easily realizable. The design, style and layouts of the hotels were reproduced to precise specifications. For example bedroom size was standard throughout Europe at twenty-four metres square. Since the Novotel chain was positioned as a 3-star chain world-wide, certain facilities such as bedroom furniture, fixtures and fittings or outside amenities such as swimming pools and amounts of free car parking space were (and still are) always available at all Novotel units. The service intangibles were conceptualized as standardized service levels to be delivered at all locations world-wide. These were implemented by means of centralized design and centralized control of service standards.

International standardization: 1987–92

Maintaining universal service standards as the chain grew rapidly over a twenty-five-year period became more and more problematic, especially when many new staff were recruited from other hotel groups with different working practices. Therefore a management process to monitor standard procedures was introduced in 1987 that became known as the '95 Bolts'. This process was intended to be, and duly became, a template for organizational routines. It was a hierarchical system, designed and controlled by central headquarters. It emphasized structural elements of service and was top-down in both concept and style. The '95 Bolts' were ninety-five points or regulations applied to the thirteen main points of staff/customer interaction. These key service encounters included: reservation, arrival/access, parking, check-in, hall, bedroom, bathroom/WC, evening meal, breakfast, shops, bar, outdoor games/the swimming-pool, and checkout. Each of these important service encounter interaction points were divided into a series of compulsory regulations for staff, including how to set out a bedroom; how to lay a place setting in the restaurant; how to welcome a guest. A booklet containing the 95 Bolts was issued to all staff and was the induction 'Bible' for new staff. An internal team of inspectors enforced the process. They visited each hotel approximately twice each year to carry out monitoring of standards. They functioned in the same way as 'mystery shoppers' in that they made reservations, arrived, stayed and departed incognito. On completion of their stay they would make themselves known to the hotel general manager (GM) for review and discussion. Percentage grades were awarded and recommendations made.

It was a rigid process which did deliver consistent international standards. It was certainly based on well-understood routines and shared values, developed and reinforced through induction and training programmes. However, the nature of the routines espoused by Novotel's value system and reinforced by Novotel's training programmes were highly inflexible systems and routines designed to prevent initiative or responsiveness and to maximize a rigid standardization.

Such standardization provided Novotel with many business benefits. These benefits included cost reductions arising from the economies of scale from standardization of recruitment, facilities or training, as well as economies of scope from shared marketing or hotel design. Standard design of hotels and guest bedrooms allowed basic housekeeping and maintenance functions also to be standardized. Training of staff in all basic functions could therefore be simplified and standardized. Indeed, one of the features of the Accor Group was the 'Academie Accor' set up in 1985, as the centre for all staff training within the Group. Its 'campus' was located on the site of Group corporate headquarters just outside Paris. From there, all training was centrally designed and centrally delivered to reinforce the standard routines. Its objective was control of the service encounter to ensure that the staff delivered international consistency.

Taking the notion of international consistency of standards one stage further, the Novotel senior management developed an approach to staffing described as 'multi-skilling' ('multi-competence'). The idea behind multi-competence was to develop staff to specific service levels for each hotel task such that they could work anywhere in the Novotel international network with transferable skills. This was later more fully developed into the multi-layered competence measurement system of 'Progress Novotel'.

Thus two key managerial processes were seen as core competencies at this stage by Novotel management. They were the processes related to the delivery of international standardization and those that generated a more efficient and cost-effective workforce. Unfortunately in terms of the business as a whole, these were competencies that were internally focused on costs and service levels, rather than externally focused on customers or markets.

Inflexible routines, inappropriate competencies: the early 1990s

Gradually the internal system to monitor standards and ensure international transferability and consistency had become locked into a standardization which customers no longer valued. Unlike the 1970s and 1980s when a 3-star international chain was an innovative concept, by the early 1990s there were many other 3-star chains (e.g. Marriott 'Courtyard') which had imitated Novotel's original concept and positioning. The early focus on competencies to support centralized standardization, whilst internally effective for an organization in a new niche in a period of rapid market development, now represented a lost business opportunity to meet more sophisticated customer needs. The competencies supported by the 95 Bolts had been intended to build and achieve rigidity and procedure to support international uniformity. They were replaced by a more adaptive system in 1992.

The new set of core competencies which Novotel management identified and built from 1992 onwards represented a shift in the Novotel business concept away from international standardization of the service offering and towards an international hospitality business with local identity and discretion. It resulted from a series of industry and business reviews, carried out in the light of worsening performance by the Novotel group. These reviews resulted in Novotel management recognizing a need to change the focus of their international strategy and its mode of implementation. The period from business start-up in 1967 to 1987 was about rapid growth of a business based upon identification of an unfilled market gap at the 3-star level ('Understanding the Industry'). Internally, the organization built core competencies based upon shared values about international standardization for that segment ('Understanding the Organization'). Introducing the 95 Bolts in 1987 was a tightening of the existing competencies, based on the existing business concept, based on the historical analysis of the industry niche. Both the 1987 and the 1992 actions involved an additional element, namely 'Interpreting the Business Context' and making judgments about current market needs.

The 1992 reappraisal led to a rejection of standardization of the international service offering as their source of competitive advantage, together with the internal core competencies which had been developed to support it. Instead an entrepreneurial, customer-focused hotel network was to be created by extending zones of discretion to junior staff throughout the network. Culturally the organization understood this internally as strategic change, but not cultural change. Instead it marked a return to its original entrepreneurial culture. A new corporate mission 'Back to the Future' ('Retour vers le Futur') was adopted to reflect the abandonment of the centralized approach to standardization and a return to Novotel's entrepreneurial roots of responsiveness to the customer. The core shared value on which this cultural renaissance and shift of business concept were based was the concept of 'hospitality'. The next section analyses these changes in more detail.

International responsiveness: after 1992

Hospitality as the central business concept was Novotel's response to the external business and industry contexts with which it had gradually lost touch. 'Hospitality' as a potential source of competitive advantage is dependent on the service encounter. It is not a resource but a competence, since it is about how you do things ('doing') rather than what resources you have available ('having') (Bogaert *et al.* 1994). It led to a changed emphasis for the competencies needed by the firm. This core value of hospitality was already embedded in the philosophy of the Novotel corporate parent, the Accor Group: 'hospitality is more than a word, a concept, hospitality is a frame of mind. . . . Because what you give is what you get' (*Accor Annual Report* 1992). To begin implementing the hospitality concept, a new style of organization and new working practices were required. Various initiatives to build new core competencies were begun. These involved surfacing and sharing tacit knowledge where possible, such as local knowledge or transferable best practice and developing shared values about new managerial and staff responsibilities and styles.

For example, from 1992, the relationship of the hotel General Manager (GM) and his staff team was redefined as enabling instead of hierarchical. Inter-functional groups were set up across hotels and countries. Cross-country GM interest groups were established to share ideas, innovations or best practice. These GM interest groups were constructed around common hotel types within the Novotel chain, such as all GM's of motorway locations, or airport locations, or city centre locations. The hierarchical mode of decision-making was replaced by devolution to individual service units (hotels). *Ad hoc* teams set themselves up for specific tasks and purposes both within and between hotels and regions. Teams and groups were mainly voluntary, informal, cross-functional, both inter- and intra-regional. Their objective was the pooling and sharing of knowledge throughout the group. Sharing and flexibility became part of the emergent values of the revised Novotel. One and a half layers of management were eliminated leaving only one direct reporting layer between GM's and the (then) two co-presidents of Novotel. The role of the GM was rethought and redefined. In the revised strategy the role of the GM was to be primarily interactive and social ('Maitre de Maison'), similar in idea to the social role of a ship's captain. All GM's were required to go through an assessment activity incorporating role-play in such situations as conflict-resolution with subordinates or guests since these were now the types of social and interpersonal competencies required in that role. Novotel changed its strategic direction from a central control structure directed towards uniformity to a less formal, more innovative system.

The process of competence development in Novotel

Novotel's' own view of its competencies derives from a blend of continuity and change. Continuity arising from history of ownership, management, and strategic intent; change demonstrated by its willingness to adapt to market and competitive pressures and move to a devolved loose-tight structure (Peters and Waterman 1982). In 1992 'the hotel was at a cross-roads where one reorients or declines'.[1] After 1992 Novotel redefined its core competencies around its new/old business concept of 'hospitality' and 'welcome'. GMs and other senior managers use such phrases as 'comes from the heart' and 'giving a piece of yourself' as personal interpretations of this service concept.

However, any service concept must be rooted within shared values, tacit knowledge and flexible routines. The approach adopted after 1992 was founded on delegation and horizontal integration, not on vertical control. This loose–tight system needed 'not a reliance on structure but on interrelationships with each other. That is where the strength is.' Within this process of delegation 'style is important' together with the 'ability to implement and project' by all staff levels. Uniformity was expected in high standards of service throughout the group, with flexibility and discretion in how the standards were achieved. Uniformity was measured by the system of 'Progress Novotel' which set minimum standards and grades for every task within the hotels. Each task is assessed for competence at each stage or grade. All staff can progress from grade to grade. Their progression is rewarded financially. It also provides the basis for world-wide transferability of staff throughout the Novotel chain. 'Progress Novotel provides us with a clear competitive advantage because it enables us by having closely defined criteria . . . for the person, for example, on the front desk and for that person to become multi-skilled and multi-competent.'

Novotel 's management processes for developing the new competencies affected both the structure of Novotel's corporate headquarters, as well as operations and routines in every hotel in the chain. This switch to a proactive competence management process transformed, although in differing degrees and over different timescales, the relationship around all three sides of Novotel's service triangle (i.e. between management, employee and customer). The main elements in these changes are given in Figure 15.1 (page 328) as Novotel's 'New Service Triangle'.

The hospitality concept contains such intangibles as 'greeting', 'welcome" and warmth of personal interactions. Internal routines must be able to deliver these service intangibles to the customer on a routine basis. Novotel uses tangibles where possible to support intangibles. For example, the physical layout of their hotels (part of service design) is intended to lead the customer immediately to the 'hospitable' public spaces of bar and restaurant, which are always on the entry floor adjacent to reception. The hospitality concept is further implemented by other policies such as staff exchanges (between countries, locations and type of customer mix) which ensure an international mix of hotel staff to interact sympathetically with an international client mix. Such policies also provide a means of motivating staff in an industry where labour-turnover is typically high and service delivery is dependent on staff motivation.

Figure 15.1 shows some of the means by which this process was carried out. Figure 15.1 features staff 'progress groups'; formal group-wide training programmes at the Academie Accor; 'quick' meetings (so

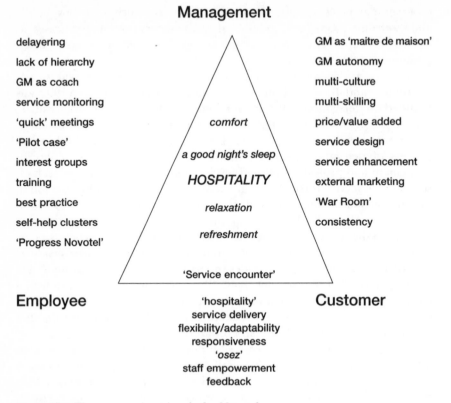

Management

delayering

lack of hierarchy

GM as coach

service monitoring

'quick' meetings

'Pilot case'

interest groups

training

best practice

self-help clusters

'Progress Novotel'

comfort

a good night's sleep

HOSPITALITY

relaxation

refreshment

'Service encounter'

GM as 'maitre de maison'

GM autonomy

multi-culture

multi-skilling

price/value added

service design

service enhancement

external marketing

'War Room'

consistency

Employee

Customer

'hospitality'
service delivery
flexibility/adaptability
responsiveness
'*osez*'
staff empowerment
feedback

Figure 15.1 The new service triangle for Novotel

called because they lasted for no more than five minutes and could be called by any staff member or manager to discuss an issue); GM interest groups, formed by GMs of similar types of hotels within the Novotel group; the best-practice 'Pilot Cases' of management practice from anywhere in the group that were made available throughout the company and named after the style of briefcases carried by airline pilots; the system of international staff exchanges; and the information flows to and from the co-presidents' 'War Room' at corporate headquarters, a room whose walls were covered with data on every Novotel throughout the world. Many of these processes have already been discussed. Of particular interest for the hospitality service concept is the shared value '*osez*', given on the 'service encounter' axis of Figure 15.1. This is from the French verb '*oser*', to dare. Roughly translated the shared value means: 'go on, dare to do it'. This is an important shared value for encouraging flexible routines.

A different example of the creation of flexible routines may be taken from Novotel's external and internal marketing strategy. Novotel operates within both the individual and corporate business and leisure markets. Its special promotions and advertising themes address these different segments. For example Dolphi, a baby dolphin, is the marketing and promotional symbol for children's events world-wide. However, although all locations world-wide will use the co-ordinated symbol and marketing materials for this (or any other) segment, hotel general managers at different locations and in different countries are encouraged to tailor promotions to local holidays and lifestyles. This is a classic example of global integration combined with local responsiveness (Bartlett and Ghoshal 1989, 1993) to create an organizational network, rather than an organizational hierarchy.

Some broader summary points of organizational changes and their resulting contribution to the building of new competencies at Novotel may now be given.

- Removal of layers of management significantly changed the internal organization structure. It led to reduction in headcount of management staff (which reduced costs) and reinforced the greater discretionary powers of the hotel GMs.
- Flattening the hierarchy changed information flows throughout the company. More relevant information could be conveyed faster to relevant people. It became easier to reconstruct organizational routines more appropriate to the changed competitive dynamics.
- The role of Headquarters changed. It began to act as an information co-ordinator and channel. The centre (HQ) now filters useful information to all hotels which they store as the 'Pilot Case' file for shared reference. This change supports of many other changes. Since corporate HQ is no longer a 'centralizer'; it has become a provider of resources for building competencies, rather than a consumer of them.
- Collaboration across and between levels has increased. GMs organize self-help clusters; training sessions are shared across the group; 'reflective clubs' (*Clubs de Réflection*) have been created in some hotels as mixed informal groupings of staff meeting to discuss innovations. They contain staff from across all service areas in the hotels and discussion covers the hotel as a whole, not the specific responsibility of any individual staff (club) member. These are collaborative routines that are inherently concerned with flexibility, sharing knowledge and reinforcing shared values.
- The role of the GM has changed to that of coach, developing the competencies of his team to enable them to deliver the hospitality concept. GMs time has been released for interaction with both staff and guests.
- Increased autonomy for all staff has given added responsibility, greater awareness of the business as a whole and encouraged cross-functional links. Day-to-day operational issues are dealt with in five-minute 'quick' meetings both on a routine and an *ad hoc* basis. This has released staff time for guests.

These six points contain the most significant changes that took place. Some developments had unexpected negative consequences. The flatter hierarchy for example, has created a short career path and loss of promotion opportunities for senior managers, which the organization is still struggling to address.

Analysis of Novotel's core competencies

We will now consider whether these changes led to a more defensible competitive position for Novotel. This would only be so if the new competencies were able to meet the requirements of distinctiveness that I described earlier. Since there is a high path dependency in the developments described, Novotel's new competencies should be distinctive and difficult to imitate and should therefore yield some competitive advantage. Following the terms of the mainstream resource-based literature (Barney 1986; Grant 1991; Peteraf 1993), these distinctive competencies must:

1   be hard to imitate
2   draw on combinations of resources
3   integrate individual functional capabilities
4   blend 'hard' and 'soft' elements.

The section following will show to what extent these criteria are illustrated at Novotel. However, to these four criteria, a fifth may be added:

5   core competence should lead to competitive advantage

Core competencies must not only be appropriate, but also distinctive, in order to lead to competitive advantage for the firm.

Let us return to the list of six major changes in Novotel from the previous section to see to what extent they reflect the five core competence criteria:

1   de-layering
2   changed information flows
3   headquarters as information and knowledge channel
4   increased vertical and horizontal collaboration between levels and business units
5   the role of the GM has changed to that of coach
6   flexible working routines for all managers and staff.

De-layering is easy to imitate, but the purpose of this structural change for Novotel was as an input to the other five changes. Without this flattening of the hierarchy, much of the integration across roles and functions, feedback and collaboration, would not have been achievable.

All of the remaining five change factors involve complexity: integration of functions and roles; drawing on combinations of resources; and blending 'hard and soft' elements. Recasting of the information flows enabled co-ordination and other horizontal linkages. A focus on collaboration emphasized team-working, shared responsibilities and coaching. Headquarters became an information co-ordinator. Working methods were broadened leading to multi-skilling and multi-competence. The sum of all these changes was complex in terms of the implications for team-working, learning, and individual behaviour. The impact of them was to blend the 'hard and soft' elements of organizational process to develop new, more relevant, competencies.

By definition, factors 2–6 are hard to imitate since they each involve complex combinations of both explicit and tacit resources. As is commonly the case, core competence criteria 1–4 tend to blend together in practice, which is what causal ambiguity highlights (Reed and DeFillippi 1990). The links between resources, competencies and performance are indirect rather than direct. At Novotel, as in other organizations, these indirect, complex linkages include the history and experience held within that particular firm.

While standardization requires the setting of explicit criteria for service delivery, in practice service concepts and delivery are dynamic rather than static in character ('in a hotel every day is different') and therefore the repertoire of skills and behaviours requires continuous updating and adjustment. Thus, post-1992, such initiatives as 'Progress Novotel' created a new foundation for service delivery. Service delivery is underpinned by a complexity of detail. Integration of this complexity was being achieved through delegated, multi-skilled team-working. Such internal resources as the 'Pilot Case' or the 'War Room' at the Novotel headquarters at Evry outside Paris acted as additional integrating mechanisms. They monitored continuously the interaction between core competencies and external industry context. The management style became more devolved, with accountability and responsibility shared among peer groups, in sharp distinction to the division of labour and specialization inherent in the previous command and control organization. The intent was to provide a distinctive service environment which, in a myriad of ways (some big, most quite small), contributed to a distinctive offering by Novotel in all its markets.

It is clear from Novotel's internal reviews and subsequent actions that these processes of building new competencies were intended to lead to an improved industry position and enhanced profitability. To judge the fifth criterion (i.e. whether these changes were perceived as leading to competitive advantage), it is certainly the case that these competencies were better suited to current industry dynamics in the international hotel sector where demand has been static at best and customer expectations becoming more sophisticated. The changes the company made from 1992 onward were a market-driven attempt to retain the benefits of consistency while injecting new processes to also achieve greater flexibility. Their purpose was to be more responsive to customers and thereby consolidate or improve external market positioning. Novotel's industry performance in the current market-place, and throughout the 1990s, has not been especially strong. This indicates that what these changes have achieved is to develop competencies that are core, but not distinctive. In other words, they are likely to be merely competencies that are necessary for survival in the demanding international hotel industry without providing the basis for any distinctive competitive advantage for Novotel.

Conclusion: the core competence management process in service multinationals

In this chapter I have provided an analysis of competence development in one service multinational. At first, Novotel was an innovator in its sector. It failed to remain so. Path dependency necessitates a commitment by management to competence management as a long-term process. Novotel did embark on a far-reaching internal re-alignment of its core competencies and its management processes, leading to a radically revised strategy and organization structure. However, the changes it made were sufficient to allow it survive within its sector, but not to gain any competitive advantage over competitors from superior performance. This suggests therefore that the competencies that Novotel developed were relevant core competencies for its sector, but not distinctive competencies. Nevertheless, the stages in the internal process of evaluation, identification and building of new competencies which Novotel underwent, provides a useful lesson that competencies are not static but dynamic and therefore must be actively managed and developed over time.

Core competence management in service MNCs relies upon shared values and a shared knowledge base within which both managers and staff are able to act. In this sense the service triangle for a given firm rests upon its core competencies. A dynamic (that is, continuously evolving) service triangle in terms of customer responsiveness, organizational cohesion and technical competence can only be achieved in the context of the firm's core competences. At Novotel, the trigger for changes in the shared values and the development of new core competencies and a loose–tight structure, came from interpretation of the industry dynamics and the business context. Novotel's efforts provide an imperfect but useful benchmark.

Notes

The author wishes to thank the managers and staff of the Novotel Corporation in Europe and the USA for their time and assistance in contributing to this research. Particular thanks are due to Mr Michael Flaxman and Ms Dominique Colliat.

1 The direct and indirect quotations in this section are taken from interview transcripts of the author and from a video (BBC / OU, 1996) containing interviews of Novotel management and staff carried out by the author.

References

Amit, R. and Schoemaker, P. (1993) 'Strategic Assets and Organisational Rents', *Strategic Management Journal* 14: 33–46.

Barney, J. (1986) 'Strategic Factor Markets: Expectations, Luck and Business Strategy', *Management Science* 32: 1231–41.

—— (1991) 'Firm Resources and Sustained Competitive Advantage', *Journal of Management* 17: 99–120.

Bartlett, C. A. and Ghoshal, S. (1989) *Managing Across Borders*, London: Hutchinson.

—— (1993) 'Beyond the M-Form: Toward a Managerial Theory of the Firm', *Strategic Management Journal* 14, special issue, winter: 23–46

BBC Open University (1996) 'The Passion for Distinctiveness', video, OUB039H, B820/TV1.

Bogaert, I., Martens, A. and Van Cauwenbergh, A. (1994) 'Strategy as a Situational Puzzle: the Fit of Components', in G. Hamel and A. Heene (eds) *Competence Based Competition*, Chichester: Wiley.

Bowen, D. E., Chase, R. B. and Cummings, T. G. (1990) *Service Management Effectiveness*, Oxford: Jossey-Bass.

Czepiel, J. A., Solomon, M. R. and Suprenant, C. (eds) (1985) *The Service Encounter*, Lexington, Mass.: Heath Publishing.

Erramilli, M. K.(1990) 'Entry Mode Choice in Service Industries', *International Marketing Review* 7 (5): 50–62.

Grant, R. M. (1991) 'The Resource-Based Theory of Competitive Advantage: Implications for Strategy Formulation', *California Management Review*, spring: 114–35.

Normann, R. (1984) *Service Management*, Chichester: Wiley.

Penrose, E. (1959) *The Theory of the Growth of the Firm*, Oxford: Basil Blackwell.

Peteraf, M. (1993) 'The Cornerstones of Competitive Advantage: a Resource-Based View', *Strategic Management Journal* 14: 179–91.

Peters, T. J. and Waterman, R. H. (1982) *In Search of Excellence*, New York: Harper and Row.

Porter, M. (1980) *Competitive Strategy*, New York: Free Press.

Prahalad, C. K. and Hamel, G. (1990) 'The Core Competence of the Corporation', *Harvard Business Review*, May–June: 71–91.

Reed, R. and DeFillippi, R. (1990) 'Causal Ambiguity, Barriers to Imitation, and Sustainable Competitive Advantage', *Academy of Management Review* 15: 88–102.

Wernerfelt, B. (1984) 'A Resource-Based View of the Firm', *Strategic Management Journal* 5: 171–80.

Zeithaml, V. A.and Bitner, M. J. (1996) *Services Marketing*, New York: McGraw-Hill.

Index